Twin Star Exorcists

ONMYOJI

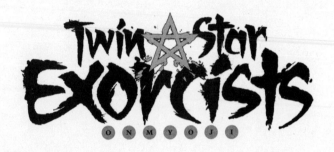

Twin ★ Star Exorcists

O N M Y O J I

9

WITHDRAWN

STORY & ART
YOSHIAKI SUKENO

Character Introduction

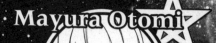

Mayura Otomi

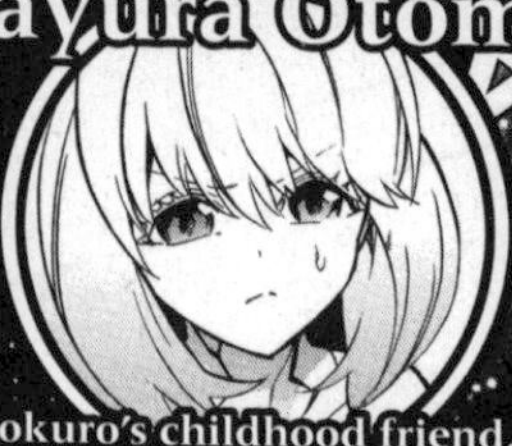

Rokuro's childhood friend. During a fierce battle in Magano, her commitment to protecting others earned her the spiritual protector White Tiger.

Seigen Amawaka

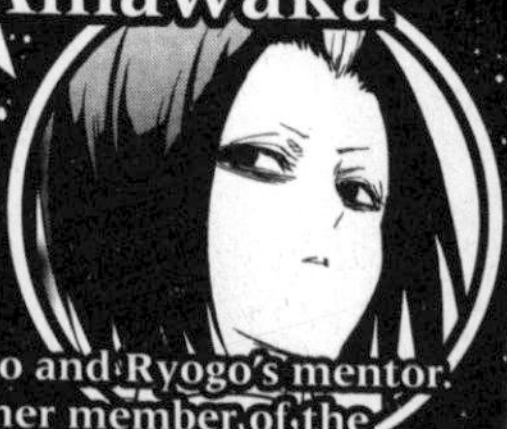

Rokuro and Ryogo's mentor. A former member of the Twelve Guardians, the strongest of the exorcists. He is also Mayura's father.

Rokuro Enmado

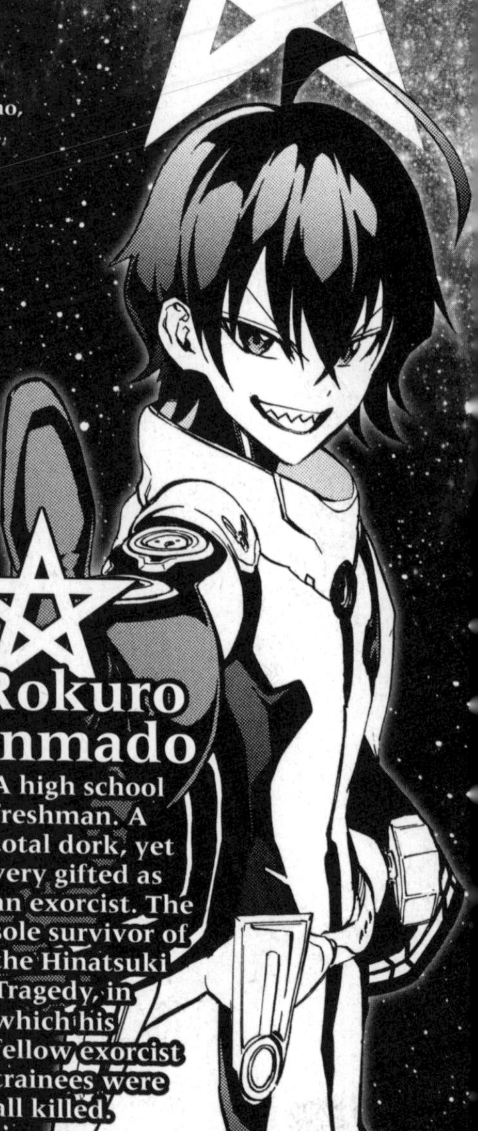

A high school freshman. A total dork, yet very gifted as an exorcist. The sole survivor of the Hinatsuki Tragedy, in which his fellow exorcist trainees were all killed.

Story Thus Far...

Kegare are creatures from Magano, the underworld, and it is the duty of an exorcist to hunt, exorcise and purify them. Rokuro and Benio are the Twin Star Exorcists, fated to bear the Prophesied Child who will defeat the Kegare. For the past two years, the unlikely pair have been living together and training in preparation for going to Tsuchimikado Island, the front line of the battle against the Kegare. But first, they must undergo the Ascertainment Ritual to determine if they are qualified...

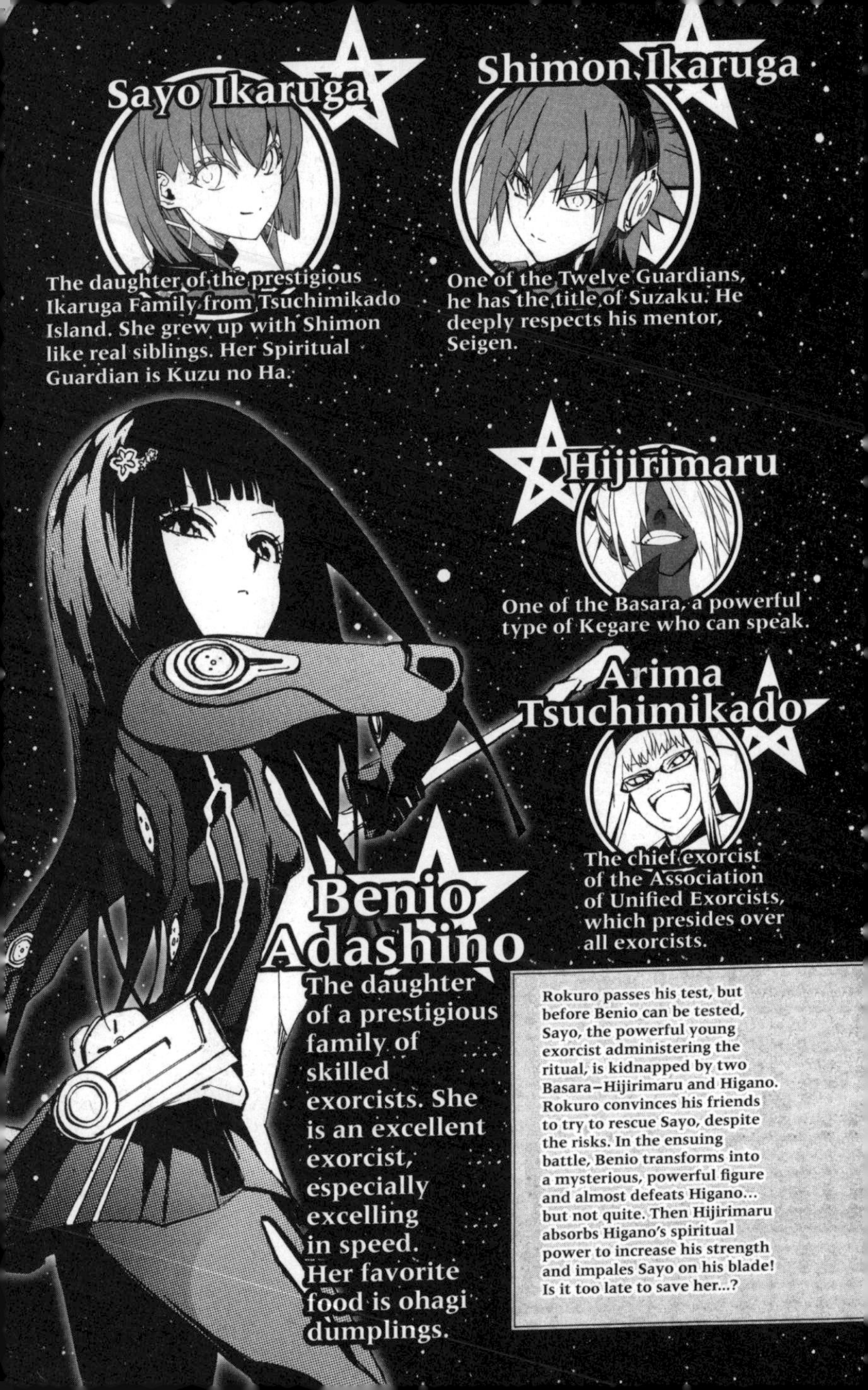

Sayo Ikaruga
The daughter of the prestigious Ikaruga Family from Tsuchimikado Island. She grew up with Shimon like real siblings. Her Spiritual Guardian is Kuzu no Ha.
Shimon Ikaruga
One of the Twelve Guardians, he has the title of Suzaku. He deeply respects his mentor, Seigen.
Hijirimaru
One of the Basara, a powerful type of Kegare who can speak.
Arima Tsuchimikado
The chief exorcist of the Association of Unified Exorcists, which presides over all exorcists.
Benio Adashino
The daughter of a prestigious family of skilled exorcists. She is an excellent exorcist, especially excelling in speed. Her favorite food is ohagi dumplings.
Rokuro passes his test, but before Benio can be tested, Sayo, the powerful young exorcist administering the ritual, is kidnapped by two Basara—Hijirimaru and Higano. Rokuro convinces his friends to try to rescue Sayo, despite the risks. In the ensuing battle, Benio transforms into a mysterious, powerful figure and almost defeats Higano... but not quite. Then Hijirimaru absorbs Higano's spiritual power to increase his strength and impales Sayo on his blade! Is it too late to save her...?

Twin☆Star Exorcists

ONMYOJI

EXORCISMS

9

ONMYOJI have worked for the Imperial Court since the Heian era. In addition to exorcising evil spirits, as civil servants they performed a variety of roles, including advising nobles by foretelling the future, creating the calendar, observing the movements of the stars, measuring time…

#30 The Encroachment of Magano

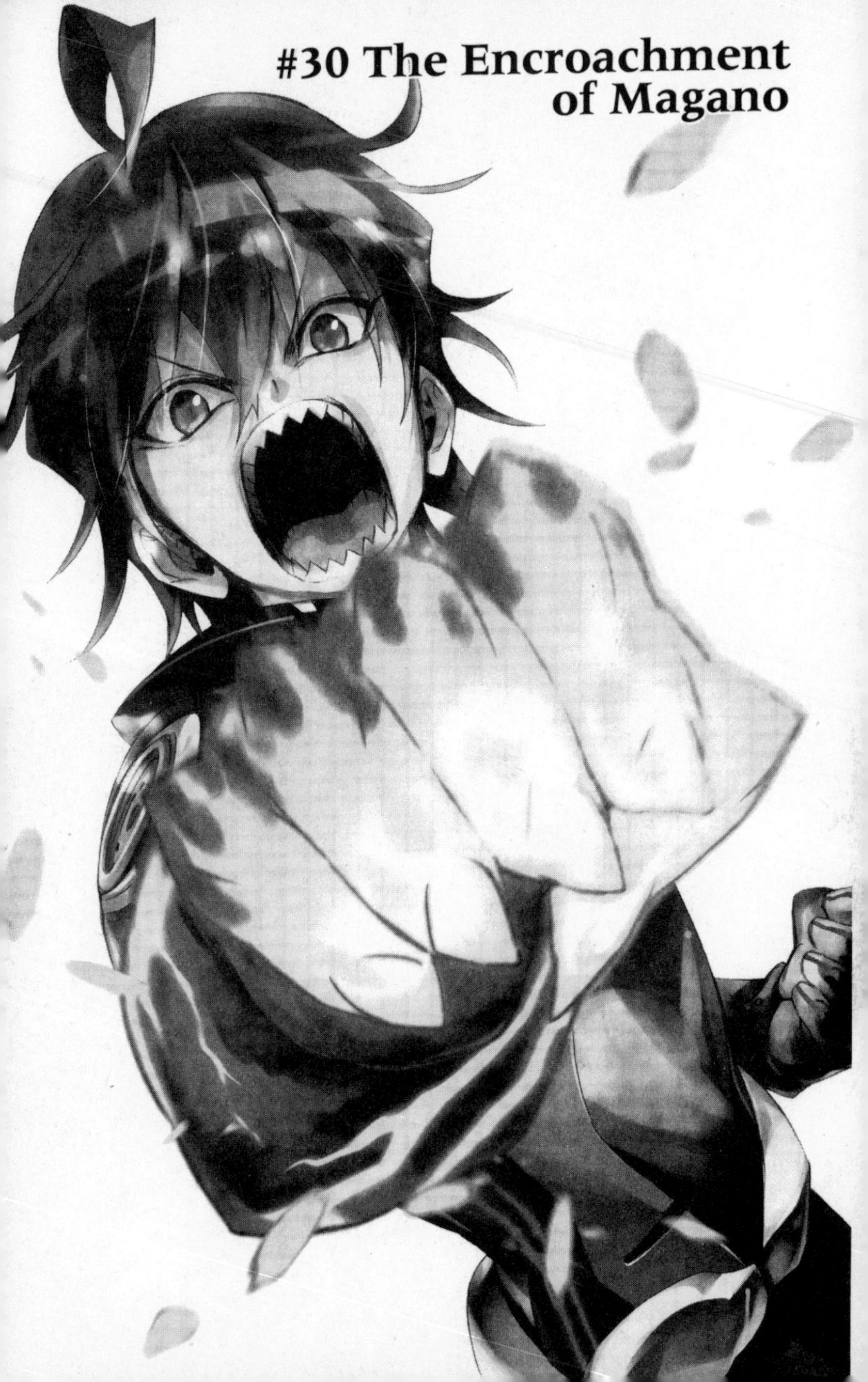

Twin Star Exorcists

O N M Y O J I

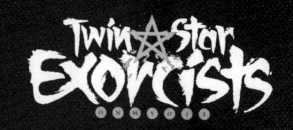

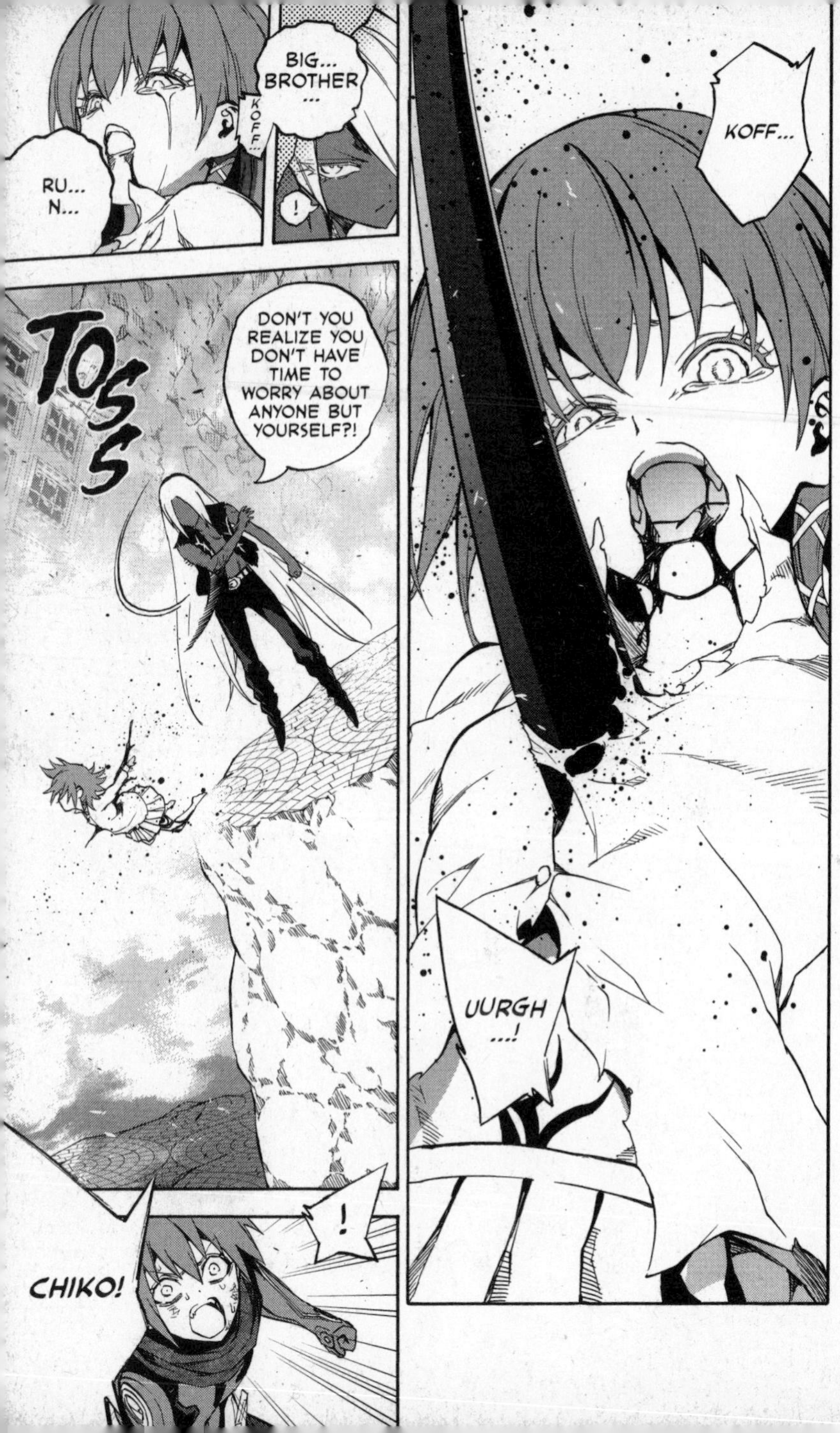
KOFF...
UURGH ...!
BIG... BROTHER ...
KOFF...
!
RU... N...
DON'T YOU REALIZE YOU DON'T HAVE TIME TO WORRY ABOUT ANYONE BUT YOURSELF?!
TOSS
!
CHIKO!

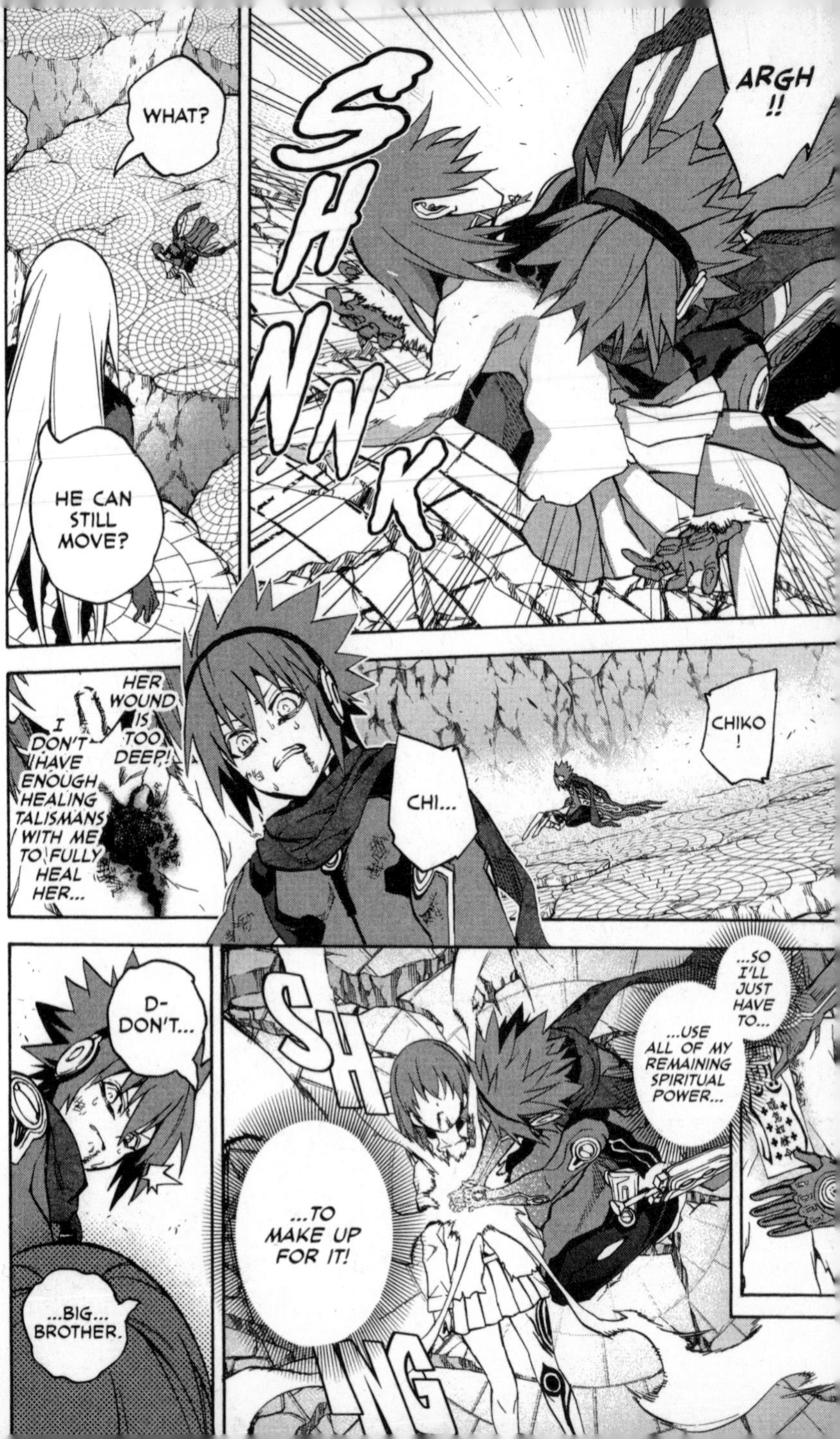

SHNNK
ARGH!!
WHAT?
HE CAN STILL MOVE?
CHIKO!
CHI...
HER WOUND IS TOO DEEP!
I DON'T HAVE ENOUGH HEALING TALISMANS WITH ME TO FULLY HEAL HER...
...SO I'LL JUST HAVE TO...
...USE ALL OF MY REMAINING SPIRITUAL POWER...
...TO MAKE UP FOR IT!
SH
NG
D-DON'T...
...BIG... BROTHER.

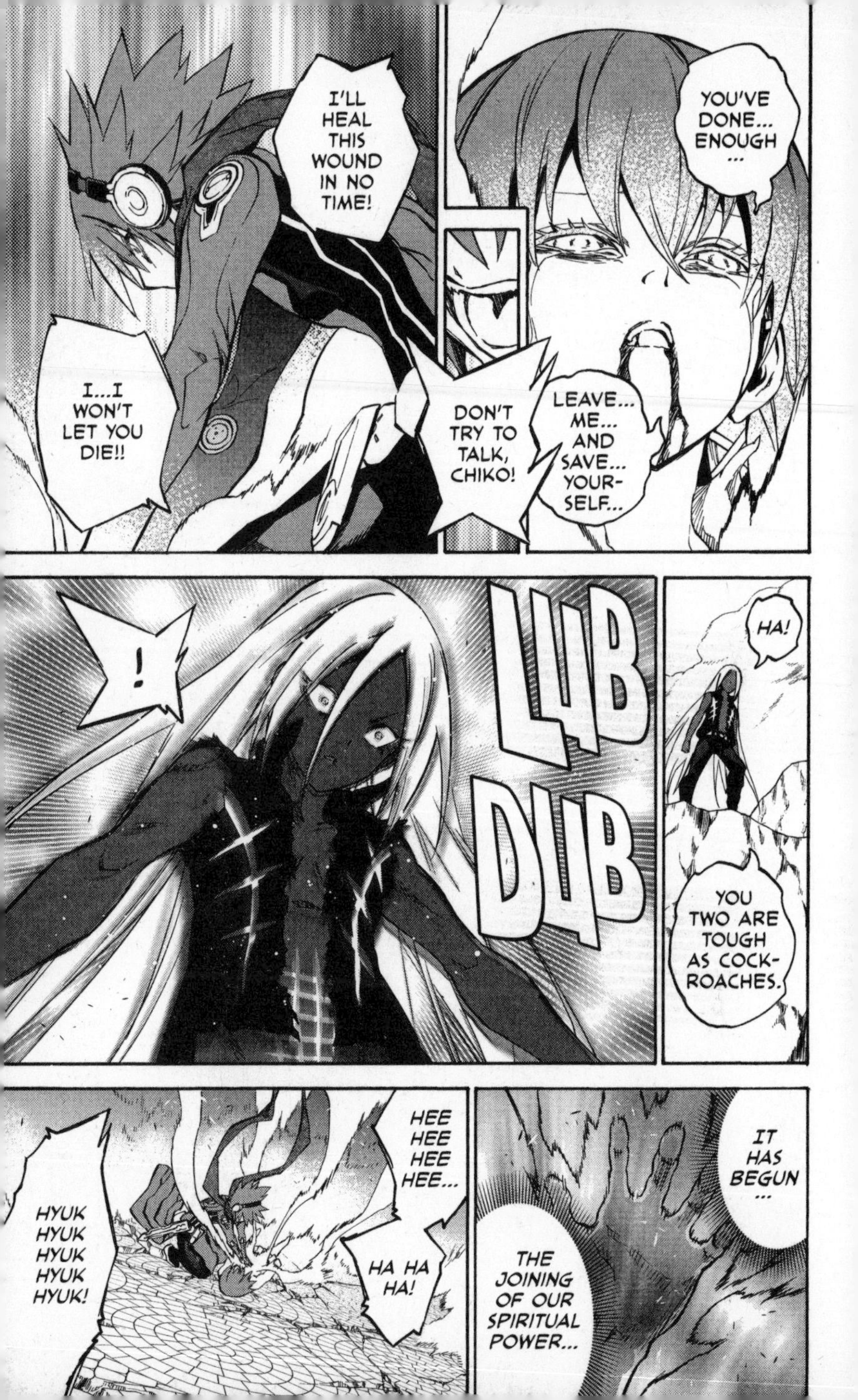

YOU'VE DONE... ENOUGH ...
LEAVE... ME... AND SAVE... YOURSELF...
DON'T TRY TO TALK, CHIKO!
I'LL HEAL THIS WOUND IN NO TIME!
I...I WON'T LET YOU DIE!!
HA!
YOU TWO ARE TOUGH AS COCKROACHES.
LUB DUB
!
IT HAS BEGUN ...
THE JOINING OF OUR SPIRITUAL POWER...
HEE HEE HEE HEE...
HA HA HA!
HYUK HYUK HYUK HYUK HYUK!

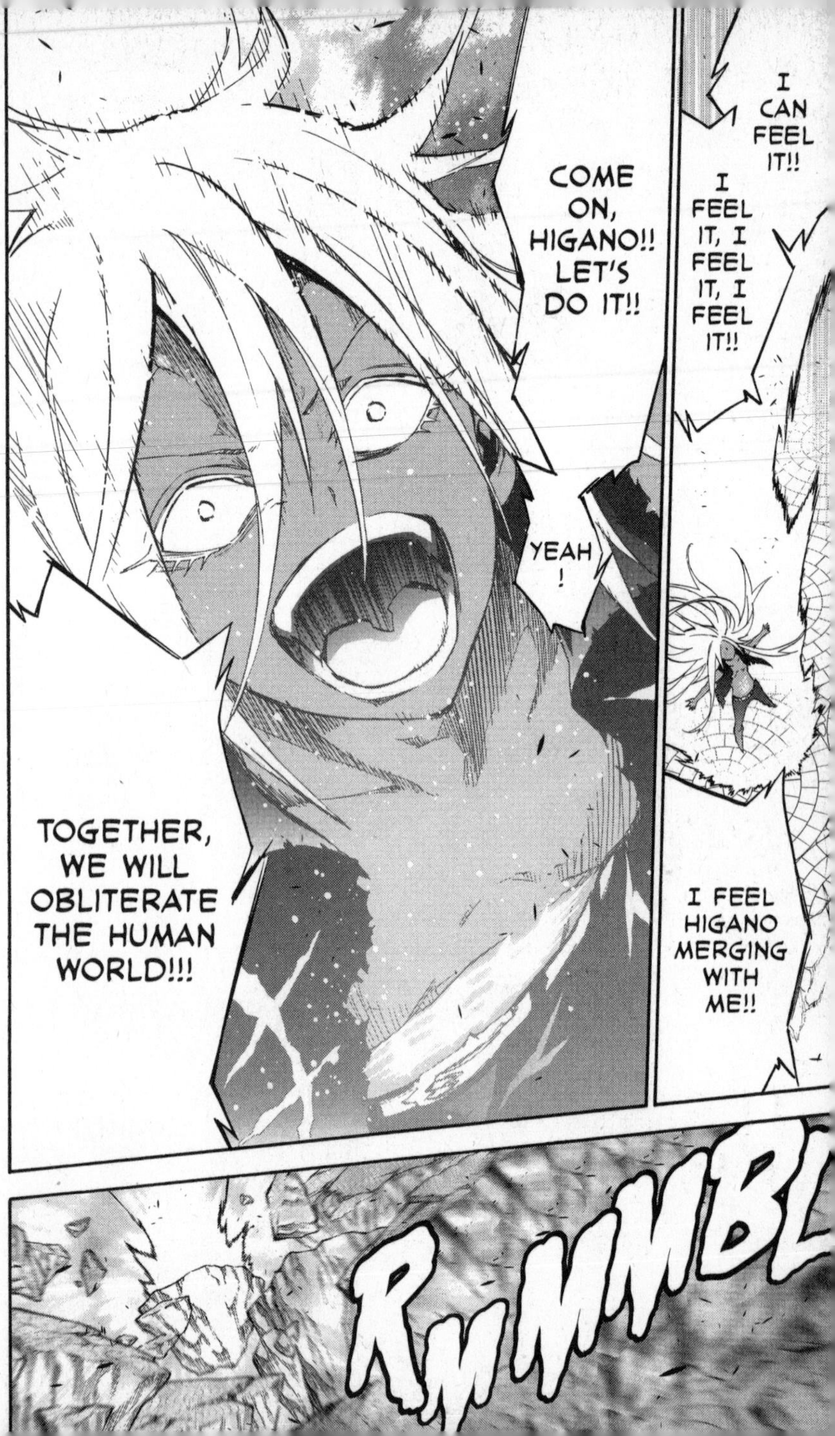
I CAN FEEL IT!!
I FEEL IT, I FEEL IT, I FEEL IT!!
I FEEL HIGANO MERGING WITH ME!!
COME ON, HIGANO!! LET'S DO IT!!
YEAH!
TOGETHER, WE WILL OBLITERATE THE HUMAN WORLD!!!
RUMMBL

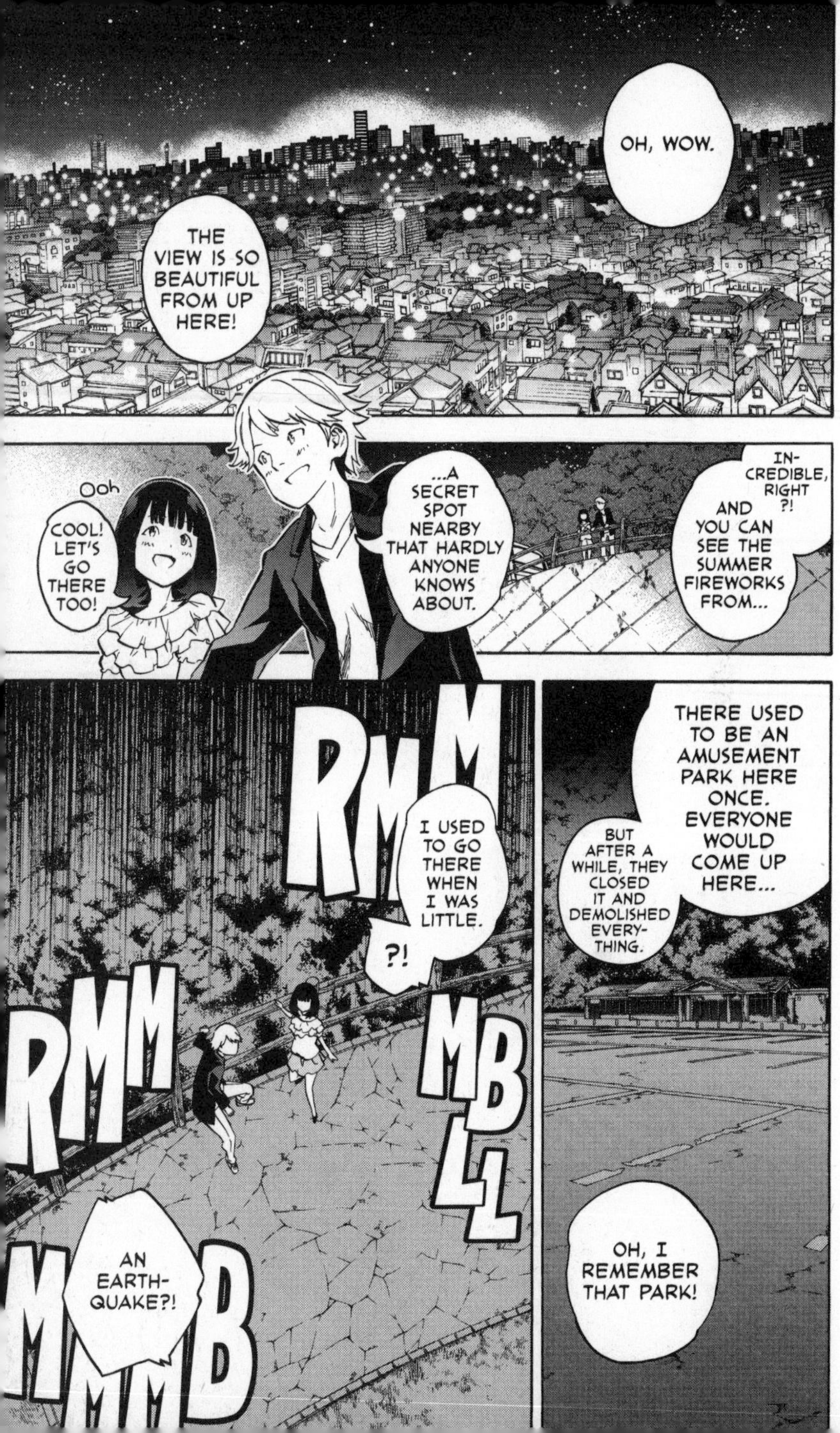
OH, WOW.
THE VIEW IS SO BEAUTIFUL FROM UP HERE!
IN-CREDIBLE, RIGHT?!
AND YOU CAN SEE THE SUMMER FIREWORKS FROM...
...A SECRET SPOT NEARBY THAT HARDLY ANYONE KNOWS ABOUT.
Ooh
COOL! LET'S GO THERE TOO!
THERE USED TO BE AN AMUSEMENT PARK HERE ONCE. EVERYONE WOULD COME UP HERE...
BUT AFTER A WHILE, THEY CLOSED IT AND DEMOLISHED EVERY-THING.
OH, I REMEMBER THAT PARK!
RMM
I USED TO GO THERE WHEN I WAS LITTLE.
?!
MBLL
RMMM
AN EARTH-QUAKE?!
MMMMB

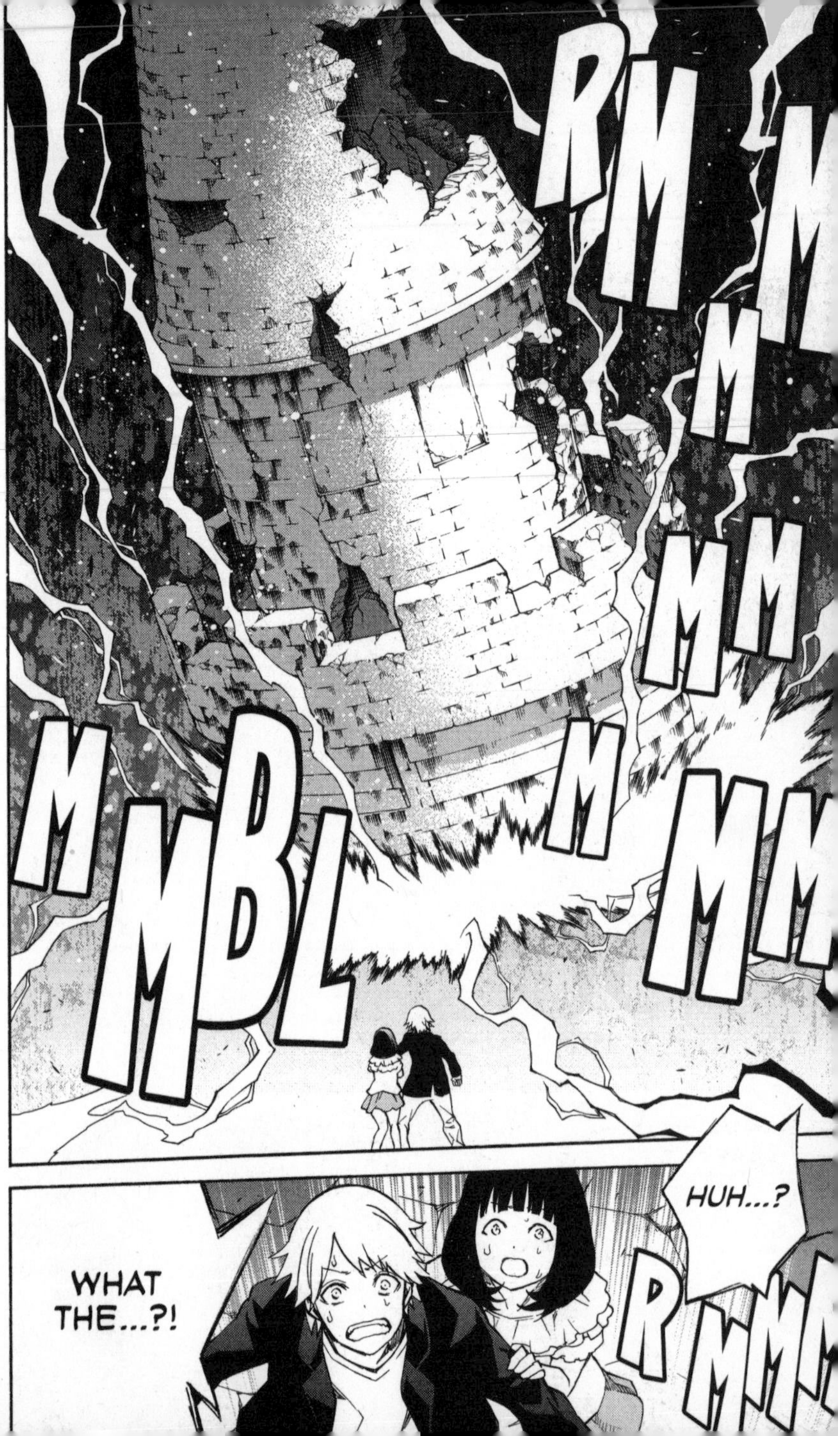
RMMM
MMM
MMMM
MMMBL
HUH...?
WHAT THE...?!
RMMMM

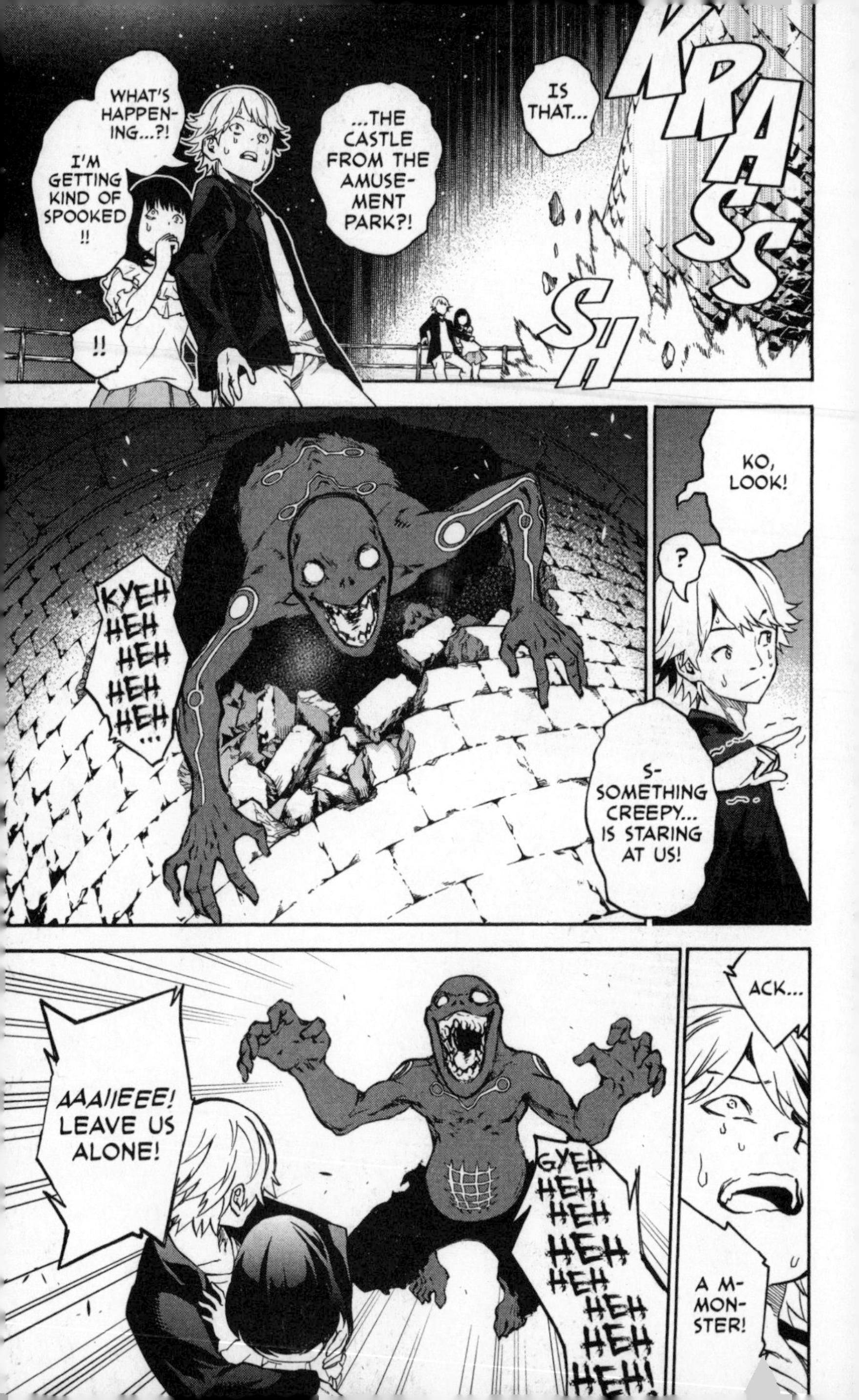
KRASSSH
IS THAT...
...THE CASTLE FROM THE AMUSEMENT PARK?!
WHAT'S HAPPENING...?!
I'M GETTING KIND OF SPOOKED!!
!!
KO, LOOK!
?
S-SOMETHING CREEPY... IS STARING AT US!
KYEH HEH HEH HEH HEH...
ACK...
A M-MONSTER!
GYEH HEH HEH HEH HEH HEH HEH HEH!
AAAIIEEE! LEAVE US ALONE!

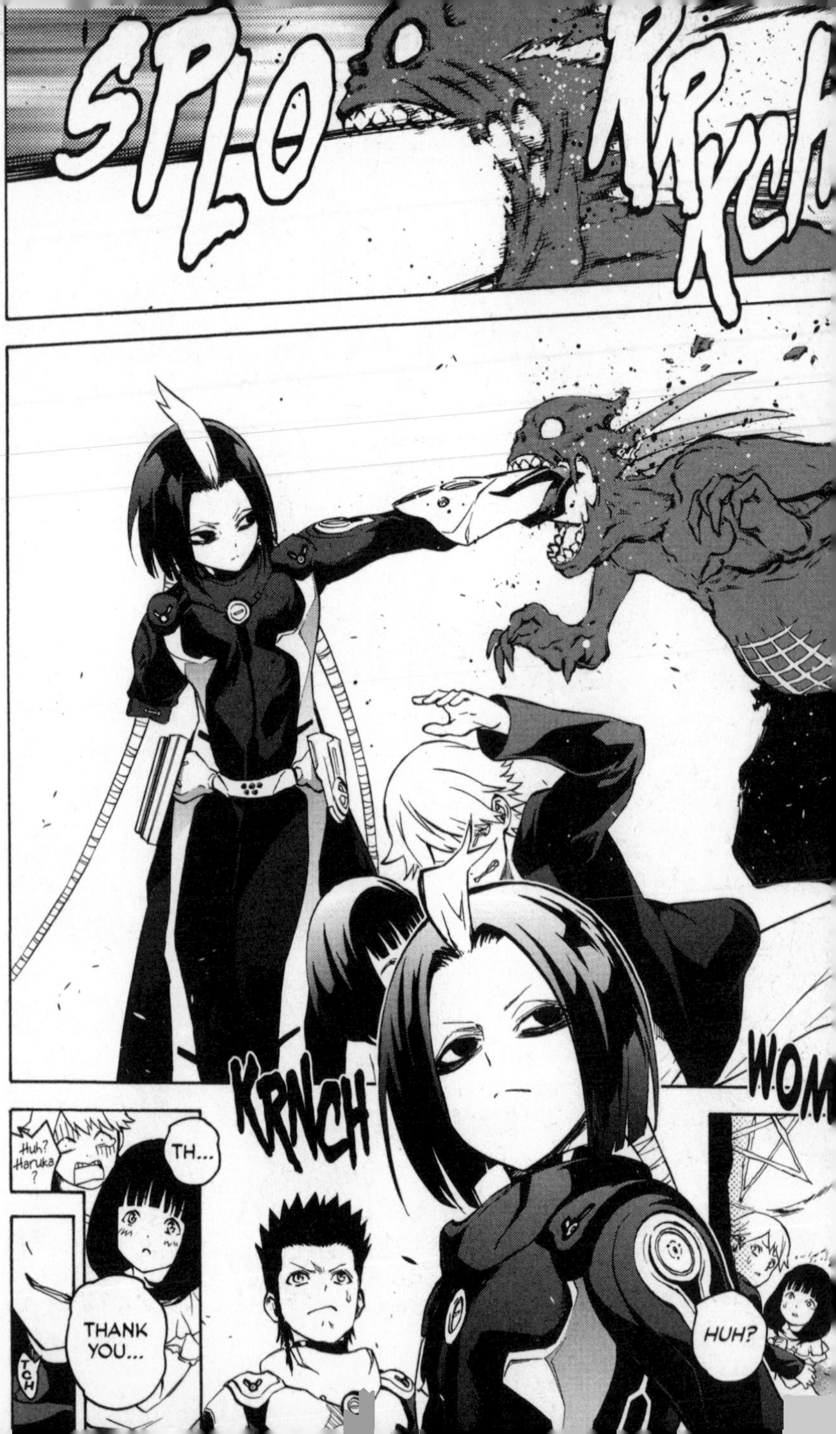
KRKCH
SPLO
WOM
KRNCH
HUH?
Huh? Haruka?
TH...
THANK YOU...
TCH

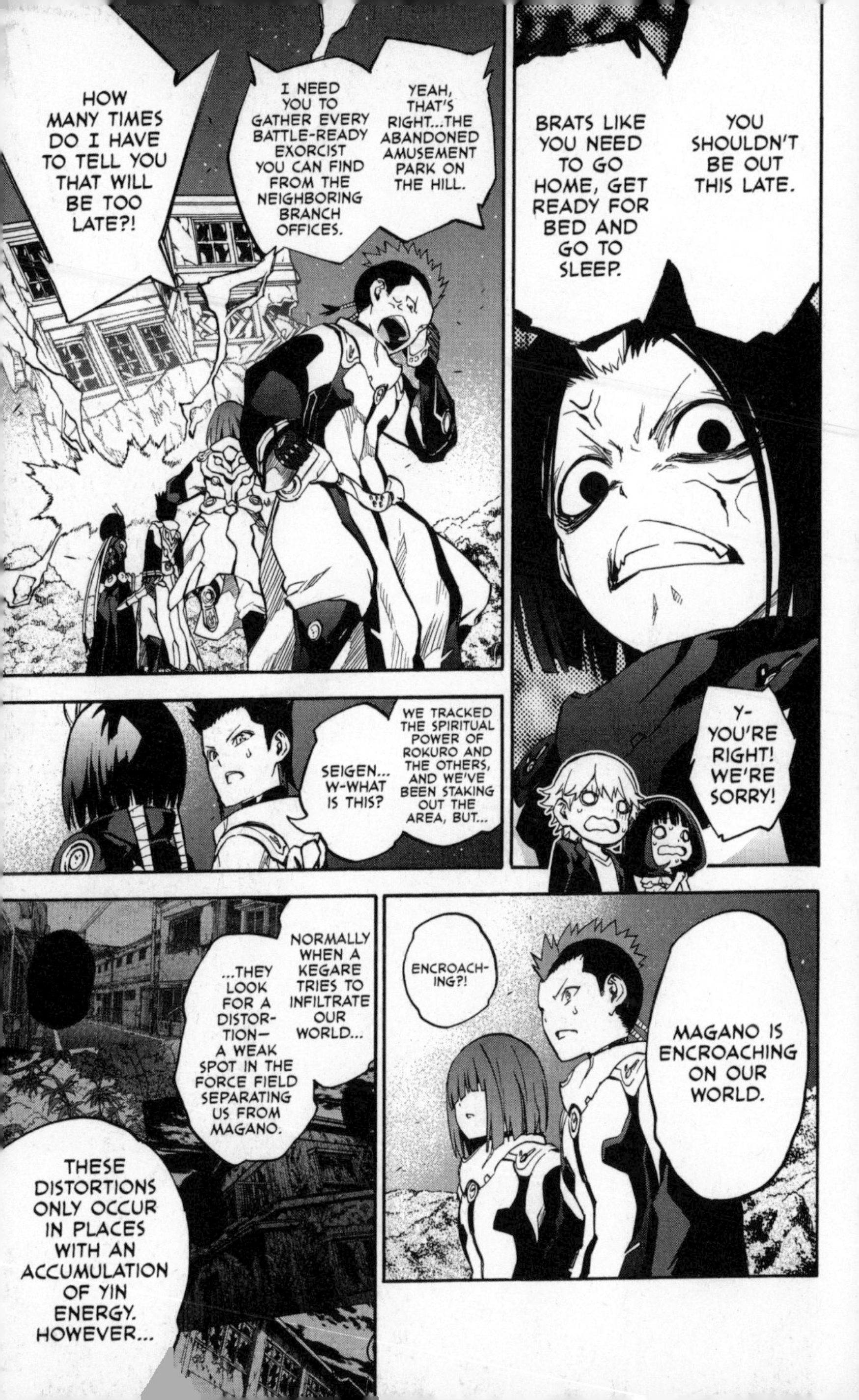
YOU SHOULDN'T BE OUT THIS LATE.
BRATS LIKE YOU NEED TO GO HOME, GET READY FOR BED AND GO TO SLEEP.
Y-YOU'RE RIGHT! WE'RE SORRY!
YEAH, THAT'S RIGHT...THE ABANDONED AMUSEMENT PARK ON THE HILL.
I NEED YOU TO GATHER EVERY BATTLE-READY EXORCIST YOU CAN FIND FROM THE NEIGHBORING BRANCH OFFICES.
HOW MANY TIMES DO I HAVE TO TELL YOU THAT WILL BE TOO LATE?!
WE TRACKED THE SPIRITUAL POWER OF ROKURO AND THE OTHERS, AND WE'VE BEEN STAKING OUT THE AREA, BUT...
SEIGEN... W-WHAT IS THIS?
MAGANO IS ENCROACHING ON OUR WORLD.
ENCROACHING?!
NORMALLY WHEN A KEGARE TRIES TO INFILTRATE OUR WORLD...
...THEY LOOK FOR A DISTORTION— A WEAK SPOT IN THE FORCE FIELD SEPARATING US FROM MAGANO.
THESE DISTORTIONS ONLY OCCUR IN PLACES WITH AN ACCUMULATION OF YIN ENERGY. HOWEVER...

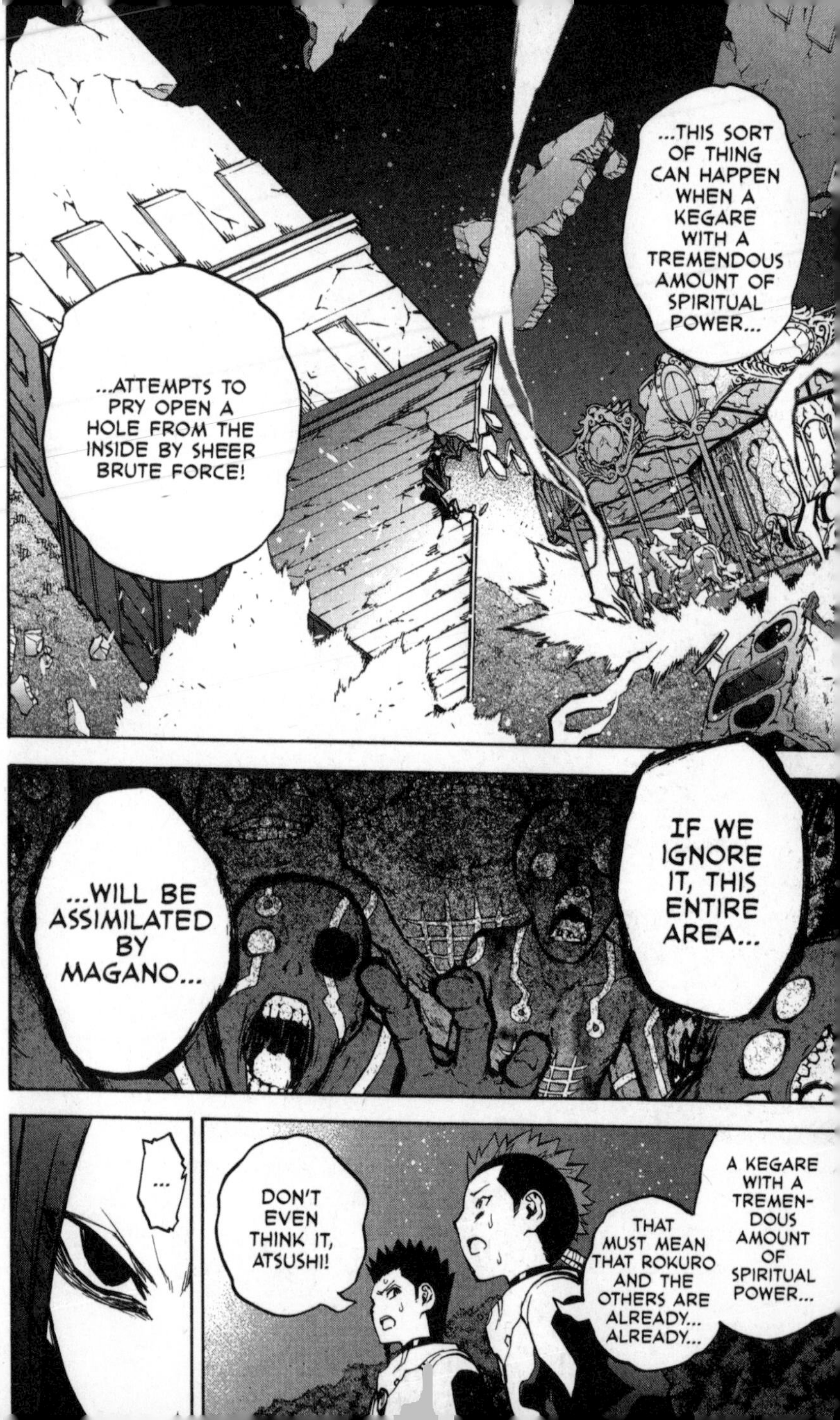
...THIS SORT OF THING CAN HAPPEN WHEN A KEGARE WITH A TREMENDOUS AMOUNT OF SPIRITUAL POWER...
...ATTEMPTS TO PRY OPEN A HOLE FROM THE INSIDE BY SHEER BRUTE FORCE!
IF WE IGNORE IT, THIS ENTIRE AREA...
...WILL BE ASSIMILATED BY MAGANO...
A KEGARE WITH A TREMENDOUS AMOUNT OF SPIRITUAL POWER...
THAT MUST MEAN THAT ROKURO AND THE OTHERS ARE ALREADY... ALREADY...
DON'T EVEN THINK IT, ATSUSHI!
...

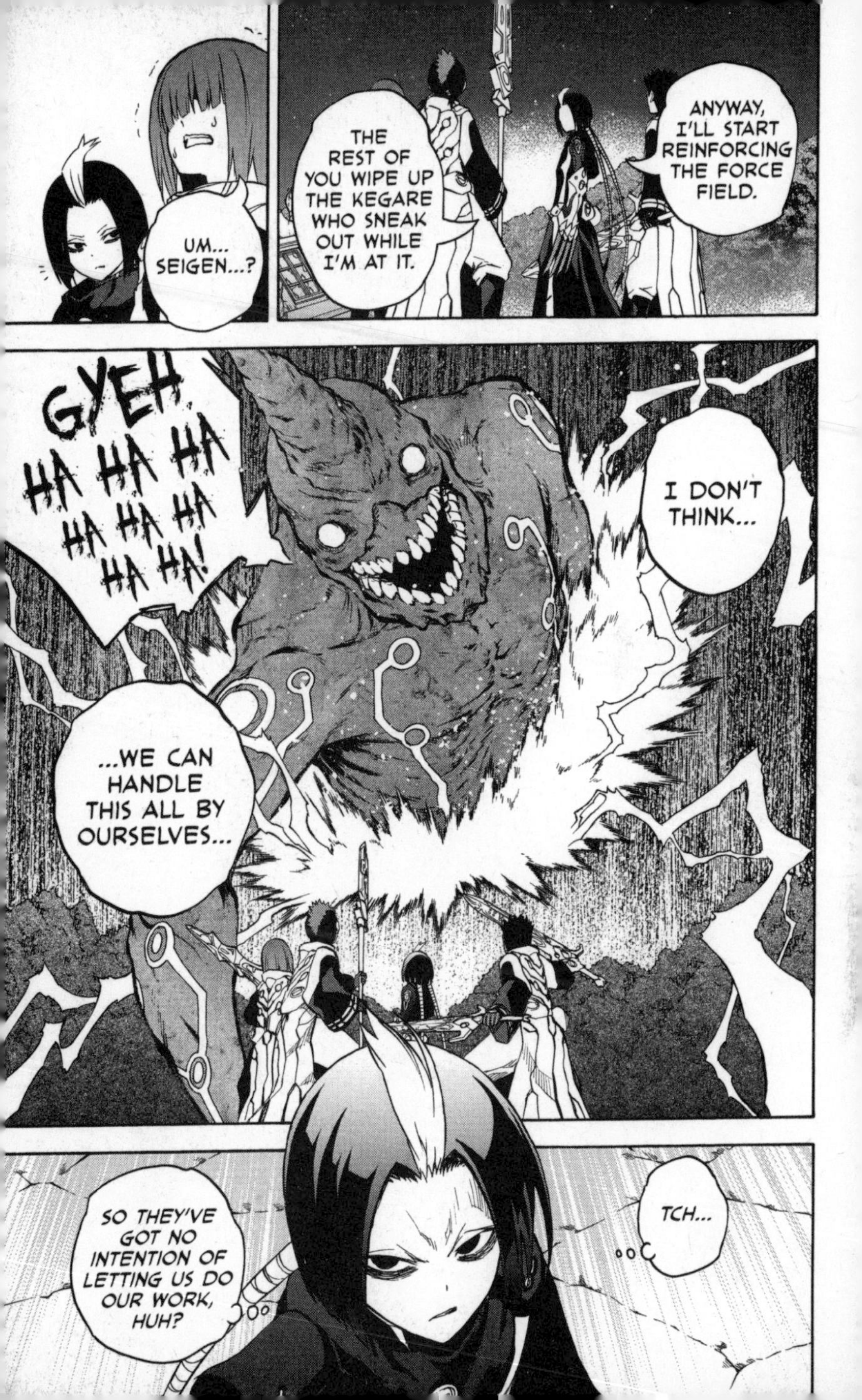
ANYWAY, I'LL START REINFORCING THE FORCE FIELD.
THE REST OF YOU WIPE UP THE KEGARE WHO SNEAK OUT WHILE I'M AT IT.
UM... SEIGEN...?
GYEH HA HA HA HA HA HA HA HA!
I DON'T THINK...
...WE CAN HANDLE THIS ALL BY OURSELVES...
TCH...
SO THEY'VE GOT NO INTENTION OF LETTING US DO OUR WORK, HUH?

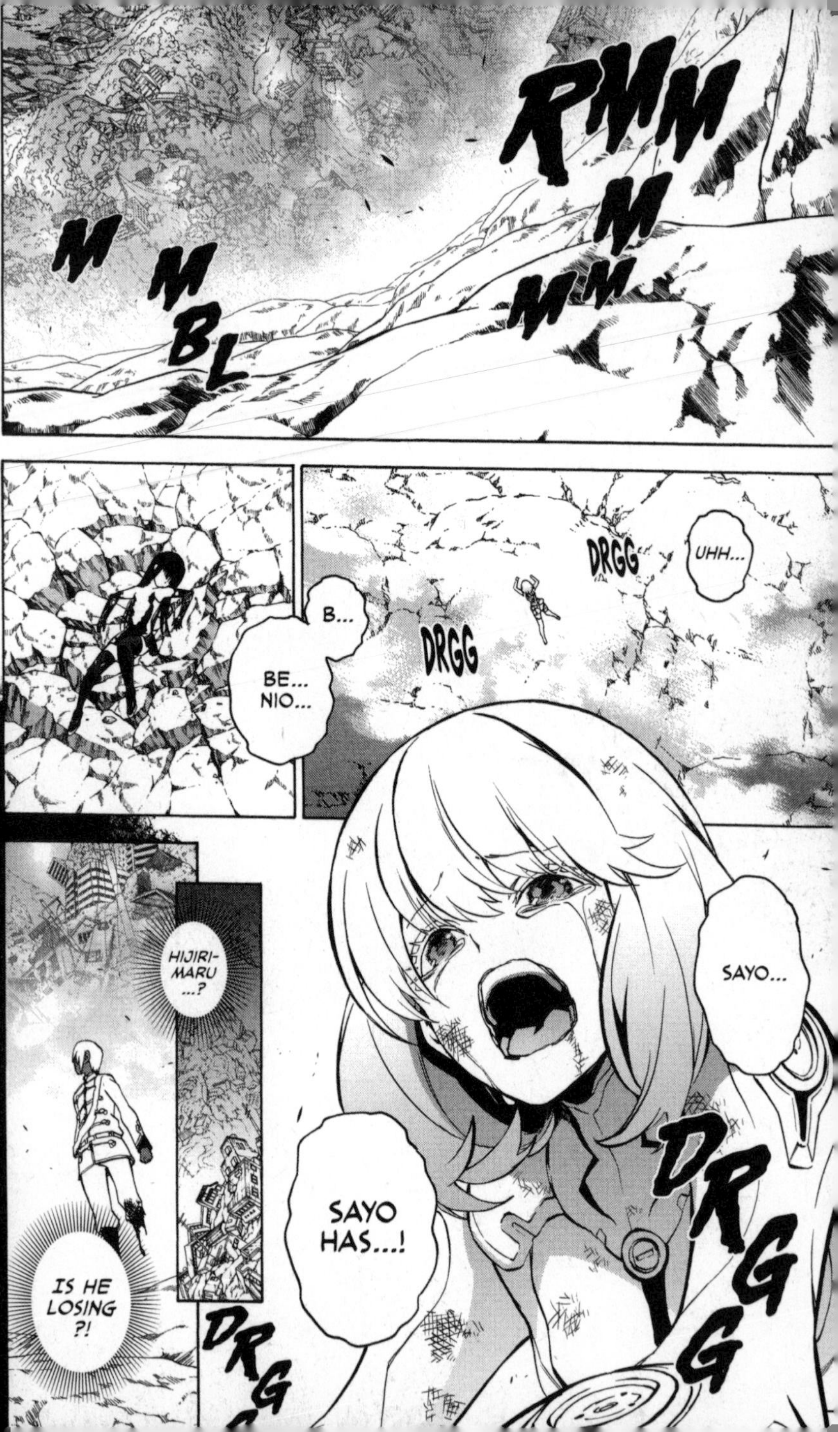
RMMMMMM
MMMBL
UHH...
DRGG
DRGG
B...
BE... NIO...
SAYO...
SAYO HAS...!
DRGG
HIJIRI-MARU ...?
IS HE LOSING ?!
DRG

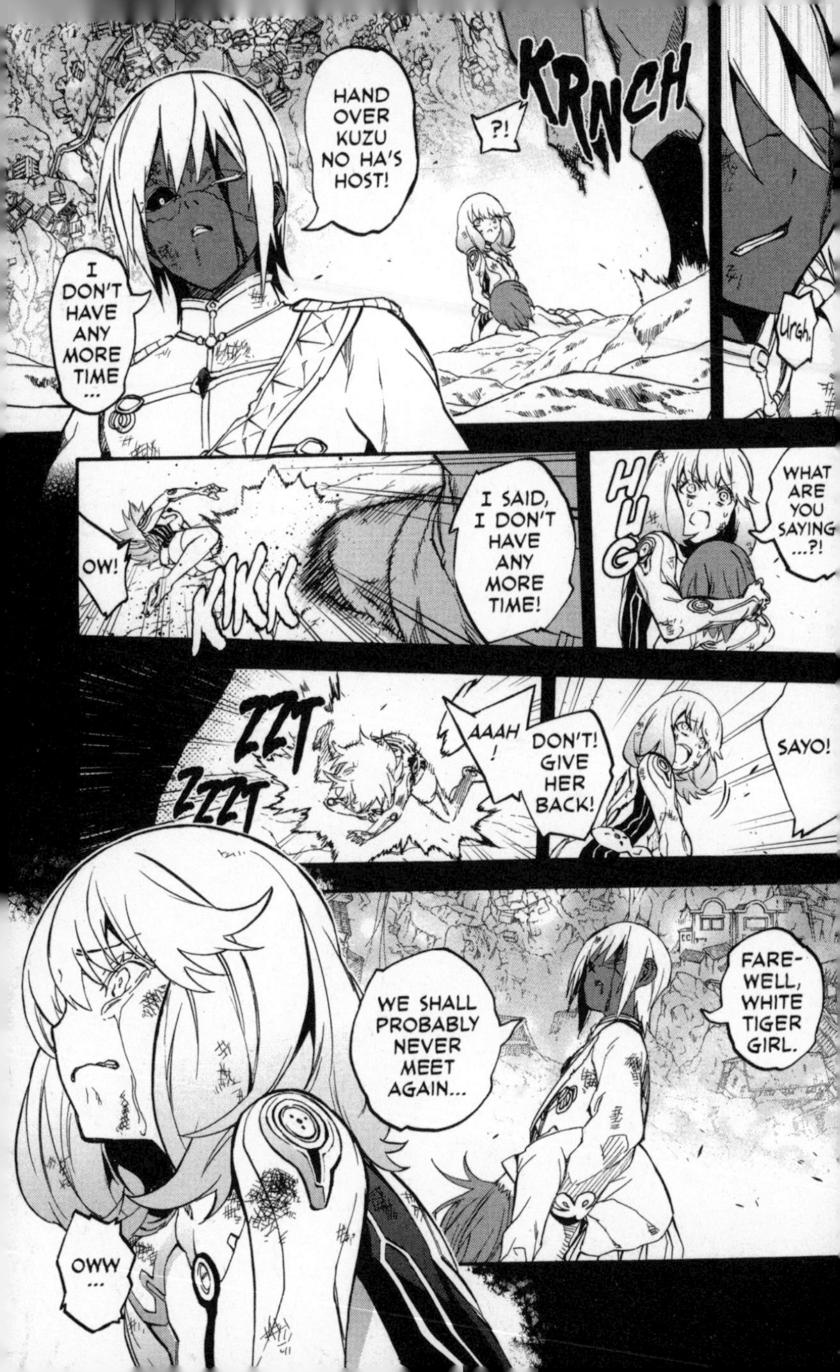
Urgh.
KRNCH
?!
HAND OVER KUZU NO HA'S HOST!
I DON'T HAVE ANY MORE TIME...
WHAT ARE YOU SAYING...?!
HUG
I SAID, I DON'T HAVE ANY MORE TIME!
KIKK
OW!
SAYO!
DON'T! GIVE HER BACK!
AAAH!
ZZZT
ZZZT
FARE-WELL, WHITE TIGER GIRL.
WE SHALL PROBABLY NEVER MEET AGAIN...
OWW...

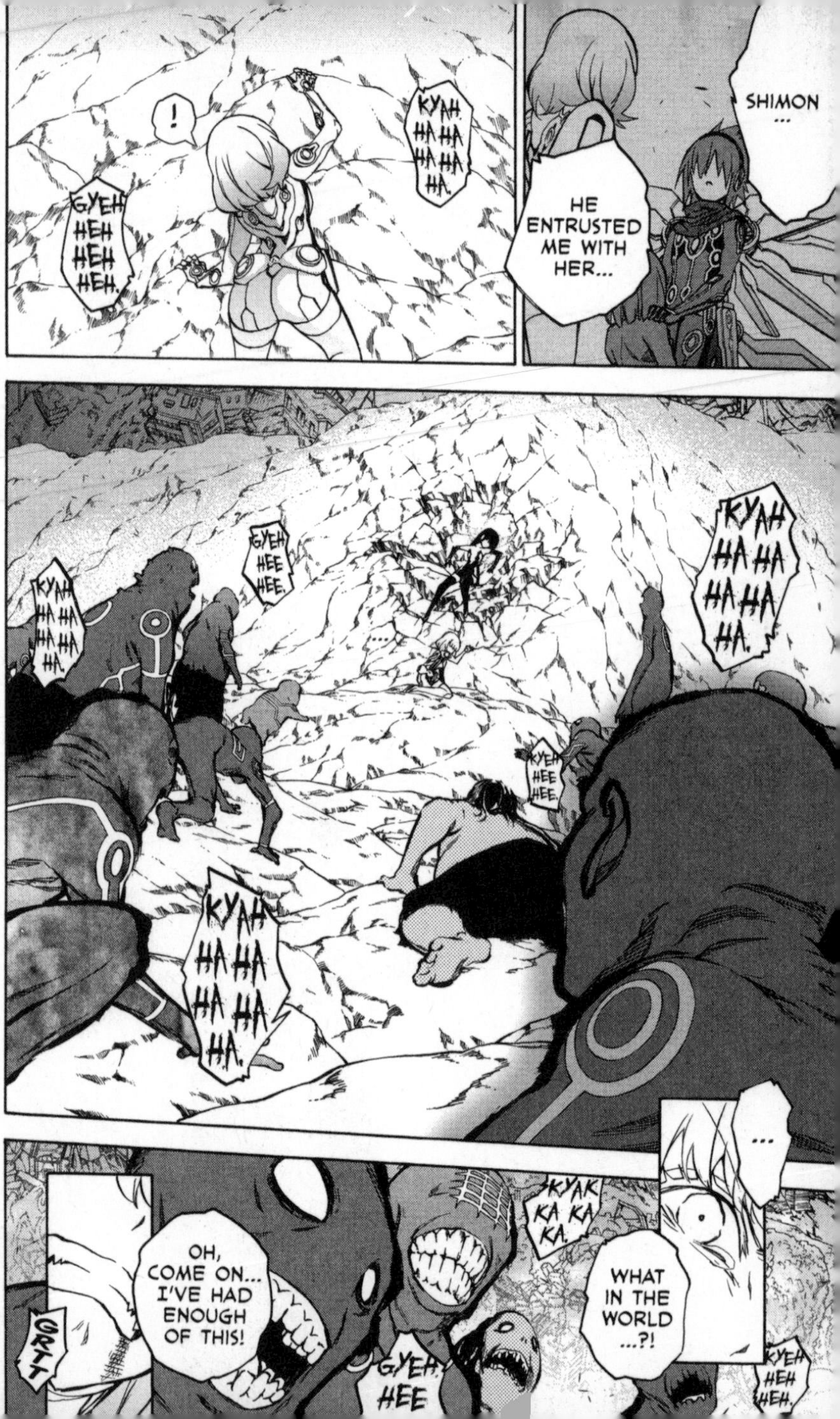
SHIMON ...
HE ENTRUSTED ME WITH HER...
KYAH HA HA HA HA HA.
!
GYEH HEH HEH HEH.
KYAH HA HA HA HA HA HA.
KYEH HEE HEE.
GYEH HEE HEE.
...
KYAH HA HA HA HA HA.
KYAH HA HA HA HA HA.
...
WHAT IN THE WORLD ...?!
KYEH HEH HEH.
KYAK KA KA KA.
OH, COME ON... I'VE HAD ENOUGH OF THIS!
GYEH HEE
GRTT

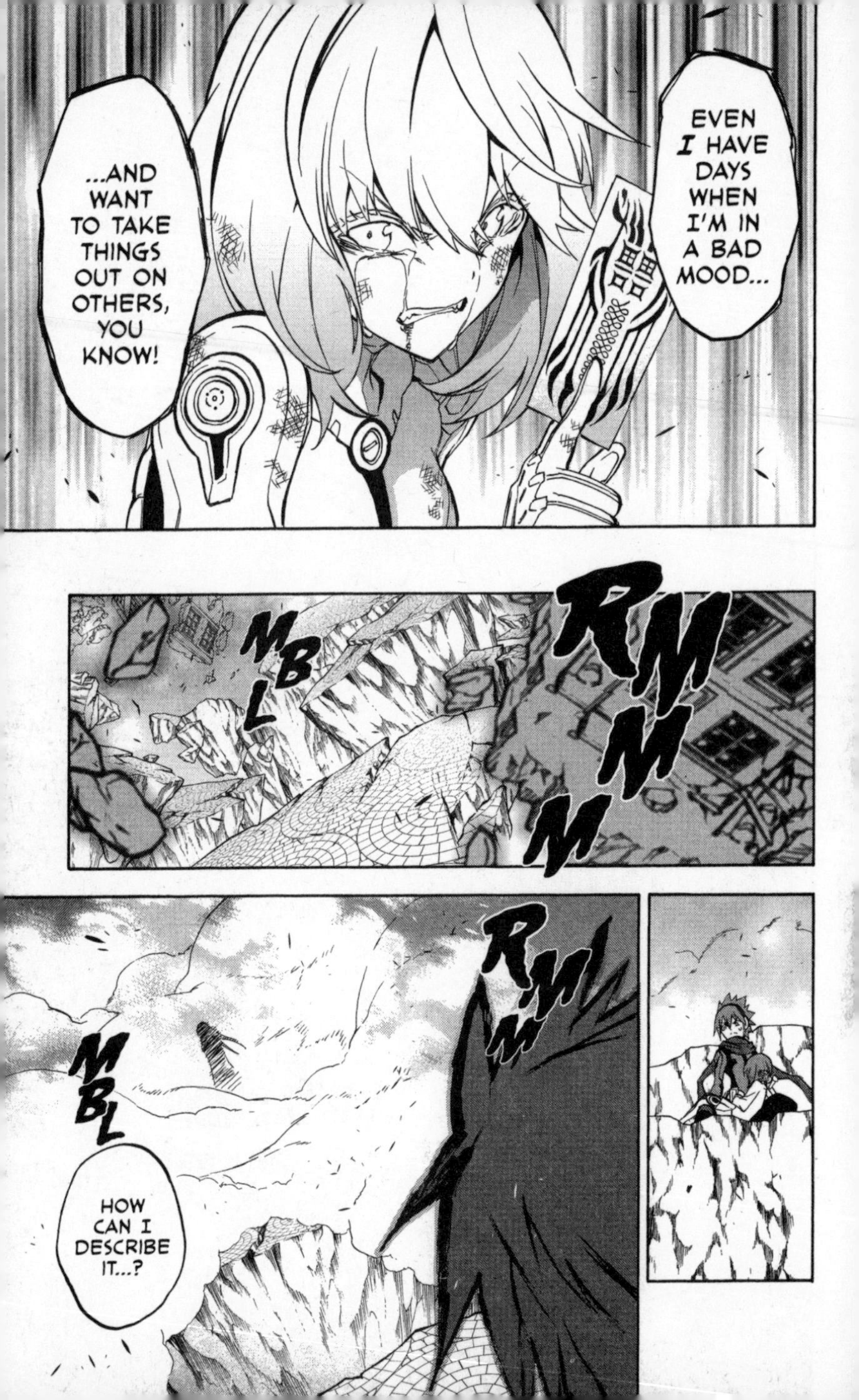
EVEN *I* HAVE DAYS WHEN I'M IN A BAD MOOD...
...AND WANT TO TAKE THINGS OUT ON OTHERS, YOU KNOW!
RMMM
MBL
RMMM
MBL
HOW CAN I DESCRIBE IT...?

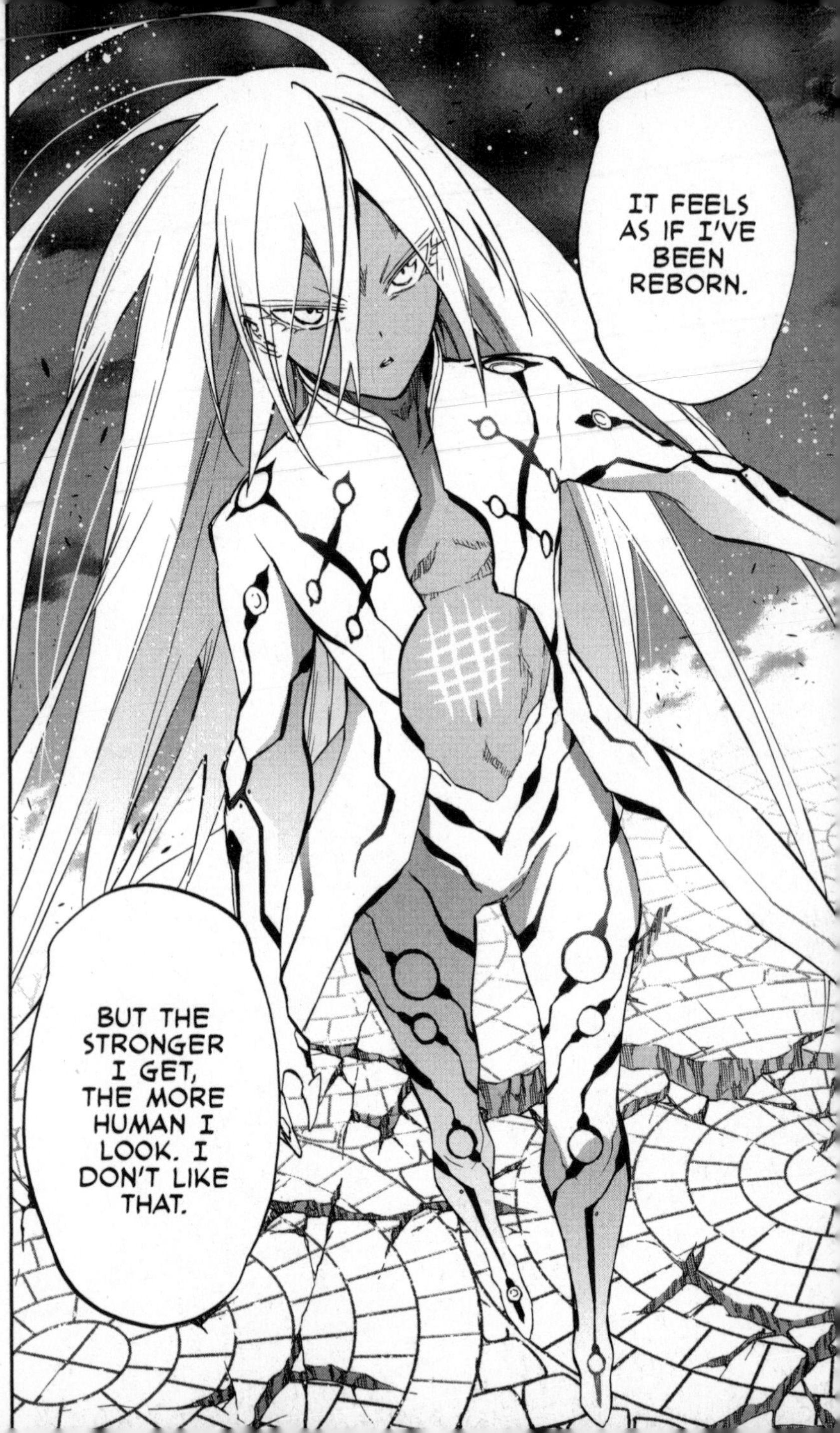
IT FEELS AS IF I'VE BEEN REBORN.
BUT THE STRONGER I GET, THE MORE HUMAN I LOOK. I DON'T LIKE THAT.

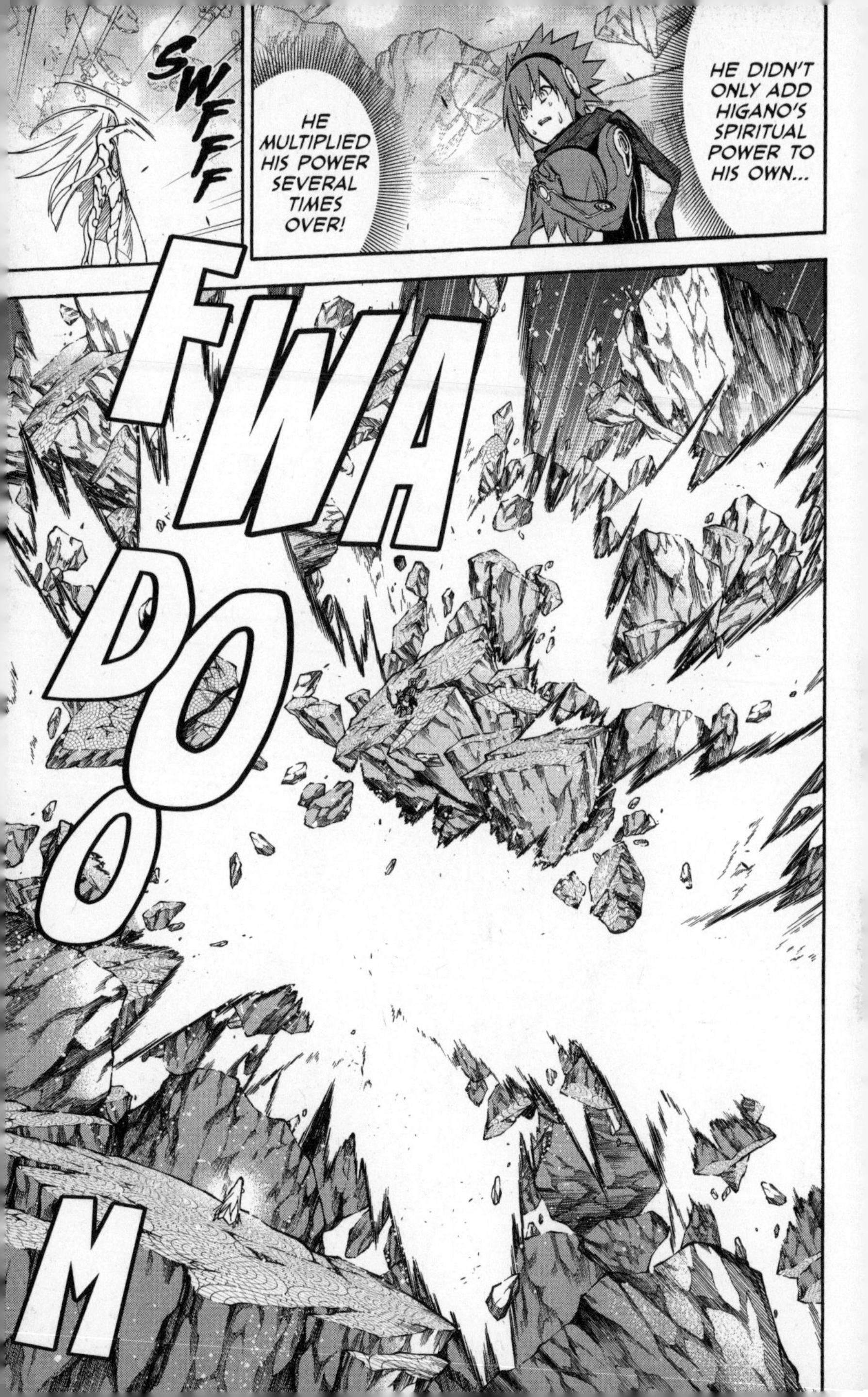
HE DIDN'T ONLY ADD HIGANO'S SPIRITUAL POWER TO HIS OWN...
HE MULTIPLIED HIS POWER SEVERAL TIMES OVER!
SWFFF
FWADOOM

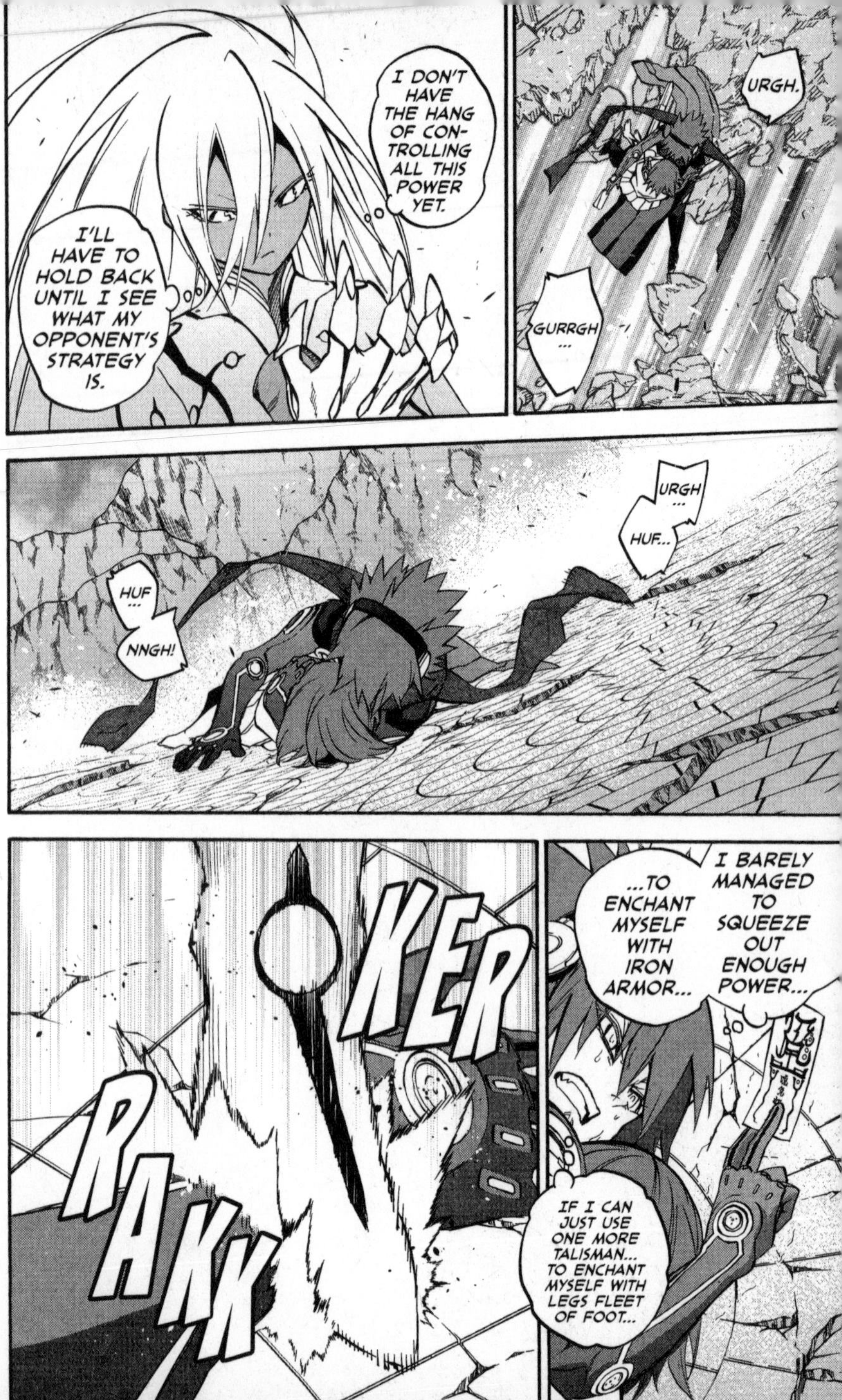
URGH.
GURRGH...
I DON'T HAVE THE HANG OF CONTROLLING ALL THIS POWER YET.
I'LL HAVE TO HOLD BACK UNTIL I SEE WHAT MY OPPONENT'S STRATEGY IS.
URGH...
HUF...
HUF...
NNGH!
I BARELY MANAGED TO SQUEEZE OUT ENOUGH POWER...
...TO ENCHANT MYSELF WITH IRON ARMOR...
IF I CAN JUST USE ONE MORE TALISMAN... TO ENCHANT MYSELF WITH LEGS FLEET OF FOOT...
KER
RAKK

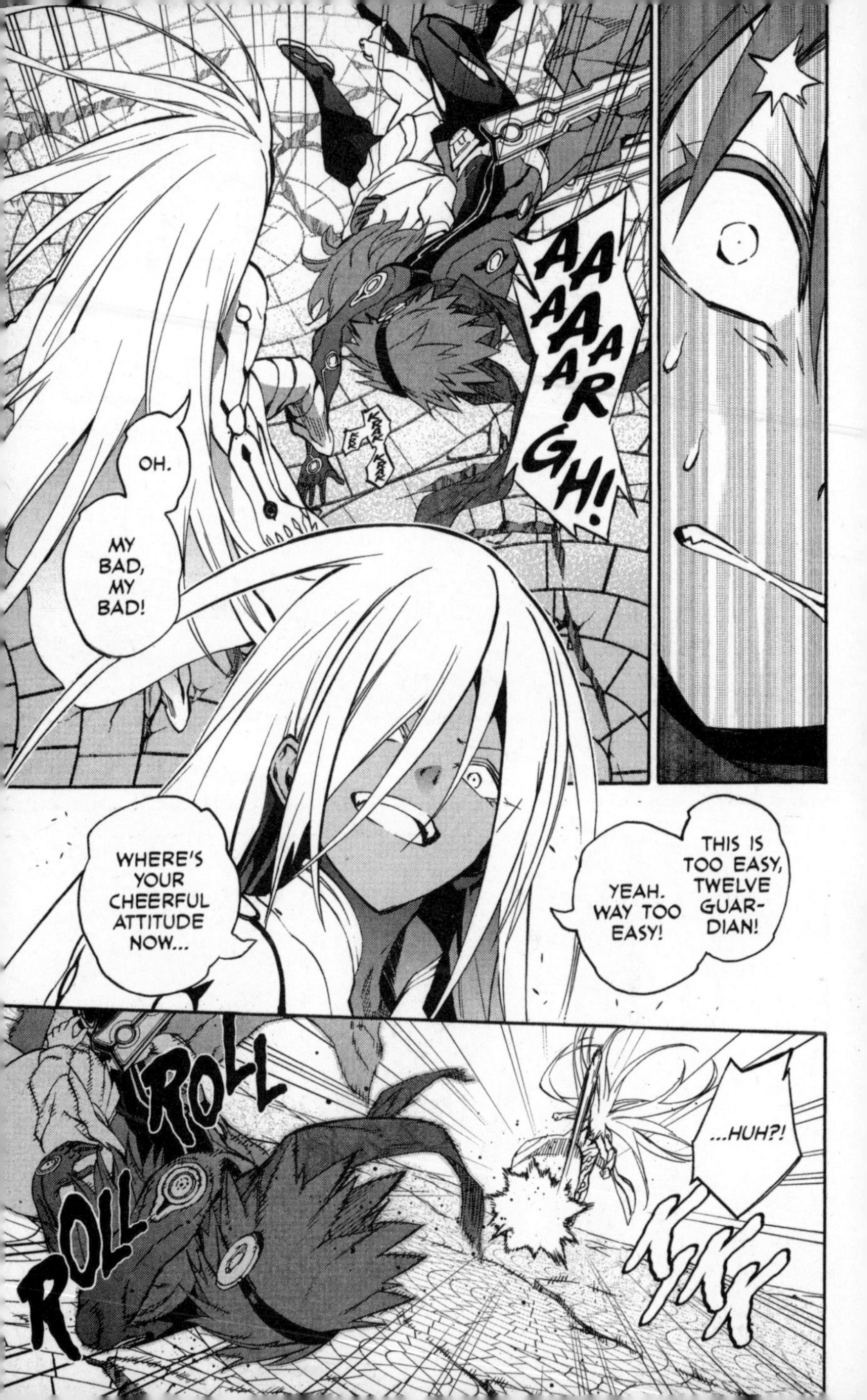
AAAAAARGH!
OH.
MY BAD, MY BAD!
THIS IS TOO EASY, TWELVE GUARDIAN!
YEAH. WAY TOO EASY!
WHERE'S YOUR CHEERFUL ATTITUDE NOW...
...HUH?!
ROLL
ROLL

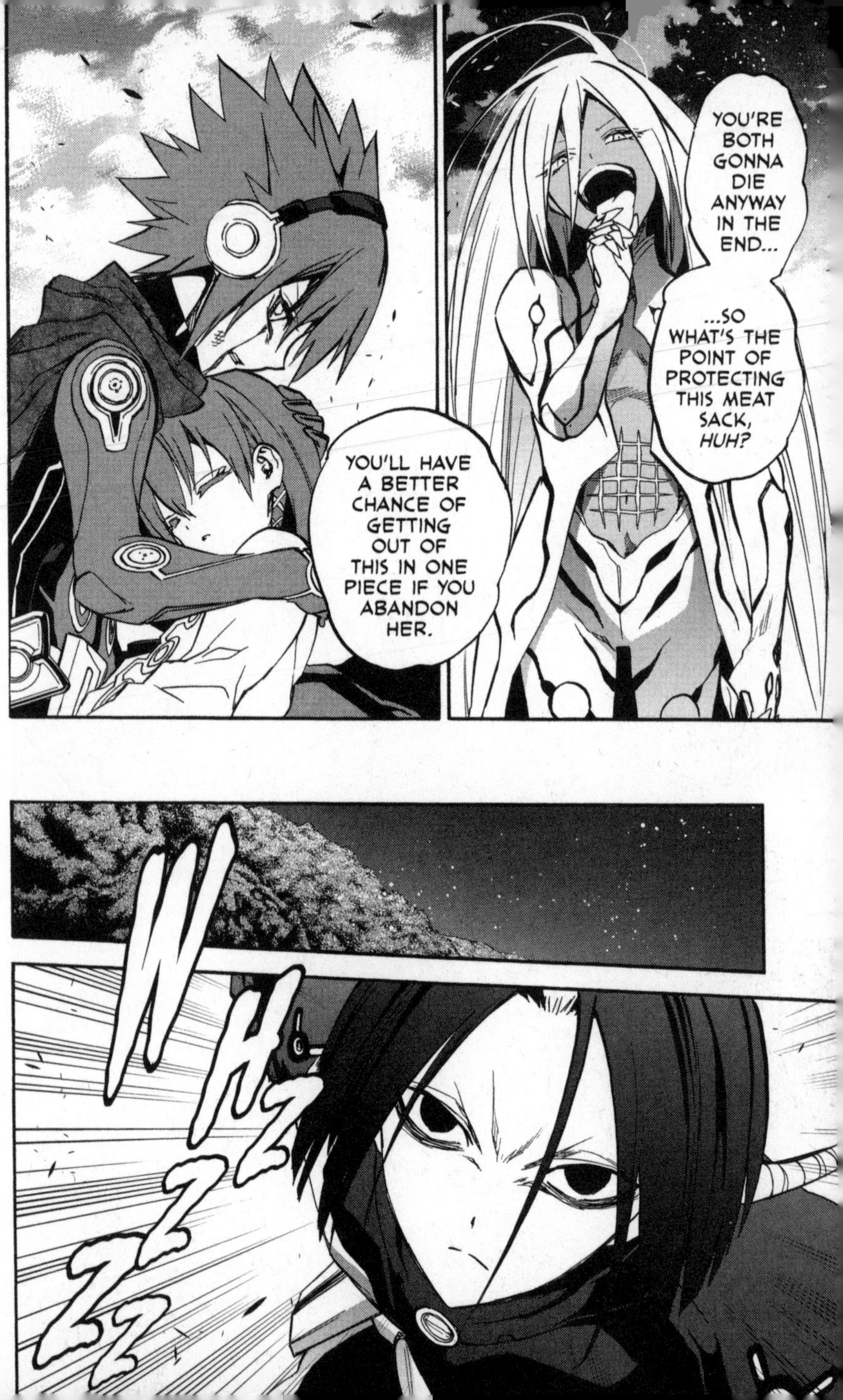
YOU'RE BOTH GONNA DIE ANYWAY IN THE END...
...SO WHAT'S THE POINT OF PROTECTING THIS MEAT SACK, *HUH?*
YOU'LL HAVE A BETTER CHANCE OF GETTING OUT OF THIS IN ONE PIECE IF YOU ABANDON HER.
WHZZZZ

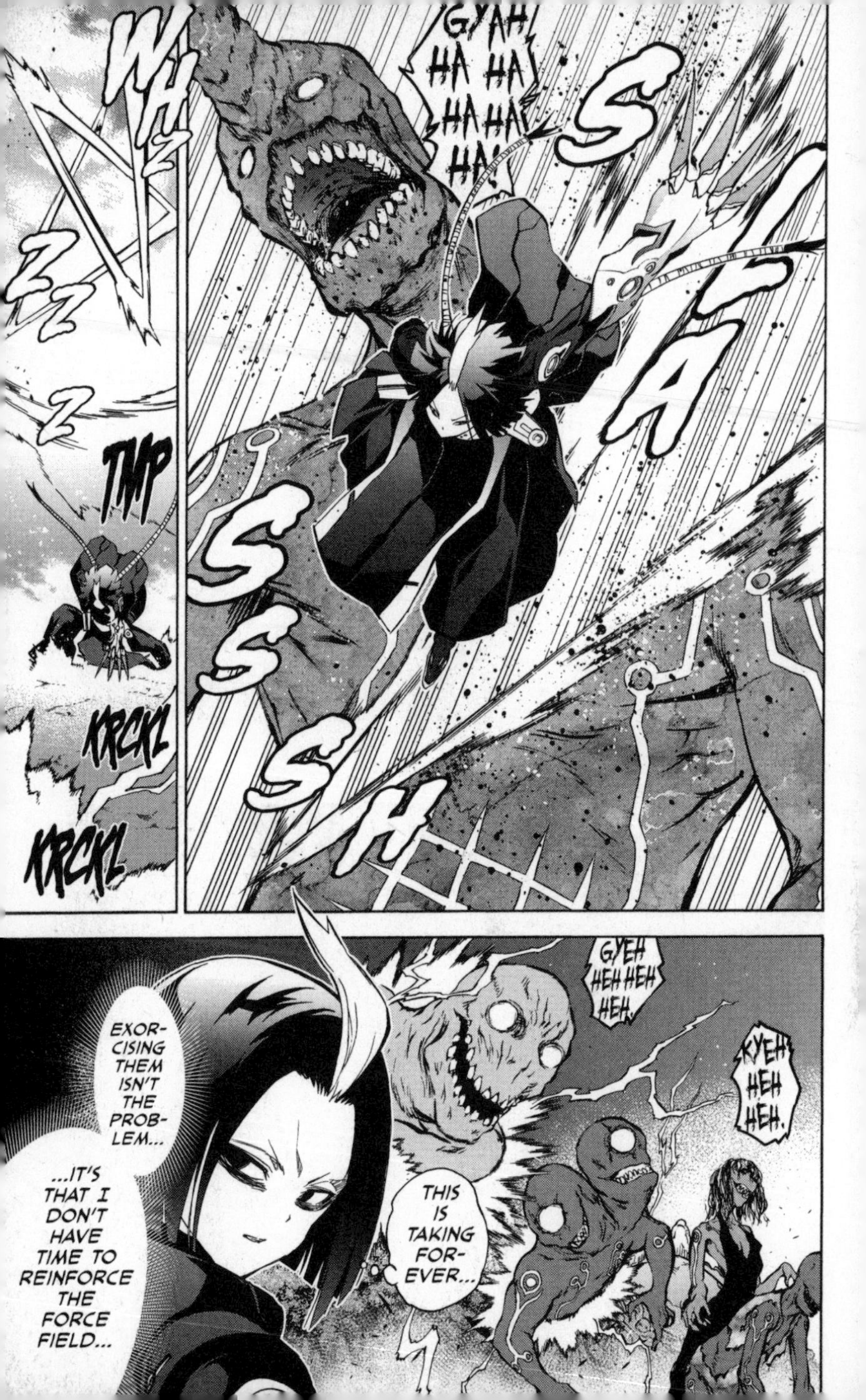
GYAH HA HA HA HA HA!
SAASSSH
WHZZZZZ
TMP
KRCKL
KRCKL
GYEH HEH HEH HEH.
KYEH HEH HEH.
EXORCISING THEM ISN'T THE PROBLEM...
...IT'S THAT I DON'T HAVE TIME TO REINFORCE THE FORCE FIELD...
THIS IS TAKING FOREVER...

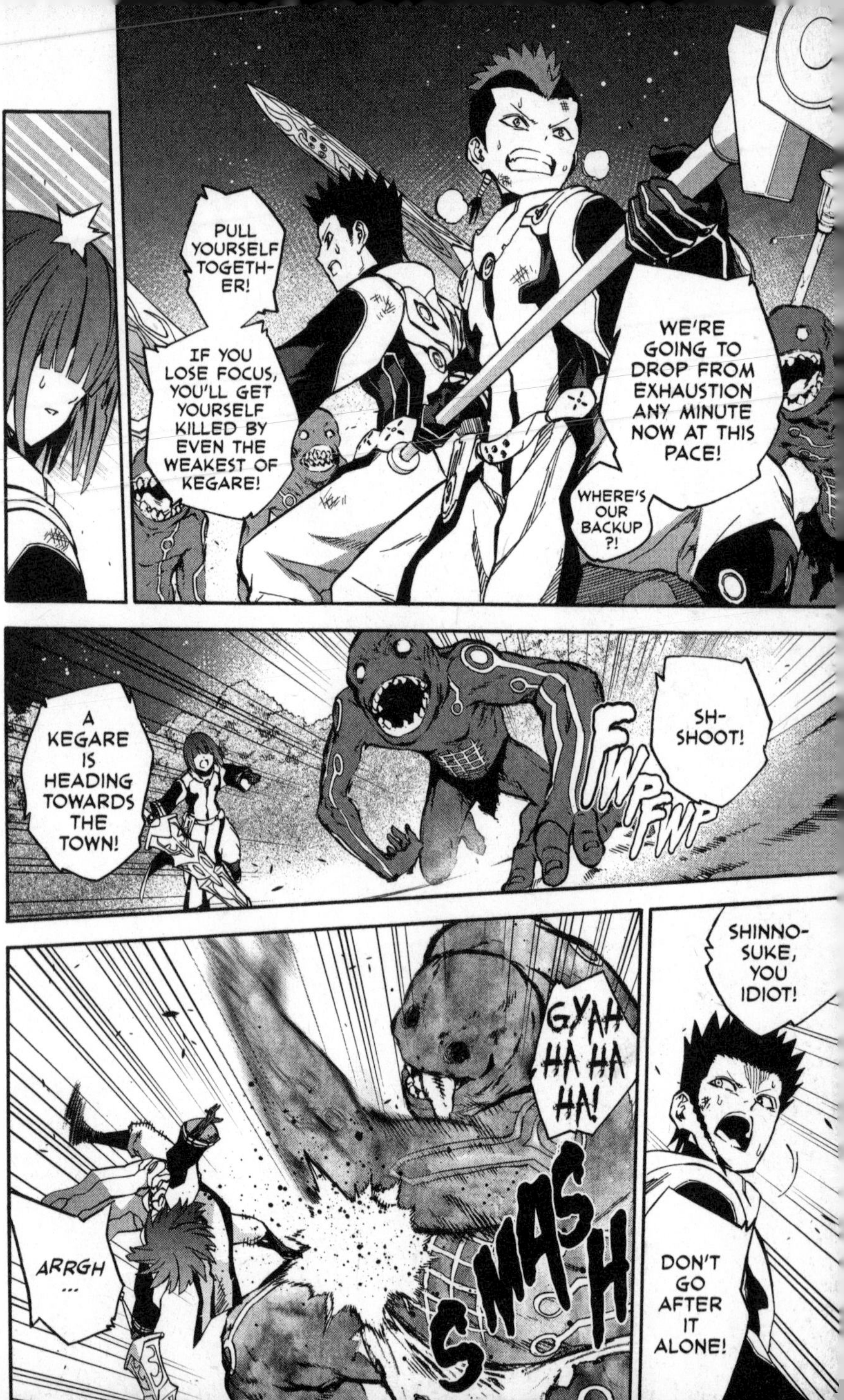

WE'RE GOING TO DROP FROM EXHAUSTION ANY MINUTE NOW AT THIS PACE!
WHERE'S OUR BACKUP?!
PULL YOURSELF TOGETH-ER!
IF YOU LOSE FOCUS, YOU'LL GET YOURSELF KILLED BY EVEN THE WEAKEST OF KEGARE!
SH-SHOOT!
FWP FWP
A KEGARE IS HEADING TOWARDS THE TOWN!
SHINNO-SUKE, YOU IDIOT!
DON'T GO AFTER IT ALONE!
GYAH HA HA HA!
SMASH
ARRGH...

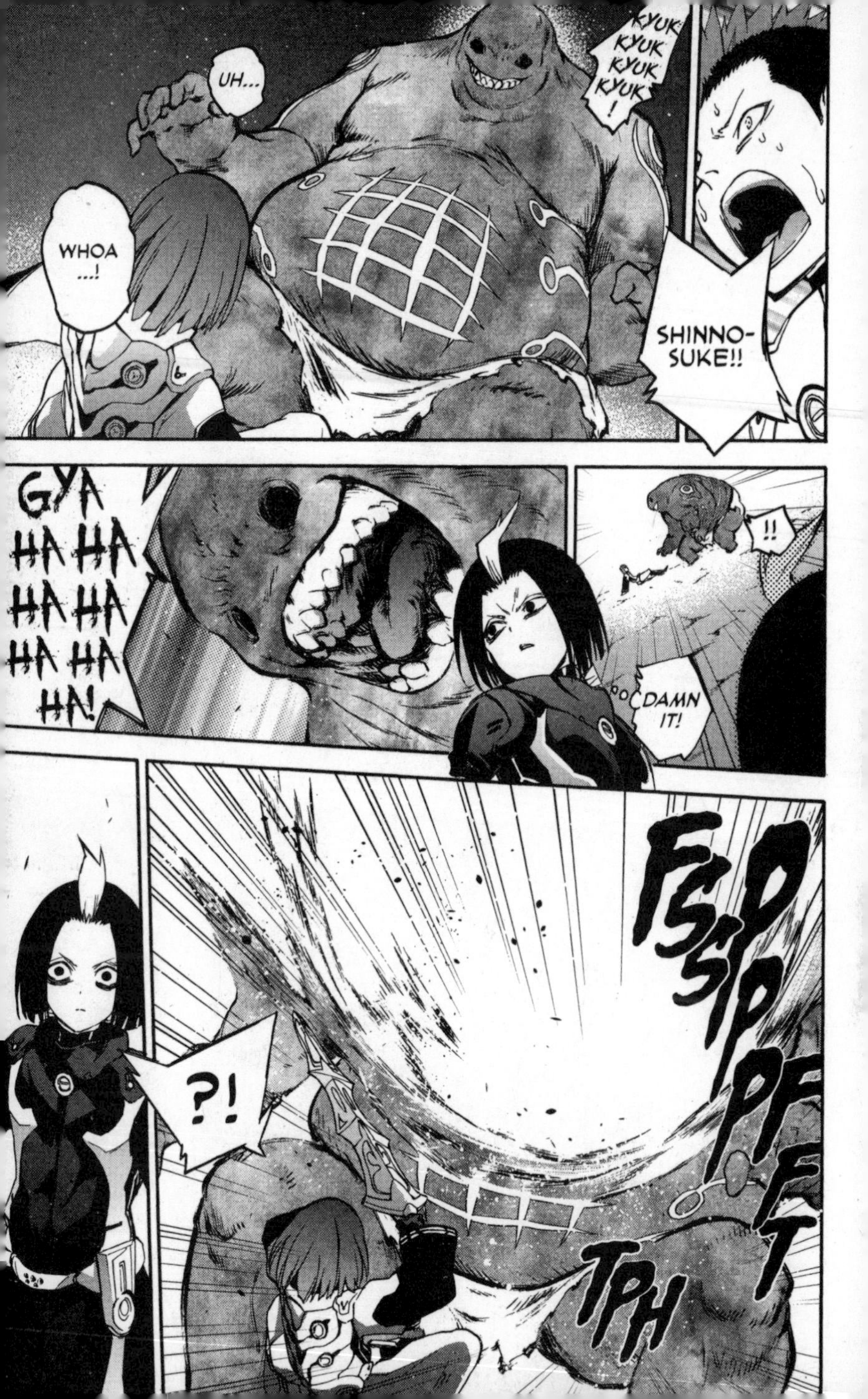
SHINNO-SUKE!!
KYUK KYUK KYUK KYUK!
UH...
WHOA ...!
!!
...DAMN IT!
GYA HA HA HA HA HA HA HA!
FSS
DPPFFT
TPH
?!

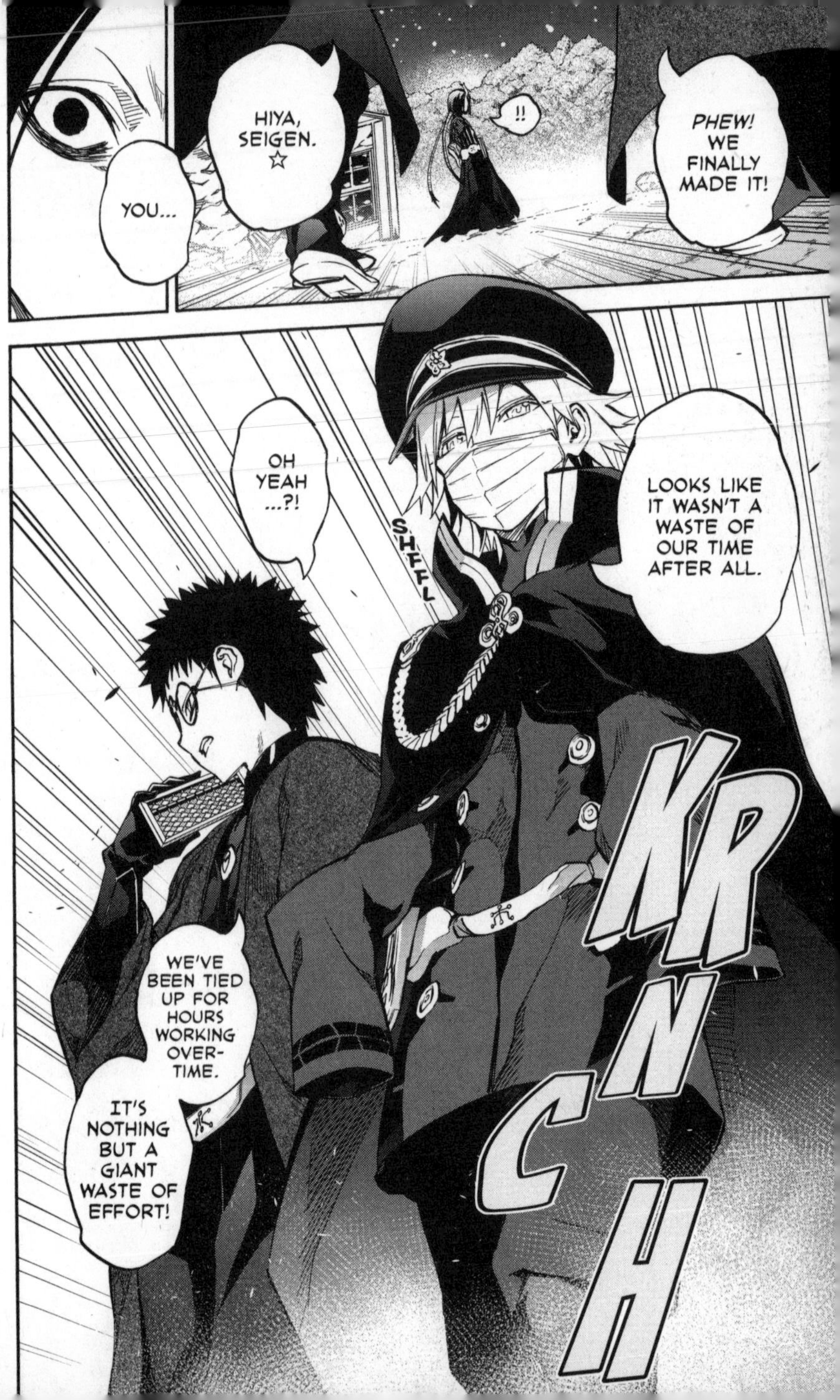
PHEW! WE FINALLY MADE IT!
HIYA, SEIGEN. ☆
!!
YOU...
LOOKS LIKE IT WASN'T A WASTE OF OUR TIME AFTER ALL.
OH YEAH ...?!
SHFFL
WE'VE BEEN TIED UP FOR HOURS WORKING OVER-TIME.
IT'S NOTHING BUT A GIANT WASTE OF EFFORT!
KRNCH

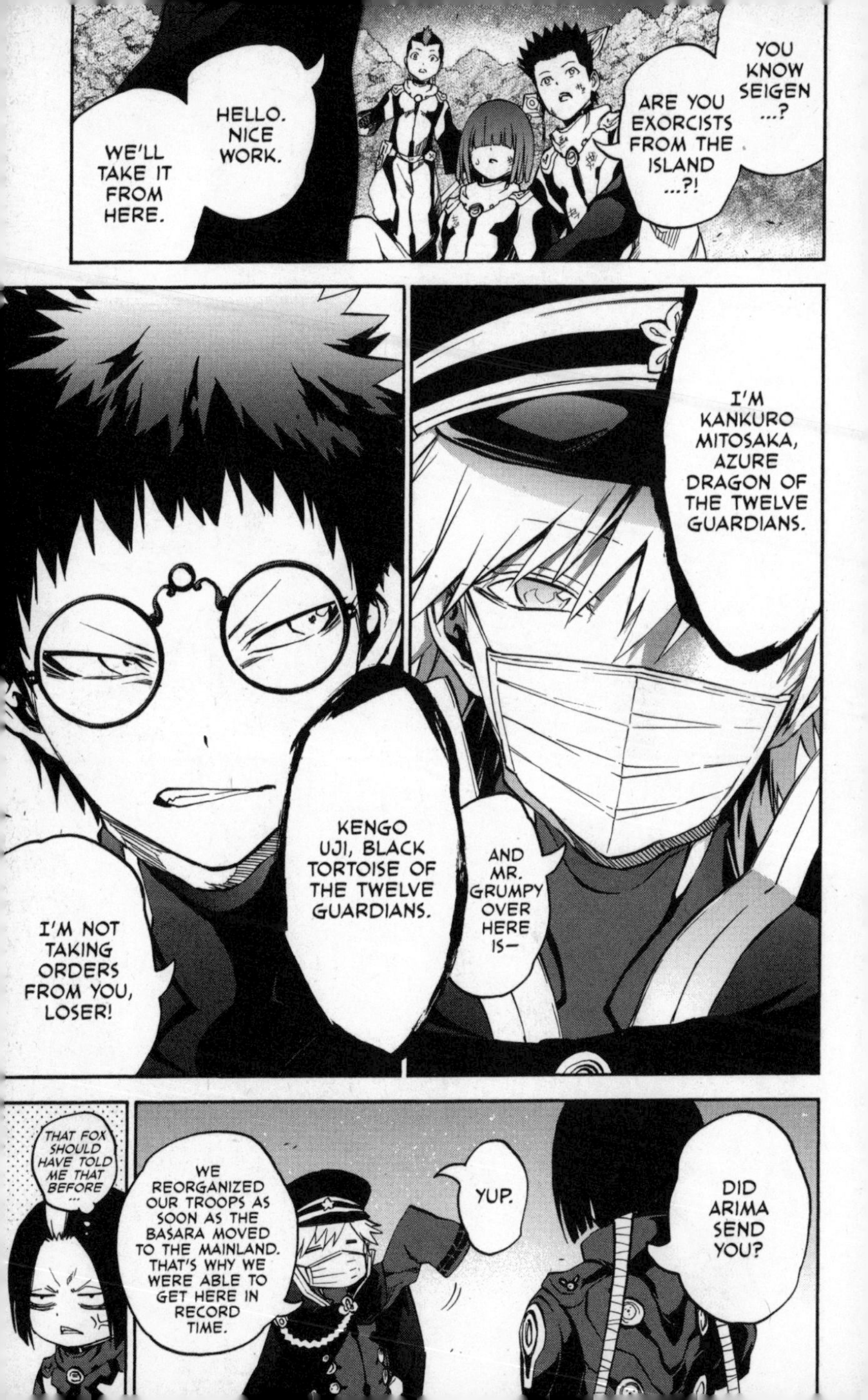
YOU KNOW SEIGEN ...?
ARE YOU EXORCISTS FROM THE ISLAND ...?!
HELLO. NICE WORK.
WE'LL TAKE IT FROM HERE.
I'M KANKURO MITOSAKA, AZURE DRAGON OF THE TWELVE GUARDIANS.
AND MR. GRUMPY OVER HERE IS—
KENGO UJI, BLACK TORTOISE OF THE TWELVE GUARDIANS.
I'M NOT TAKING ORDERS FROM YOU, LOSER!
DID ARIMA SEND YOU?
YUP.
WE REORGANIZED OUR TROOPS AS SOON AS THE BASARA MOVED TO THE MAINLAND. THAT'S WHY WE WERE ABLE TO GET HERE IN RECORD TIME.
THAT FOX SHOULD HAVE TOLD ME THAT BEFORE ...

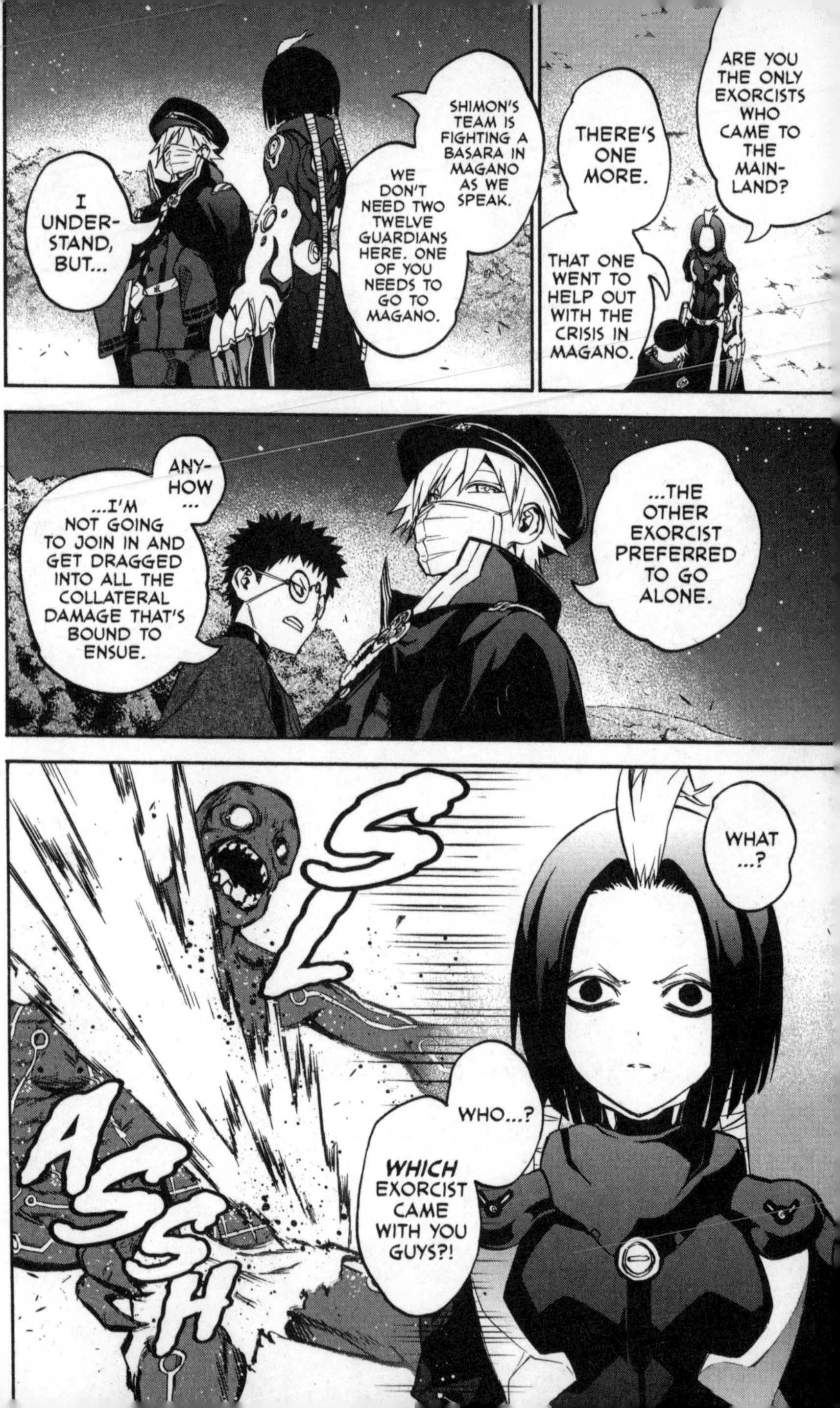
ARE YOU THE ONLY EXORCISTS WHO CAME TO THE MAIN-LAND?
THERE'S ONE MORE.
THAT ONE WENT TO HELP OUT WITH THE CRISIS IN MAGANO.
SHIMON'S TEAM IS FIGHTING A BASARA IN MAGANO AS WE SPEAK.
WE DON'T NEED TWO TWELVE GUARDIANS HERE. ONE OF YOU NEEDS TO GO TO MAGANO.
I UNDER-STAND, BUT...
...THE OTHER EXORCIST PREFERRED TO GO ALONE.
ANY-HOW...
...I'M NOT GOING TO JOIN IN AND GET DRAGGED INTO ALL THE COLLATERAL DAMAGE THAT'S BOUND TO ENSUE.
WHAT...?
WHO...?
WHICH EXORCIST CAME WITH YOU GUYS?!
SLASSH

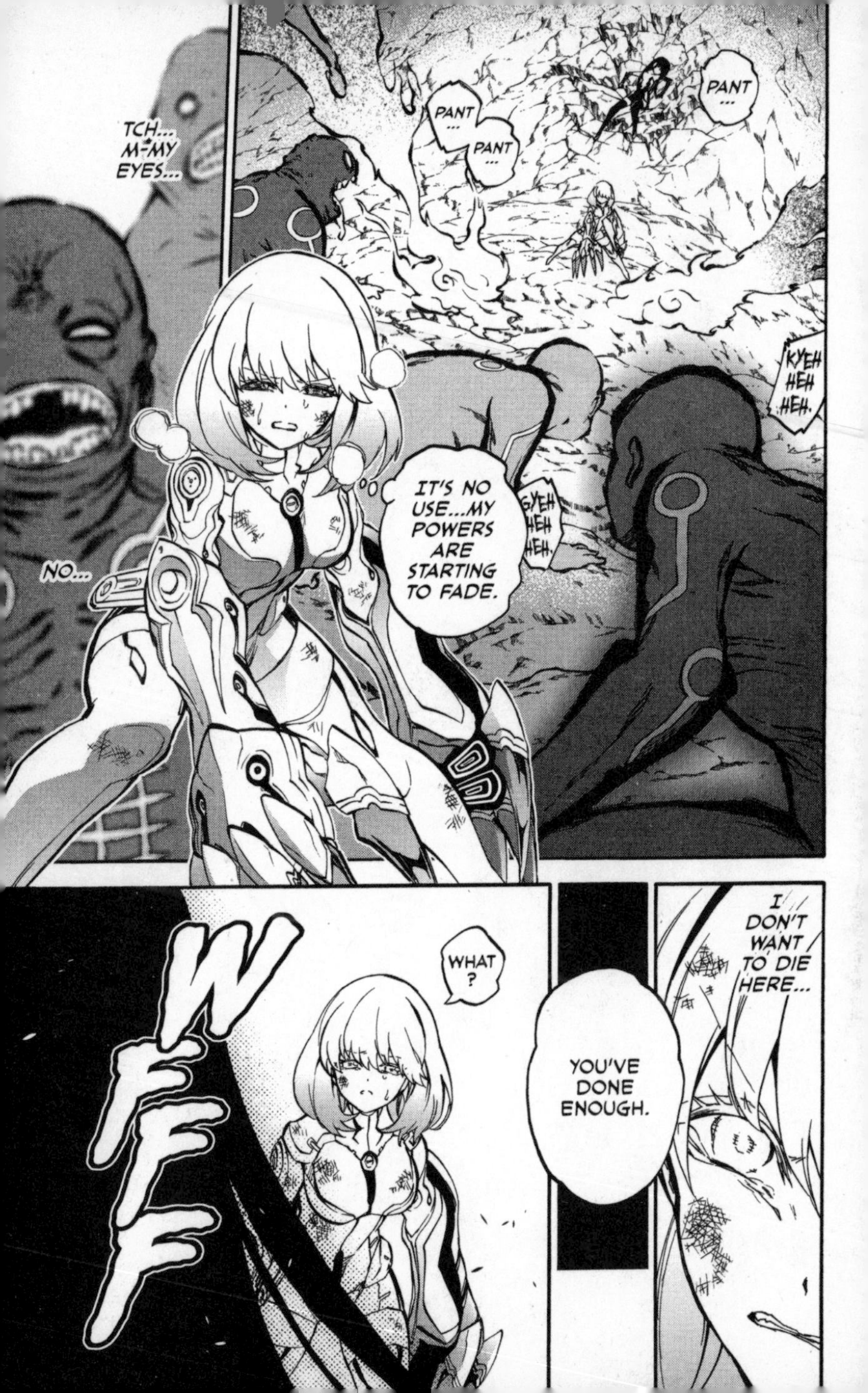
PANT...
PANT...
PANT...
TCH... M-MY EYES...
KYEH HEH HEH.
GYEH HEH HEH.
IT'S NO USE...MY POWERS ARE STARTING TO FADE.
NO...
I DON'T WANT TO DIE HERE...
YOU'VE DONE ENOUGH.
WHAT?
WFF

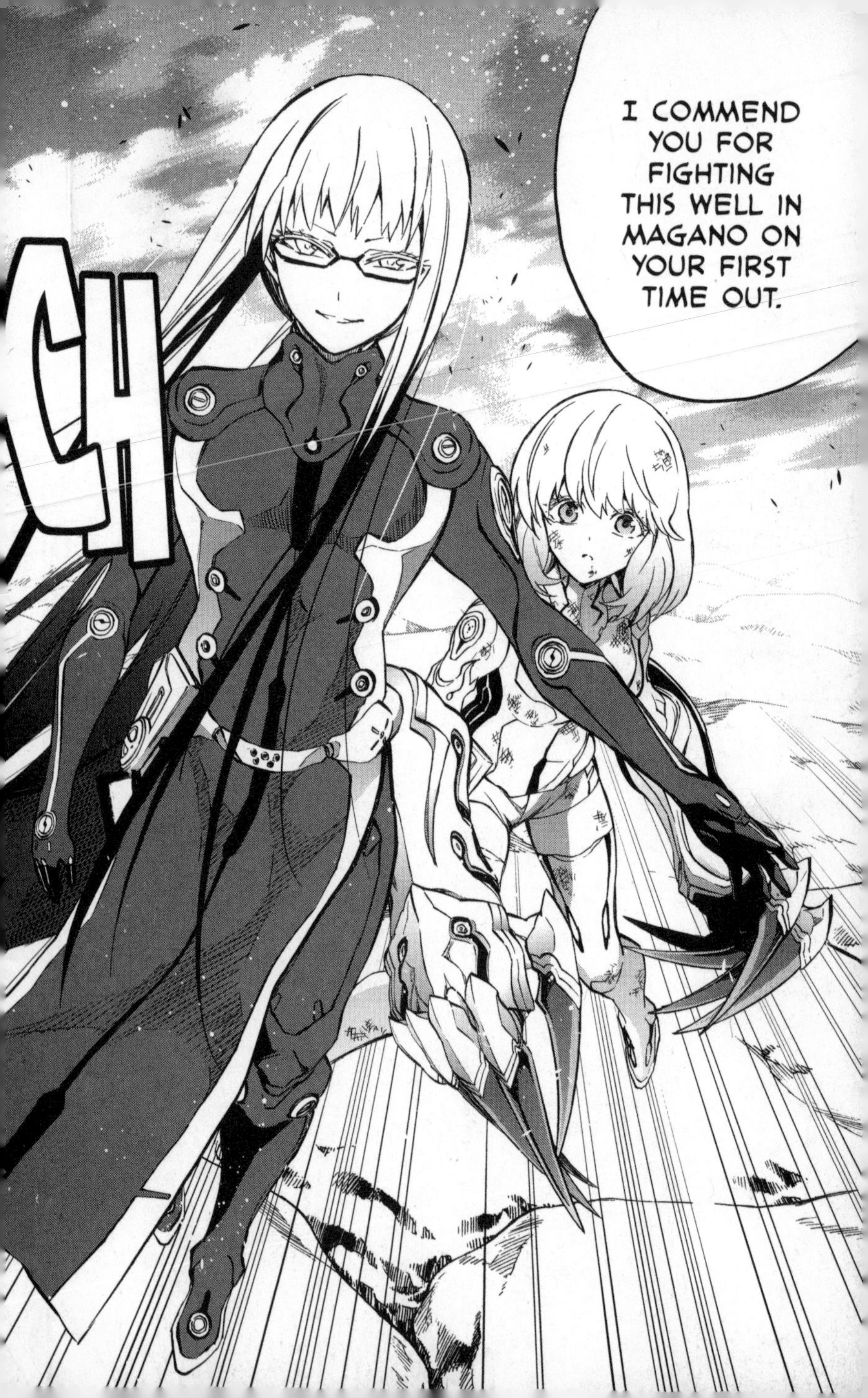
I COMMEND YOU FOR FIGHTING THIS WELL IN MAGANO ON YOUR FIRST TIME OUT.
CH

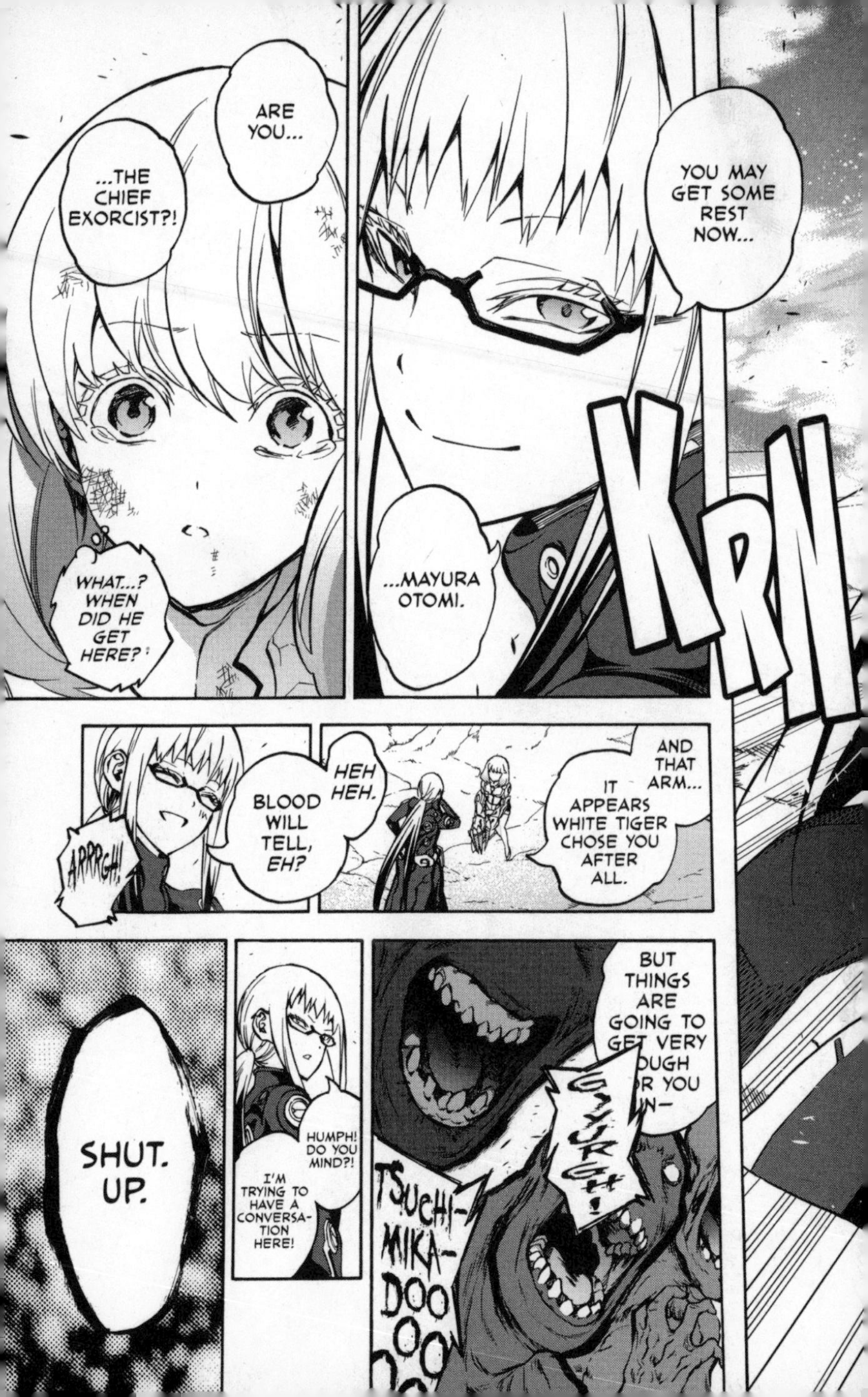
YOU MAY GET SOME REST NOW...
...MAYURA OTOMI.
KRRN
ARE YOU...
...THE CHIEF EXORCIST?!
WHAT...? WHEN DID HE GET HERE?
AND THAT ARM...
IT APPEARS WHITE TIGER CHOSE YOU AFTER ALL.
HEH HEH.
BLOOD WILL TELL, EH?
ARRRGH!
BUT THINGS ARE GOING TO GET VERY OUGH R YOU N—
GYURGH!
TSUCHI-MIKA-DOOOOO
HUMPH! DO YOU MIND?!
I'M TRYING TO HAVE A CONVERSA-TION HERE!
SHUT. UP.

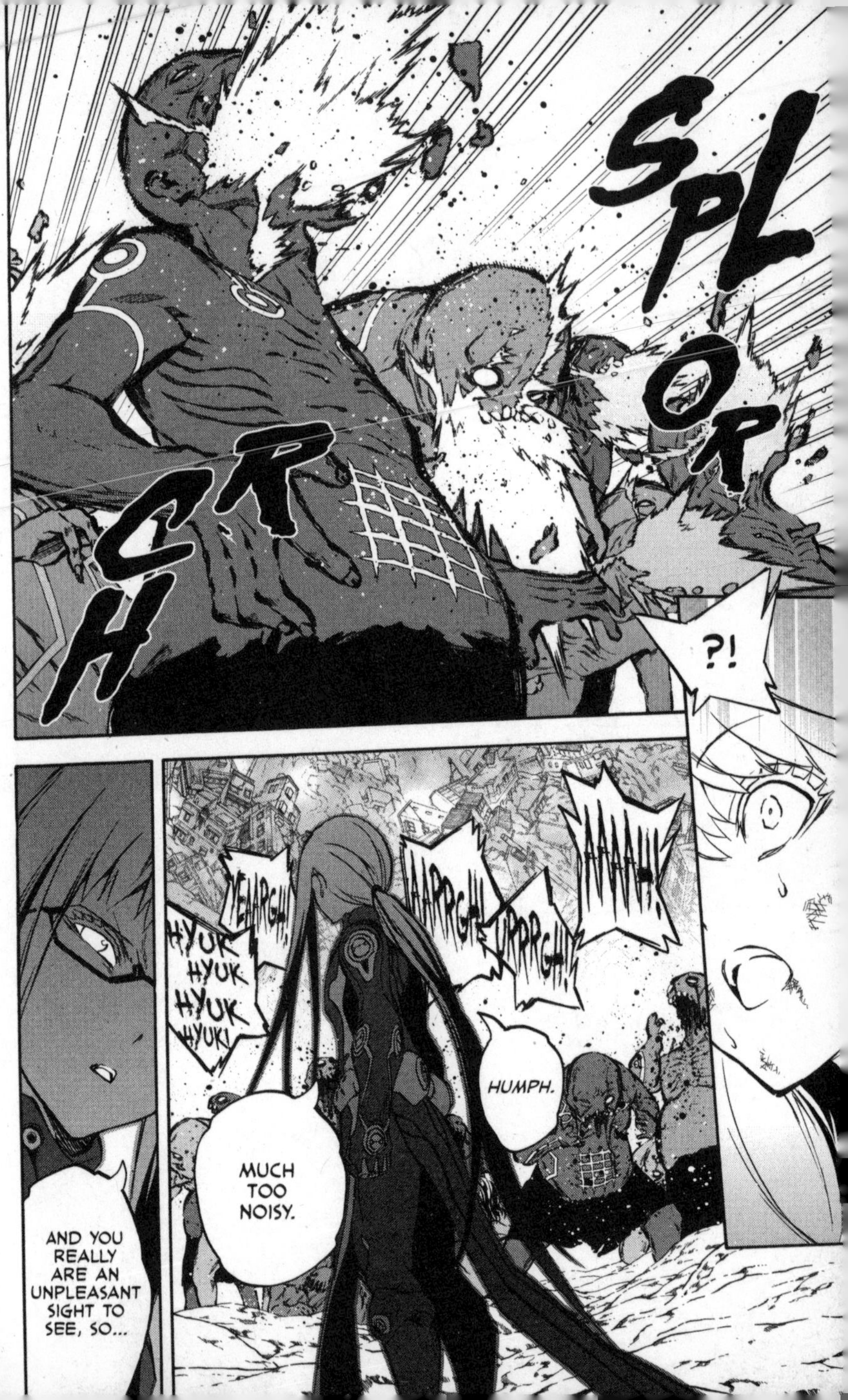
SPLORT
CRCH
?!
AAAAH!
URRRGH!
AARRGH!
YEAARGH!
HYUK HYUK HYUK HYUK!
HUMPH.
MUCH TOO NOISY.
AND YOU REALLY ARE AN UNPLEASANT SIGHT TO SEE, SO...

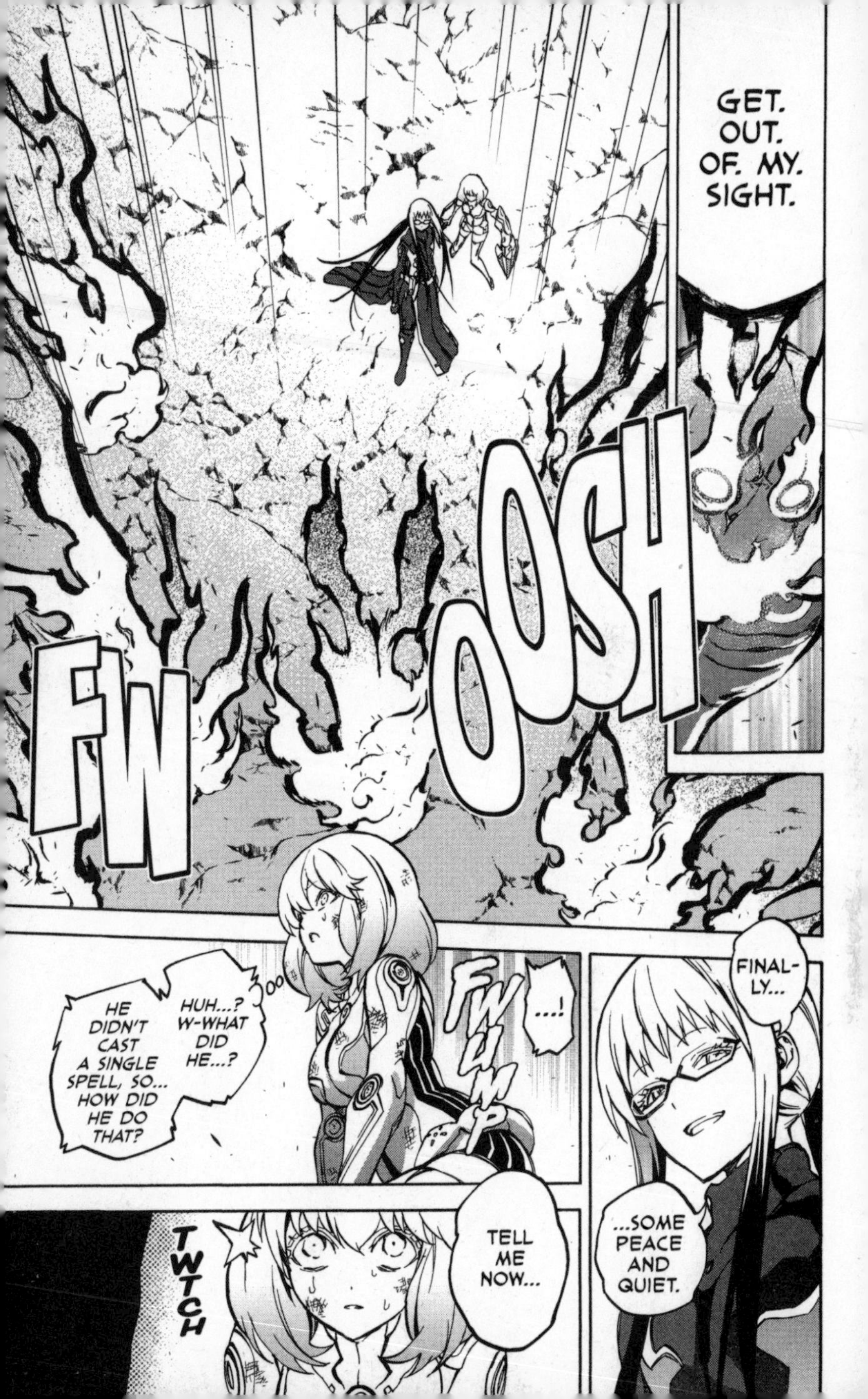
GET. OUT. OF. MY. SIGHT.
FWOOSH
FINAL-LY...
...SOME PEACE AND QUIET.
...!
FWUMP
HUH...? W-WHAT DID HE...?
HE DIDN'T CAST A SINGLE SPELL, SO... HOW DID HE DO THAT?
TELL ME NOW...
TWTCH

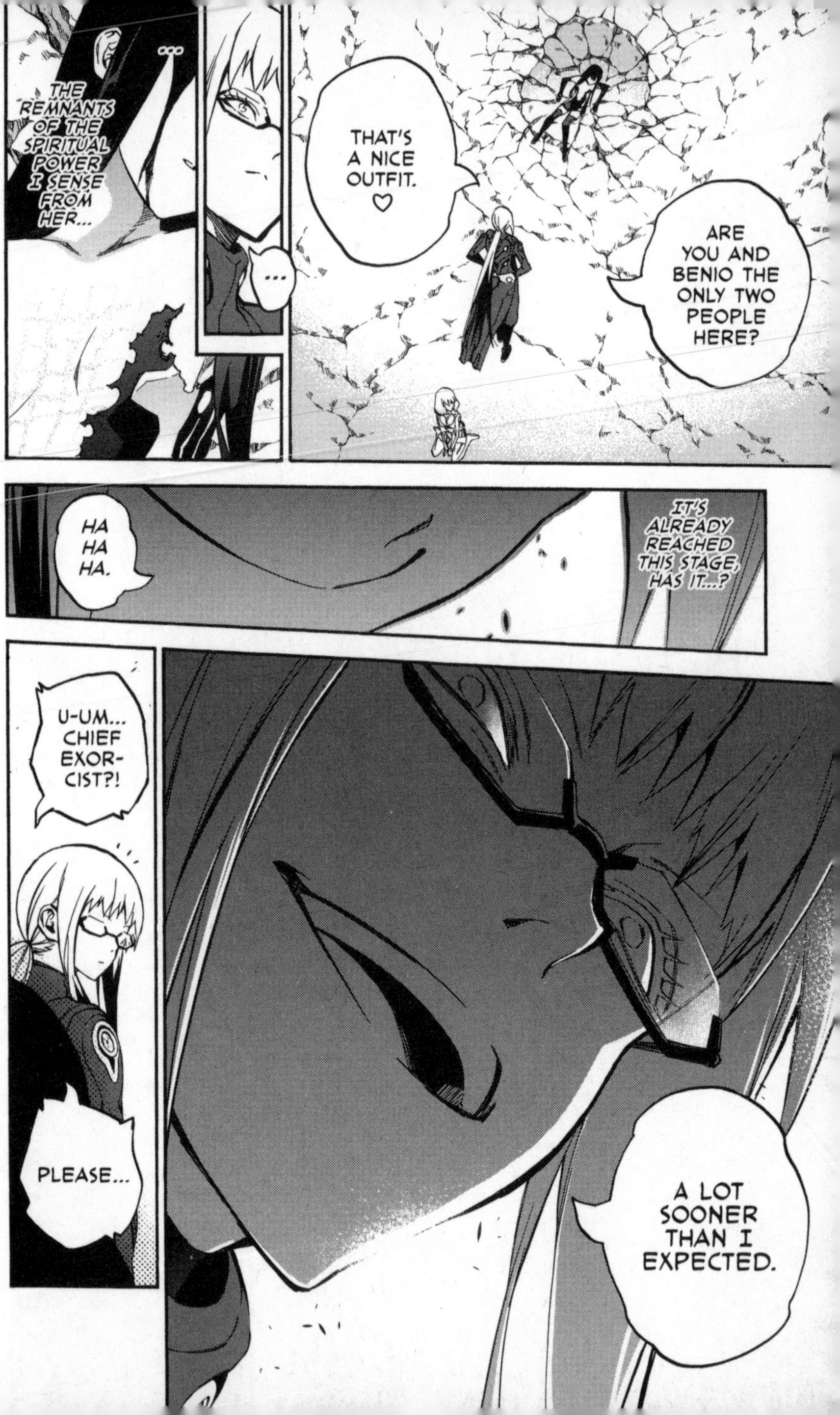
THAT'S A NICE OUTFIT. ♡
ARE YOU AND BENIO THE ONLY TWO PEOPLE HERE?
...
...
THE REMNANTS OF THE SPIRITUAL POWER I SENSE FROM HER...
IT'S ALREADY REACHED THIS STAGE, HAS IT...?
HA HA HA.
A LOT SOONER THAN I EXPECTED.
U-UM... CHIEF EXORCIST?!
PLEASE...

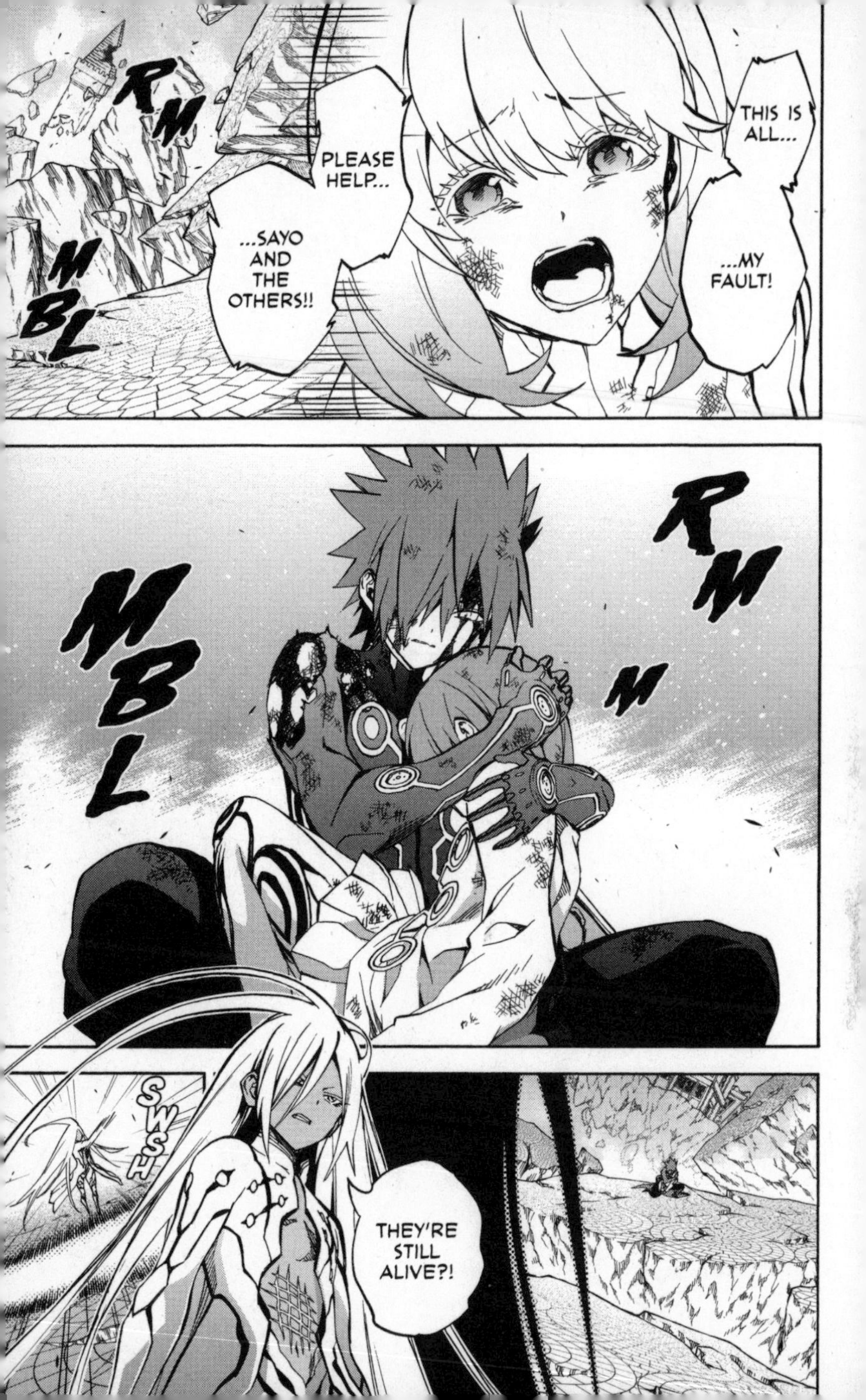
THIS IS ALL...
...MY FAULT!
PLEASE HELP...
...SAYO AND THE OTHERS!!
RM
MBL
RMM
MBL
THEY'RE STILL ALIVE?!
SWSH

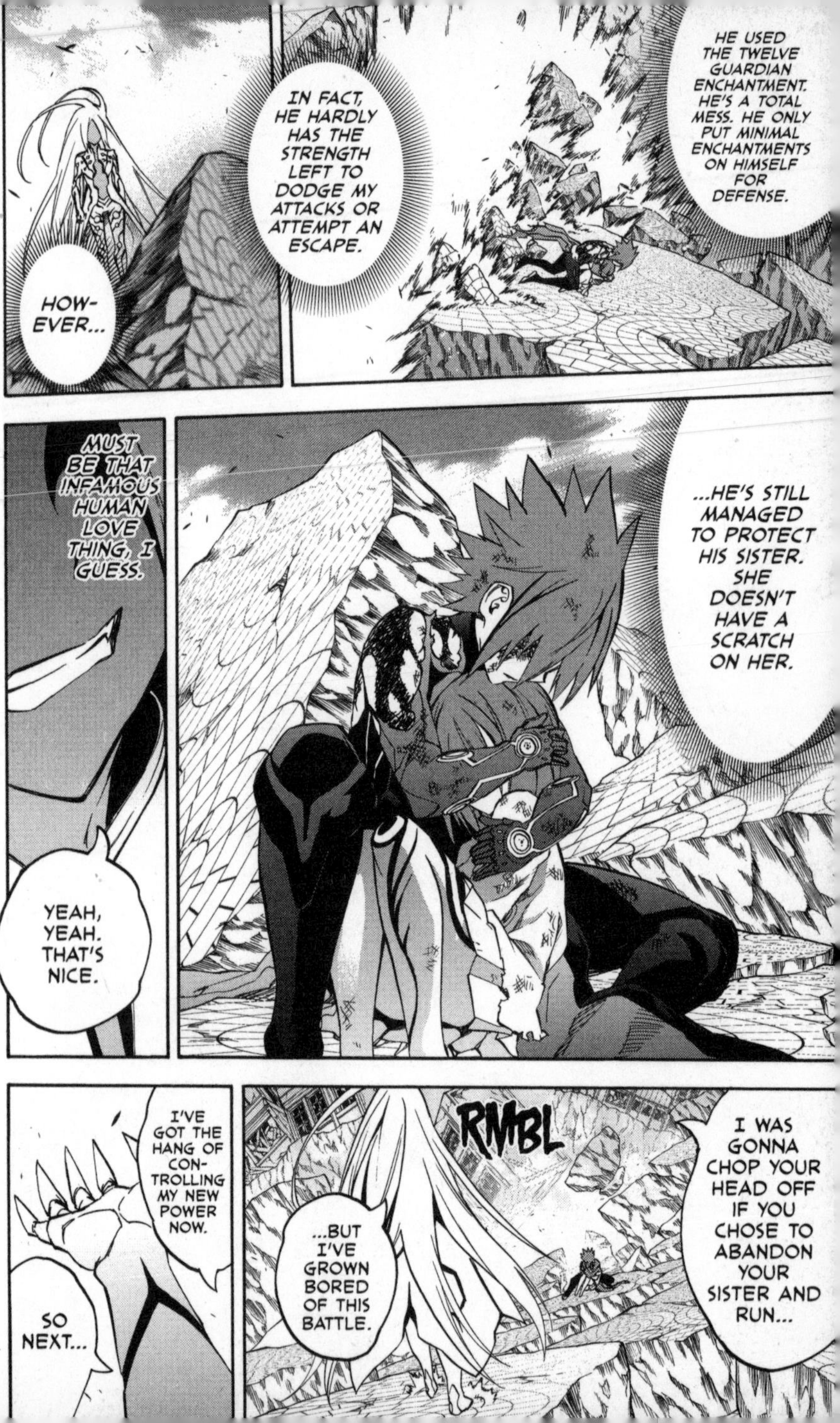
HE USED THE TWELVE GUARDIAN ENCHANTMENT. HE'S A TOTAL MESS. HE ONLY PUT MINIMAL ENCHANTMENTS ON HIMSELF FOR DEFENSE.
IN FACT, HE HARDLY HAS THE STRENGTH LEFT TO DODGE MY ATTACKS OR ATTEMPT AN ESCAPE.
HOW-EVER...
...HE'S STILL MANAGED TO PROTECT HIS SISTER. SHE DOESN'T HAVE A SCRATCH ON HER.
MUST BE THAT INFAMOUS HUMAN LOVE THING, I GUESS.
YEAH, YEAH. THAT'S NICE.
I WAS GONNA CHOP YOUR HEAD OFF IF YOU CHOSE TO ABANDON YOUR SISTER AND RUN...
RMBL
...BUT I'VE GROWN BORED OF THIS BATTLE.
I'VE GOT THE HANG OF CON-TROLLING MY NEW POWER NOW.
SO NEXT...

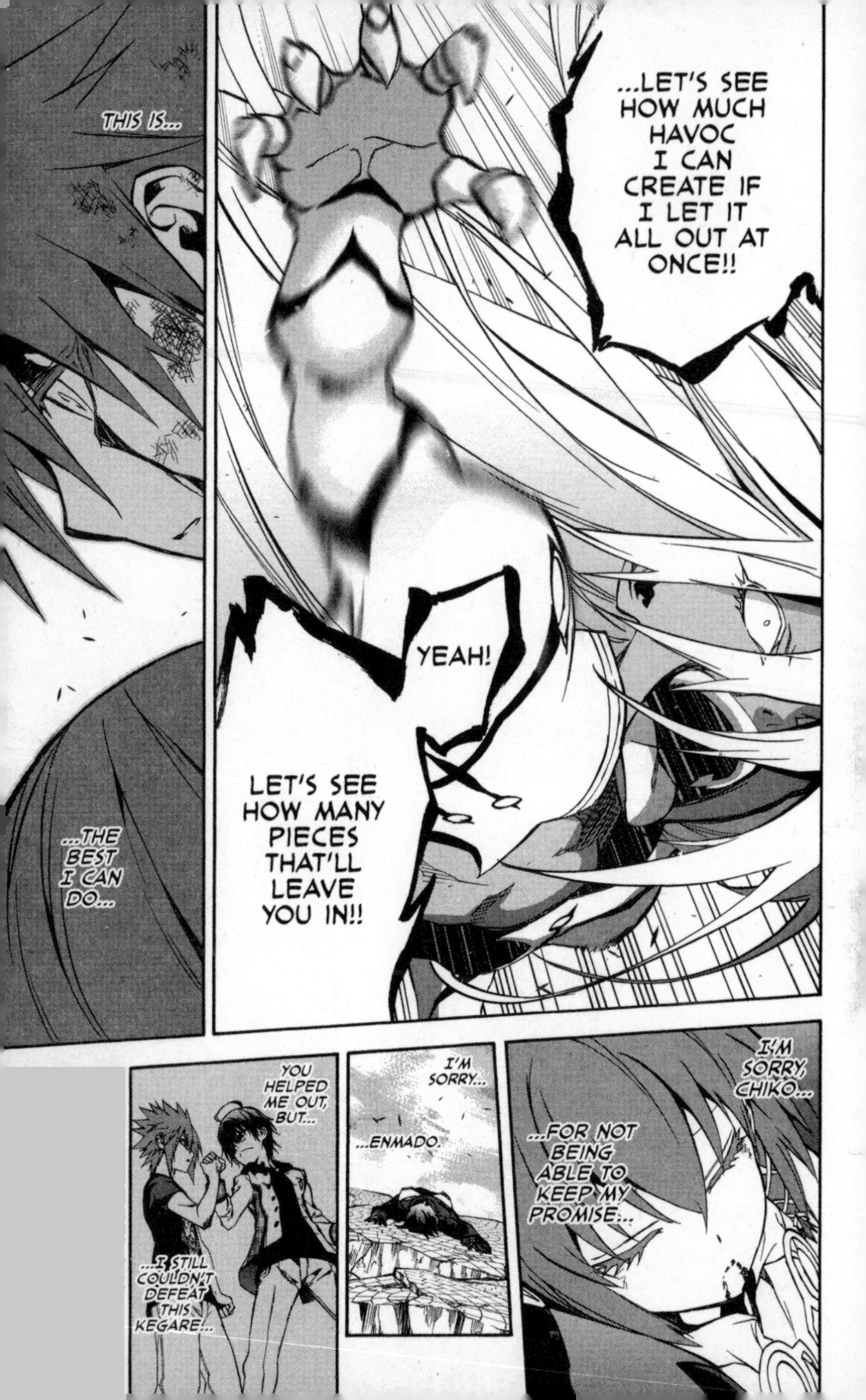
...LET'S SEE HOW MUCH HAVOC I CAN CREATE IF I LET IT ALL OUT AT ONCE!!
YEAH!
LET'S SEE HOW MANY PIECES THAT'LL LEAVE YOU IN!!
THIS IS...
...THE BEST I CAN DO...
I'M SORRY, CHIKO...
...FOR NOT BEING ABLE TO KEEP MY PROMISE...
I'M SORRY...
...ENMADO.
YOU HELPED ME OUT, BUT...
...I STILL COULDN'T DEFEAT THIS KEGARE...

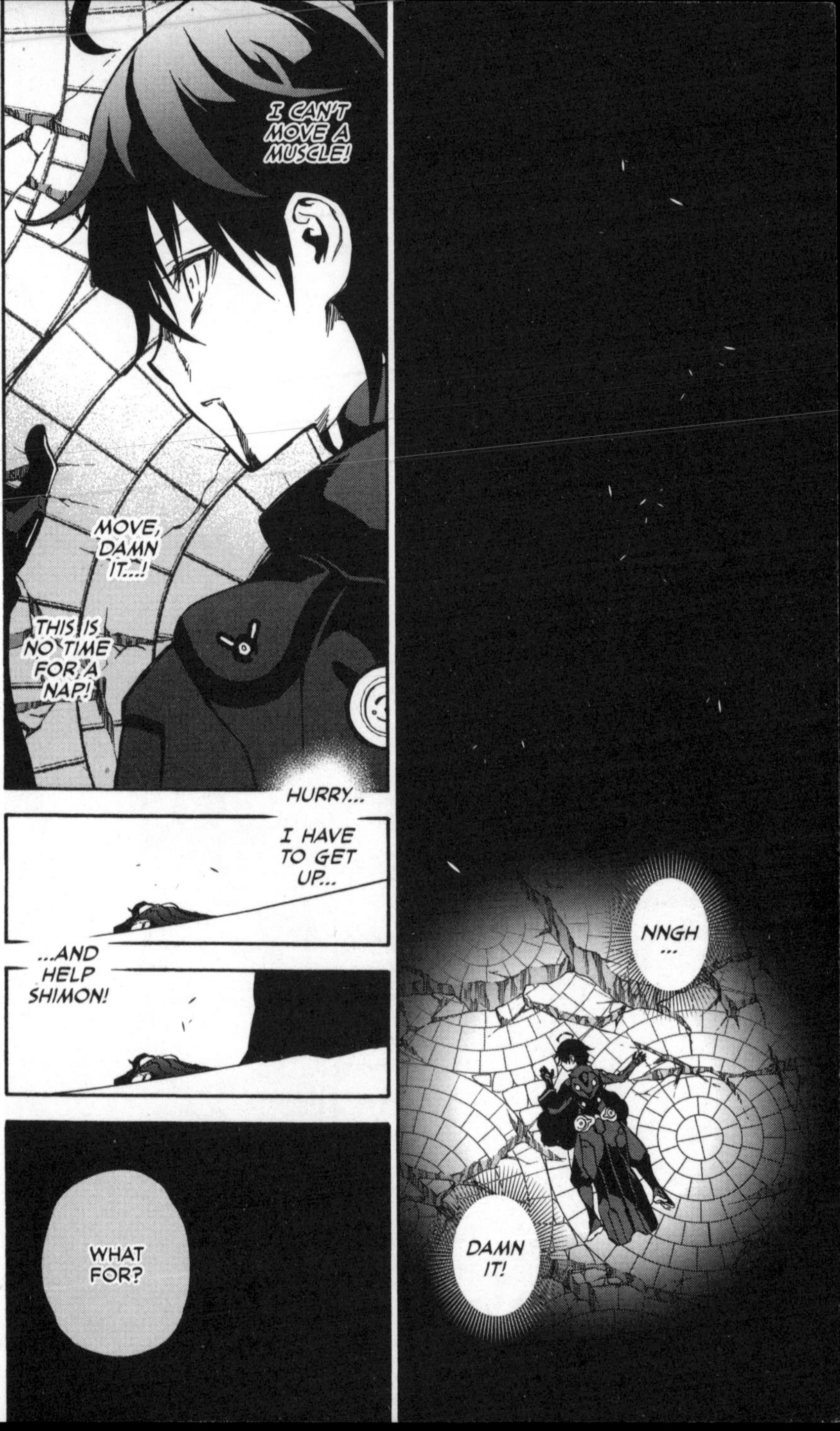
NNGH...
DAMN IT!
I CAN'T MOVE A MUSCLE!
MOVE, DAMN IT...!
THIS IS NO TIME FOR A NAP!
HURRY...
I HAVE TO GET UP...
...AND HELP SHIMON!
WHAT FOR?

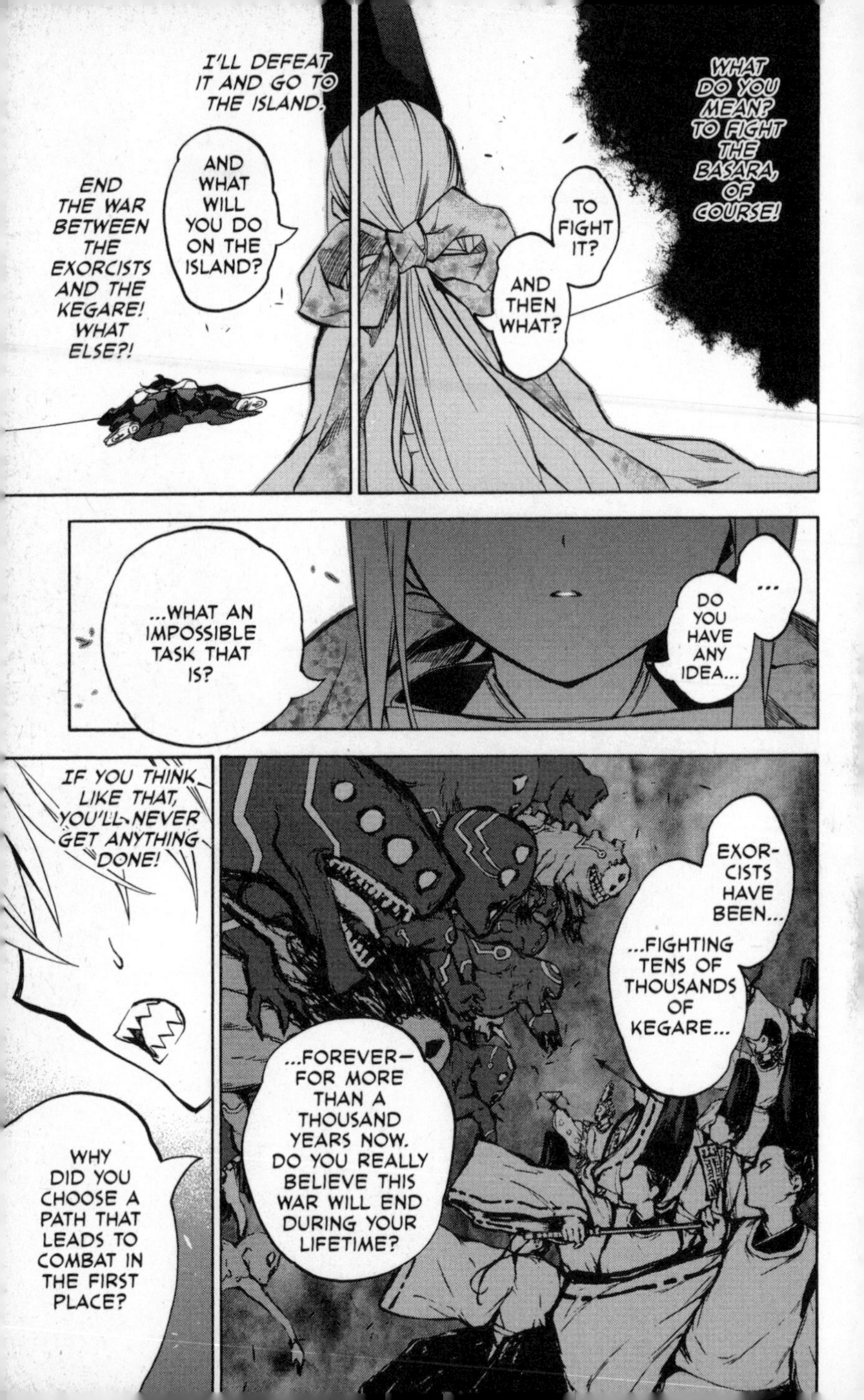
WHAT DO YOU MEAN? TO FIGHT THE BASARA, OF COURSE!
TO FIGHT IT?
AND THEN WHAT?
I'LL DEFEAT IT AND GO TO THE ISLAND.
AND WHAT WILL YOU DO ON THE ISLAND?
END THE WAR BETWEEN THE EXORCISTS AND THE KEGARE! WHAT ELSE?!
...
DO YOU HAVE ANY IDEA...
...WHAT AN IMPOSSIBLE TASK THAT IS?
EXOR-CISTS HAVE BEEN...
...FIGHTING TENS OF THOUSANDS OF KEGARE...
...FOREVER—FOR MORE THAN A THOUSAND YEARS NOW. DO YOU REALLY BELIEVE THIS WAR WILL END DURING YOUR LIFETIME?
IF YOU THINK LIKE THAT, YOU'LL NEVER GET ANYTHING DONE!
WHY DID YOU CHOOSE A PATH THAT LEADS TO COMBAT IN THE FIRST PLACE?

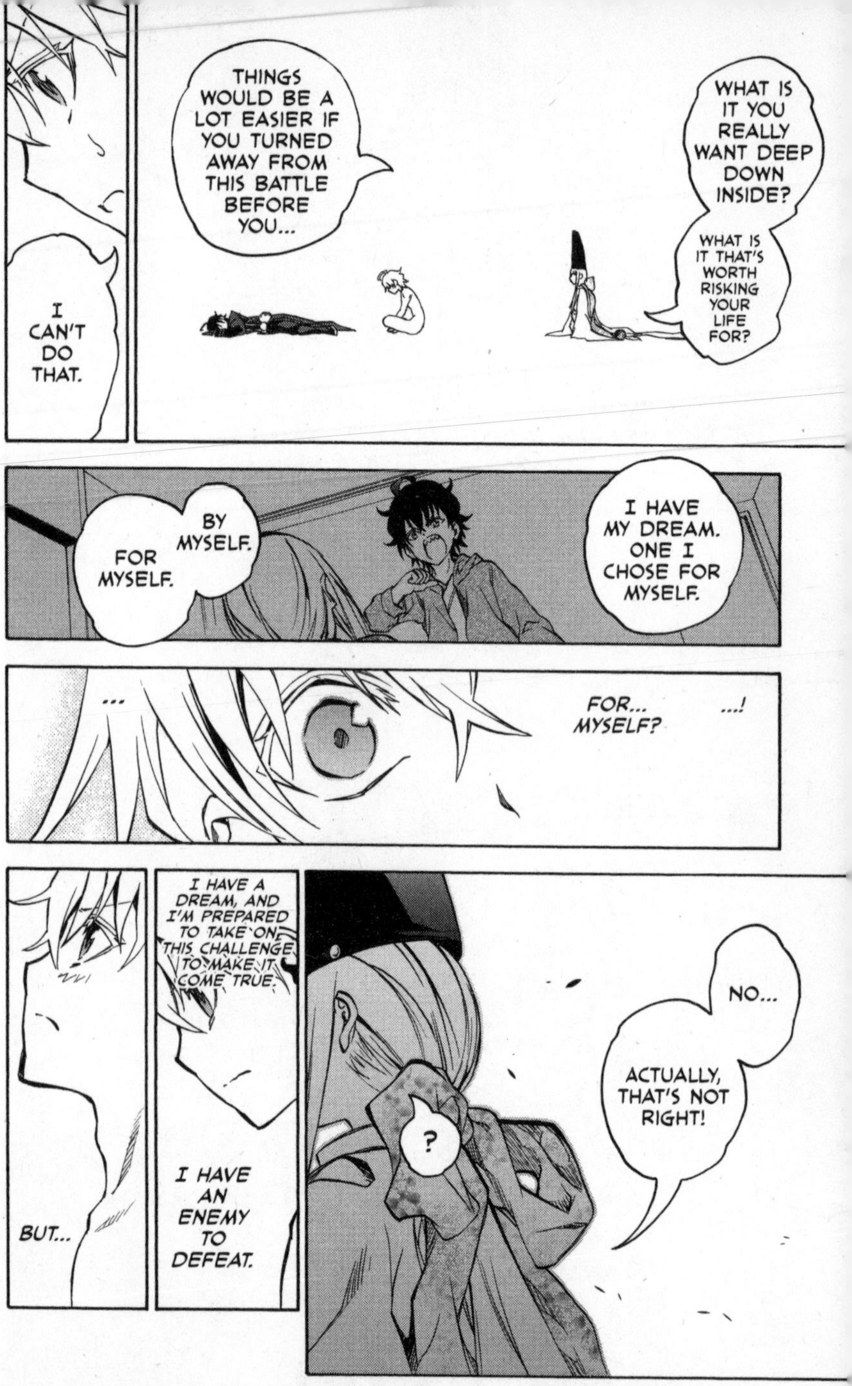
WHAT IS IT YOU REALLY WANT DEEP DOWN INSIDE?
WHAT IS IT THAT'S WORTH RISKING YOUR LIFE FOR?
THINGS WOULD BE A LOT EASIER IF YOU TURNED AWAY FROM THIS BATTLE BEFORE YOU...
I CAN'T DO THAT.
I HAVE MY DREAM. ONE I CHOSE FOR MYSELF.
BY MYSELF.
FOR MYSELF.
...!
FOR... MYSELF?
...
NO...
ACTUALLY, THAT'S NOT RIGHT!
?
I HAVE A DREAM, AND I'M PREPARED TO TAKE ON THIS CHALLENGE TO MAKE IT COME TRUE.
I HAVE AN ENEMY TO DEFEAT.
BUT...

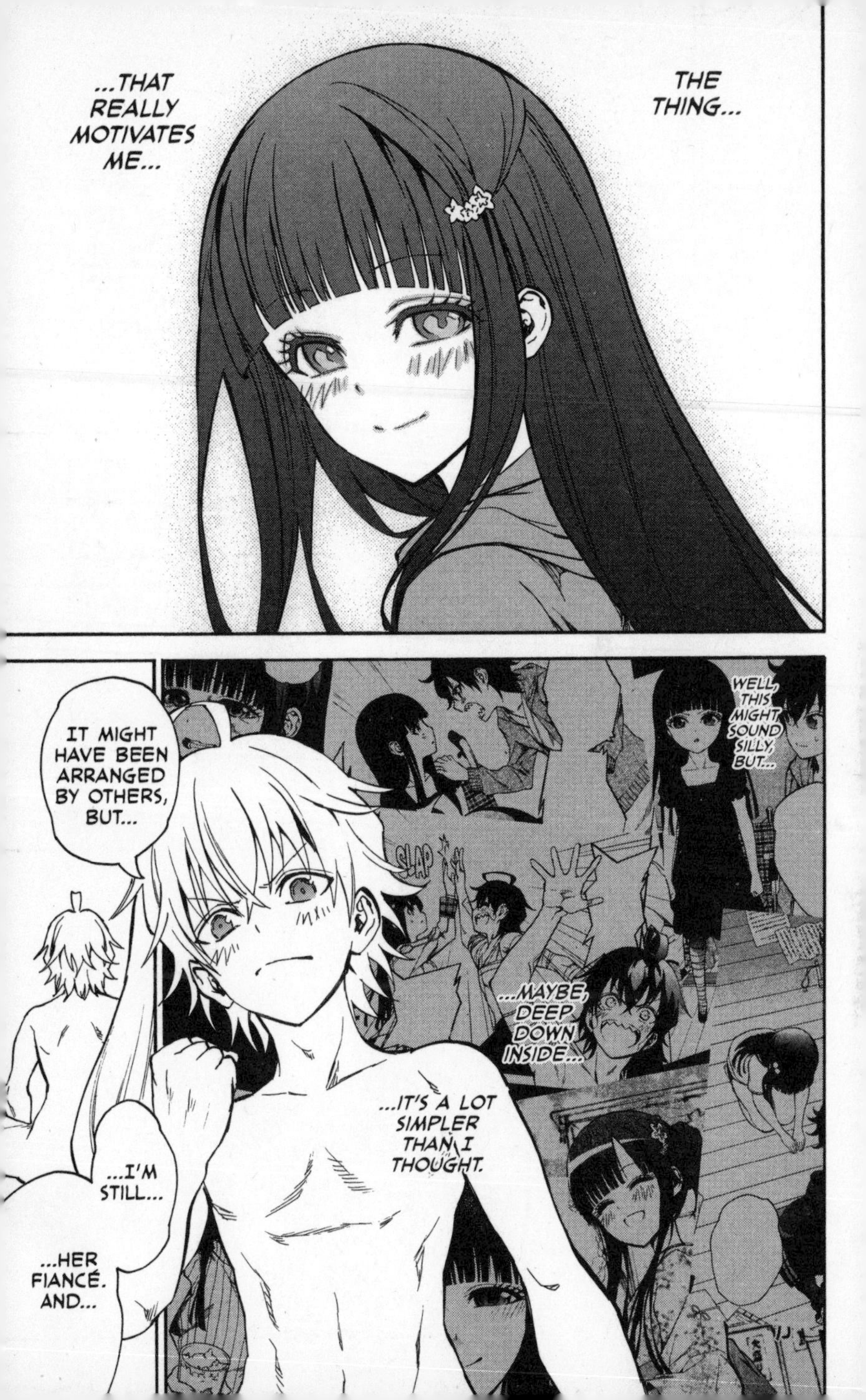
THE THING...
...THAT REALLY MOTIVATES ME...
WELL, THIS MIGHT SOUND SILLY, BUT...
IT MIGHT HAVE BEEN ARRANGED BY OTHERS, BUT...
SLAP
...MAYBE, DEEP DOWN INSIDE...
...IT'S A LOT SIMPLER THAN I THOUGHT.
...I'M STILL...
...HER FIANCÉ. AND...

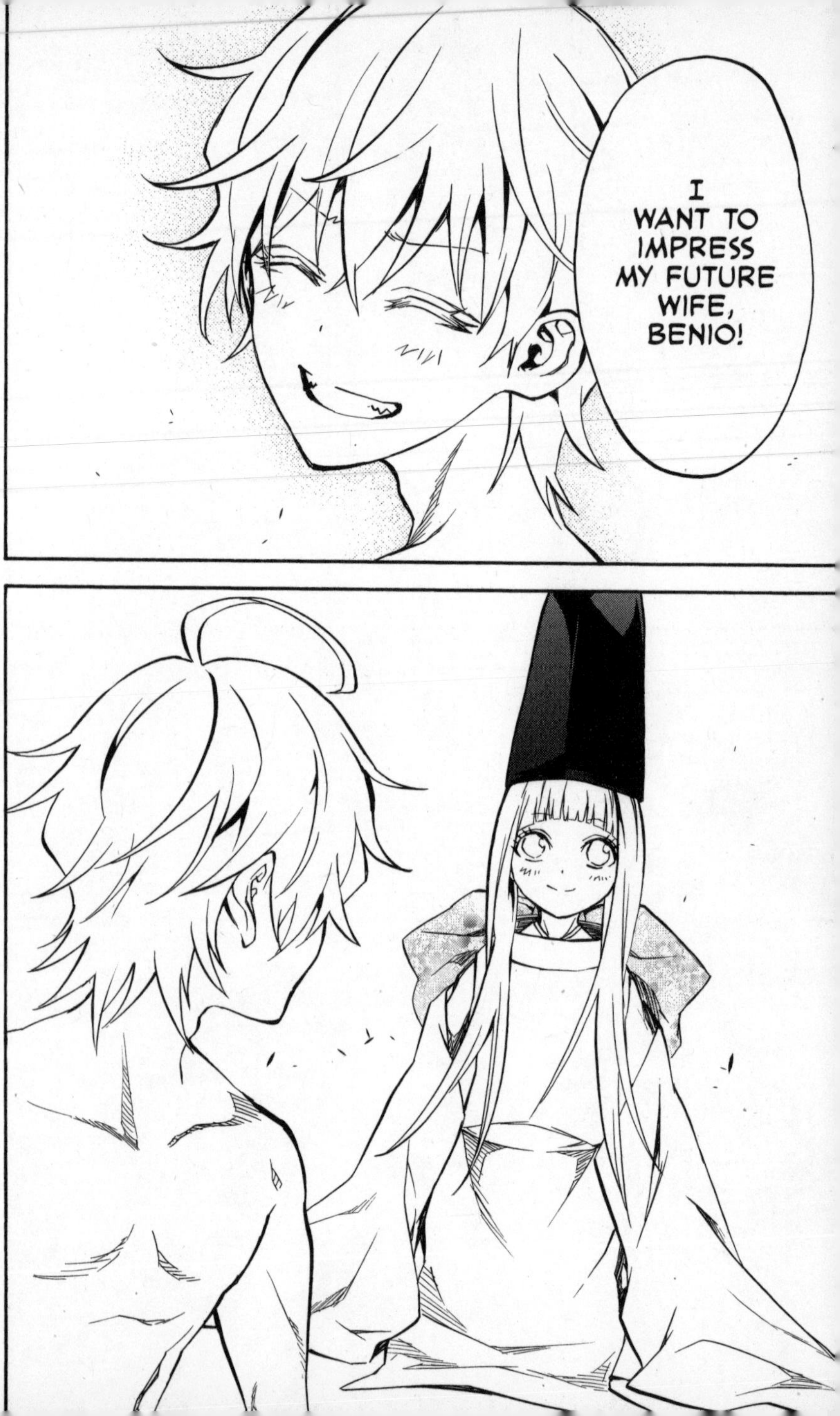
I WANT TO IMPRESS MY FUTURE WIFE, BENIO!

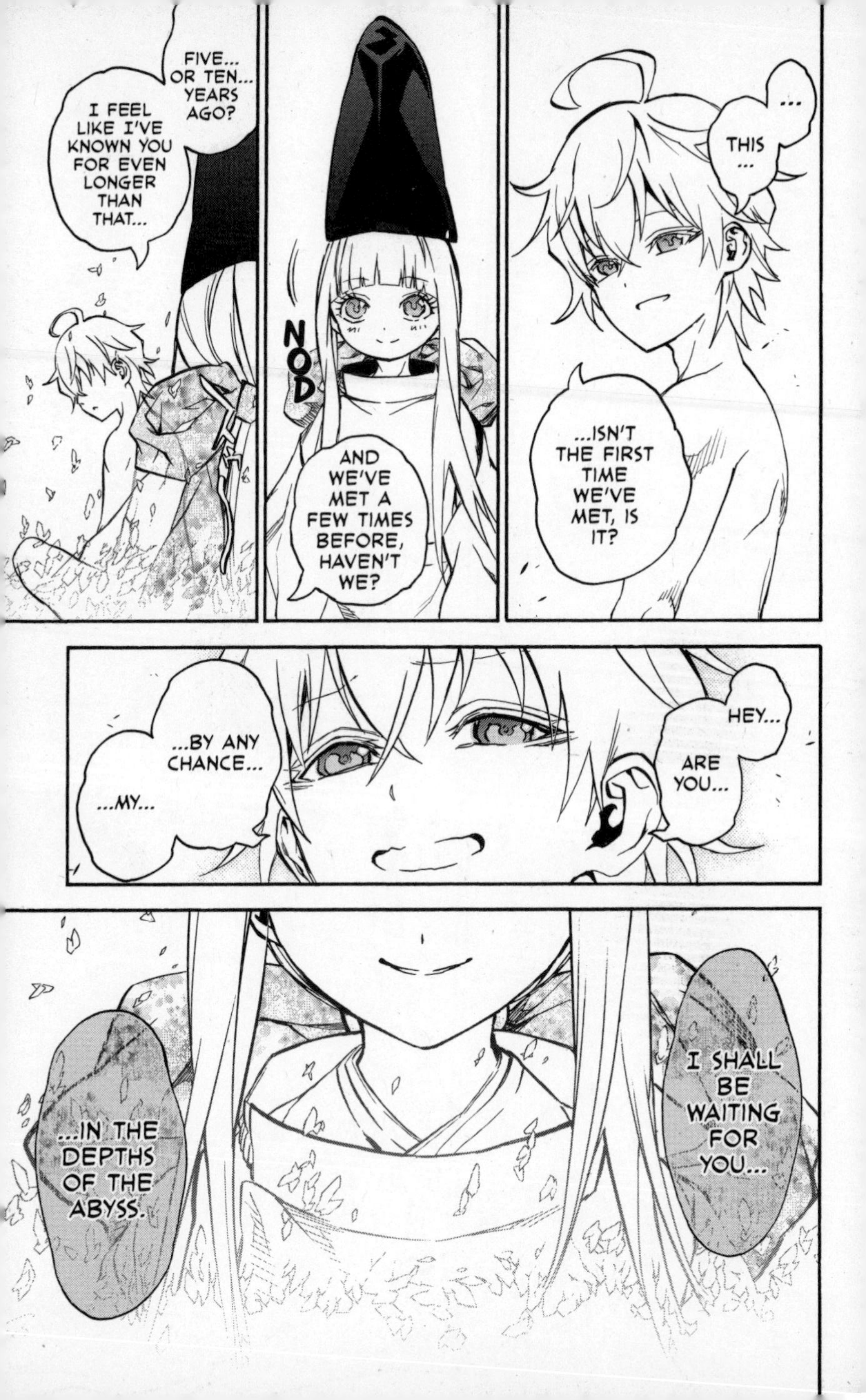
... THIS ...
...ISN'T THE FIRST TIME WE'VE MET, IS IT?
NOD
AND WE'VE MET A FEW TIMES BEFORE, HAVEN'T WE?
FIVE... OR TEN... YEARS AGO?
I FEEL LIKE I'VE KNOWN YOU FOR EVEN LONGER THAN THAT...
HEY... ARE YOU...
...BY ANY CHANCE... ...MY...
I SHALL BE WAITING FOR YOU...
...IN THE DEPTHS OF THE ABYSS.

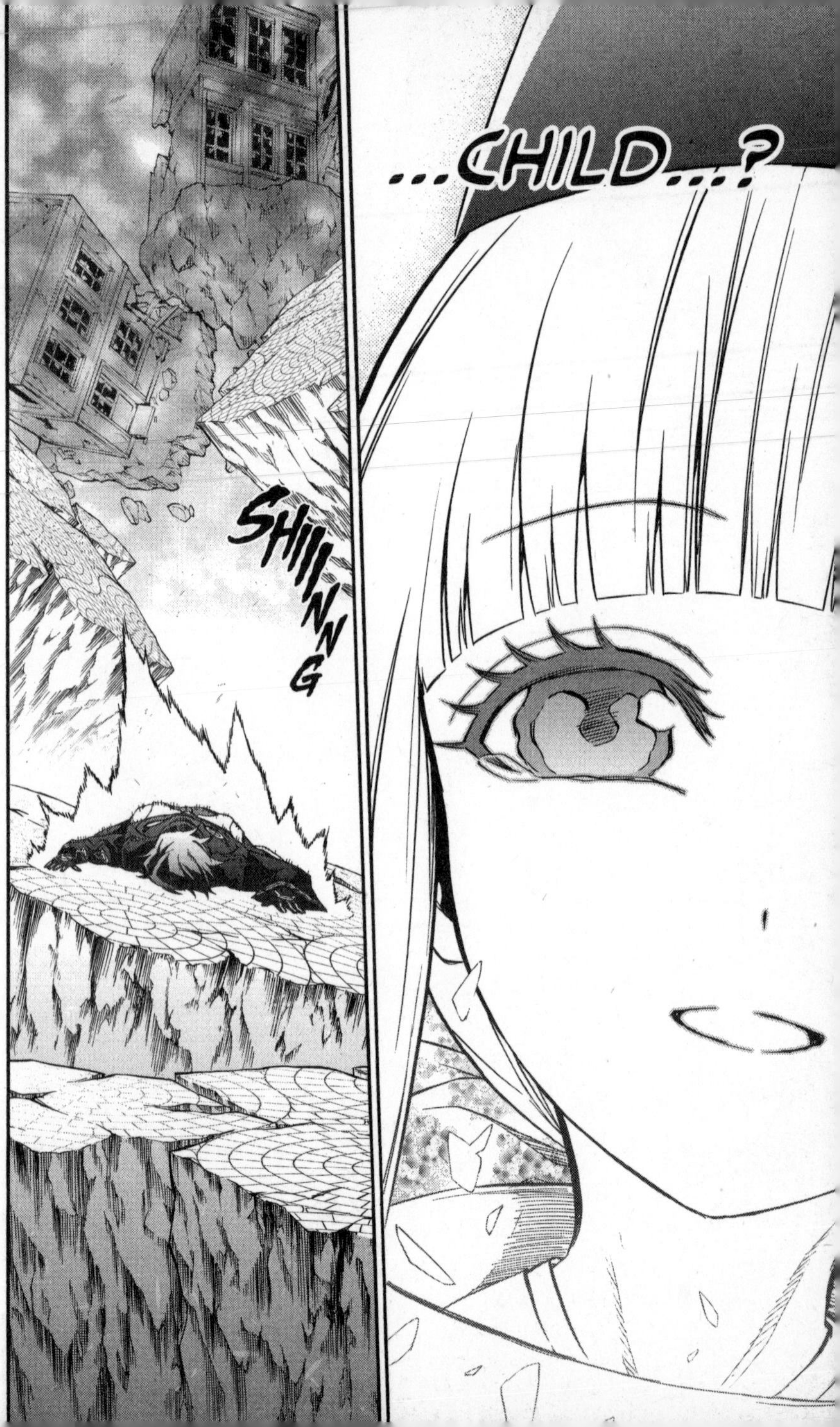
...CHILD...?
SHIIINNNG

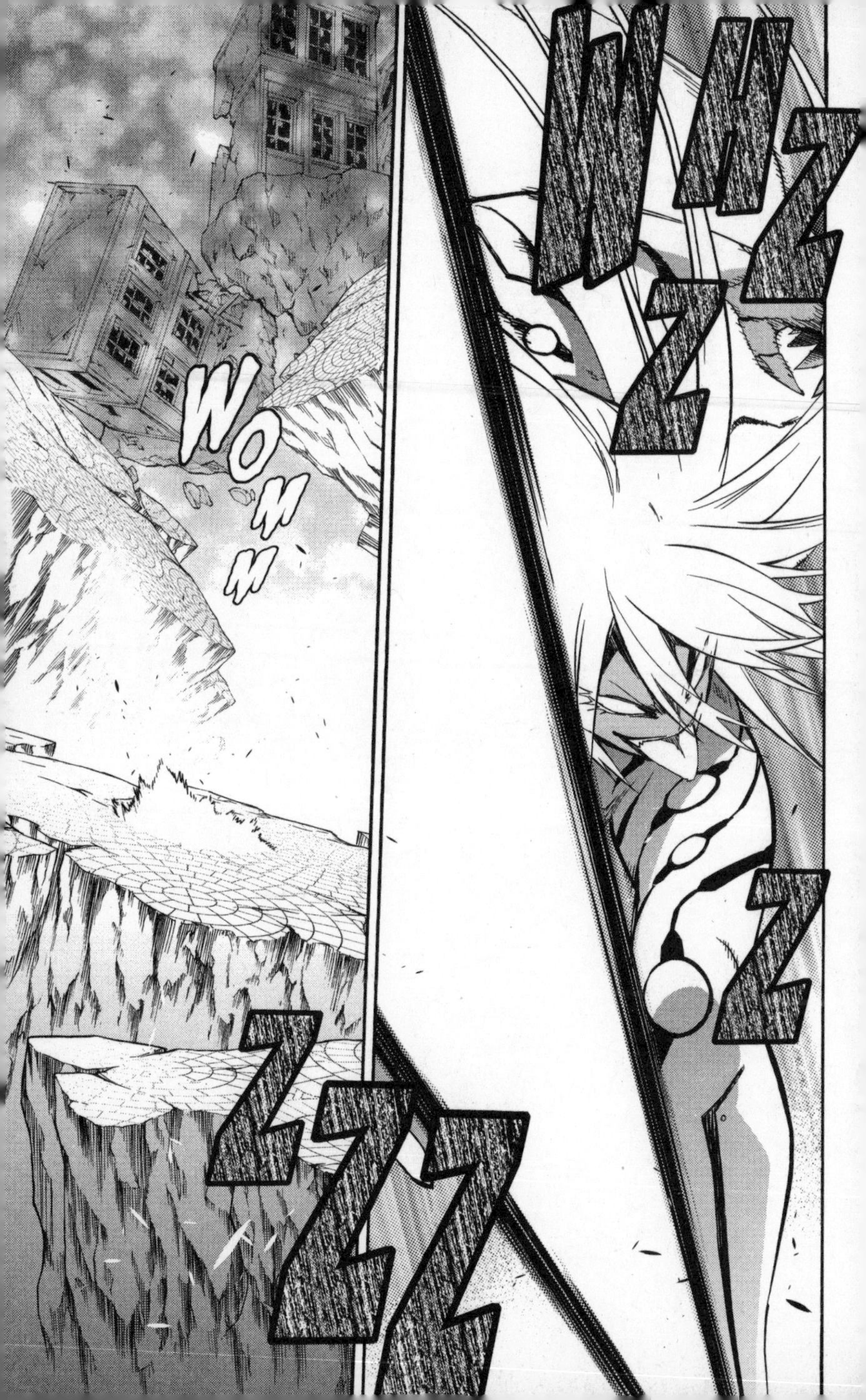

WHZZ
Z
WOMMM
ZZZZ

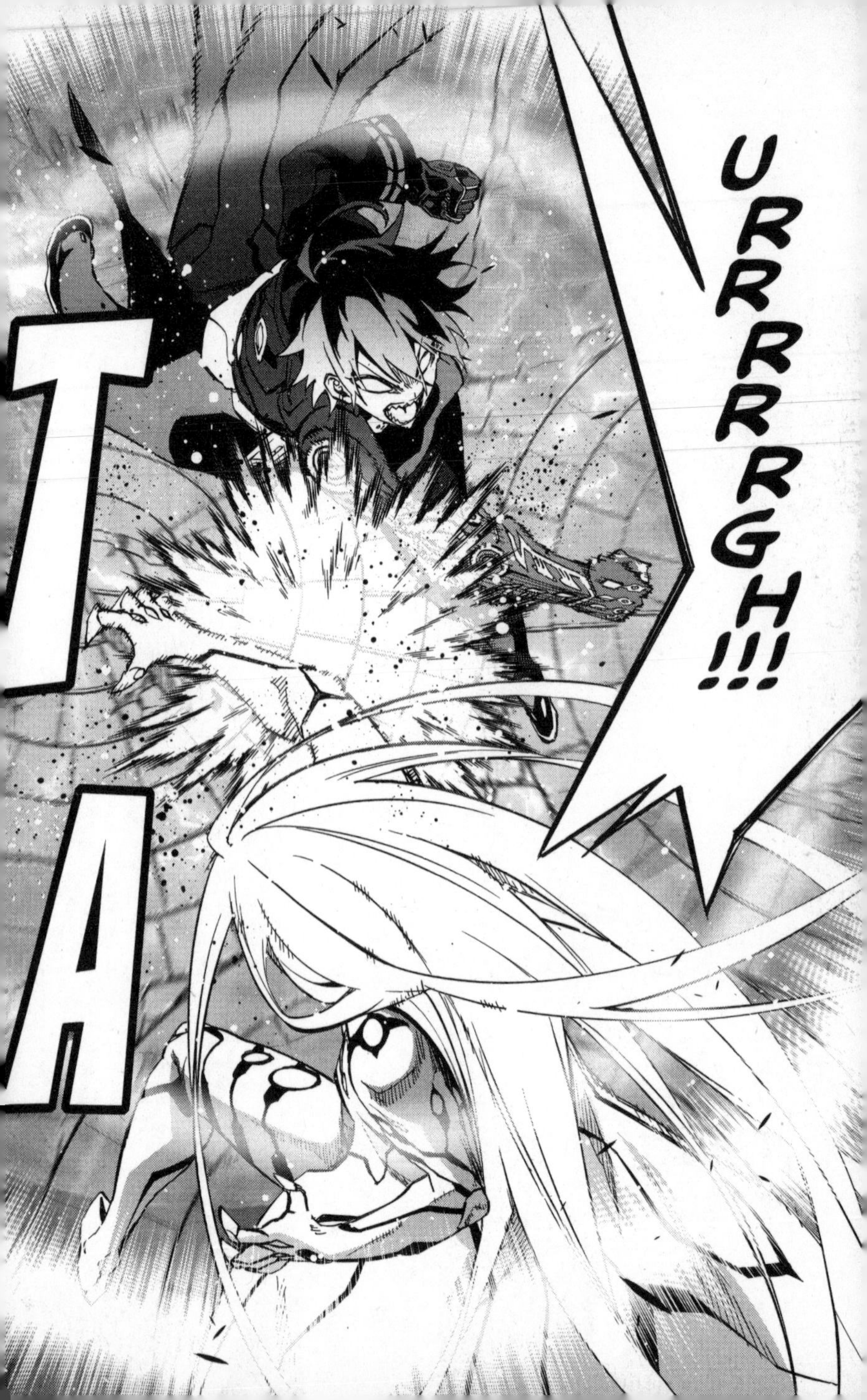
URRRRGH!!!
TA

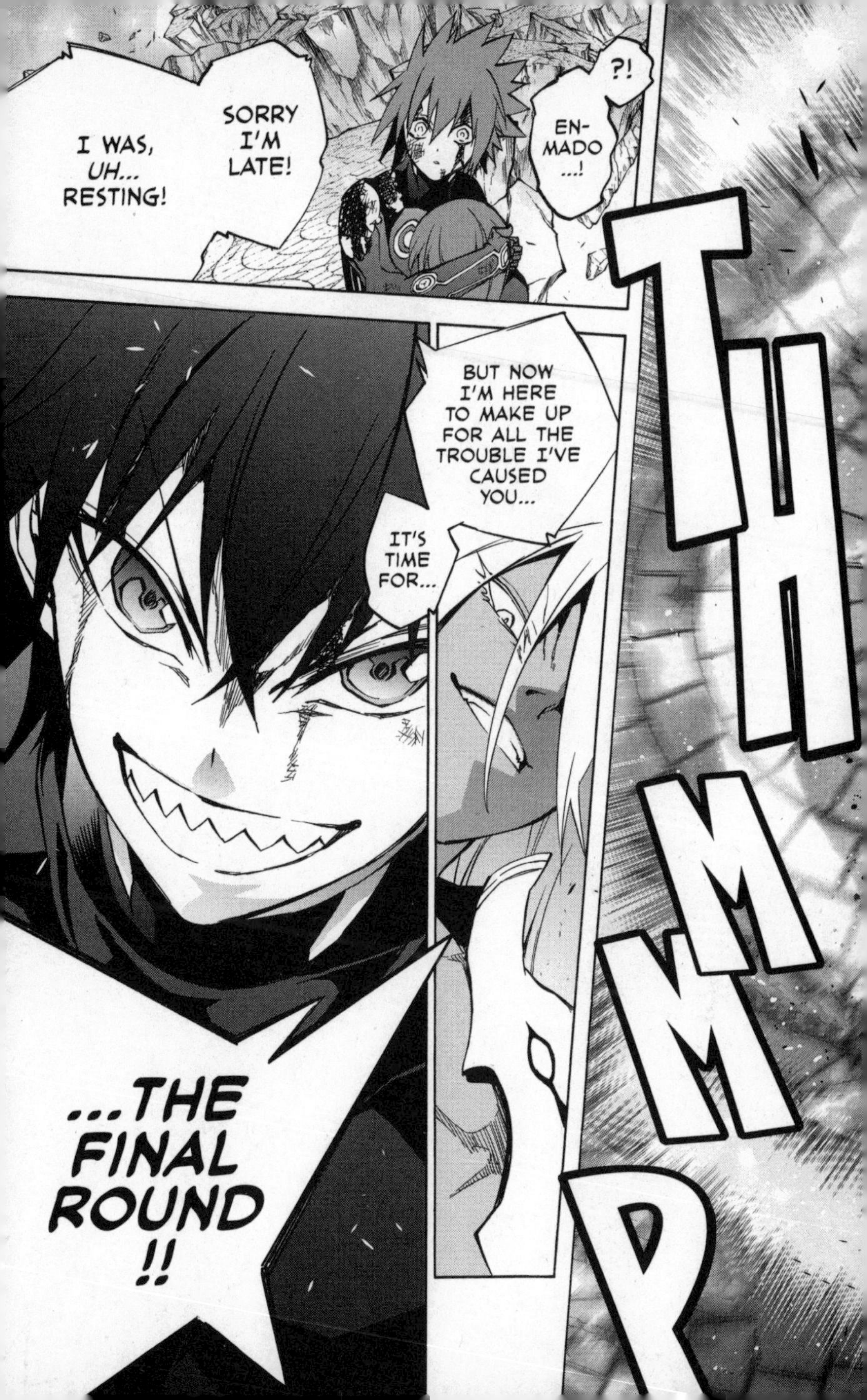
?!
EN-MADO ...!
SORRY I'M LATE!
I WAS, UH... RESTING!
THMMP
BUT NOW I'M HERE TO MAKE UP FOR ALL THE TROUBLE I'VE CAUSED YOU...
IT'S TIME FOR...
...THE FINAL ROUND!!

Twin Star Exorcists

ONMYOJI

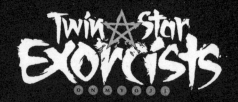

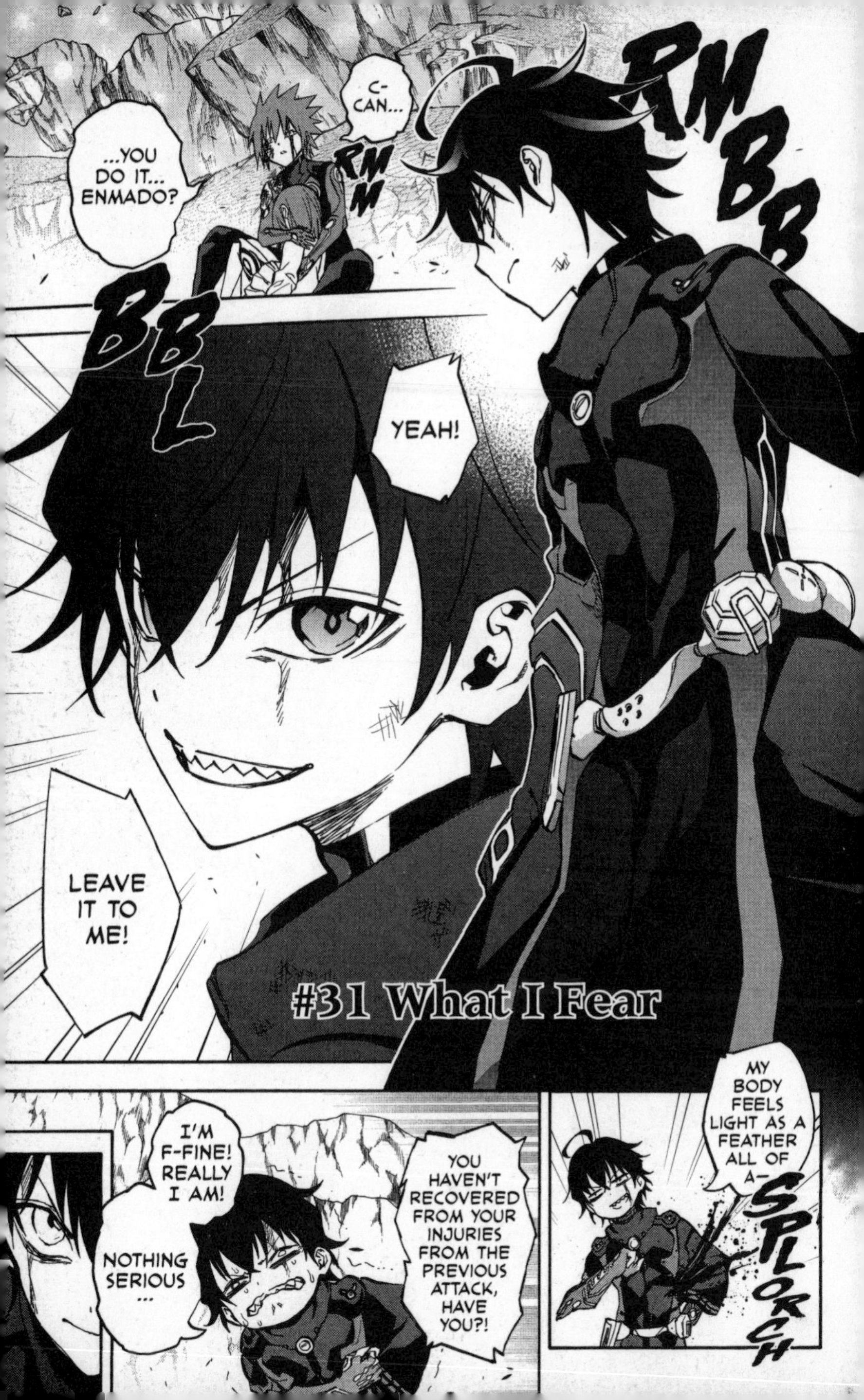
RMBB
C-CAN...
RMM
...YOU DO IT... ENMADO?
BBL
YEAH!
LEAVE IT TO ME!
#31 What I Fear
MY BODY FEELS LIGHT AS A FEATHER ALL OF A—
SPLORCH
YOU HAVEN'T RECOVERED FROM YOUR INJURIES FROM THE PREVIOUS ATTACK, HAVE YOU?!
I'M F-FINE! REALLY I AM!
NOTHING SERIOUS ...

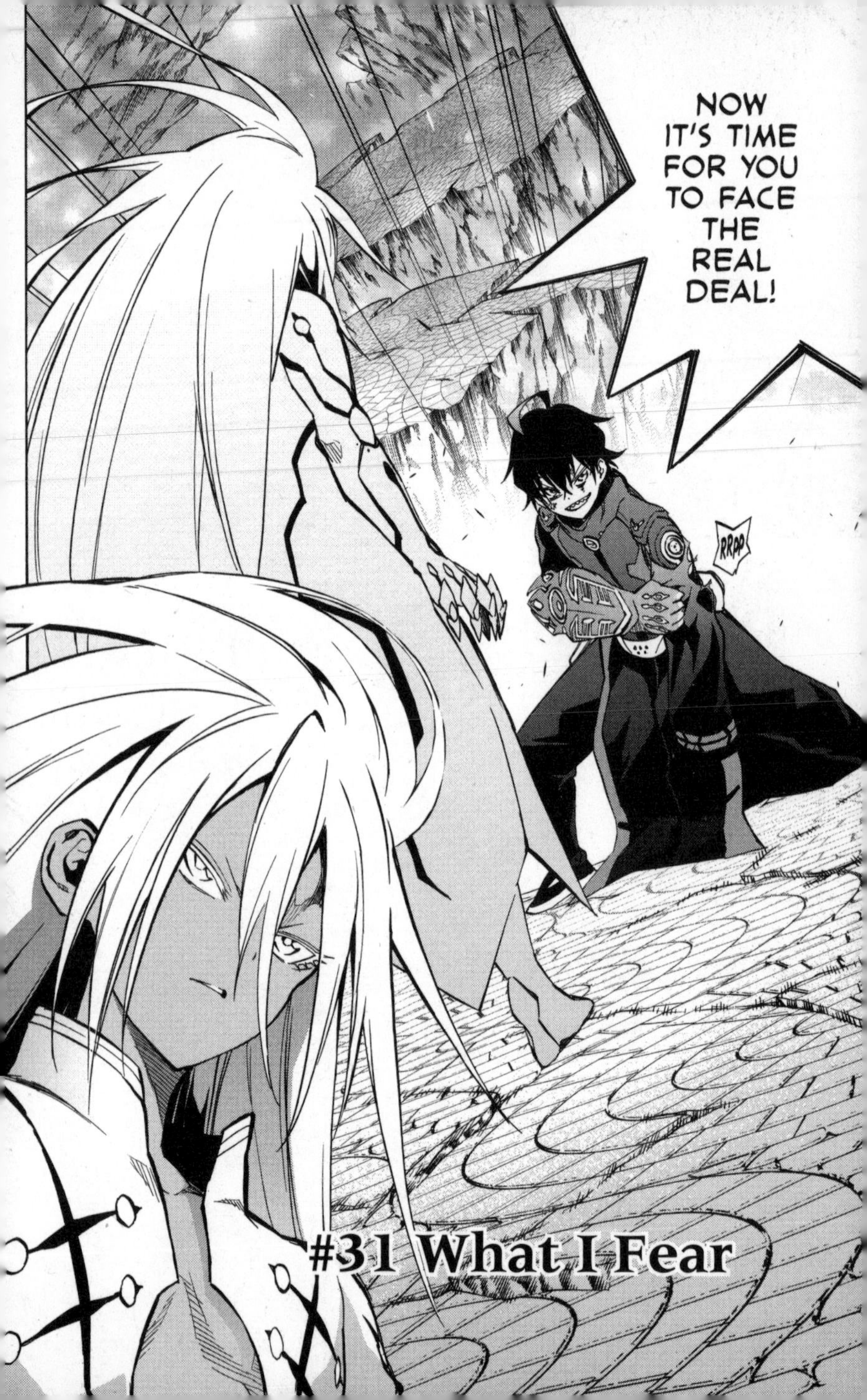
NOW IT'S TIME FOR YOU TO FACE THE REAL DEAL!
RRPP
#31 What I Fear

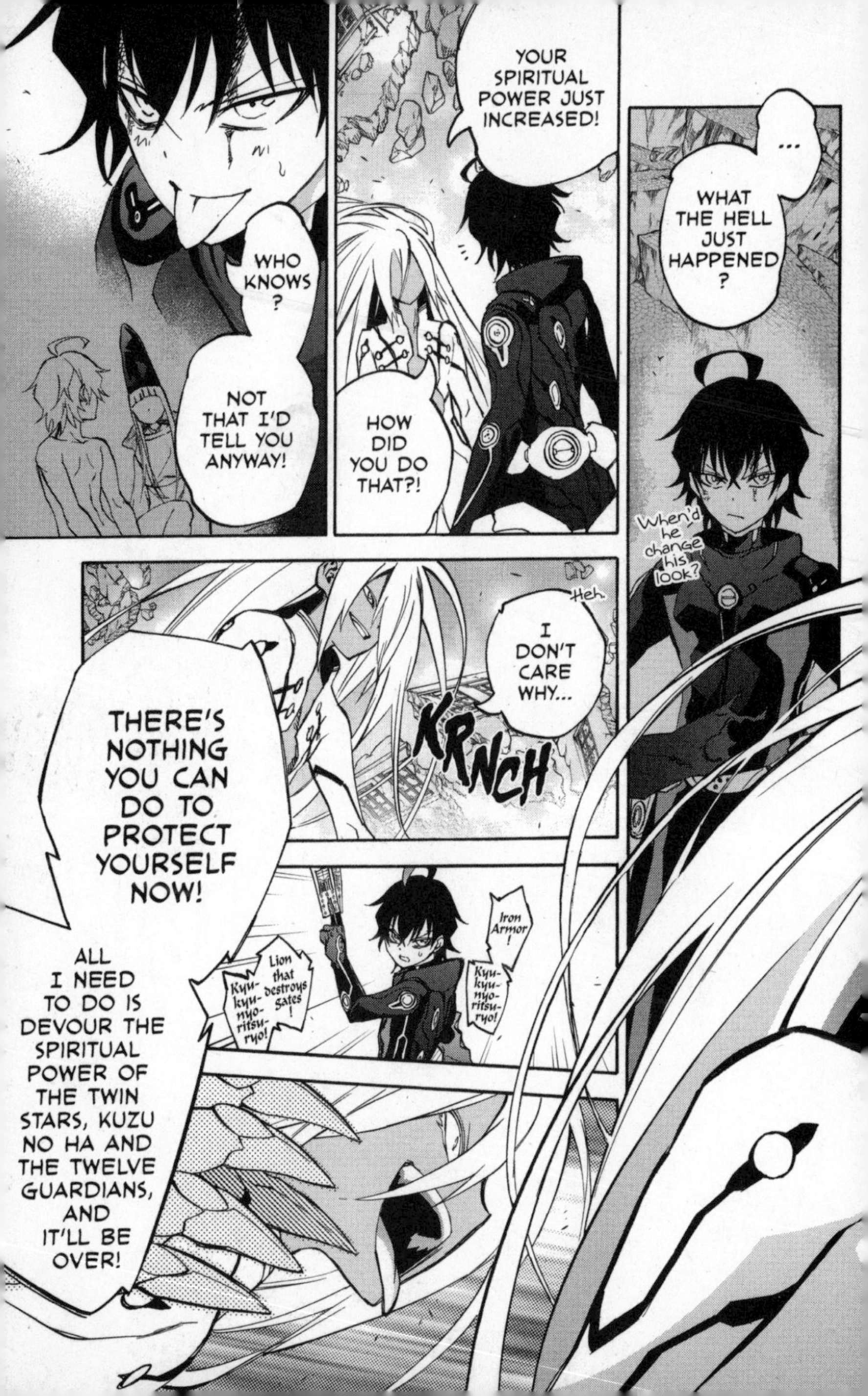
YOUR SPIRITUAL POWER JUST INCREASED!
HOW DID YOU DO THAT?!
WHO KNOWS?
NOT THAT I'D TELL YOU ANYWAY!
...
WHAT THE HELL JUST HAPPENED?
When'd he change his look?
Heh.
I DON'T CARE WHY...
KRNCH
THERE'S NOTHING YOU CAN DO TO PROTECT YOURSELF NOW!
Iron Armor!
Kyu-kyu-nyo-ritsu-ryo!
Lion that destroys gates!
Kyu-kyu-nyo-ritsu-ryo!
ALL I NEED TO DO IS DEVOUR THE SPIRITUAL POWER OF THE TWIN STARS, KUZU NO HA AND THE TWELVE GUARDIANS, AND IT'LL BE OVER!

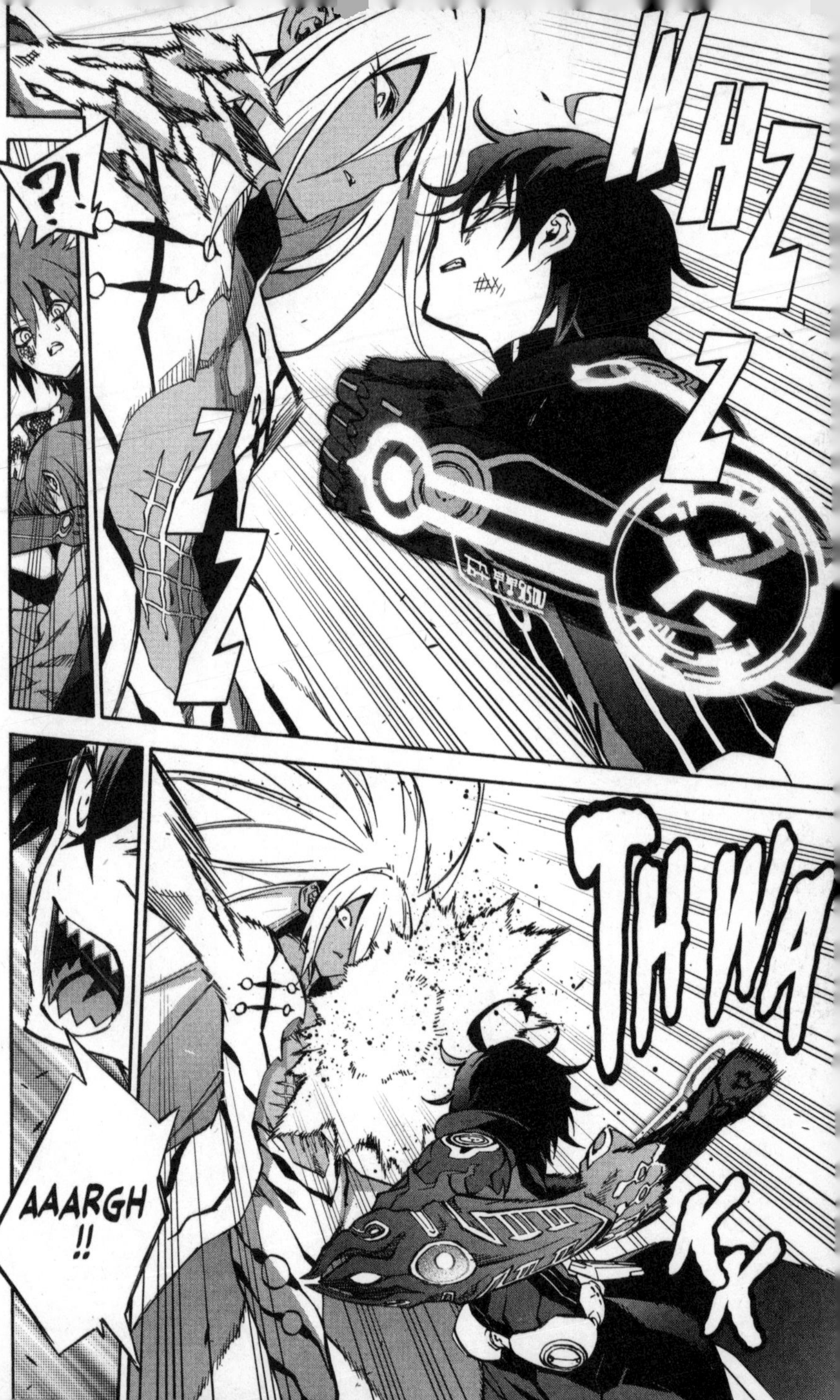
?!
WHZZZZ
THWA
AAARGH !!

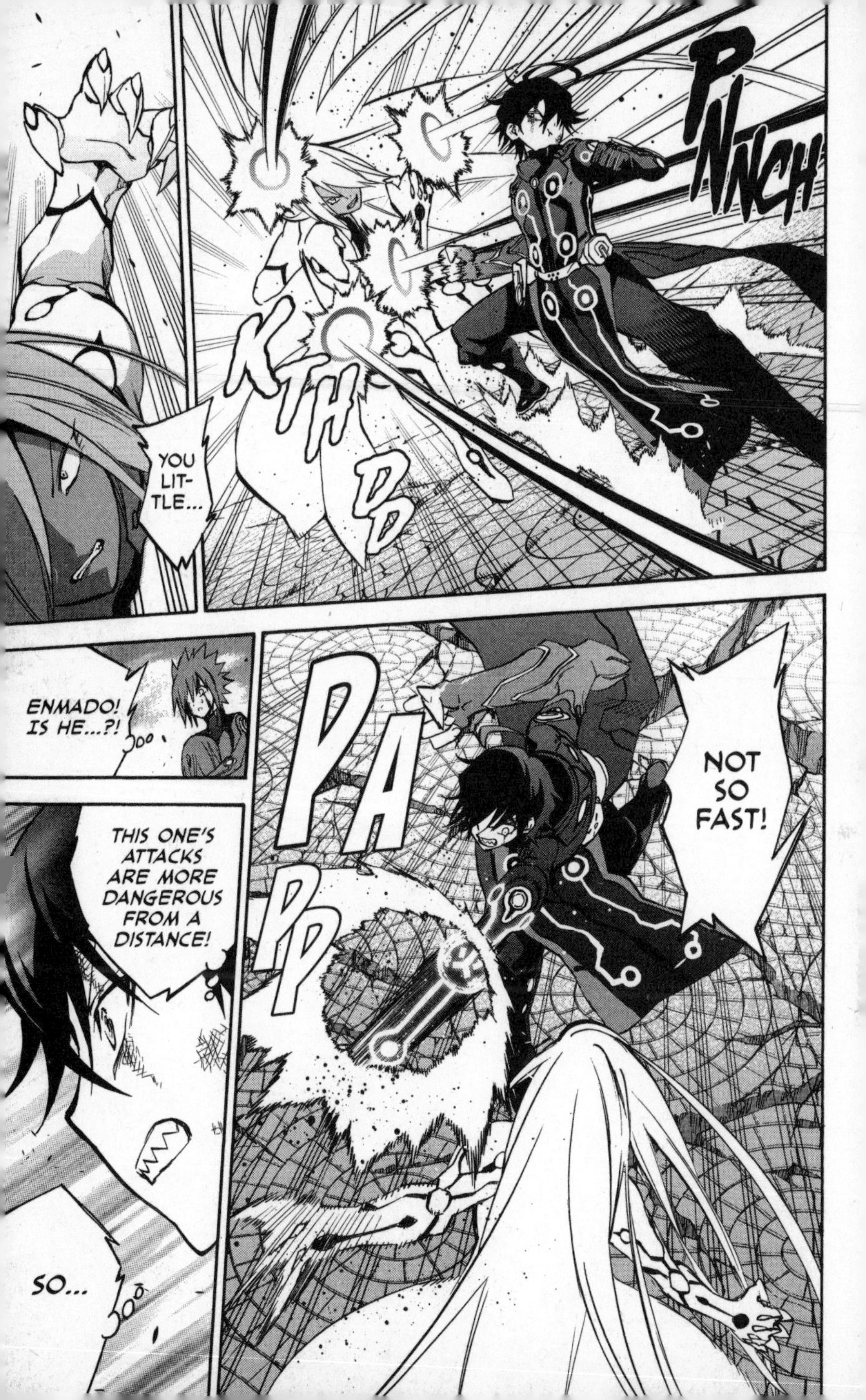
PINNCH
KTHDD
YOU LITTLE...
PAPP
NOT SO FAST!
ENMADO! IS HE...?!
THIS ONE'S ATTACKS ARE MORE DANGEROUS FROM A DISTANCE!
SO...

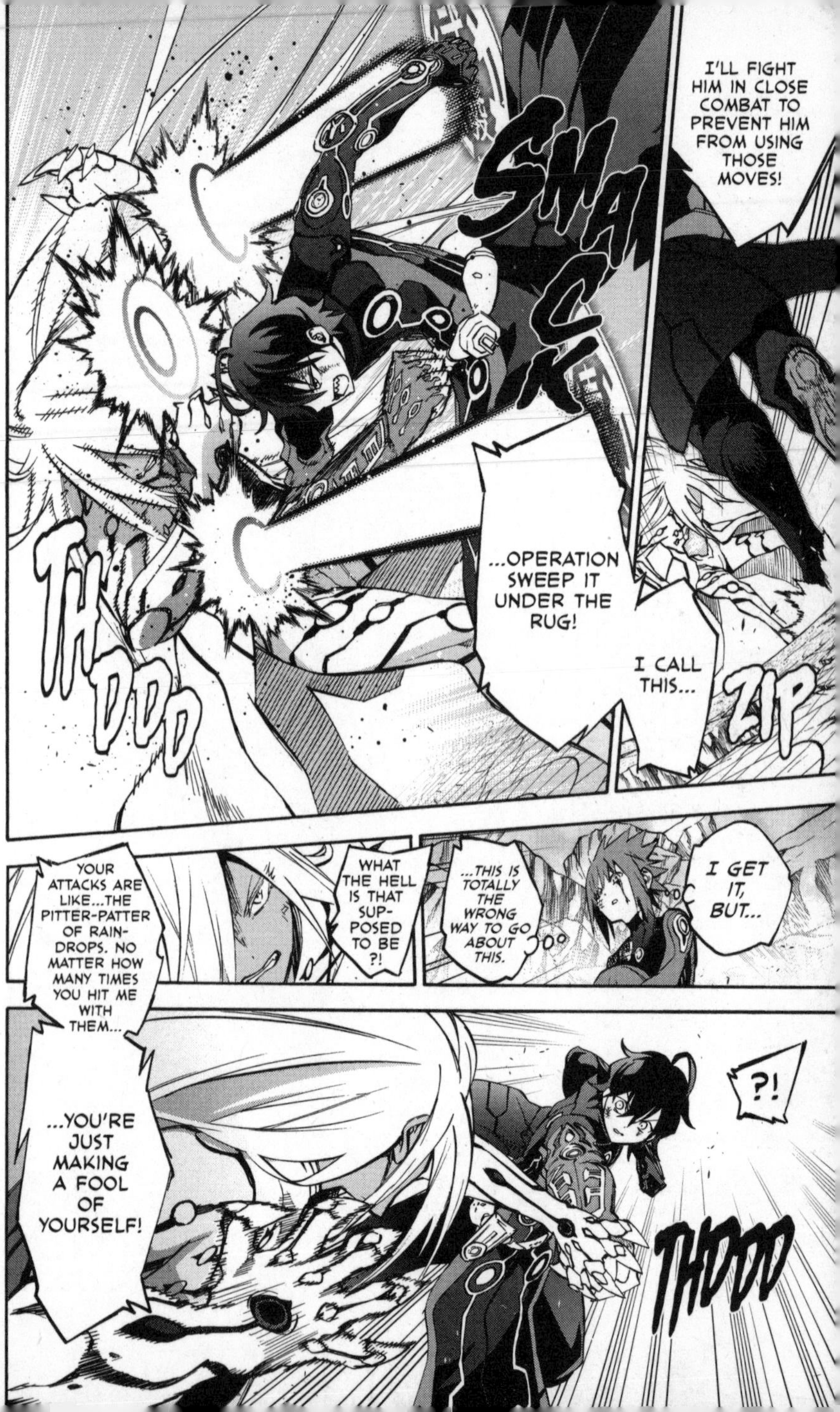
I'LL FIGHT HIM IN CLOSE COMBAT TO PREVENT HIM FROM USING THOSE MOVES!
SMACK
I CALL THIS...
...OPERATION SWEEP IT UNDER THE RUG!
ZIP
THUDDD
I GET IT, BUT...
...THIS IS TOTALLY THE WRONG WAY TO GO ABOUT THIS.
WHAT THE HELL IS THAT SUP-POSED TO BE?!
YOUR ATTACKS ARE LIKE...THE PITTER-PATTER OF RAIN-DROPS. NO MATTER HOW MANY TIMES YOU HIT ME WITH THEM...
?!
THUDDD
...YOU'RE JUST MAKING A FOOL OF YOURSELF!

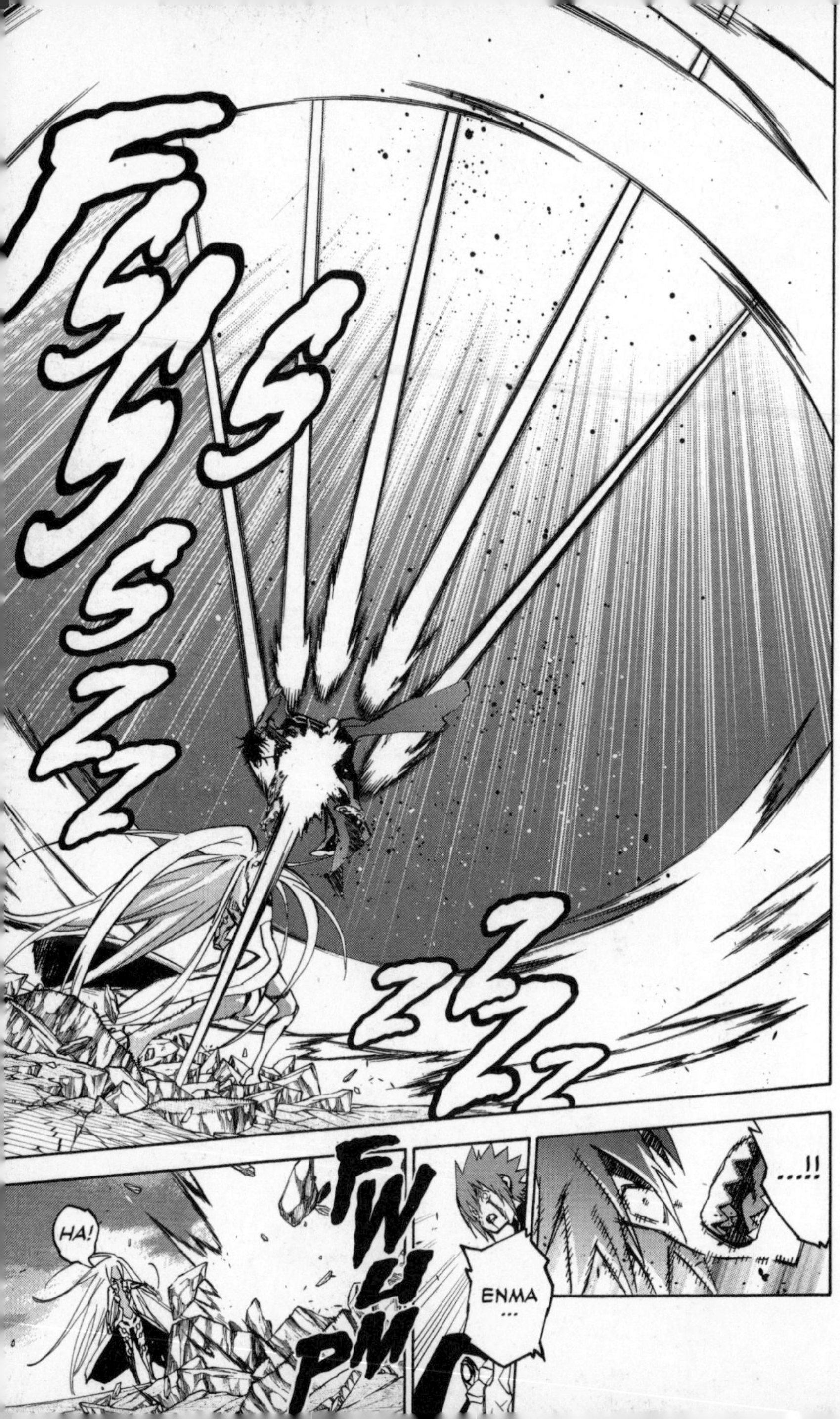
FSSSSZZ
ZZZZ
...!!
ENMA ...
FWUMP
HA!

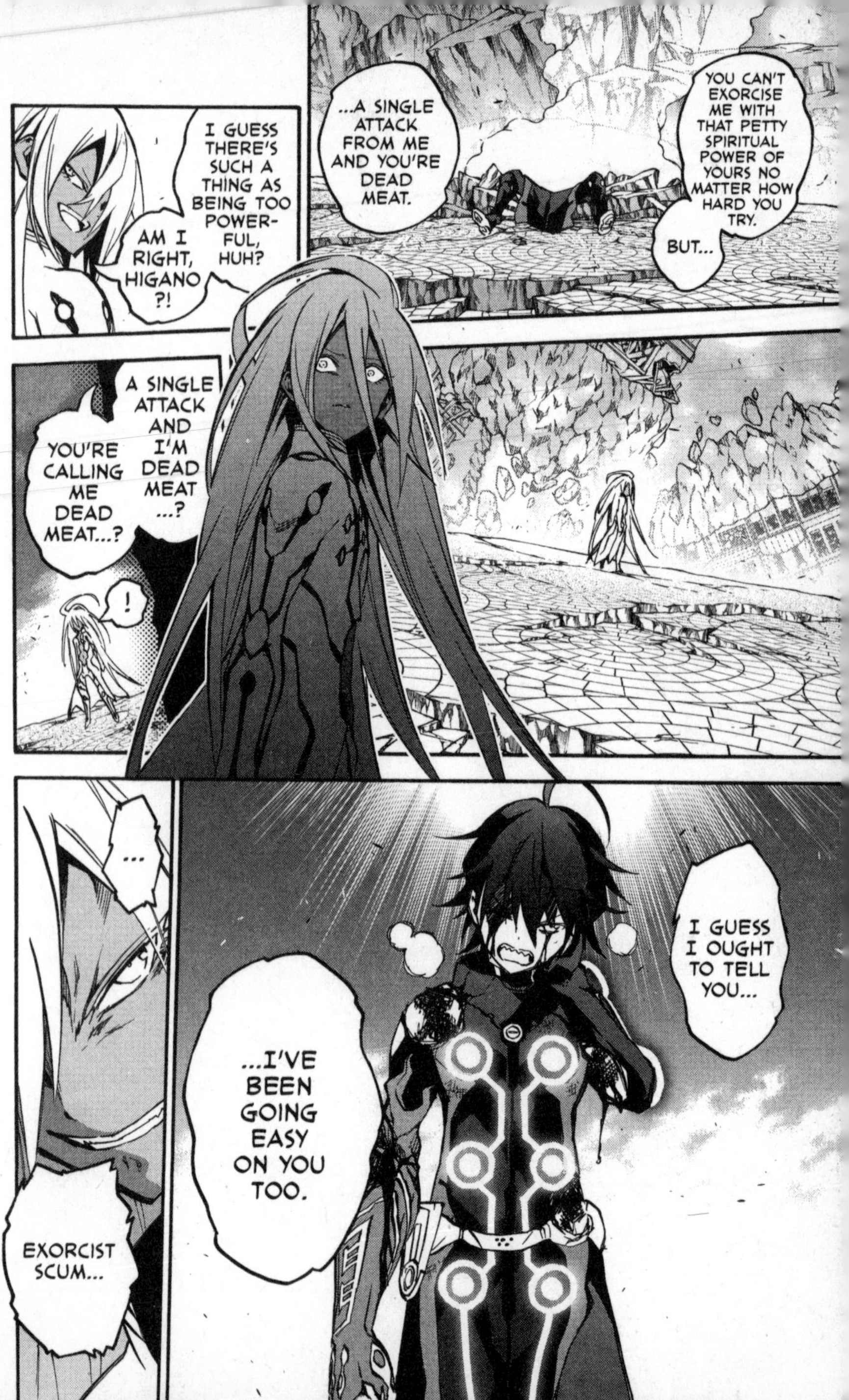
YOU CAN'T EXORCISE ME WITH THAT PETTY SPIRITUAL POWER OF YOURS NO MATTER HOW HARD YOU TRY.
BUT...
...A SINGLE ATTACK FROM ME AND YOU'RE DEAD MEAT.
I GUESS THERE'S SUCH A THING AS BEING TOO POWER-FUL, HUH?
AM I RIGHT, HIGANO?!
A SINGLE ATTACK AND I'M DEAD MEAT...?
YOU'RE CALLING ME DEAD MEAT...?
!
I GUESS I OUGHT TO TELL YOU...
...I'VE BEEN GOING EASY ON YOU TOO.
...
EXORCIST SCUM...

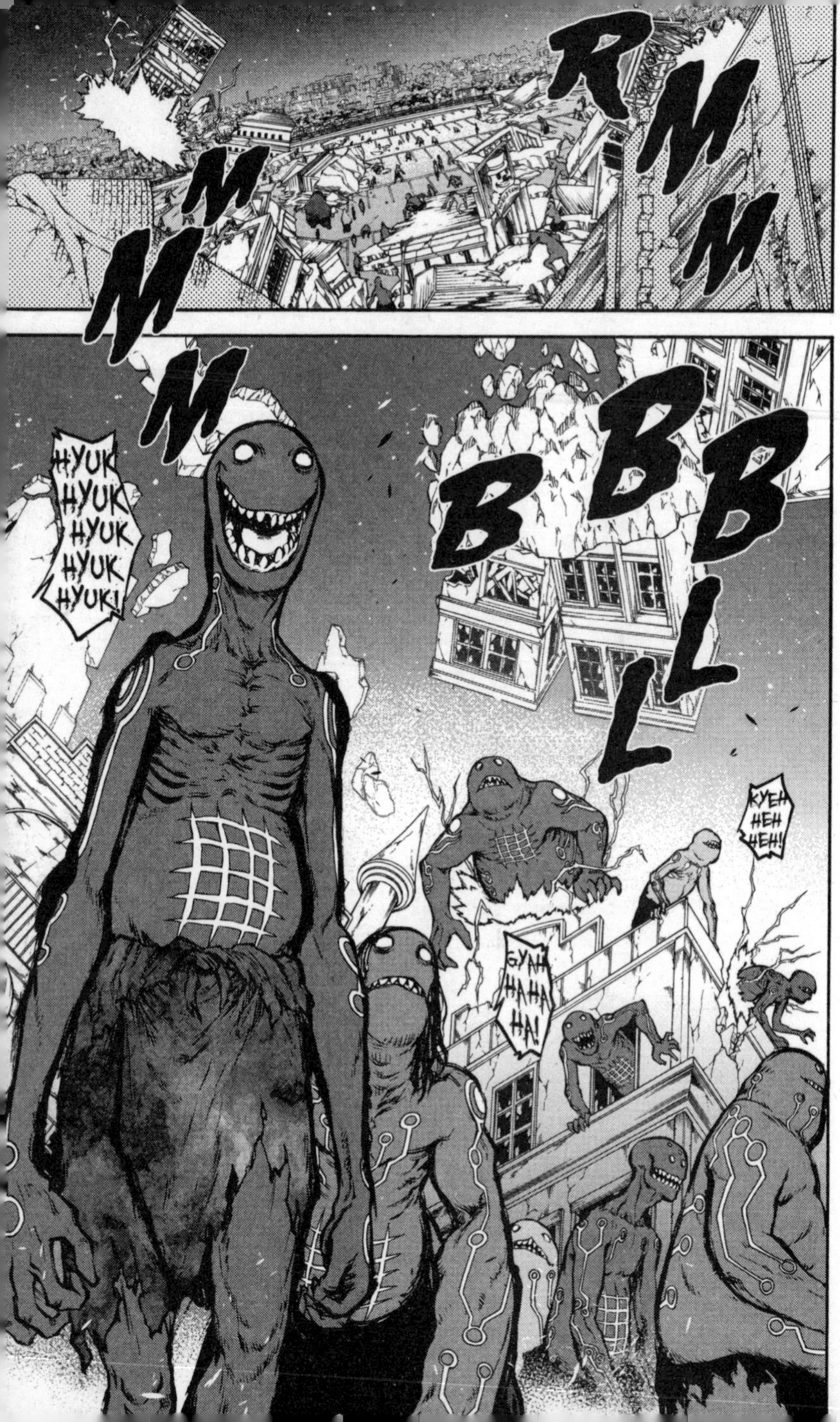
RMMM
MMMM
BBBBLLL
KYEH HEH HEH!
GYAH HAHA HA!
HYUK HYUK HYUK HYUK HYUK!

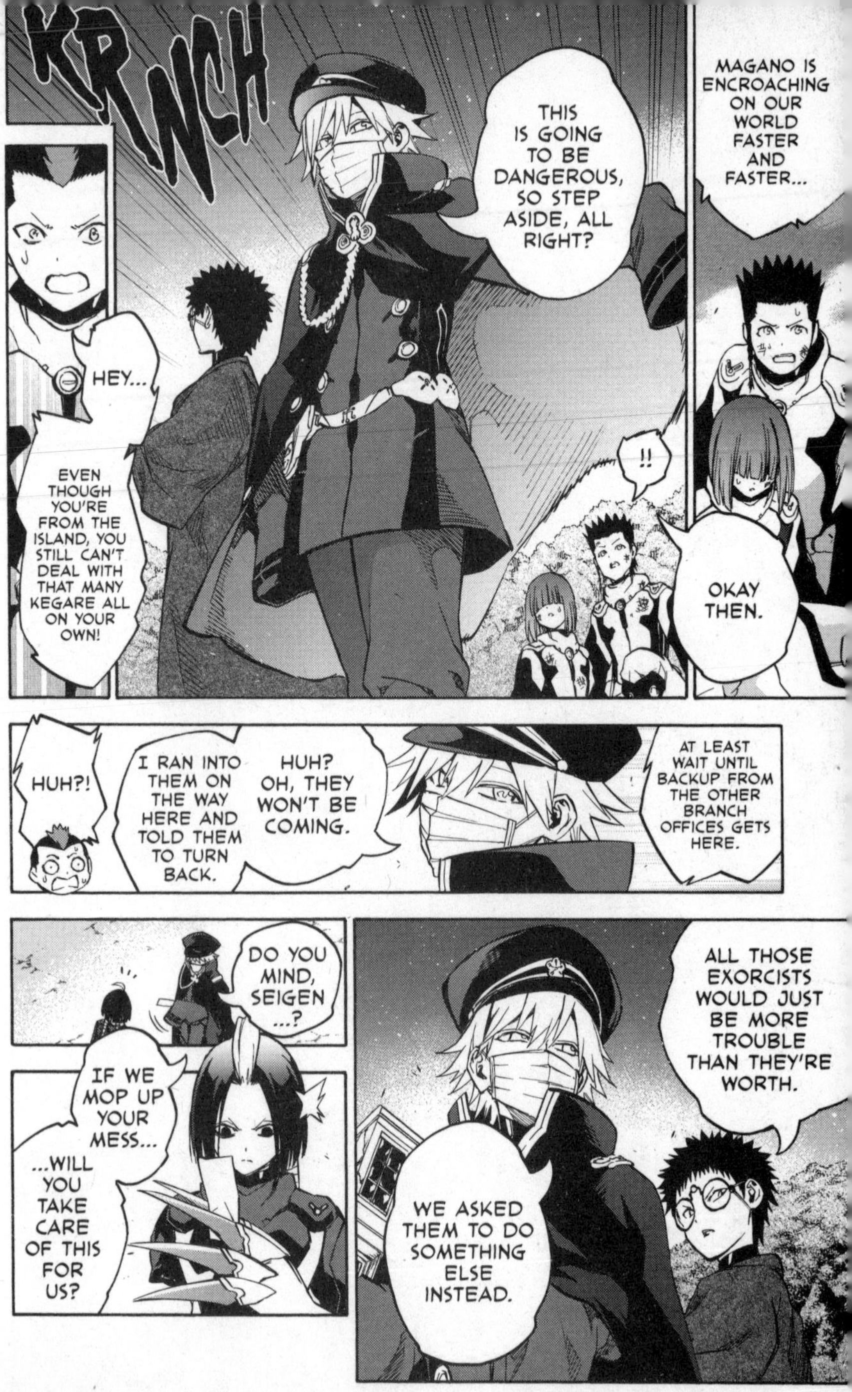
MAGANO IS ENCROACHING ON OUR WORLD FASTER AND FASTER...
OKAY THEN.
KRINCH
THIS IS GOING TO BE DANGEROUS, SO STEP ASIDE, ALL RIGHT?
!!
HEY...
EVEN THOUGH YOU'RE FROM THE ISLAND, YOU STILL CAN'T DEAL WITH THAT MANY KEGARE ALL ON YOUR OWN!
AT LEAST WAIT UNTIL BACKUP FROM THE OTHER BRANCH OFFICES GETS HERE.
HUH? OH, THEY WON'T BE COMING.
I RAN INTO THEM ON THE WAY HERE AND TOLD THEM TO TURN BACK.
HUH?!
ALL THOSE EXORCISTS WOULD JUST BE MORE TROUBLE THAN THEY'RE WORTH.
WE ASKED THEM TO DO SOMETHING ELSE INSTEAD.
DO YOU MIND, SEIGEN ...?
IF WE MOP UP YOUR MESS...
...WILL YOU TAKE CARE OF THIS FOR US?

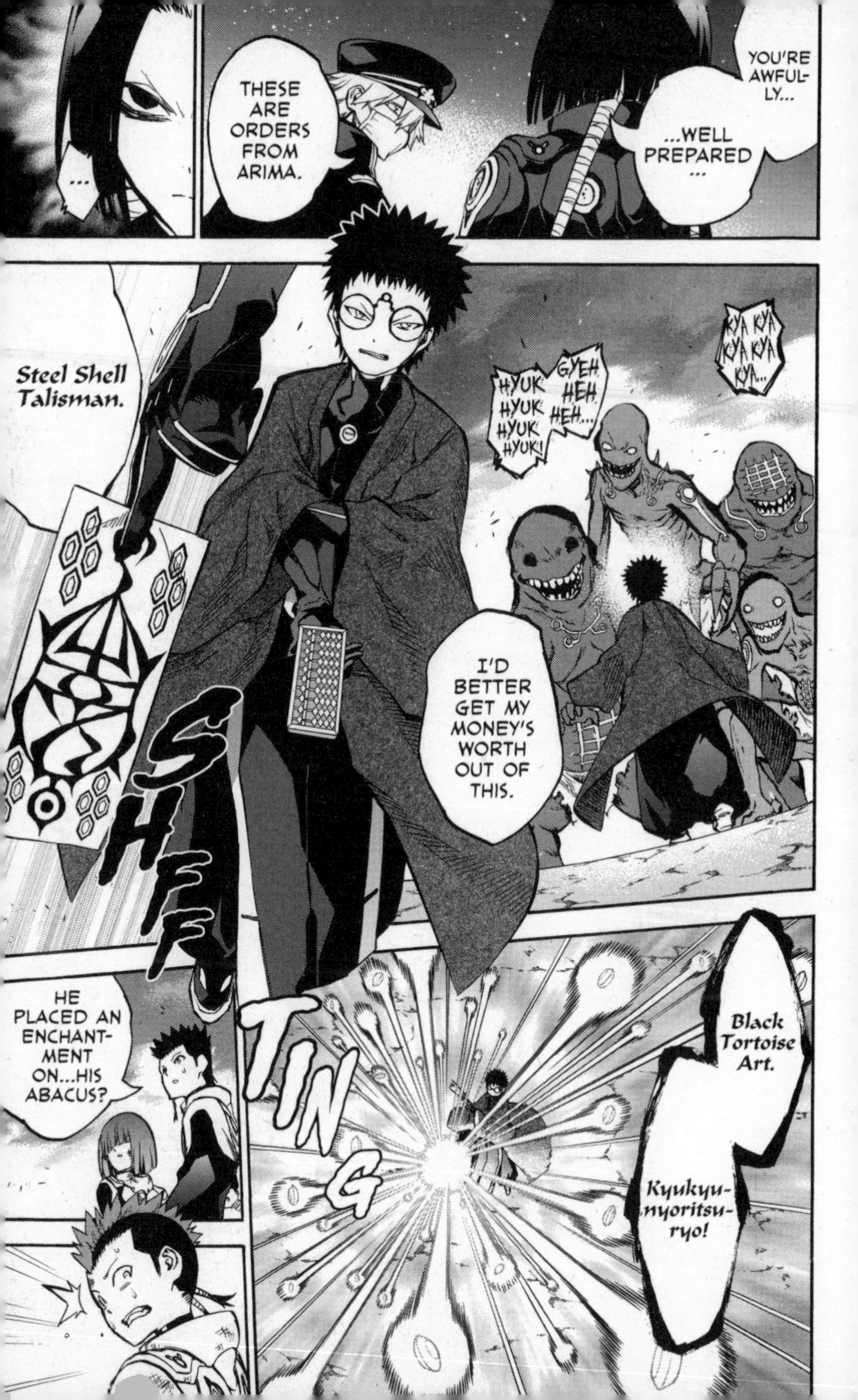
YOU'RE AWFULLY...
...WELL PREPARED...
THESE ARE ORDERS FROM ARIMA.
...
KYA KYA KYA KYA KYA...
GYEH HEH HEH...
HYUK HYUK HYUK HYUK!
I'D BETTER GET MY MONEY'S WORTH OUT OF THIS.
Steel Shell Talisman.
SHFF
Black Tortoise Art.
Kyukyu-nyoritsu-ryo!
TING
HE PLACED AN ENCHANTMENT ON...HIS ABACUS?

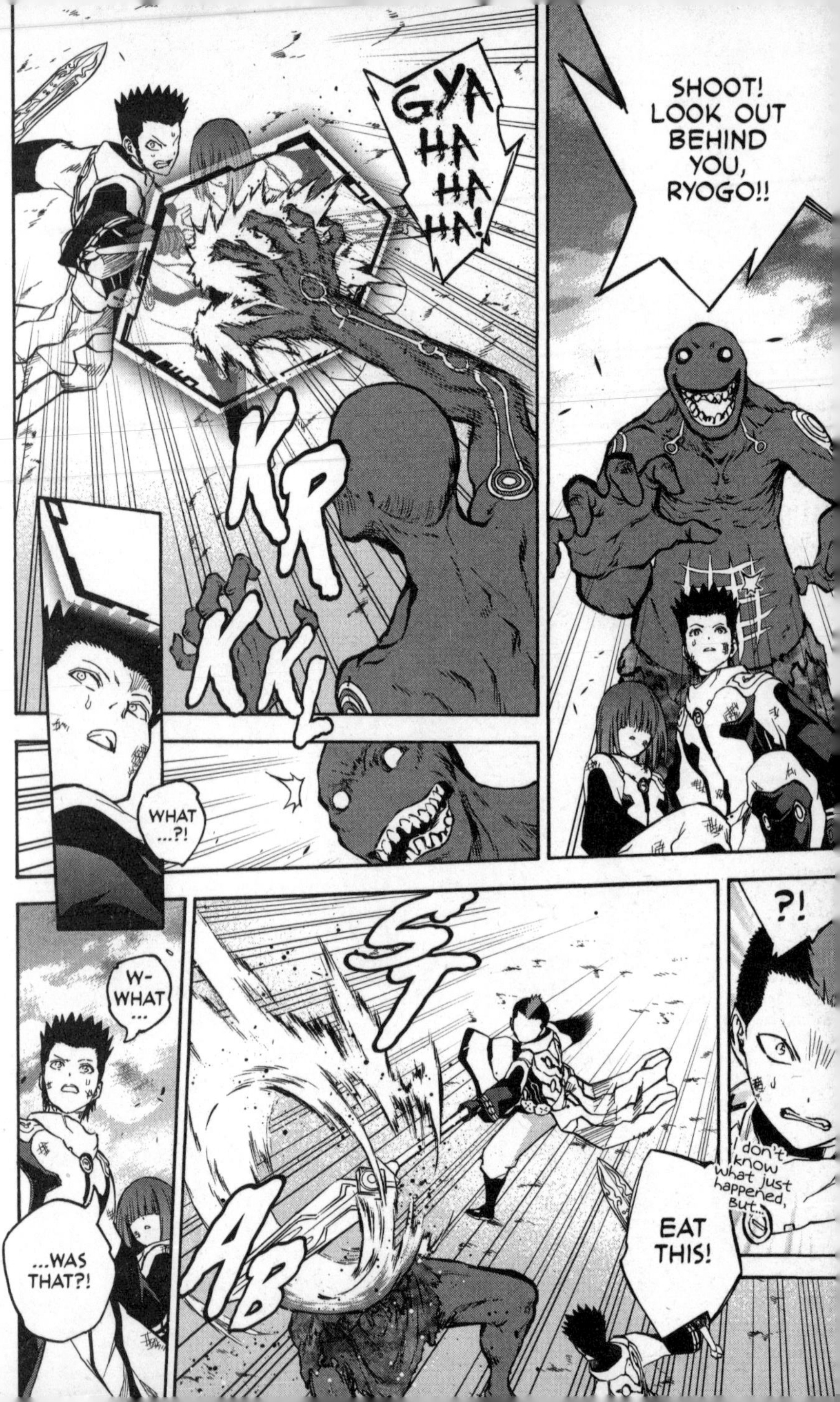
SHOOT! LOOK OUT BEHIND YOU, RYOGO!!
GYA HA HA HA!
WHAT ...?!
?!
I don't know what just happened, but...
EAT THIS!
W-WHAT ...
...WAS THAT?!

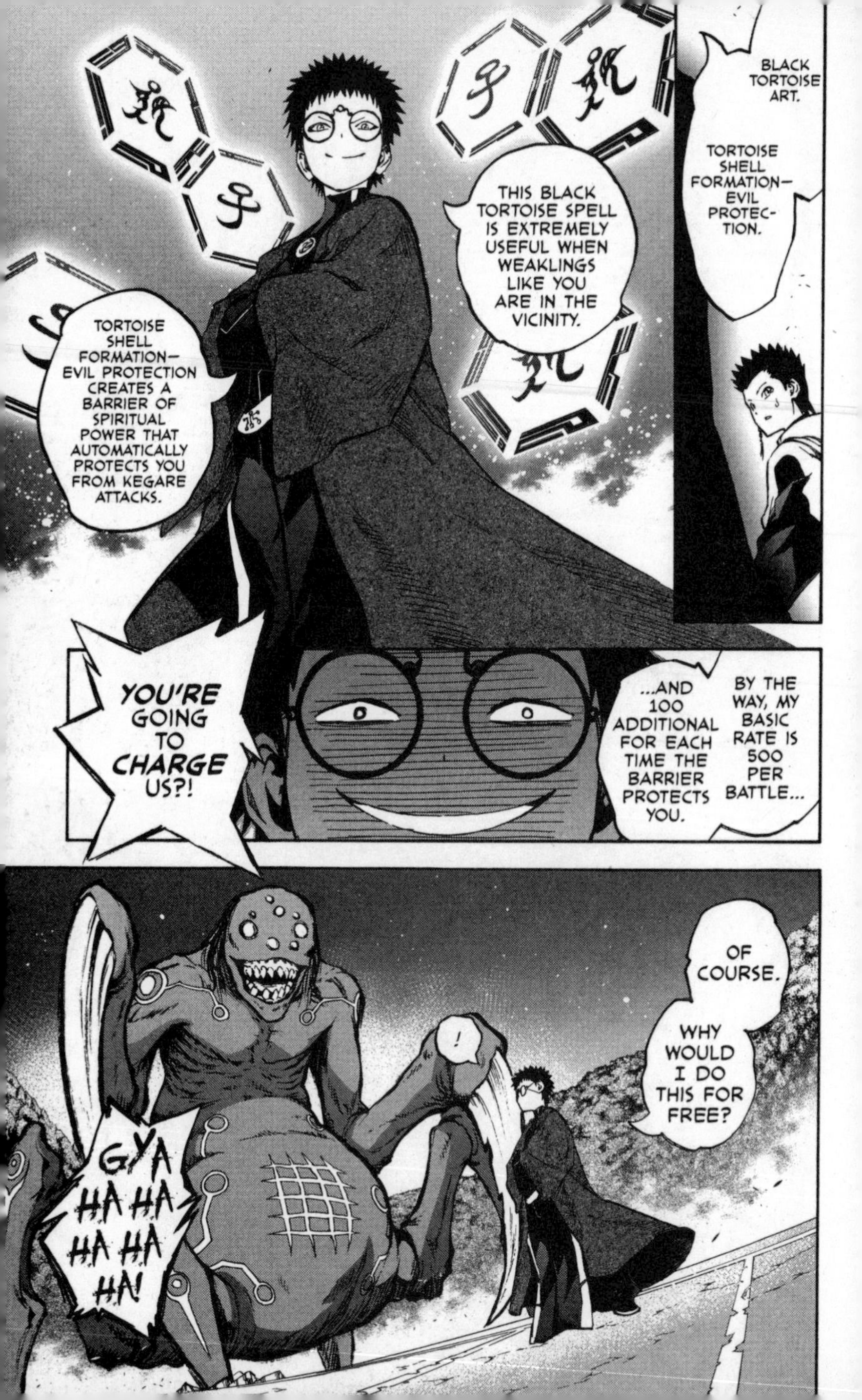
BLACK TORTOISE ART.
TORTOISE SHELL FORMATION—EVIL PROTEC-TION.
THIS BLACK TORTOISE SPELL IS EXTREMELY USEFUL WHEN WEAKLINGS LIKE YOU ARE IN THE VICINITY.
TORTOISE SHELL FORMATION—EVIL PROTECTION CREATES A BARRIER OF SPIRITUAL POWER THAT AUTOMATICALLY PROTECTS YOU FROM KEGARE ATTACKS.
BY THE WAY, MY BASIC RATE IS 500 PER BATTLE...
...AND 100 ADDITIONAL FOR EACH TIME THE BARRIER PROTECTS YOU.
YOU'RE GOING TO CHARGE US?!
OF COURSE.
WHY WOULD I DO THIS FOR FREE?
!
GYA HA HA HA HA HA HA!

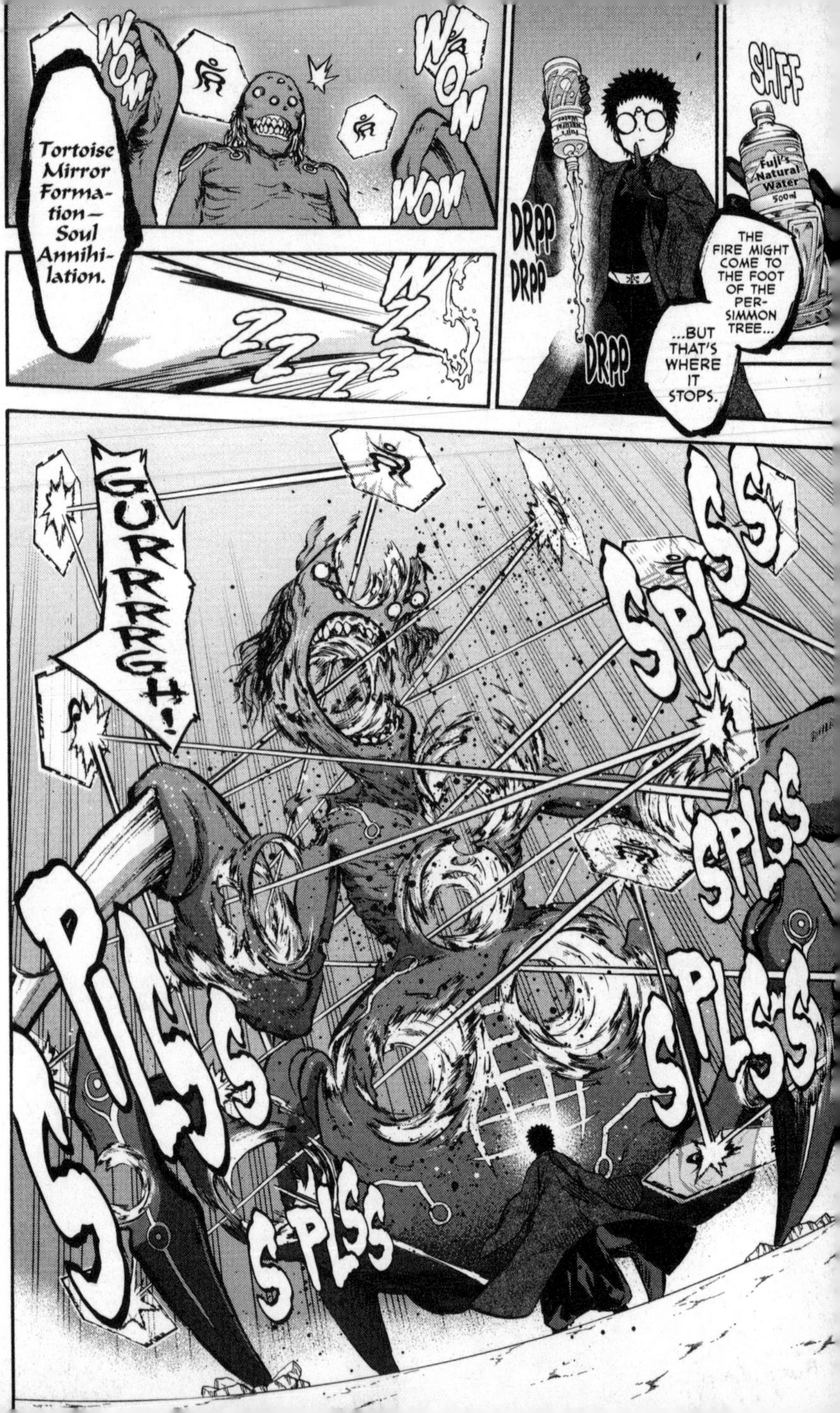

SHFF
Fuji's Natural Water 500ml
THE FIRE MIGHT COME TO THE FOOT OF THE PERSIMMON TREE...
...BUT THAT'S WHERE IT STOPS.
DRPP DRPP
DRPP
WOM
WOM
WOM
WOM
Tortoise Mirror Formation—Soul Annihilation.
WZZZZ
ZZZ
SPLSS
SPL
GURRRRGH!
SPLSS
SPLSS
SPLSS
SPLSS

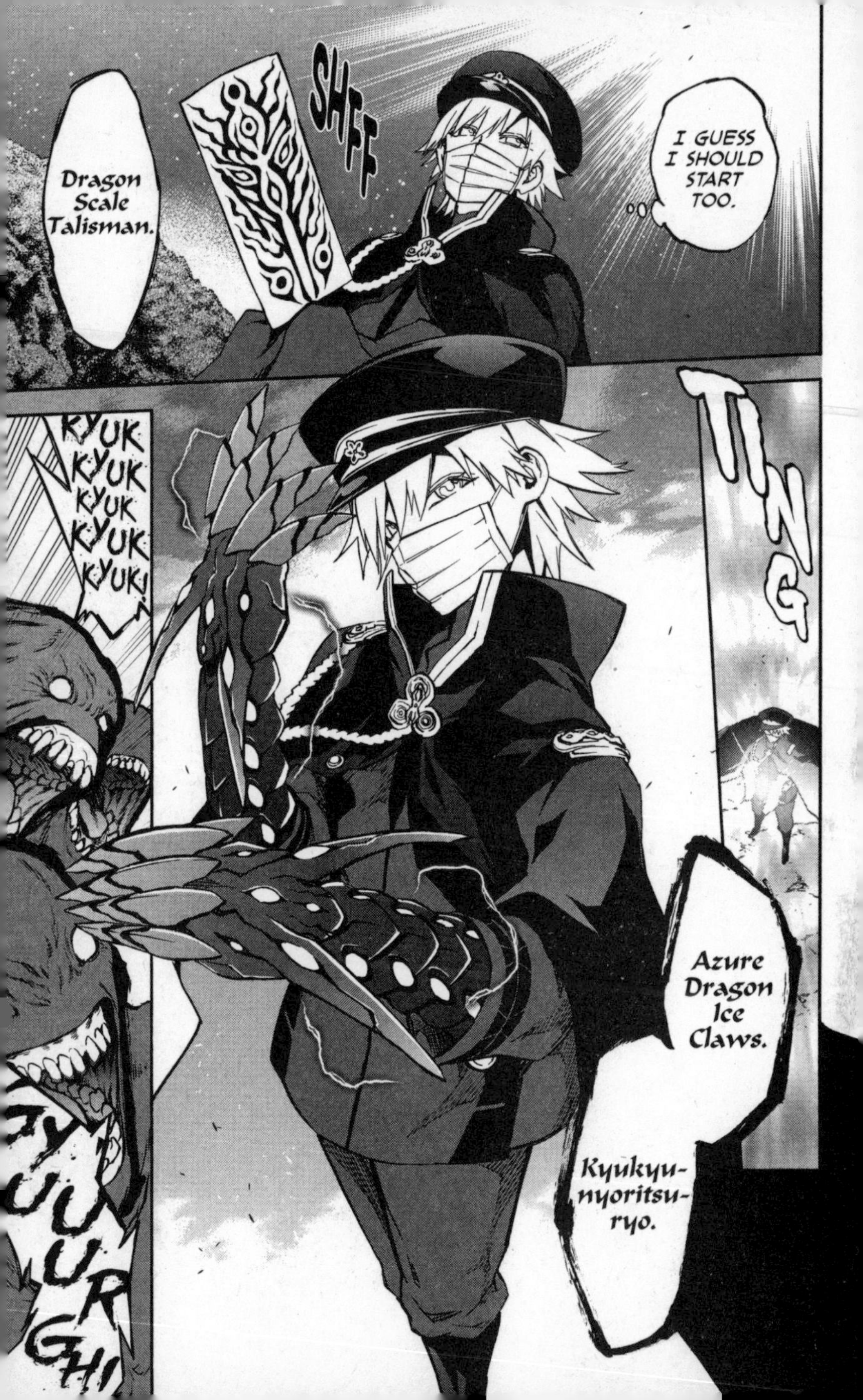
I GUESS I SHOULD START TOO.
SHFF
Dragon Scale Talisman.
TING
Azure Dragon Ice Claws.
Kyukyu-nyoritsu-ryo.
KYUK KYUK KYUK KYUK KYUK!

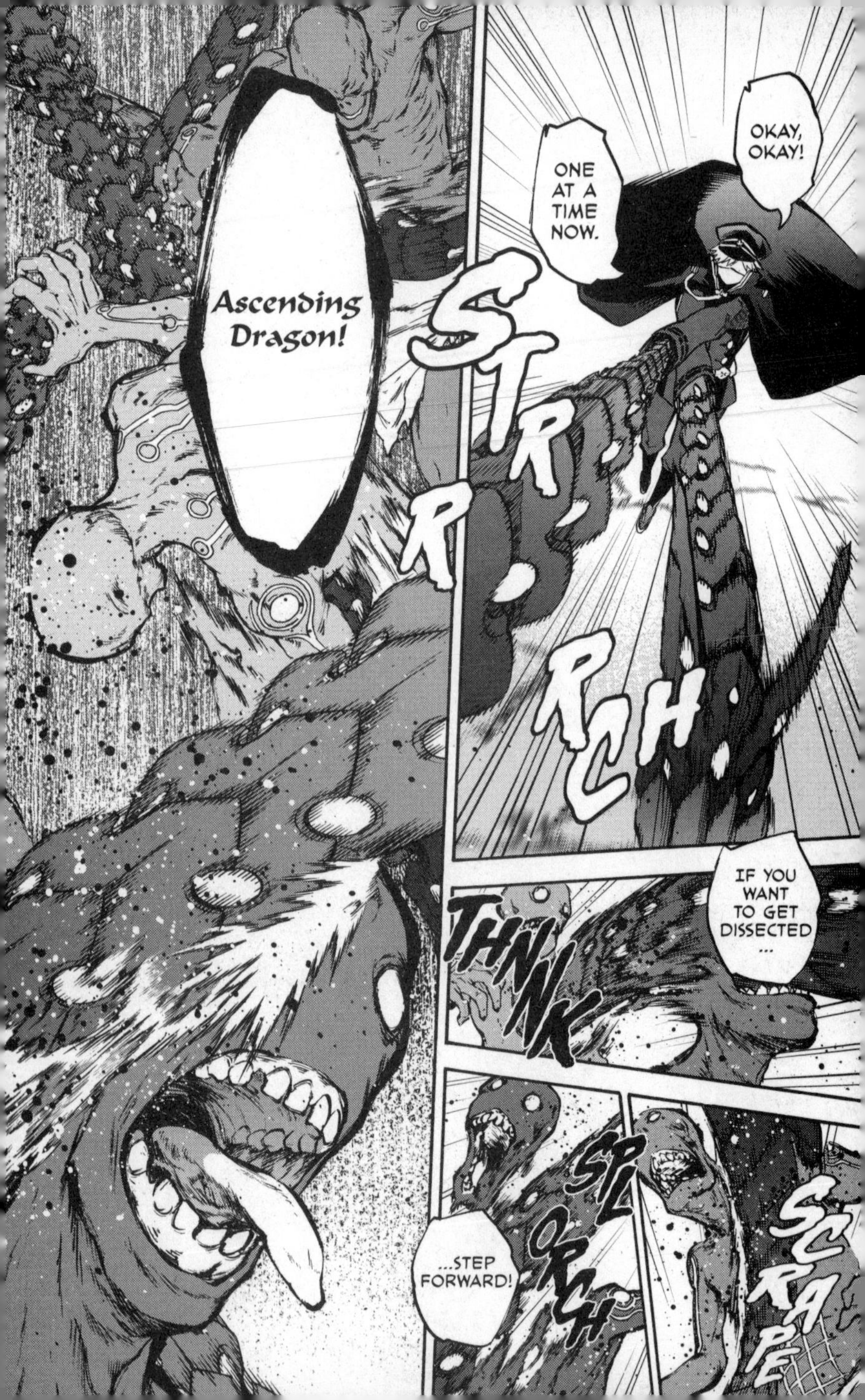
OKAY, OKAY!
ONE AT A TIME NOW.
STRRRCH
IF YOU WANT TO GET DISSECTED...
THNNK
SCRAPE
SPLORCH
...STEP FORWARD!
Ascending Dragon!

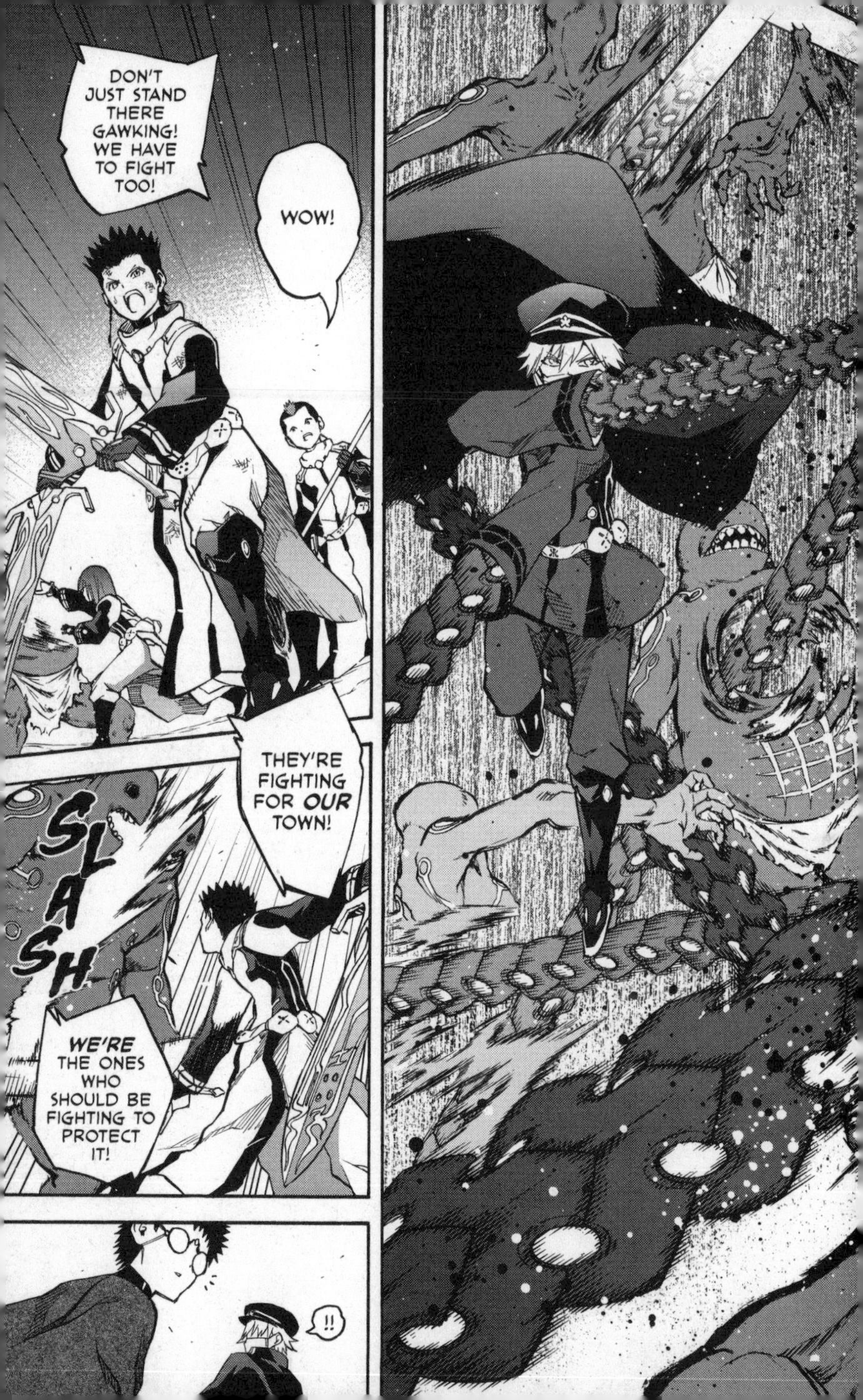
WOW!
DON'T JUST STAND THERE GAWKING! WE HAVE TO FIGHT TOO!
THEY'RE FIGHTING FOR *OUR* TOWN!
SLASH
WE'RE THE ONES WHO SHOULD BE FIGHTING TO PROTECT IT!
!!

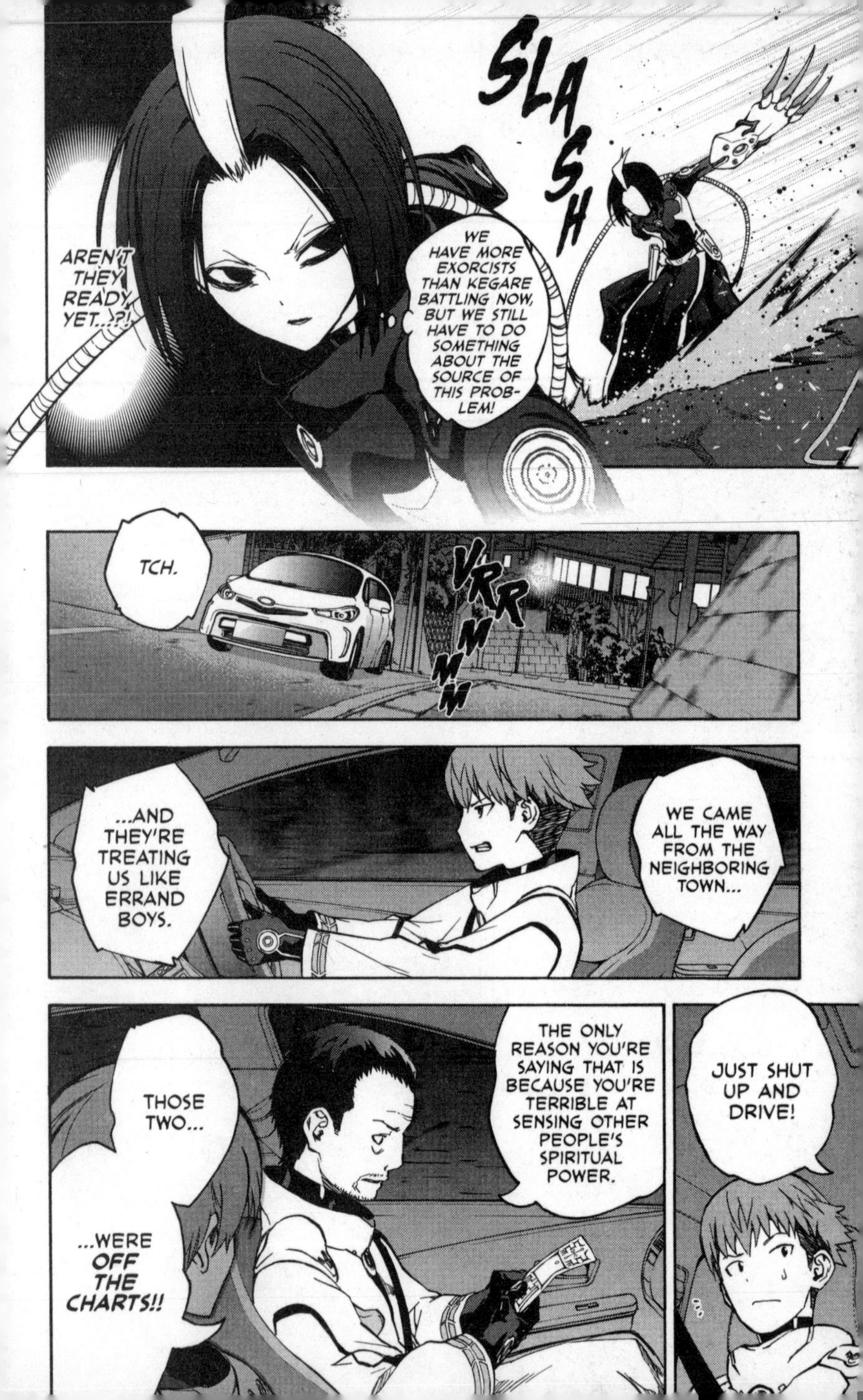
SLASH
WE HAVE MORE EXORCISTS THAN KEGARE BATTLING NOW, BUT WE STILL HAVE TO DO SOMETHING ABOUT THE SOURCE OF THIS PROB-LEM!
AREN'T THEY READY YET...?!
VRRMMMM
TCH.
WE CAME ALL THE WAY FROM THE NEIGHBORING TOWN...
...AND THEY'RE TREATING US LIKE ERRAND BOYS.
JUST SHUT UP AND DRIVE!
THE ONLY REASON YOU'RE SAYING THAT IS BECAUSE YOU'RE TERRIBLE AT SENSING OTHER PEOPLE'S SPIRITUAL POWER.
THOSE TWO...
...WERE *OFF THE CHARTS!!*

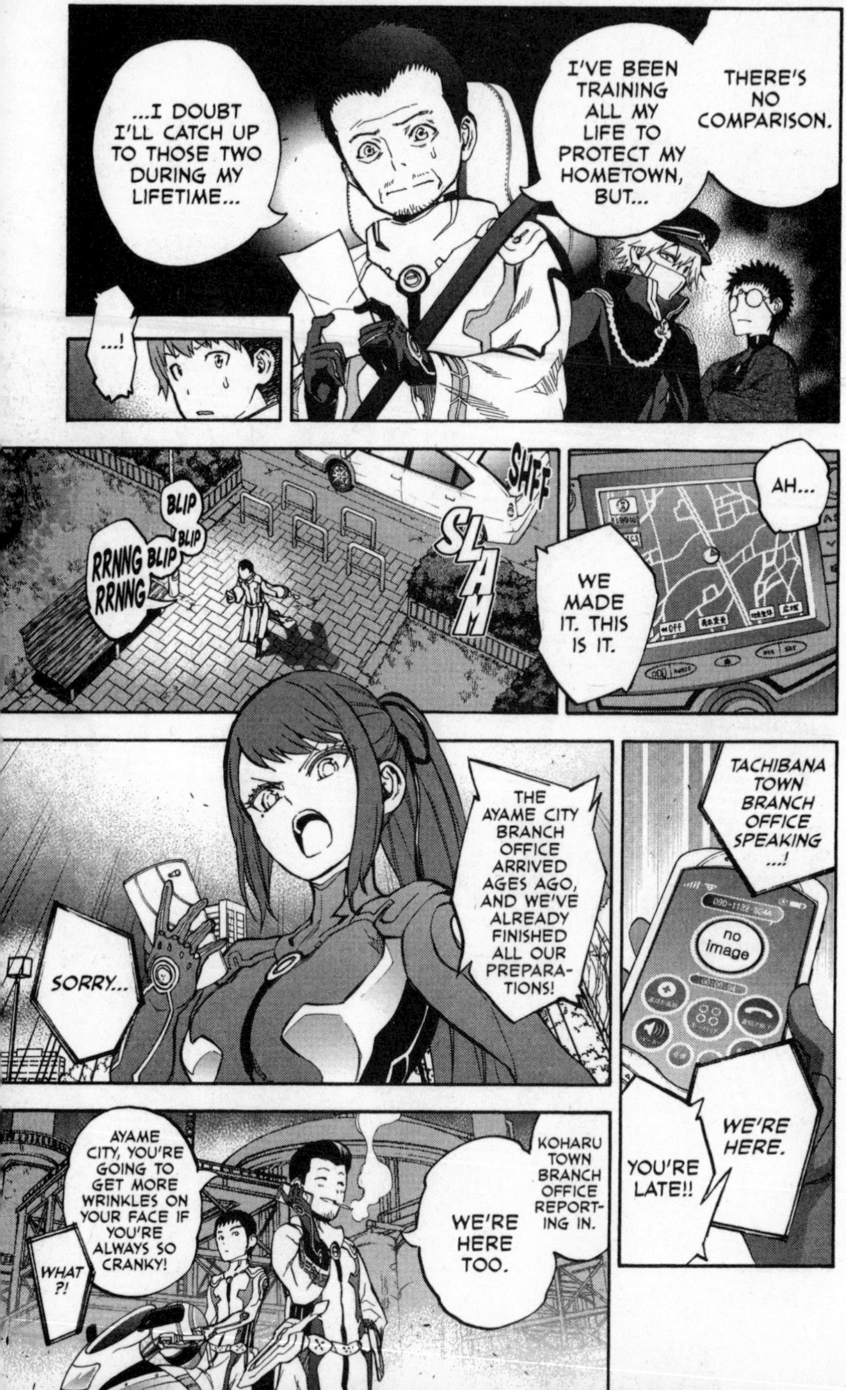
THERE'S NO COMPARISON.
I'VE BEEN TRAINING ALL MY LIFE TO PROTECT MY HOMETOWN, BUT...
...I DOUBT I'LL CATCH UP TO THOSE TWO DURING MY LIFETIME...
...!
AH...
WE MADE IT. THIS IS IT.
SHFF
SLAM
BLIP
BLIP
BLIP
RRNNG RRNNG
TACHIBANA TOWN BRANCH OFFICE SPEAKING ...!
no image
WE'RE HERE.
YOU'RE LATE!!
THE AYAME CITY BRANCH OFFICE ARRIVED AGES AGO, AND WE'VE ALREADY FINISHED ALL OUR PREPARA-TIONS!
SORRY...
KOHARU TOWN BRANCH OFFICE REPORT-ING IN.
WE'RE HERE TOO.
AYAME CITY, YOU'RE GOING TO GET MORE WRINKLES ON YOUR FACE IF YOU'RE ALWAYS SO CRANKY!
WHAT ?!

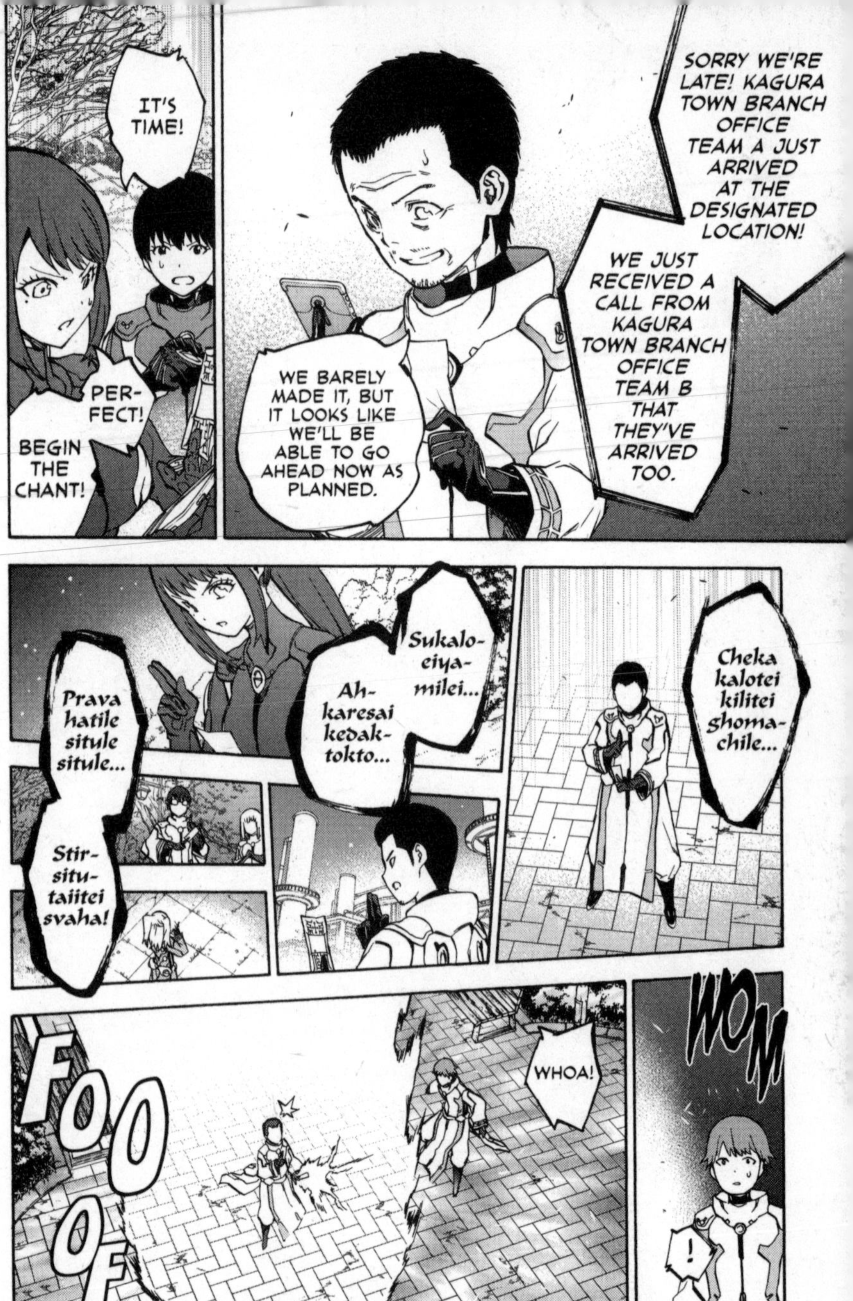
SORRY WE'RE LATE! KAGURA TOWN BRANCH OFFICE TEAM A JUST ARRIVED AT THE DESIGNATED LOCATION!
WE JUST RECEIVED A CALL FROM KAGURA TOWN BRANCH OFFICE TEAM B THAT THEY'VE ARRIVED TOO.
WE BARELY MADE IT, BUT IT LOOKS LIKE WE'LL BE ABLE TO GO AHEAD NOW AS PLANNED.
IT'S TIME!
PER-FECT!
BEGIN THE CHANT!
Cheka kalotei kilitei ghoma-chile...
Sukaloeiya-milei...
Ah-karesai kedak-tokto...
Prava hatile situle situle...
Stir-situ-taiitei svaha!
WOM
!
WHOA!
FOOOOF

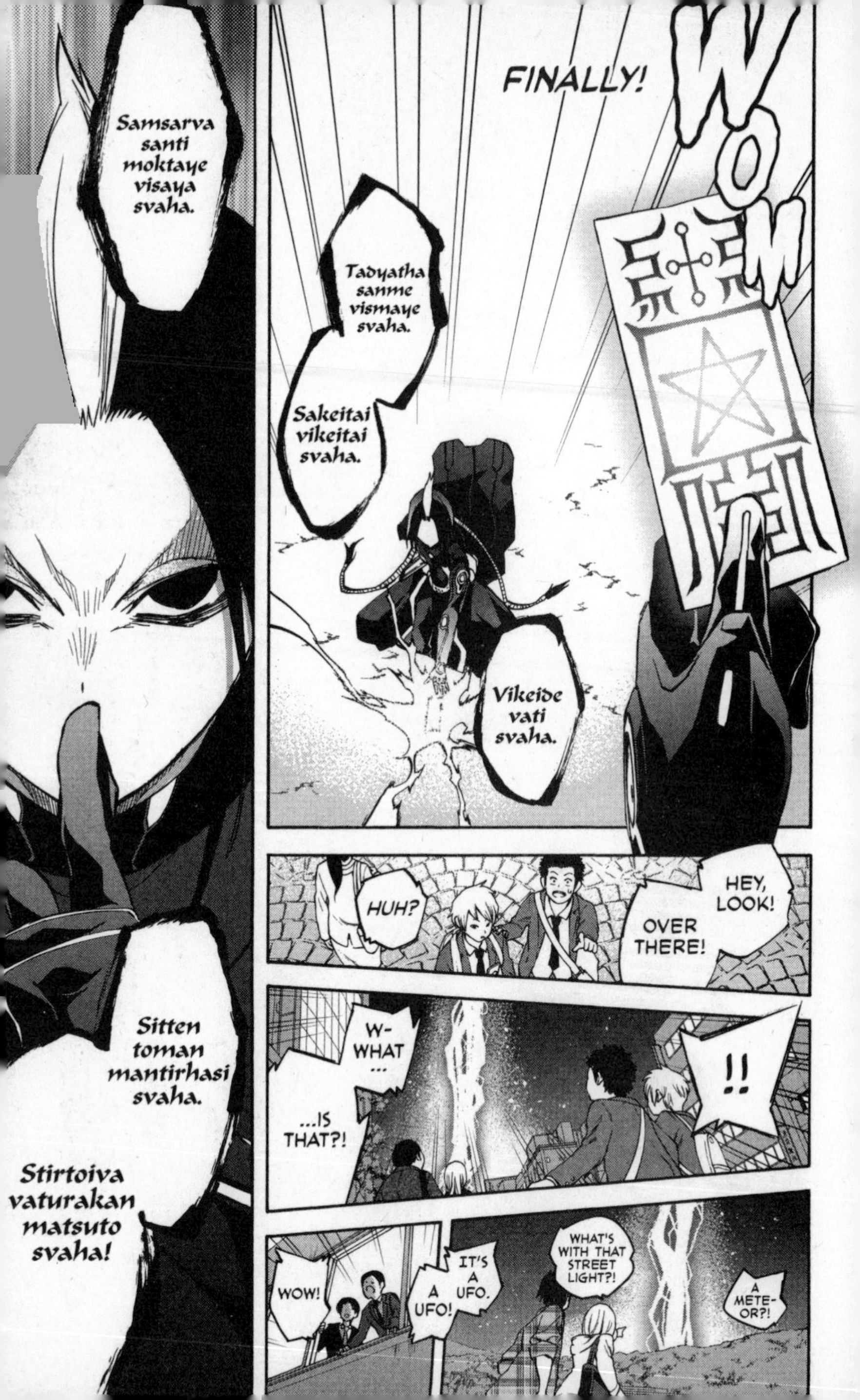
WOM
FINALLY!
Tadyatha sanme vismaye svaha.
Sakeitai vikeitai svaha.
Vikeide vati svaha.
HEY, LOOK!
OVER THERE!
HUH?
!!
W-WHAT...
...IS THAT?!
A METE-OR?!
WHAT'S WITH THAT STREET LIGHT?!
IT'S A UFO.
A UFO!
WOW!
Samsarva santi moktaye visaya svaha.
Sitten toman mantirhasi svaha.
Stirtoiva vaturakan matsuto svaha!

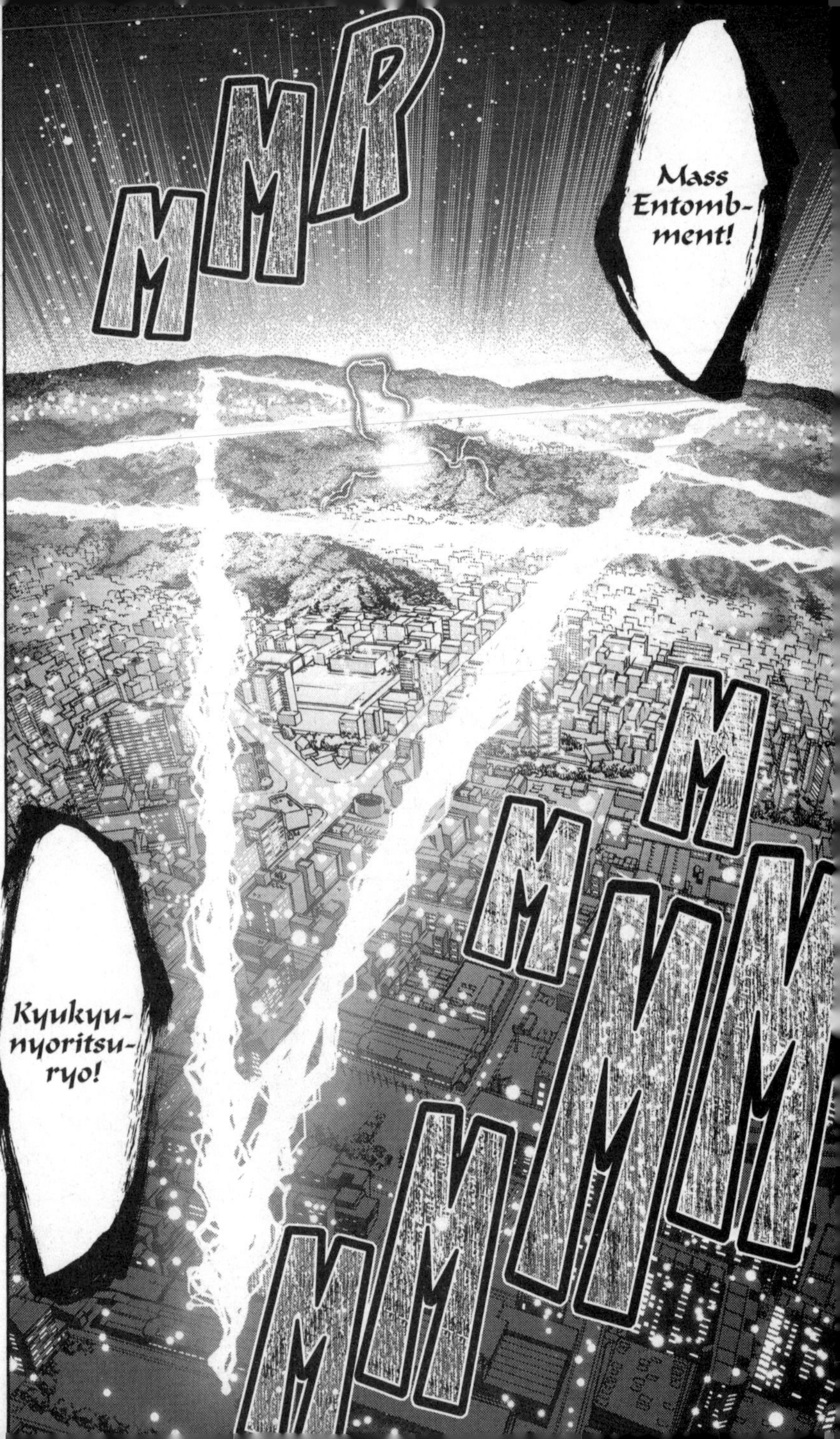

Mass Entomb-
ment!
MMMR
MMMMMMM
Kyukyu-
nyoritsu-
ryo!

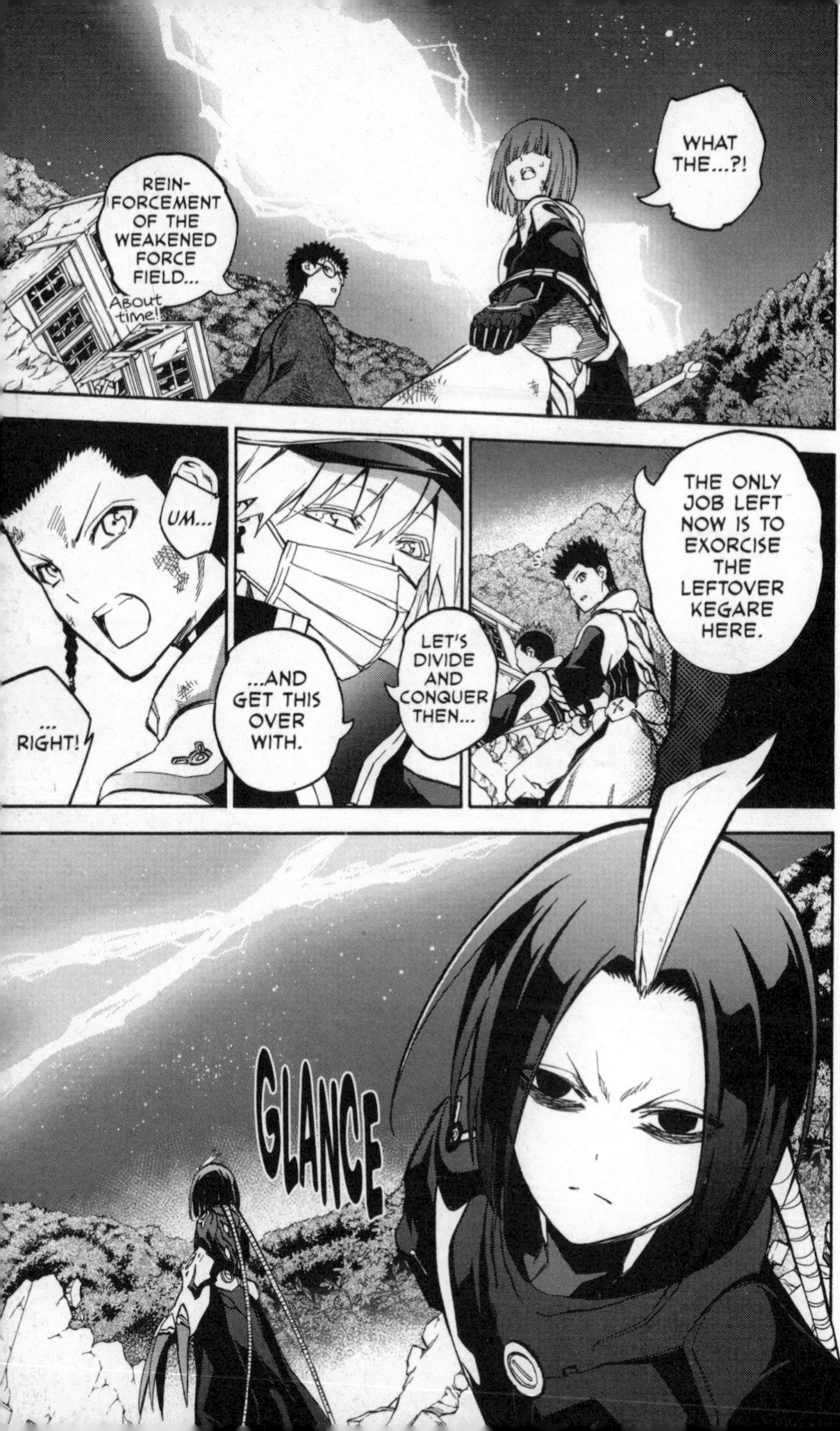
WHAT THE...?!
REIN-FORCEMENT OF THE WEAKENED FORCE FIELD...
About time!
THE ONLY JOB LEFT NOW IS TO EXORCISE THE LEFTOVER KEGARE HERE.
LET'S DIVIDE AND CONQUER THEN...
...AND GET THIS OVER WITH.
UM...
...RIGHT!
GLANCE

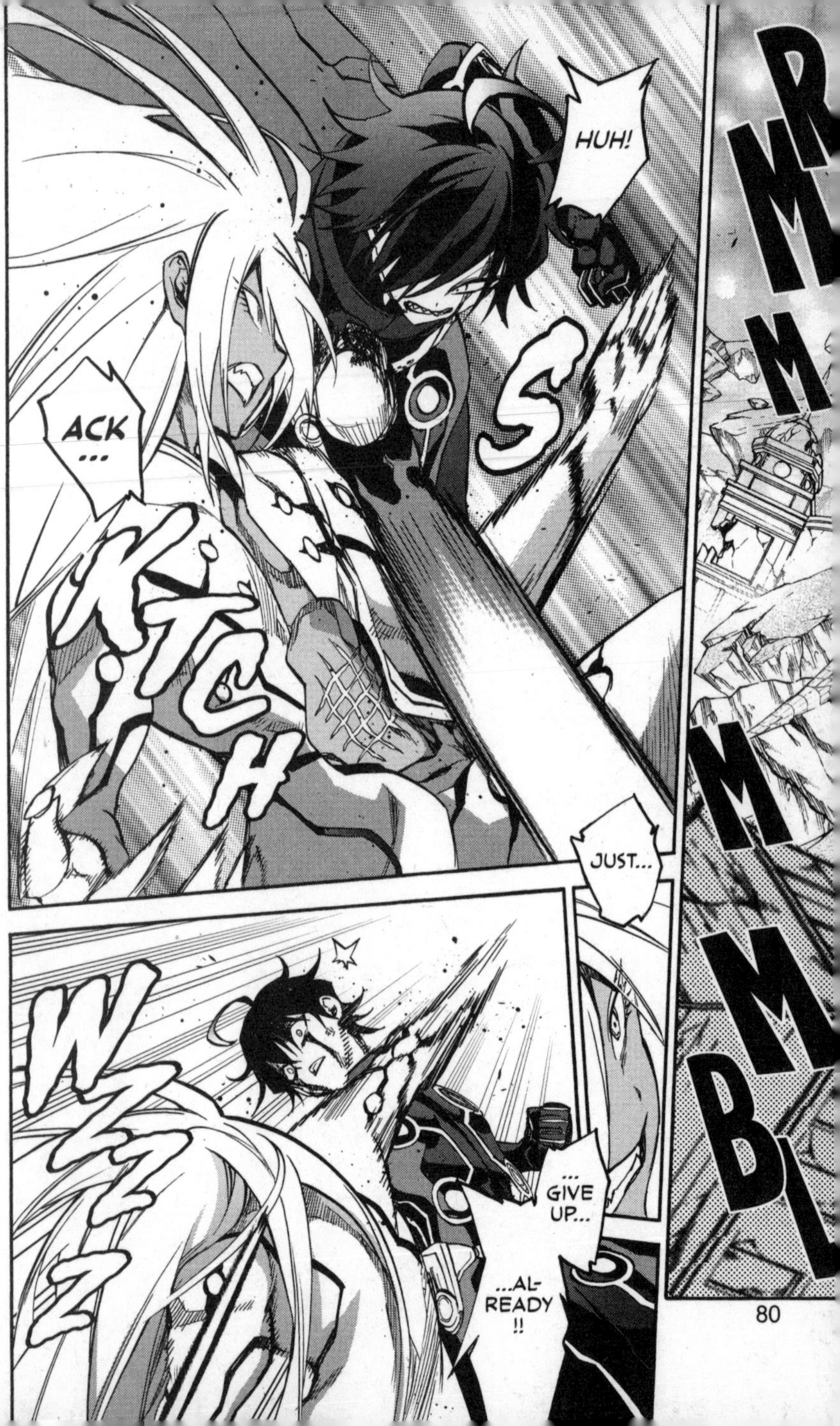
HUH!
ACK ...
JUST...
... GIVE UP...
...AL- READY !!

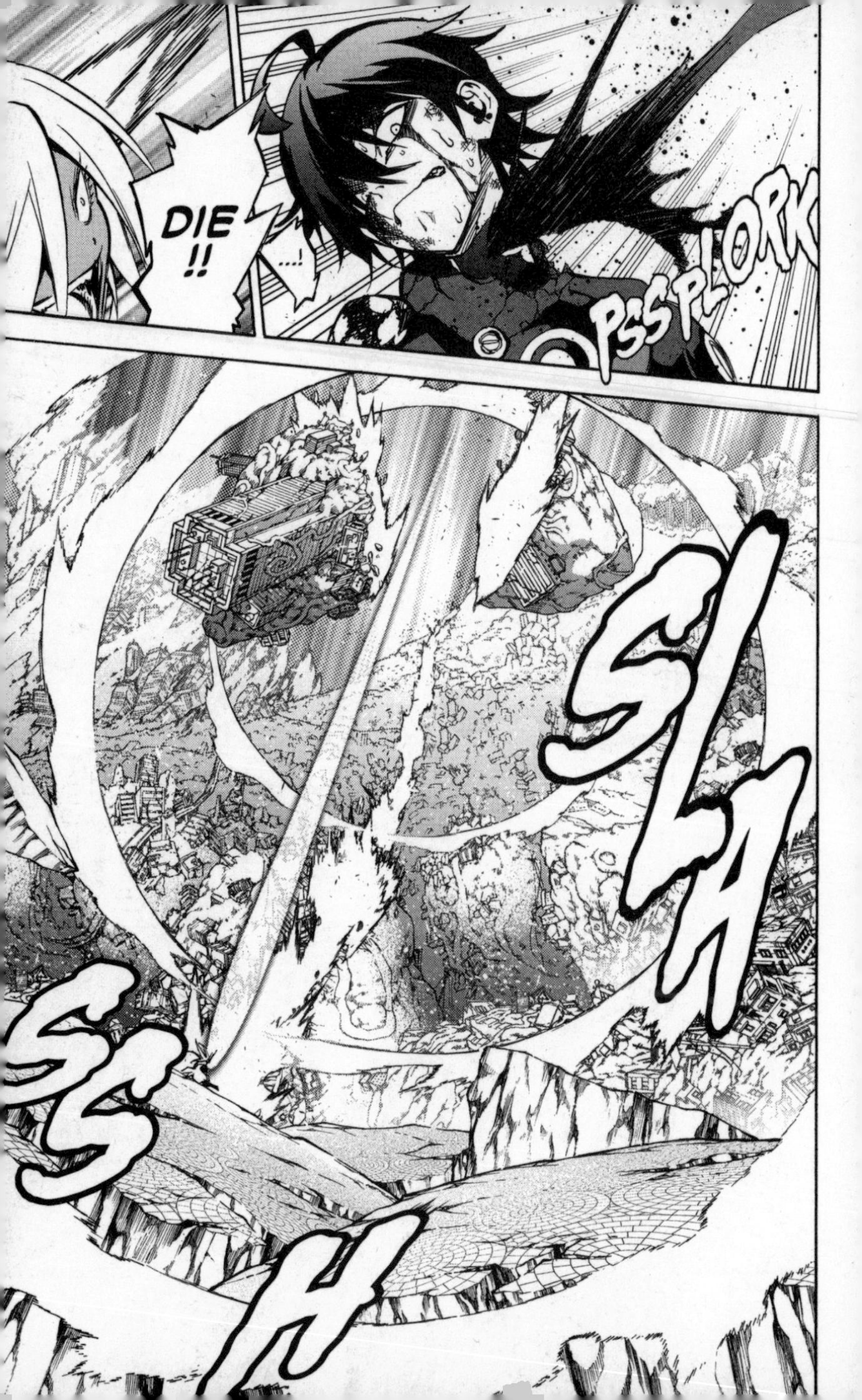
PSSPLORK
...!
DIE !!
SLASH
SSH

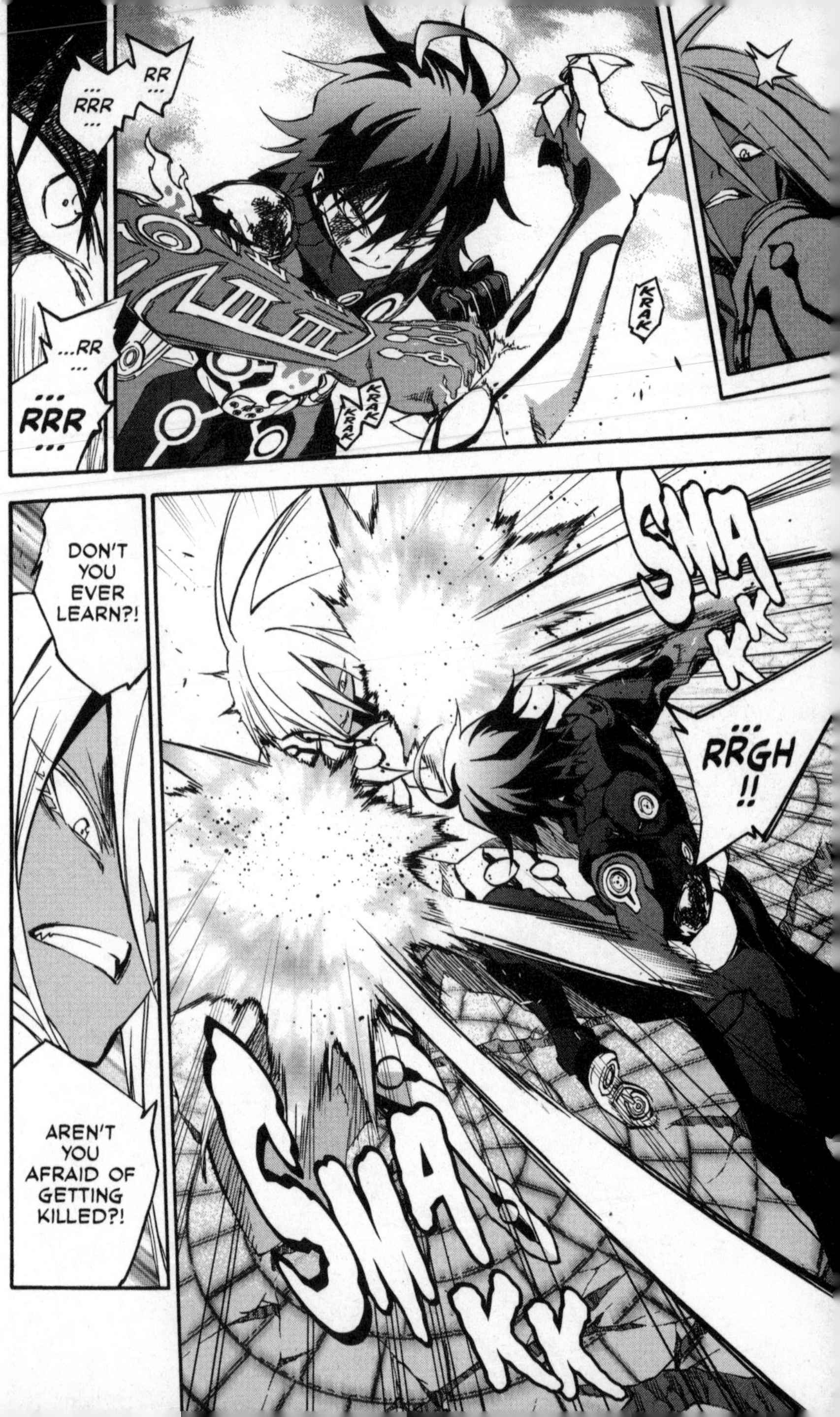
KRAK
KRAK KRAK
RR ... RRR ...
...RR ... RRR ...
SMAKK
...RRGH!!
SMAKK
DON'T YOU EVER LEARN?!
AREN'T YOU AFRAID OF GETTING KILLED?!

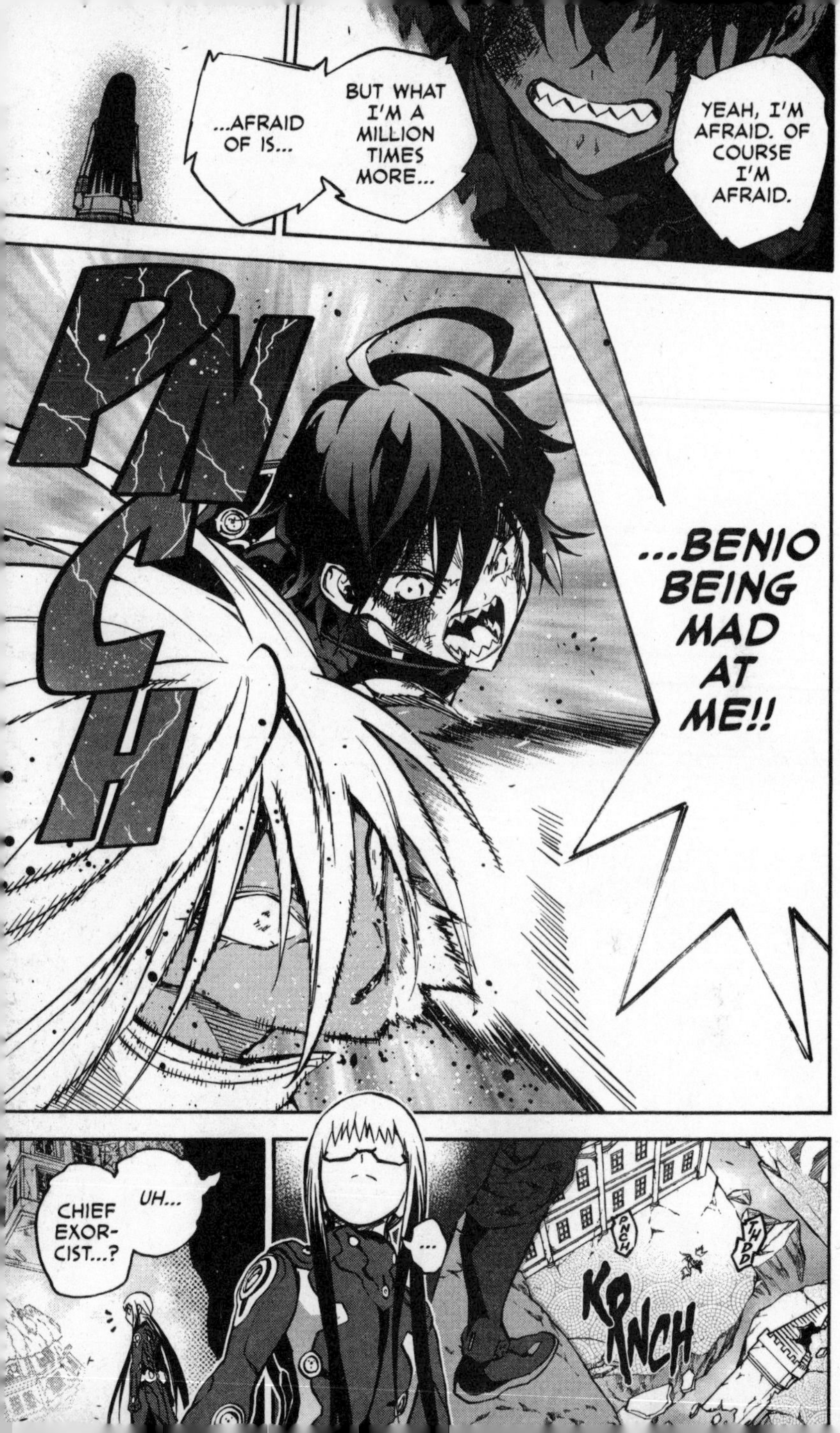
YEAH, I'M AFRAID. OF COURSE I'M AFRAID.
BUT WHAT I'M A MILLION TIMES MORE...
...AFRAID OF IS...
PNCH
...BENIO BEING MAD AT ME!!
THDD
PNCH
KRNCH
...
UH...
CHIEF EXORCIST...?

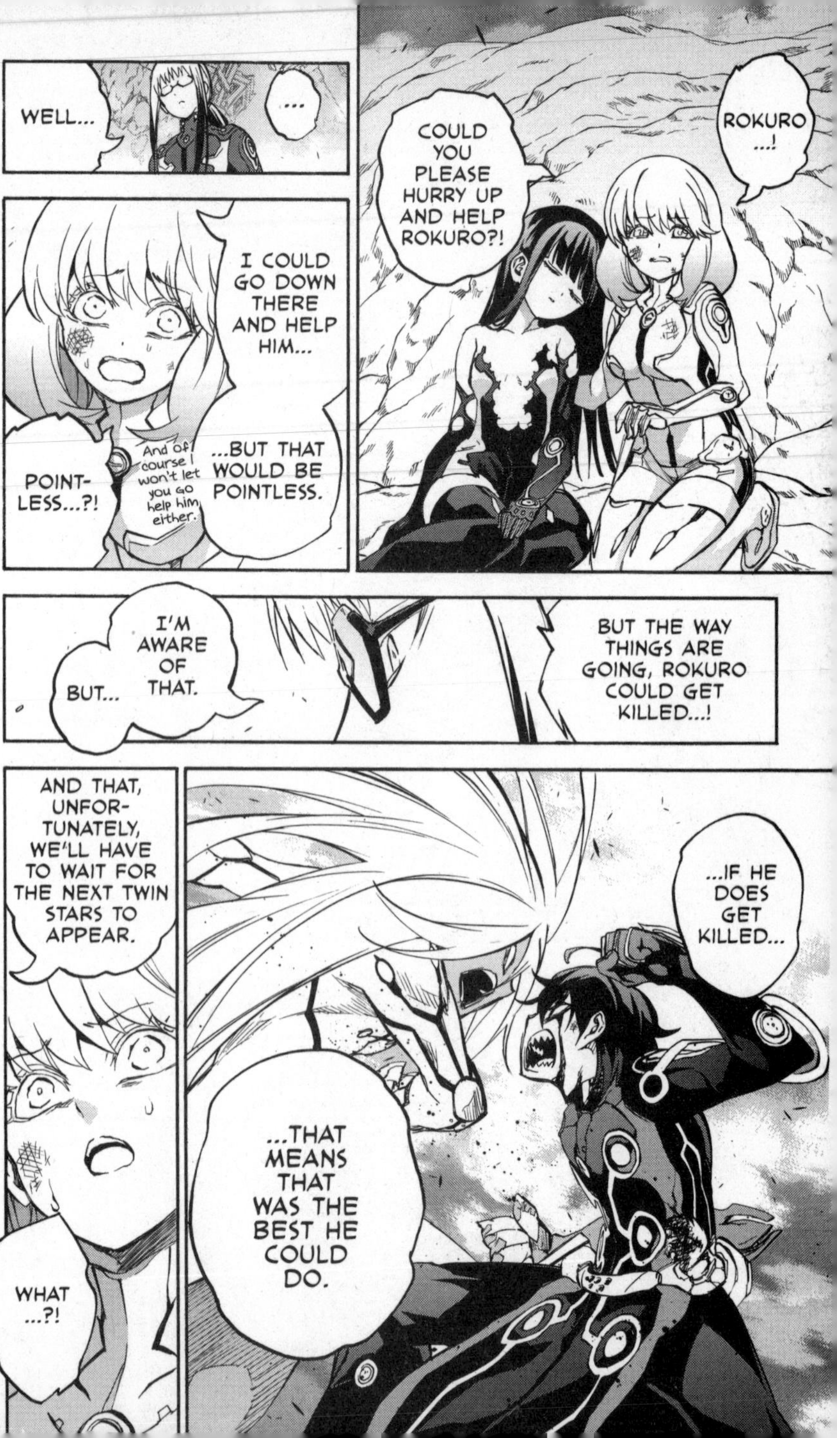
ROKURO ...!
COULD YOU PLEASE HURRY UP AND HELP ROKURO?!
....
WELL...
I COULD GO DOWN THERE AND HELP HIM...
...BUT THAT WOULD BE POINTLESS.
And of course I won't let you go help him either.
POINT-LESS...?!
BUT THE WAY THINGS ARE GOING, ROKURO COULD GET KILLED...!
I'M AWARE OF THAT.
BUT...
...IF HE DOES GET KILLED...
...THAT MEANS THAT WAS THE BEST HE COULD DO.
AND THAT, UNFOR-TUNATELY, WE'LL HAVE TO WAIT FOR THE NEXT TWIN STARS TO APPEAR.
WHAT ...?!

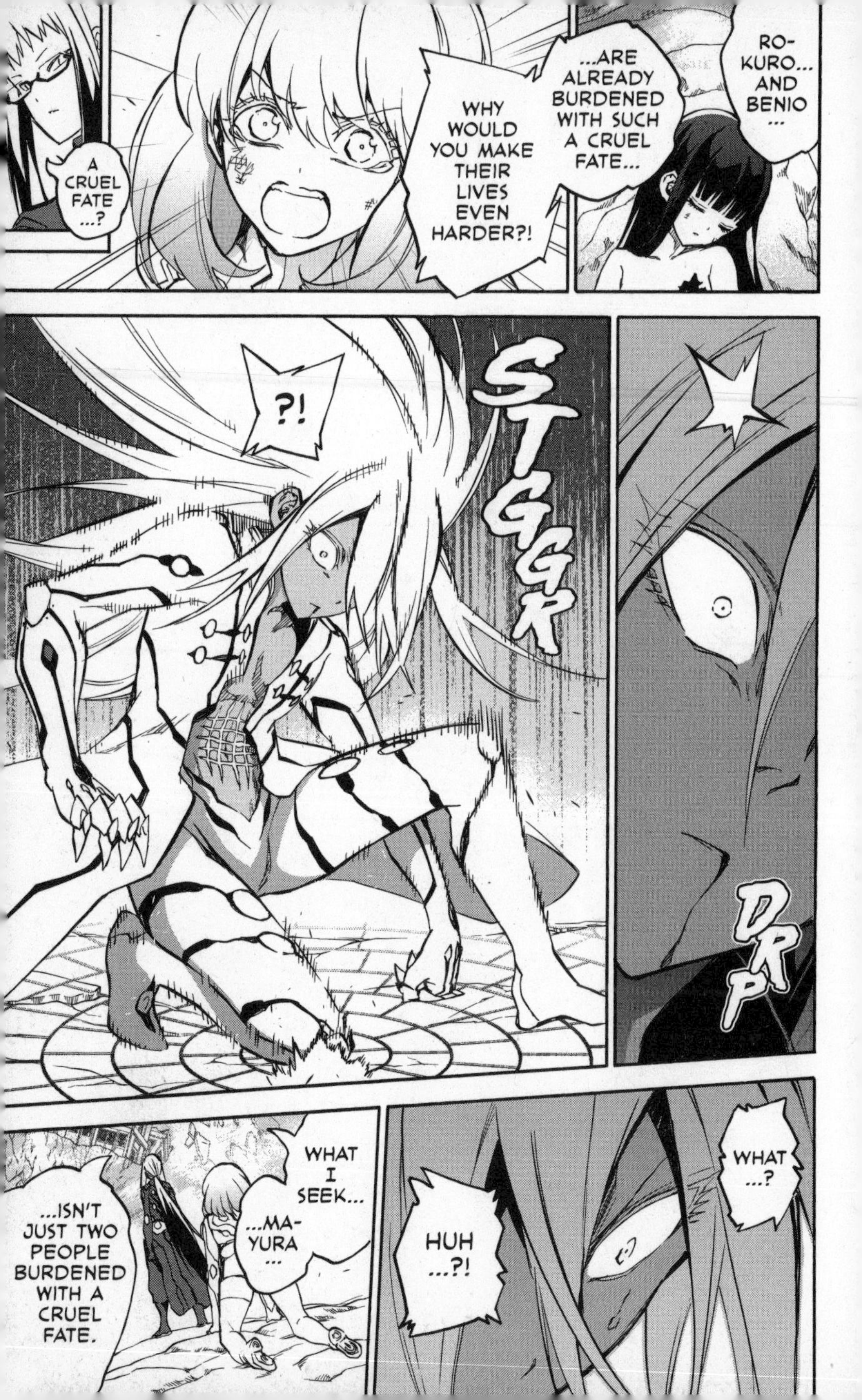
RO-KURO... AND BENIO...
...ARE ALREADY BURDENED WITH SUCH A CRUEL FATE...
WHY WOULD YOU MAKE THEIR LIVES EVEN HARDER?!
A CRUEL FATE...?
DRP
?!
STGGR
WHAT...?
HUH...?!
WHAT I SEEK...
...MA-YURA...
...ISN'T JUST TWO PEOPLE BURDENED WITH A CRUEL FATE.

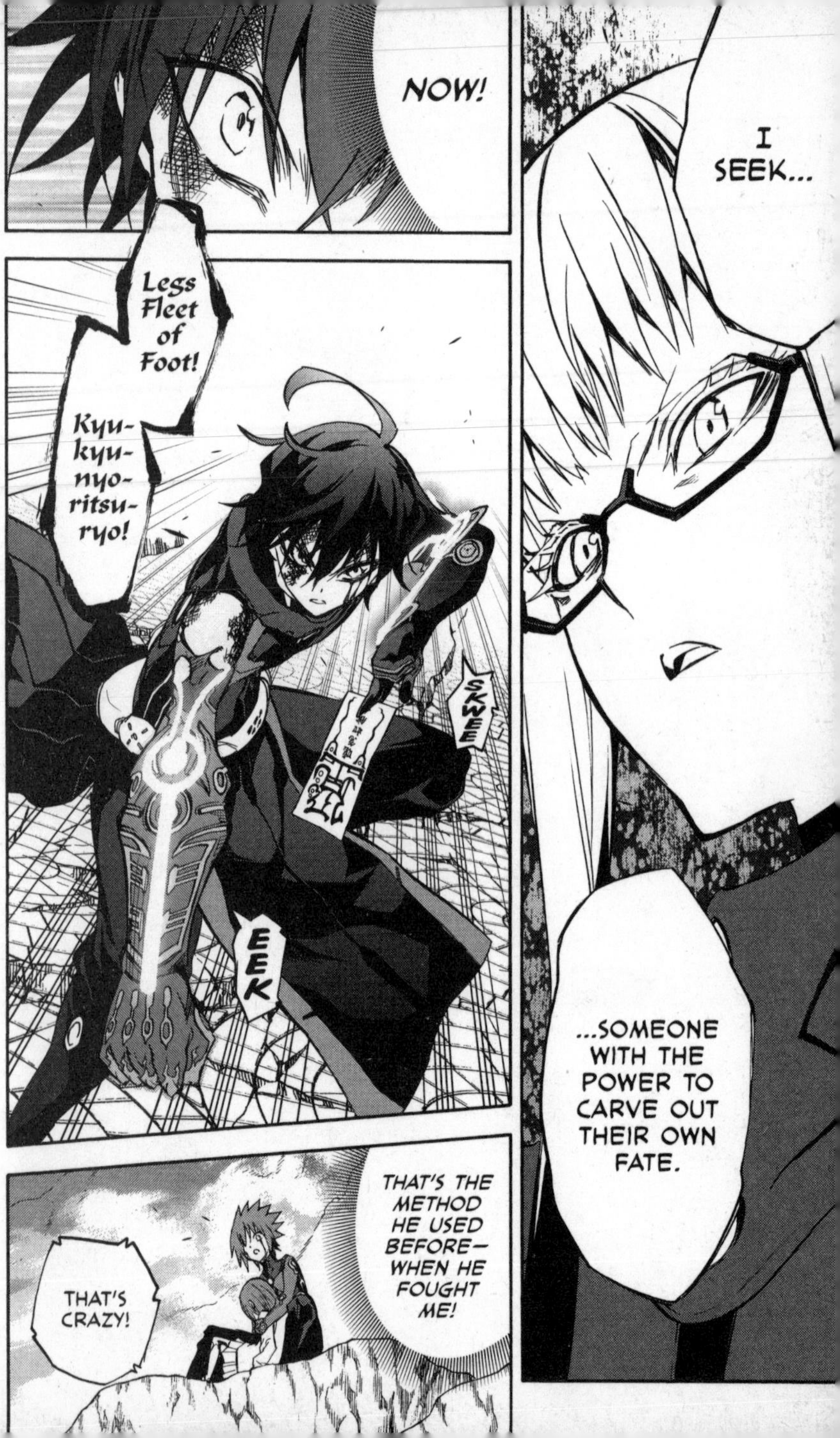
I SEEK...
...SOMEONE WITH THE POWER TO CARVE OUT THEIR OWN FATE.
NOW!
Legs Fleet of Foot!
Kyu-kyu-nyo-ritsu-ryo!
SKWEE
EEK
THAT'S THE METHOD HE USED BEFORE—WHEN HE FOUGHT ME!
THAT'S CRAZY!

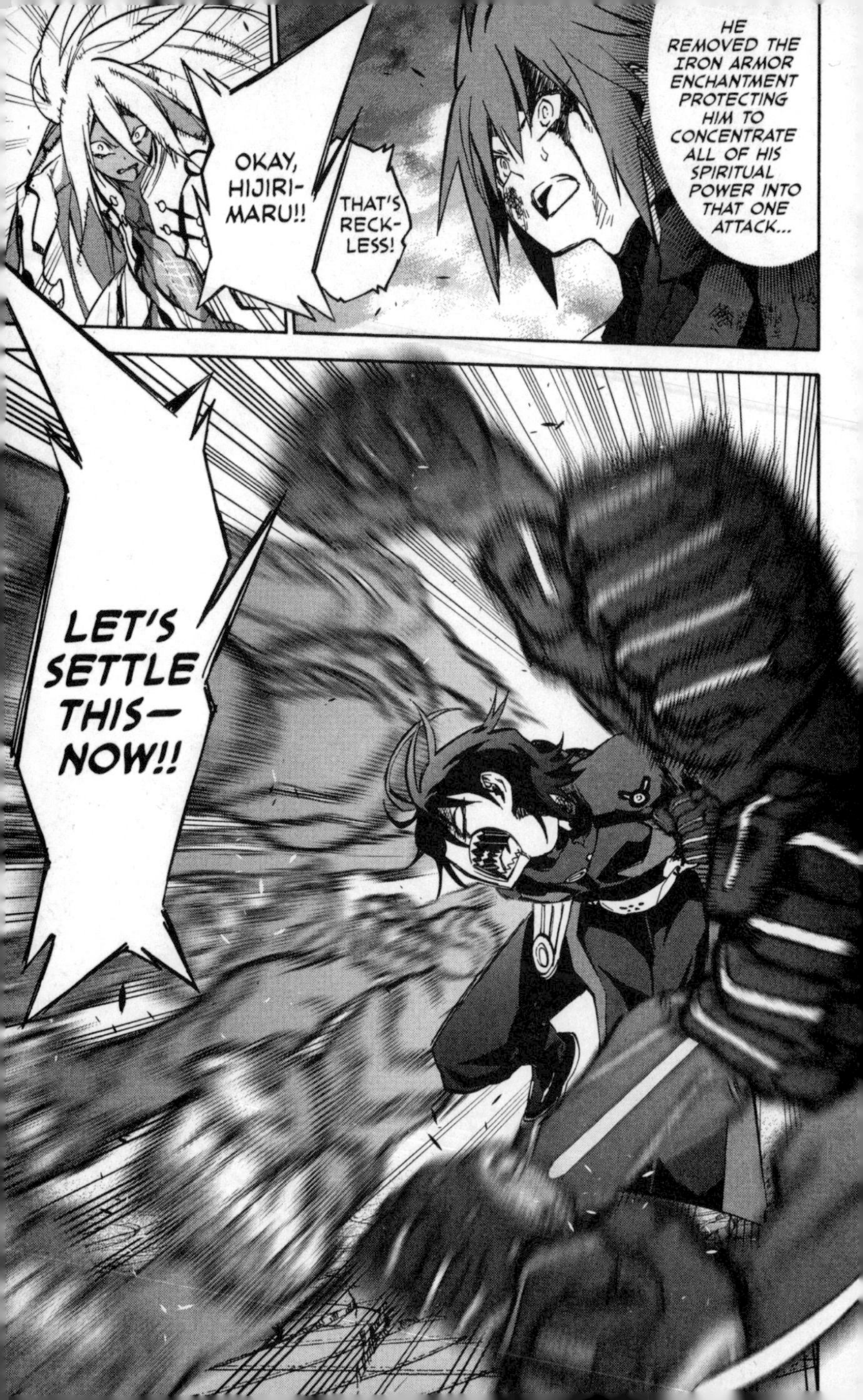
HE REMOVED THE IRON ARMOR ENCHANTMENT PROTECTING HIM TO CONCENTRATE ALL OF HIS SPIRITUAL POWER INTO THAT ONE ATTACK...
THAT'S RECK-LESS!
OKAY, HIJIRI-MARU!!
LET'S SETTLE THIS— NOW!!

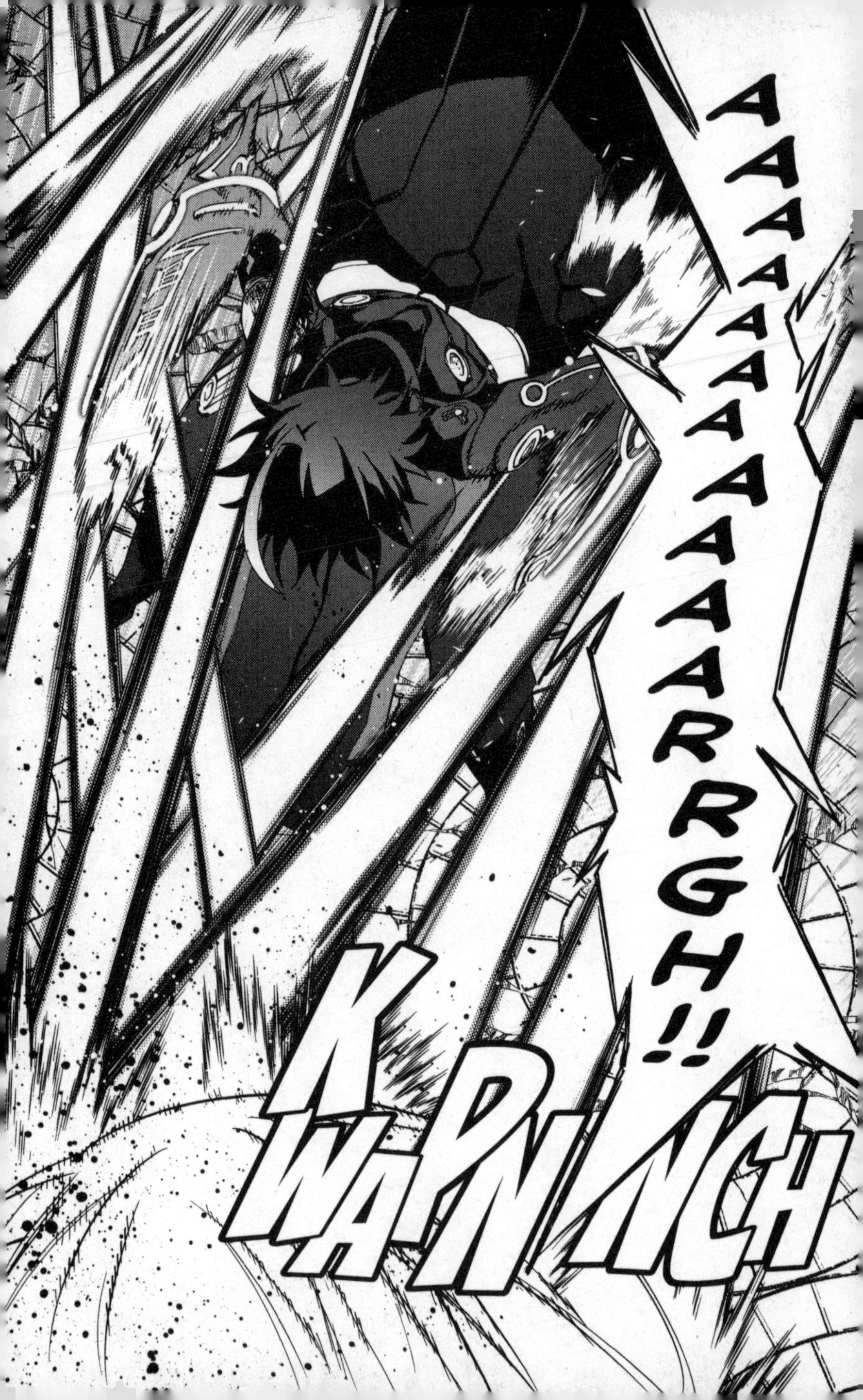
AAAAAAAAAAARRGH!!
KWAPNACH

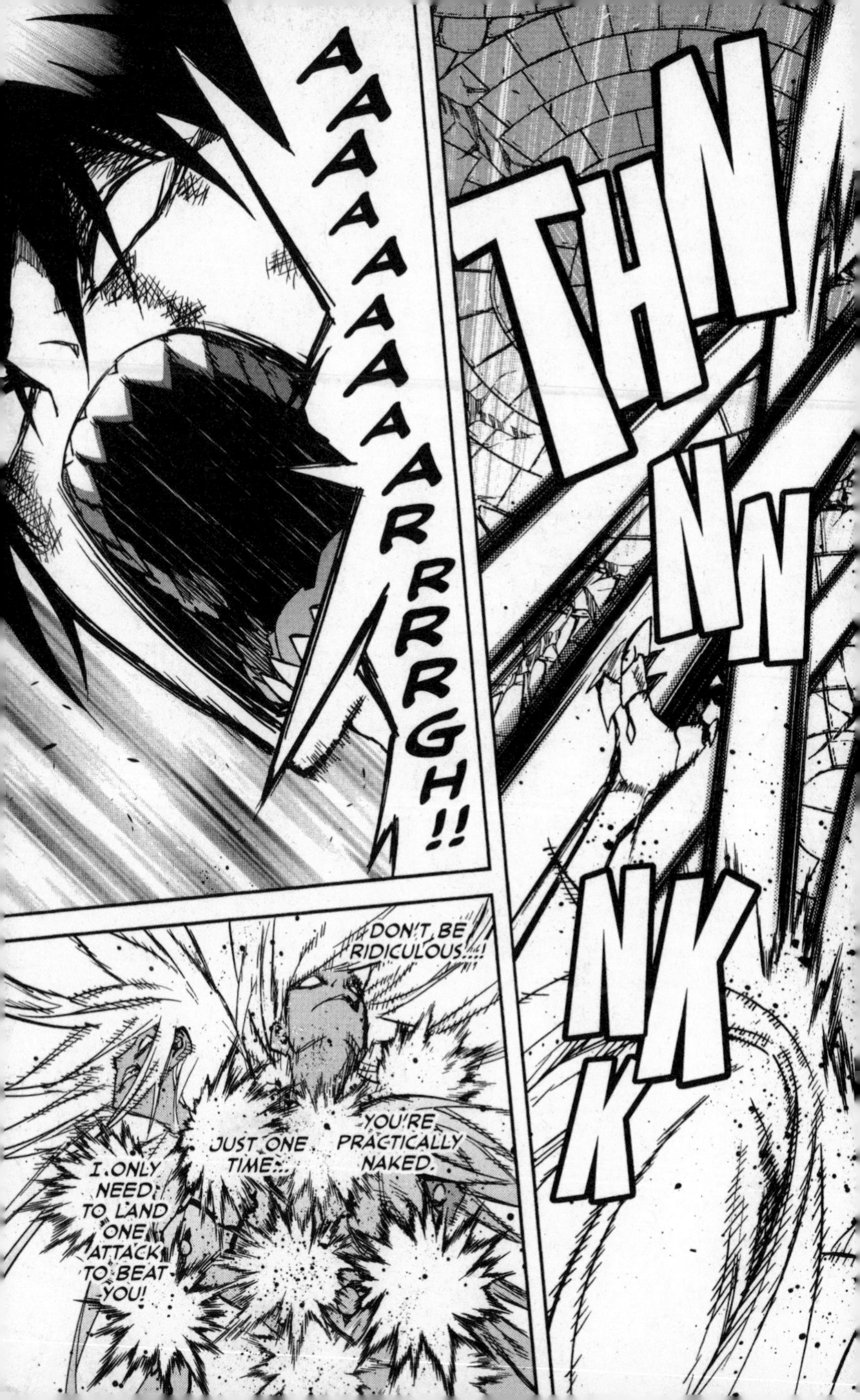
THNNNNKK
AAAAAAAAARRRRGH!!
DON'T BE RIDICULOUS...!
YOU'RE PRACTICALLY NAKED.
JUST ONE TIME...
I ONLY NEED TO LAND ONE ATTACK TO BEAT YOU!

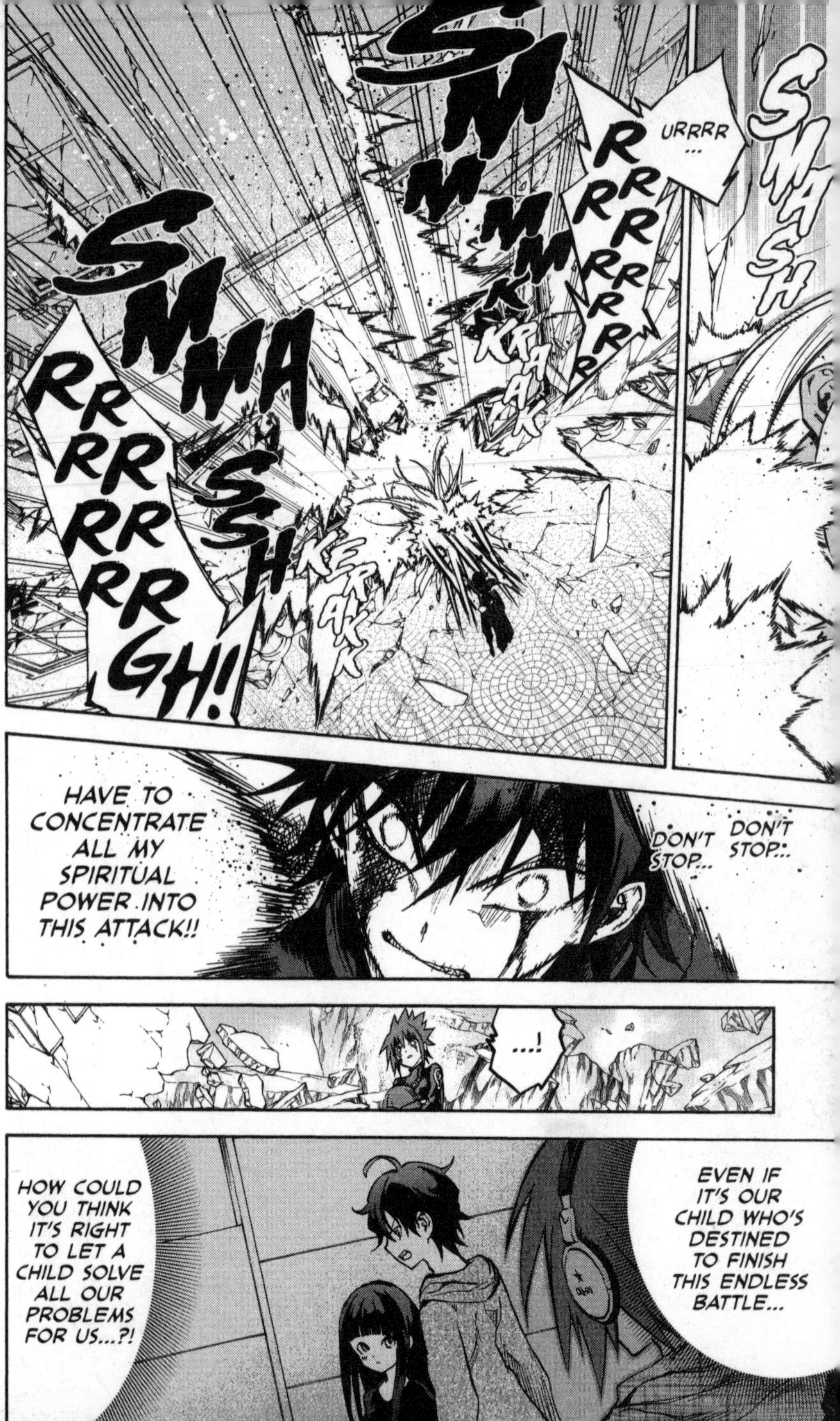
SMASH
URRRR ...
RRRRRRRRRRR
SMMMM
KRAAK
SMMASH
RRRRRRRRRRGH!
KERAKK
DON'T STOP...
DON'T STOP...
HAVE TO CONCENTRATE ALL MY SPIRITUAL POWER INTO THIS ATTACK!!
...!
EVEN IF IT'S OUR CHILD WHO'S DESTINED TO FINISH THIS ENDLESS BATTLE...
HOW COULD YOU THINK IT'S RIGHT TO LET A CHILD SOLVE ALL OUR PROBLEMS FOR US...?!

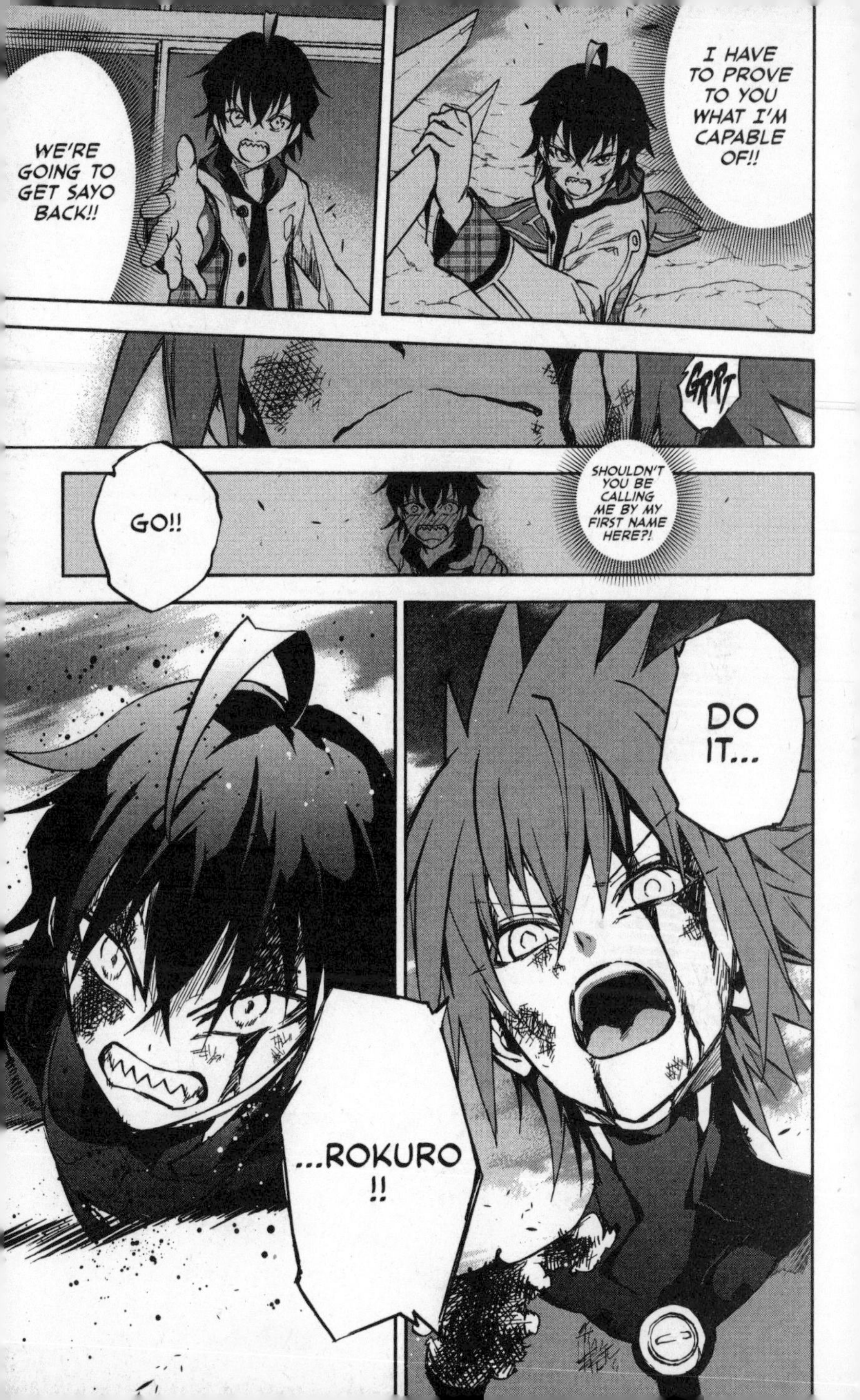
I HAVE TO PROVE TO YOU WHAT I'M CAPABLE OF!!
WE'RE GOING TO GET SAYO BACK!!
GRRT
SHOULDN'T YOU BE CALLING ME BY MY FIRST NAME HERE?!
GO!!
DO IT...
...ROKURO !!

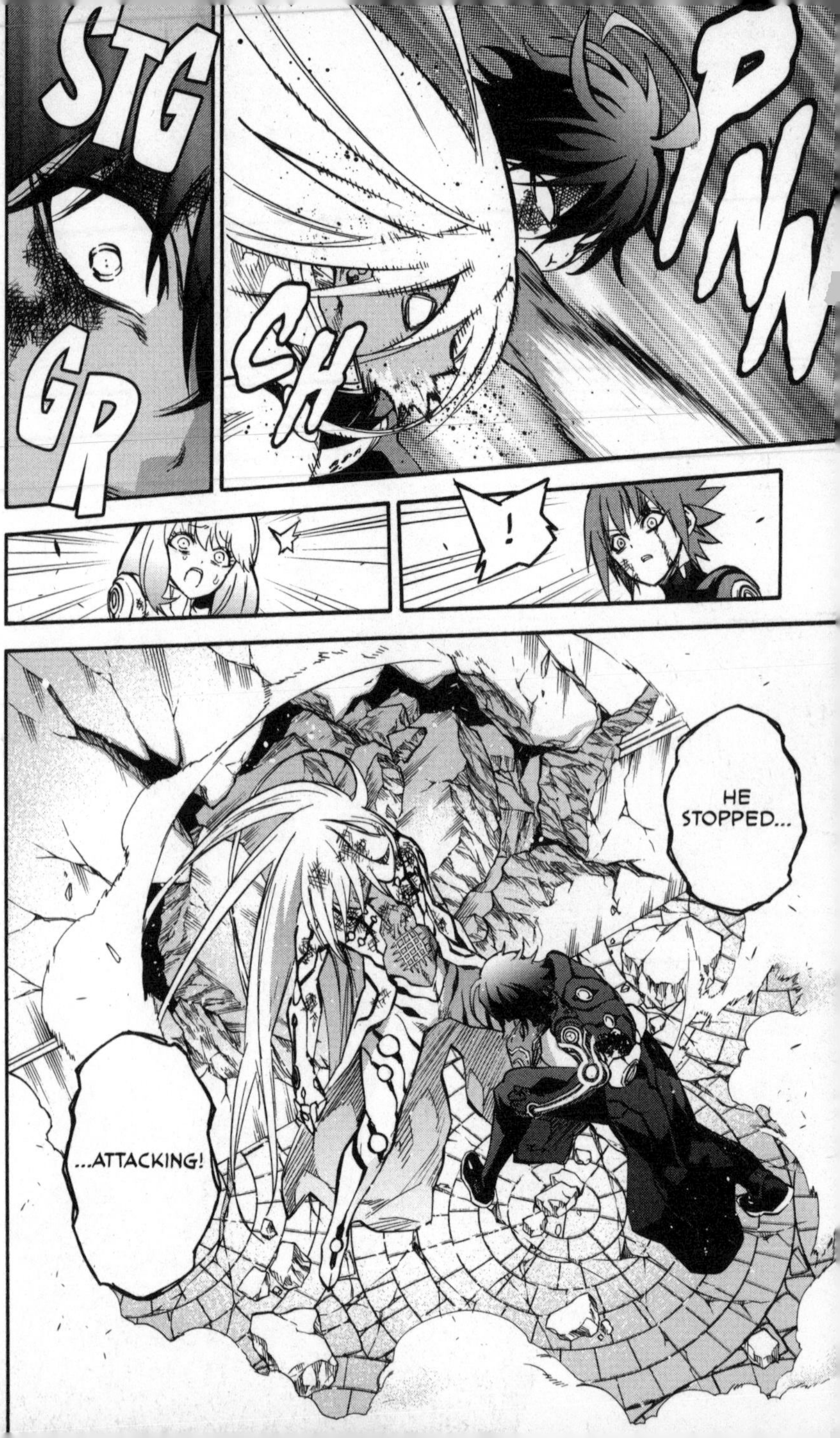
PINN
CH
STG
GR
!
HE STOPPED...
...ATTACKING!

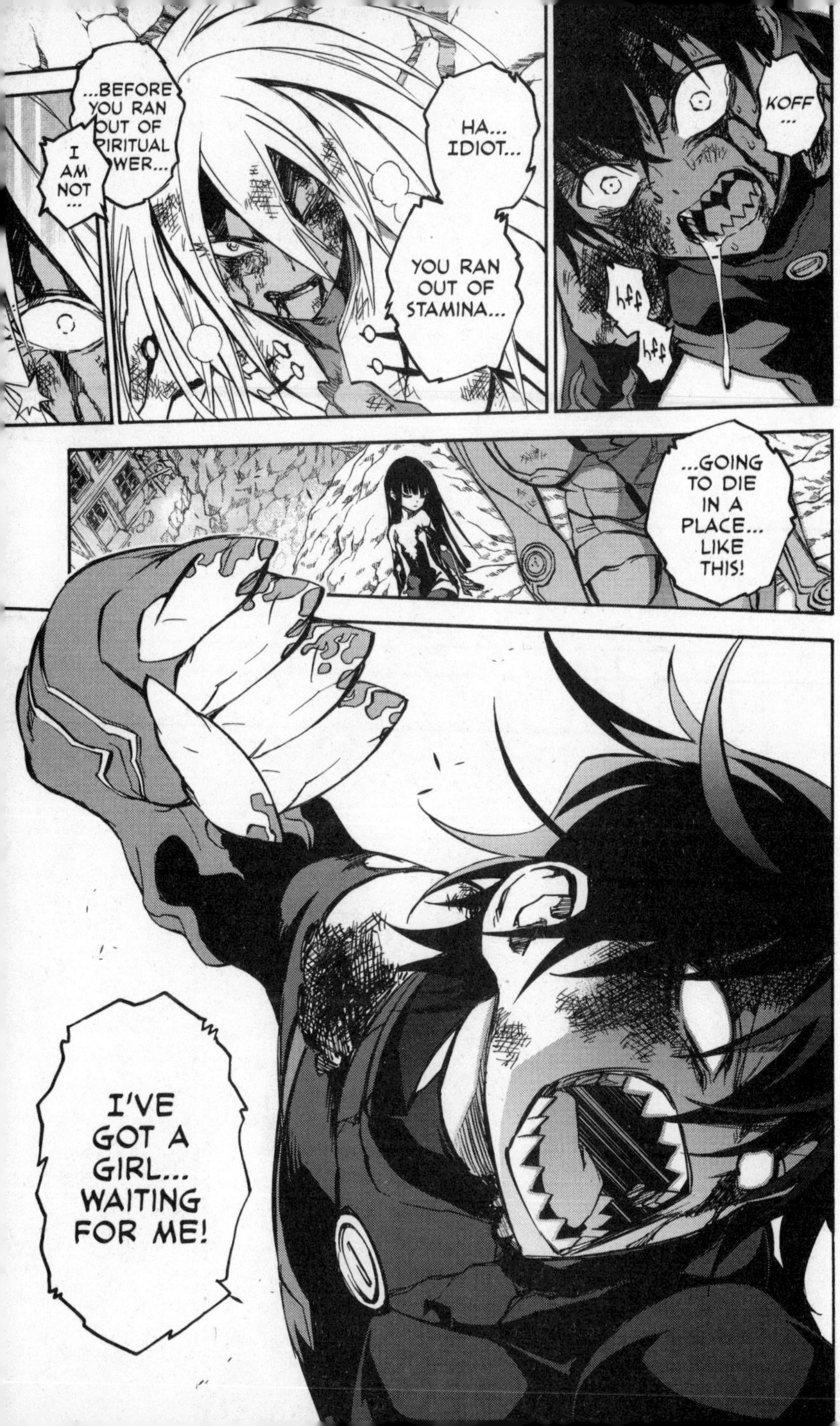
KOFF ...
hff
hff
HA... IDIOT...
YOU RAN OUT OF STAMINA...
...BEFORE YOU RAN OUT OF PIRITUAL WER...
I AM NOT ...
...GOING TO DIE IN A PLACE... LIKE THIS!
I'VE GOT A GIRL... WAITING FOR ME!

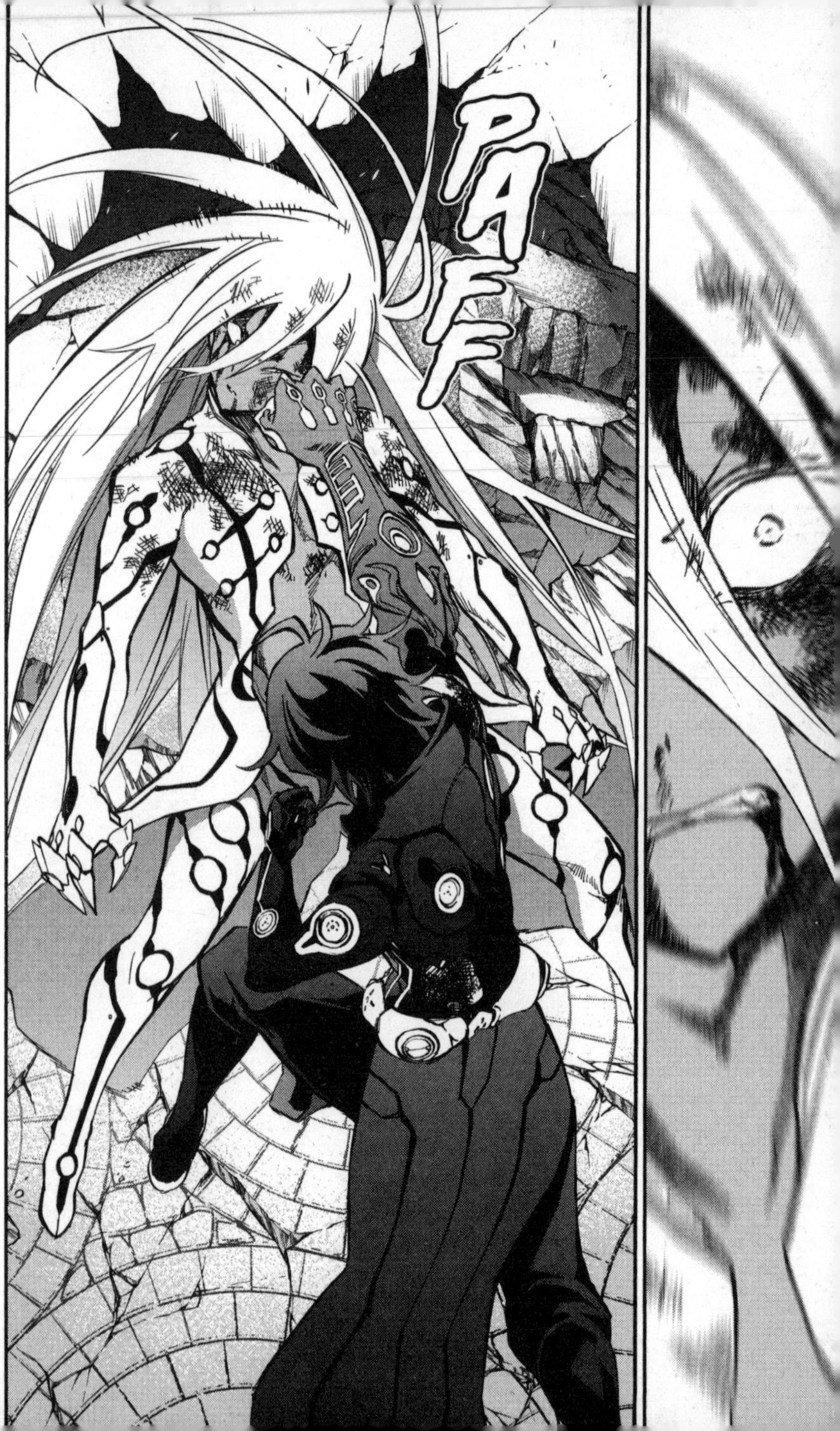
PAFF

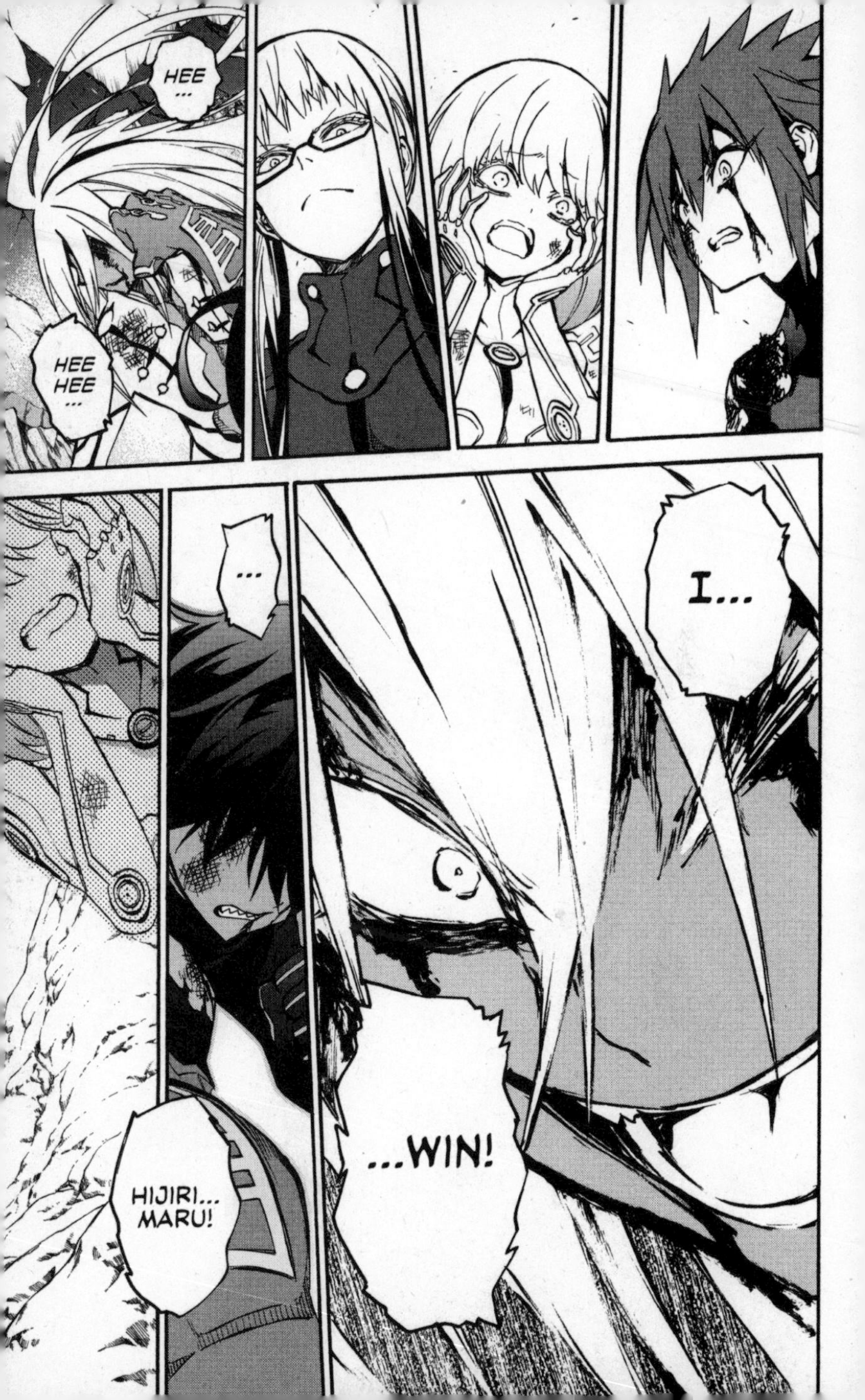
HEE ...
HEE HEE ...
I...
...WIN!
...
HIJIRI... MARU!

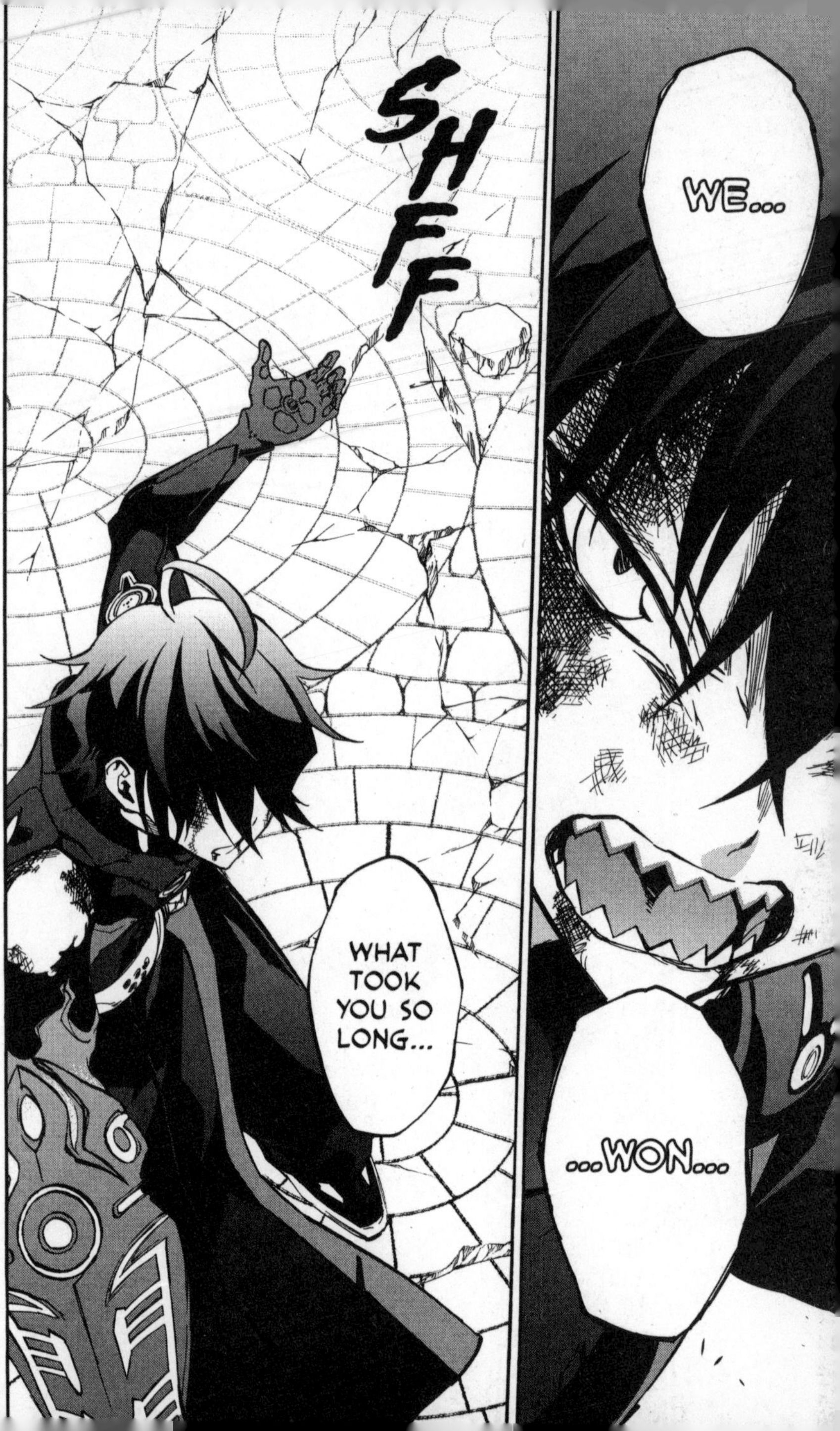
WE...
...WON...
SHFF
WHAT TOOK YOU SO LONG...

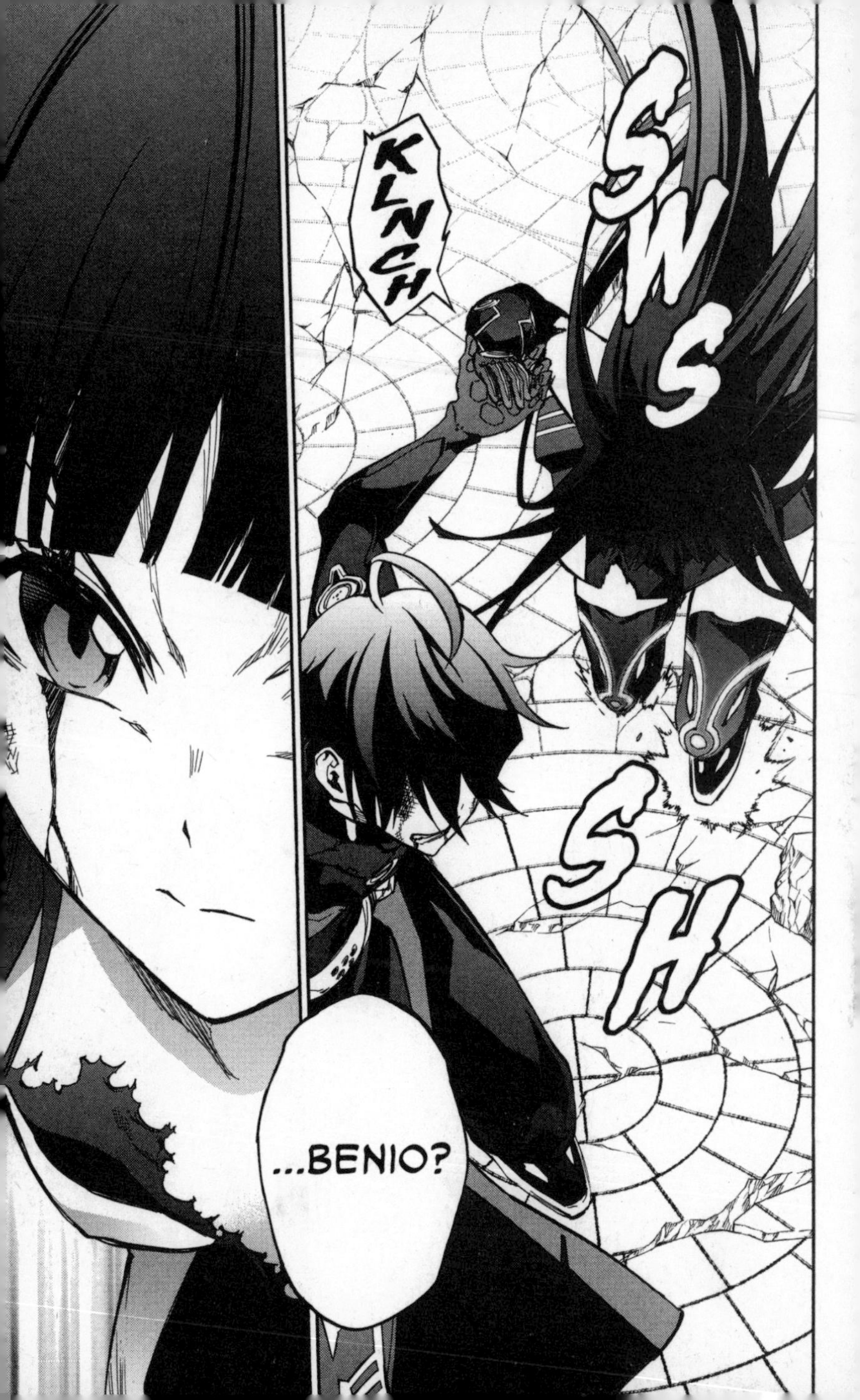
SWS
KLNCH
SH
...BENIO?

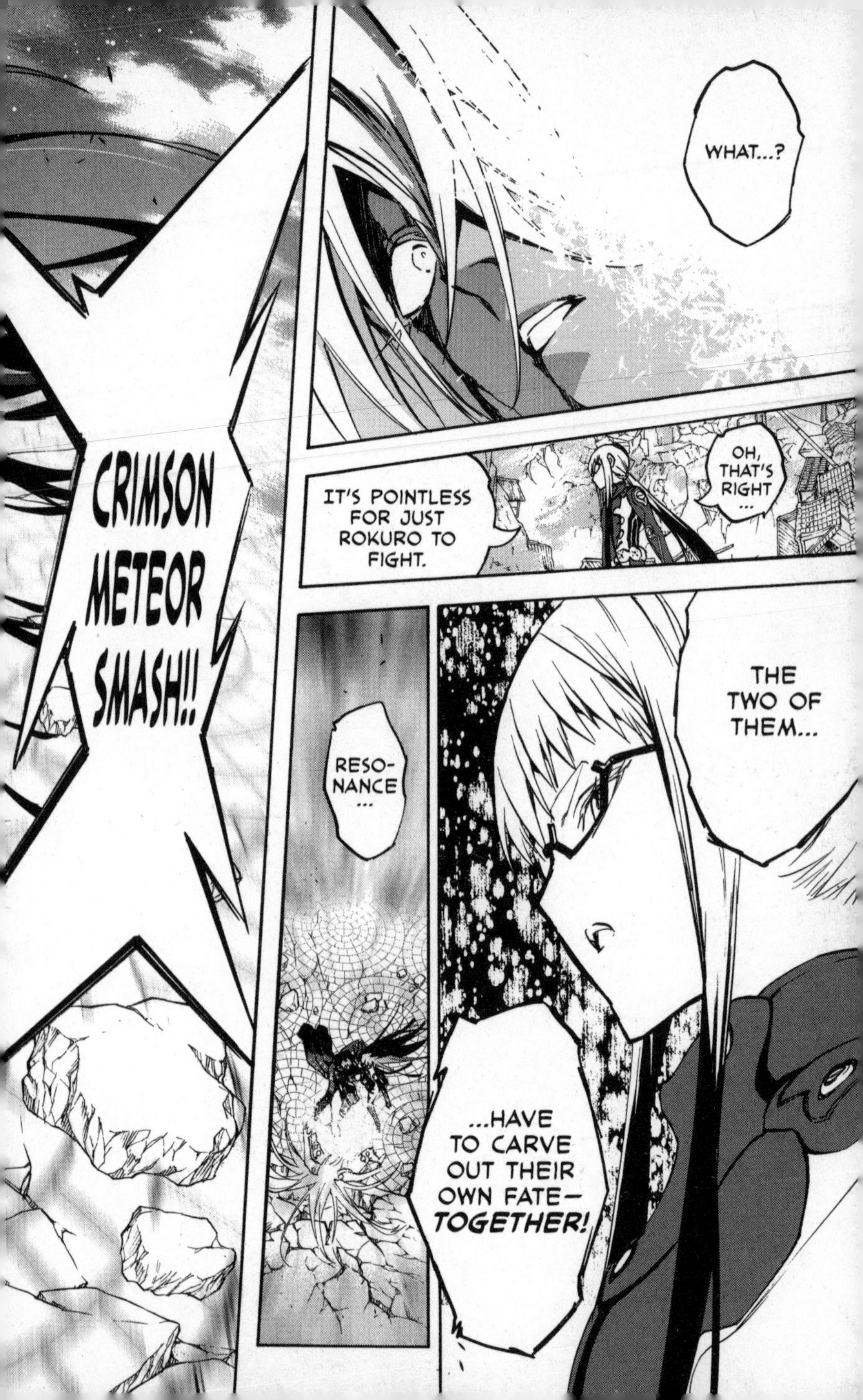
WHAT...?
OH, THAT'S RIGHT...
IT'S POINTLESS FOR JUST ROKURO TO FIGHT.
THE TWO OF THEM...
...HAVE TO CARVE OUT THEIR OWN FATE—*TOGETHER!*
RESONANCE...
CRIMSON METEOR SMASH!!

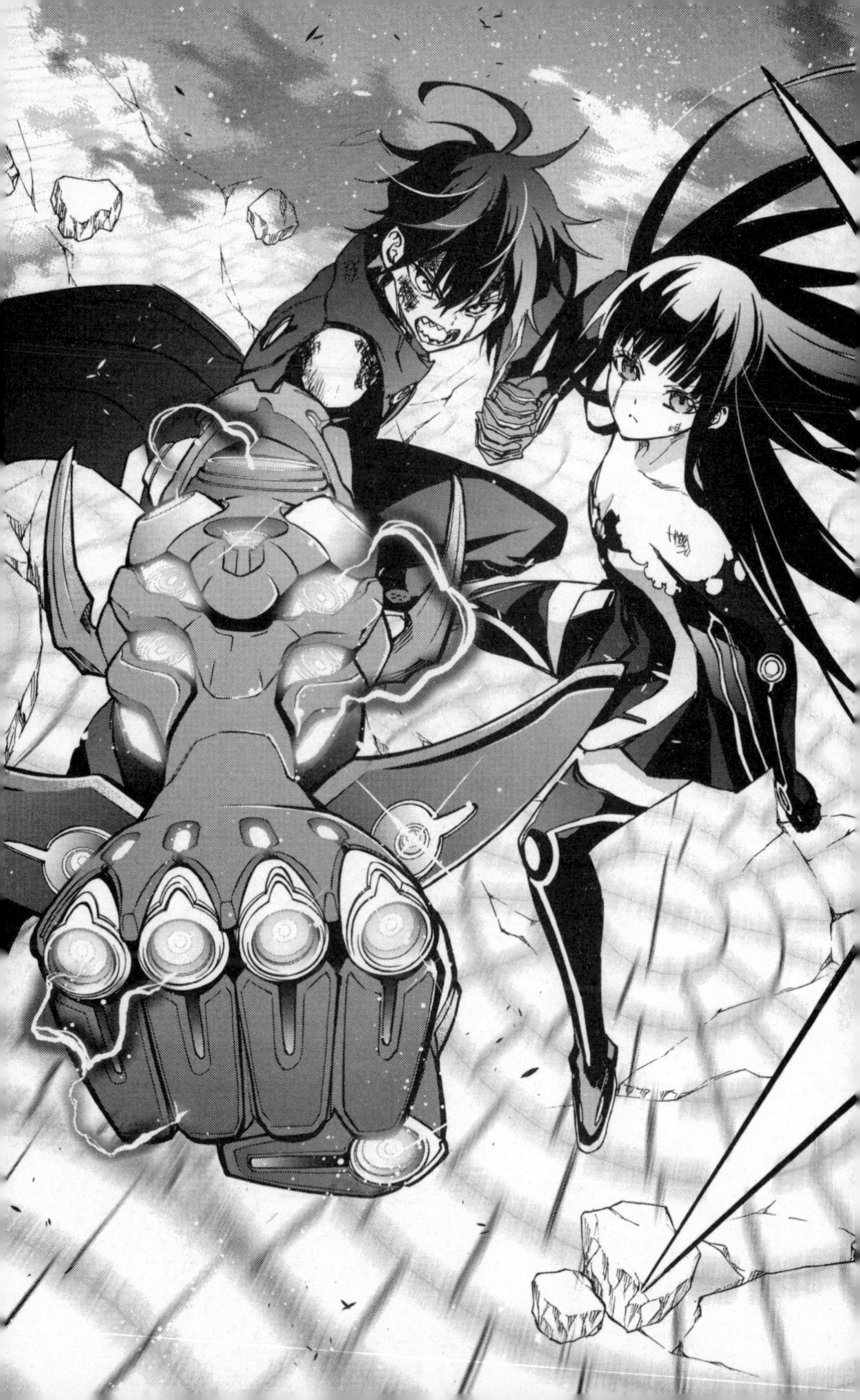

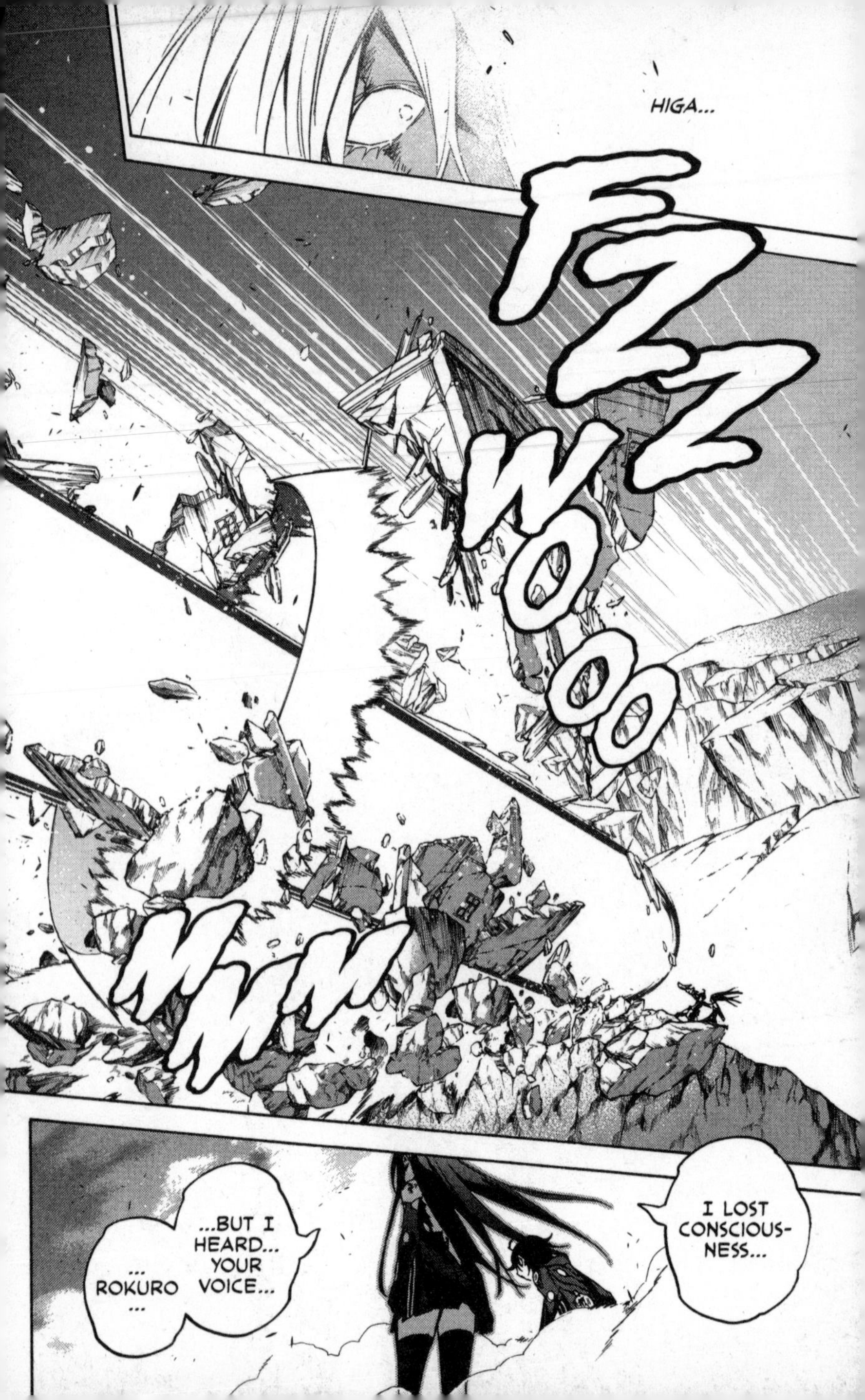
HIGA...
FZZZ
WOOOO
MMM
I LOST CONSCIOUS-NESS...
...BUT I HEARD... YOUR VOICE...
... ROKURO ...

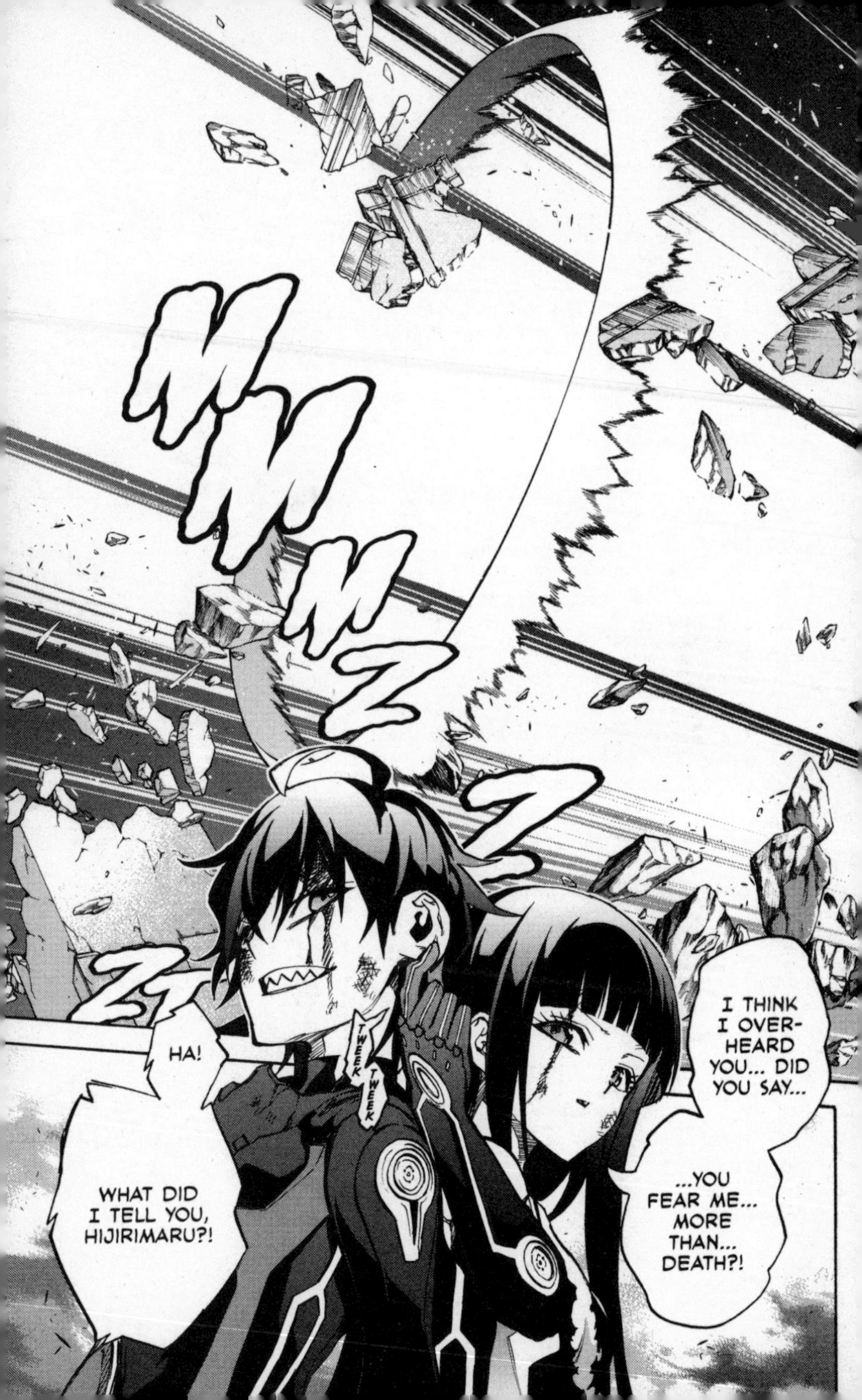
I THINK I OVER-HEARD YOU... DID YOU SAY...
...YOU FEAR ME... MORE THAN... DEATH?!
HA!
TWEEK TWEEK
WHAT DID I TELL YOU, HIJIRIMARU?!

Twin Star Questions

From the Japanese Website

Presenting to you various questions from readers answered by Sukeno Sensei on the *Twin Star Exorcists* website in Japan.

Q

Question from Rikoru-san:
We know Benio's favorite food is ohagi dumplings, but what is Rokuro's favorite food?

Answer:
Curry. Spicy stuff.

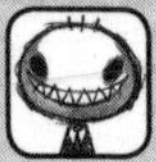

Q

Question from Sayu Neko-san:
When are Shimon Ikaruga's and Sayo's birthdays?

Answer:
Shimon's is September 13!
Sayo's is March 3!

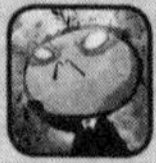

Q

Question from Hyoukane-san:
What is Shimon's hobby?

Answer:
Bonsai gardening.

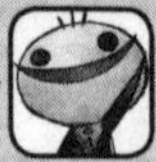

Q

Question from Biton Nenju Hansode Yaro-san:
What is the hardest part of creating names for the characters?

Answer:
I get momentary flashes of inspiration, so I've never had much trouble coming up with names. But at times, a better-sounding name will pop into my head later, and I'll regret not having come up with it earlier.

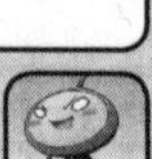

Feel free to ask questions!!!

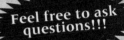

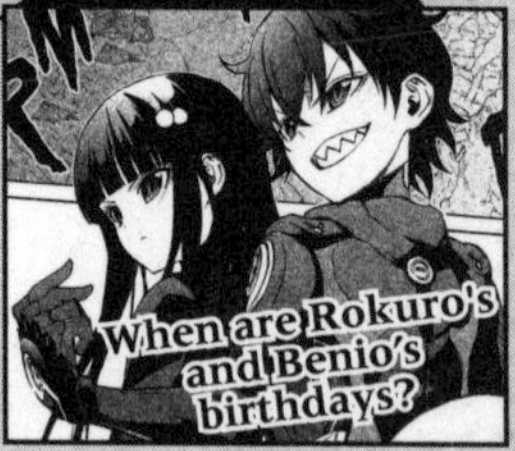
When are Rokuro's and Benio's birthdays?

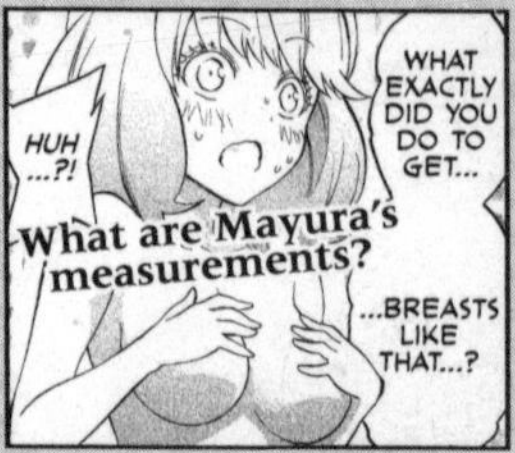
WHAT EXACTLY DID YOU DO TO GET...
HUH ...?!
What are Mayura's measurements?
...BREASTS LIKE THAT...?

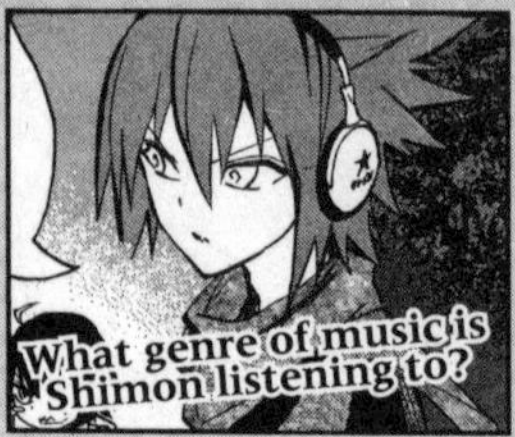
What genre of music is Shimon listening to?

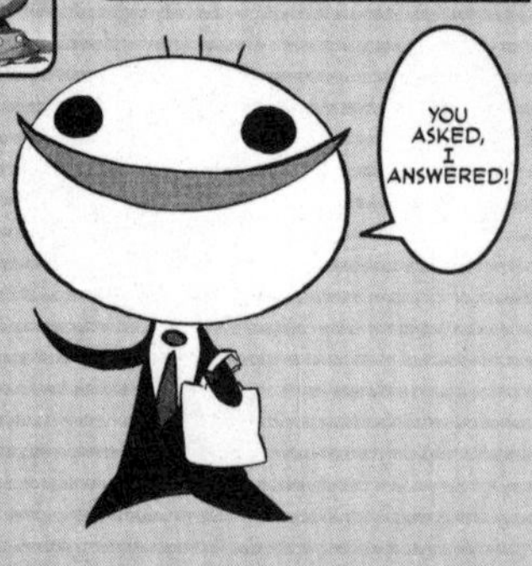
YOU ASKED, I ANSWERED!

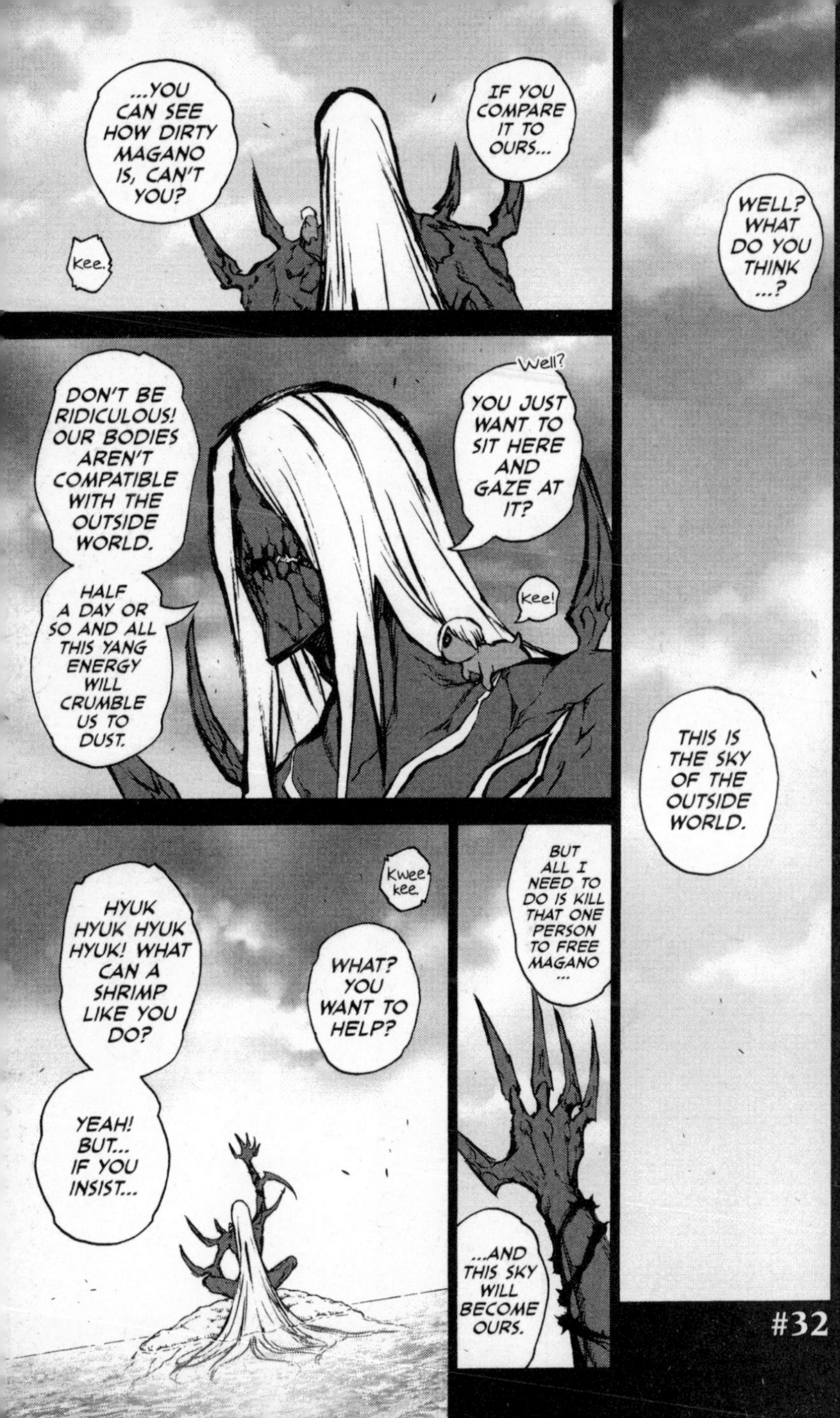
WELL? WHAT DO YOU THINK ...?
THIS IS THE SKY OF THE OUTSIDE WORLD.
IF YOU COMPARE IT TO OURS...
...YOU CAN SEE HOW DIRTY MAGANO IS, CAN'T YOU?
Kee.
Well?
YOU JUST WANT TO SIT HERE AND GAZE AT IT?
Kee!
DON'T BE RIDICULOUS! OUR BODIES AREN'T COMPATIBLE WITH THE OUTSIDE WORLD.
HALF A DAY OR SO AND ALL THIS YANG ENERGY WILL CRUMBLE US TO DUST.
BUT ALL I NEED TO DO IS KILL THAT ONE PERSON TO FREE MAGANO ...
...AND THIS SKY WILL BECOME OURS.
Kwee kee.
WHAT? YOU WANT TO HELP?
HYUK HYUK HYUK HYUK! WHAT CAN A SHRIMP LIKE YOU DO?
YEAH! BUT... IF YOU INSIST...

#32

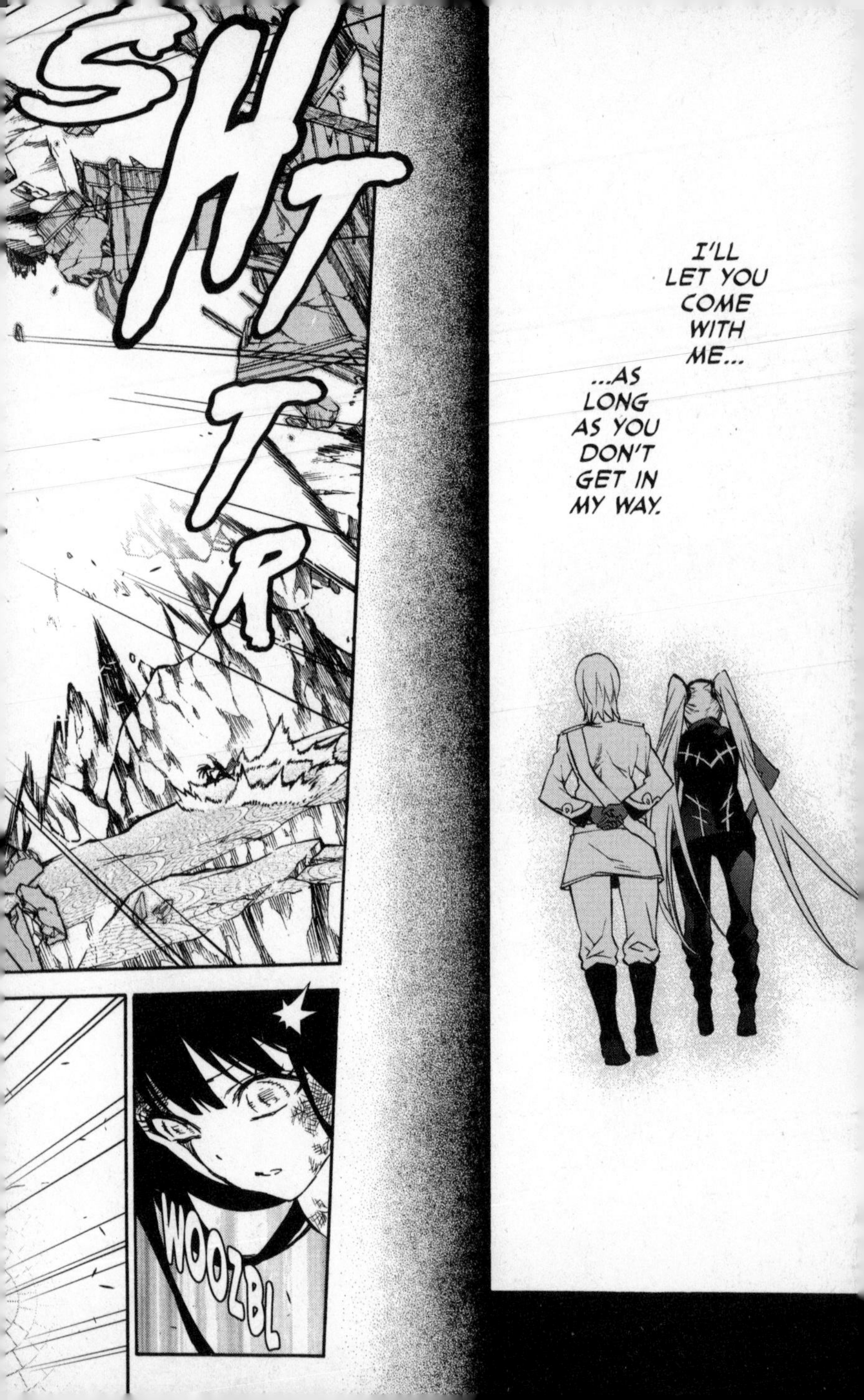
I'LL LET YOU COME WITH ME...
...AS LONG AS YOU DON'T GET IN MY WAY.
SHTTR
WOOZBL

#32 Future of the Twin Stars

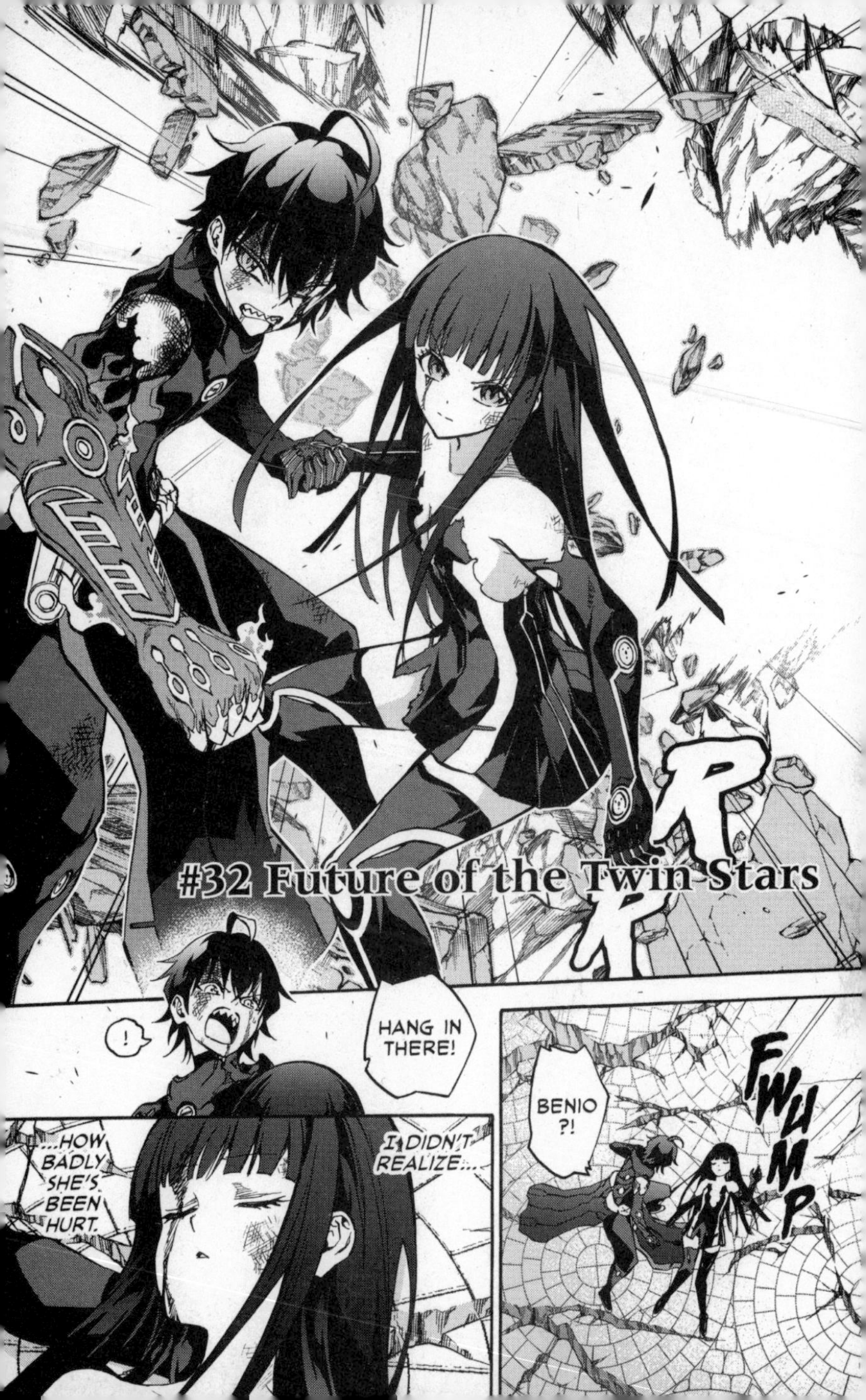
R
R
FWUMP
BENIO ?!
!
HANG IN THERE!
I DIDN'T REALIZE...
...HOW BADLY SHE'S BEEN HURT.

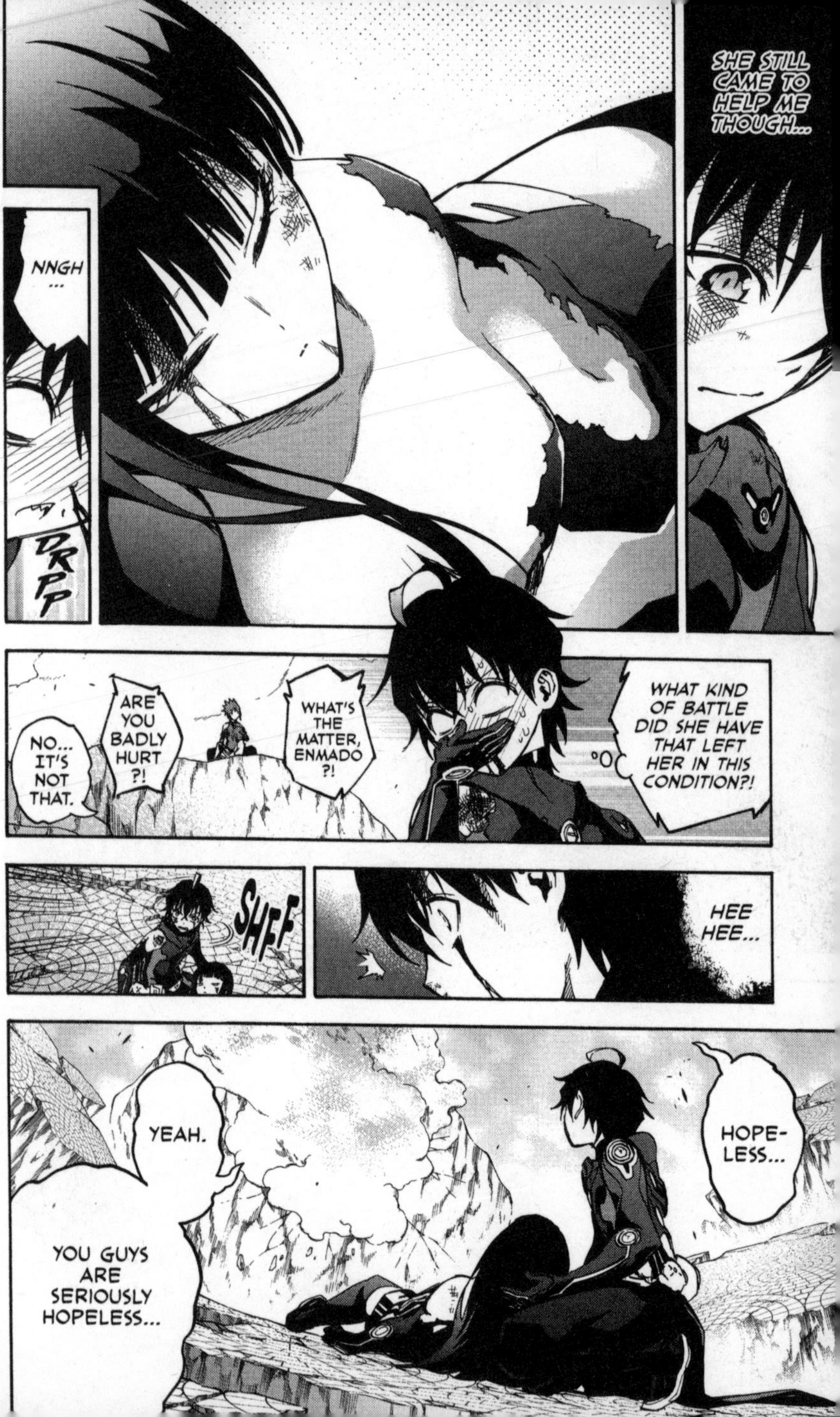
SHE STILL CAME TO HELP ME THOUGH...
NNGH ...
DRPP
WHAT KIND OF BATTLE DID SHE HAVE THAT LEFT HER IN THIS CONDITION?!
WHAT'S THE MATTER, ENMADO ?!
ARE YOU BADLY HURT ?!
NO... IT'S NOT THAT.
HEE HEE...
SHFF
HOPE-LESS...
YEAH.
YOU GUYS ARE SERIOUSLY HOPELESS...

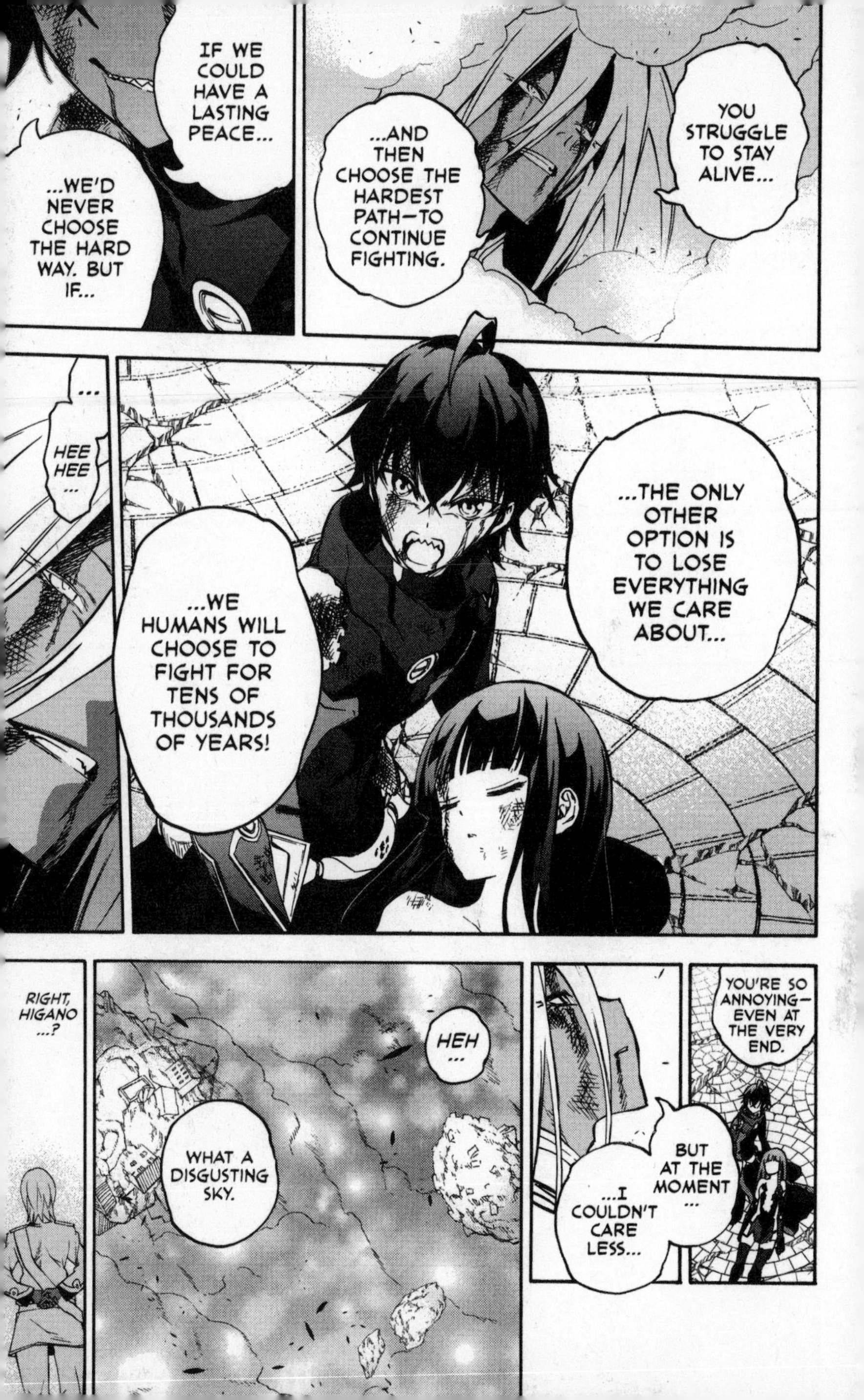
YOU STRUGGLE TO STAY ALIVE...
...AND THEN CHOOSE THE HARDEST PATH—TO CONTINUE FIGHTING.
IF WE COULD HAVE A LASTING PEACE...
...WE'D NEVER CHOOSE THE HARD WAY. BUT IF...
...THE ONLY OTHER OPTION IS TO LOSE EVERYTHING WE CARE ABOUT...
...WE HUMANS WILL CHOOSE TO FIGHT FOR TENS OF THOUSANDS OF YEARS!
...
HEE HEE ...
YOU'RE SO ANNOYING—EVEN AT THE VERY END.
BUT AT THE MOMENT ...
...I COULDN'T CARE LESS...
HEH ...
WHAT A DISGUSTING SKY.
RIGHT, HIGANO ...?

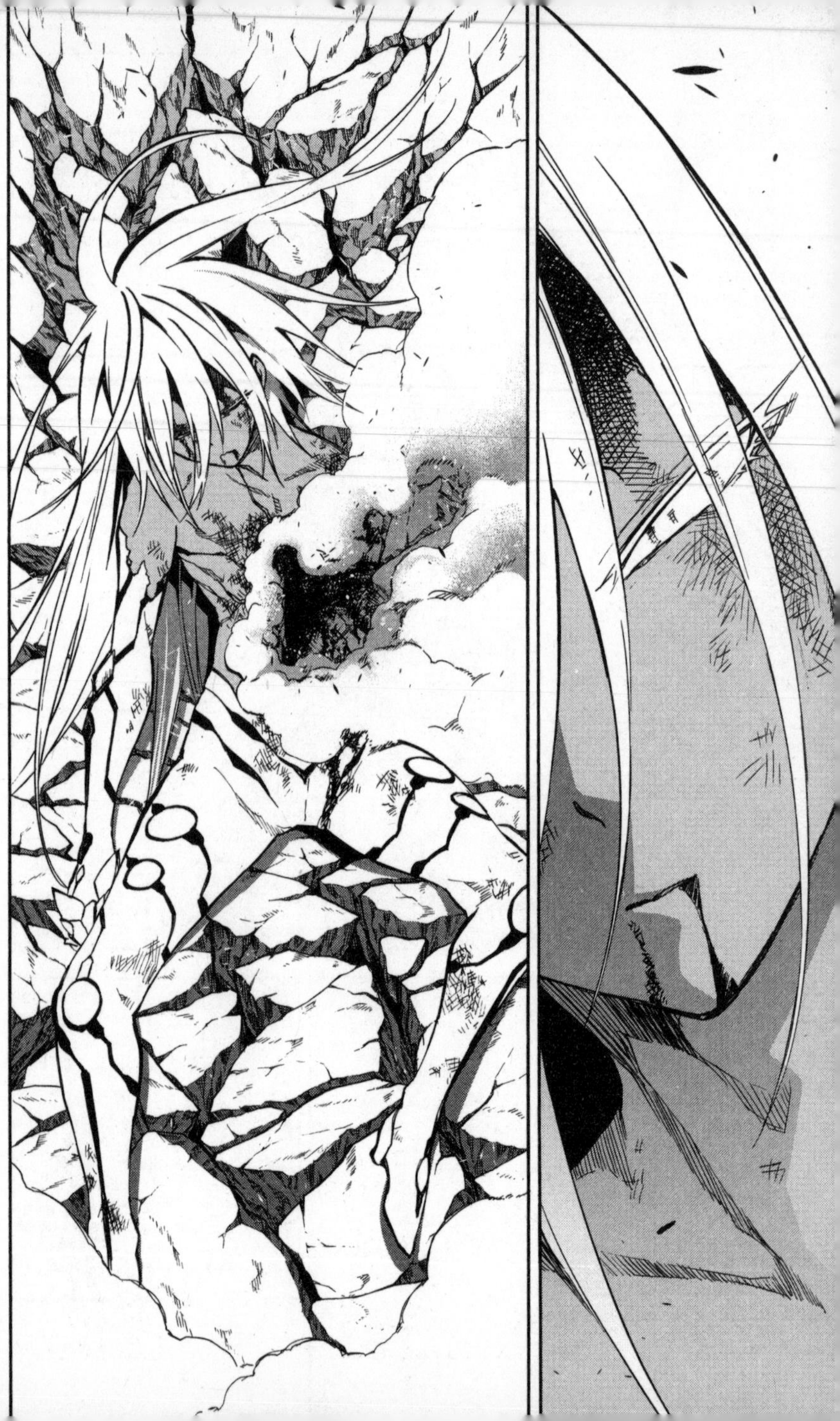

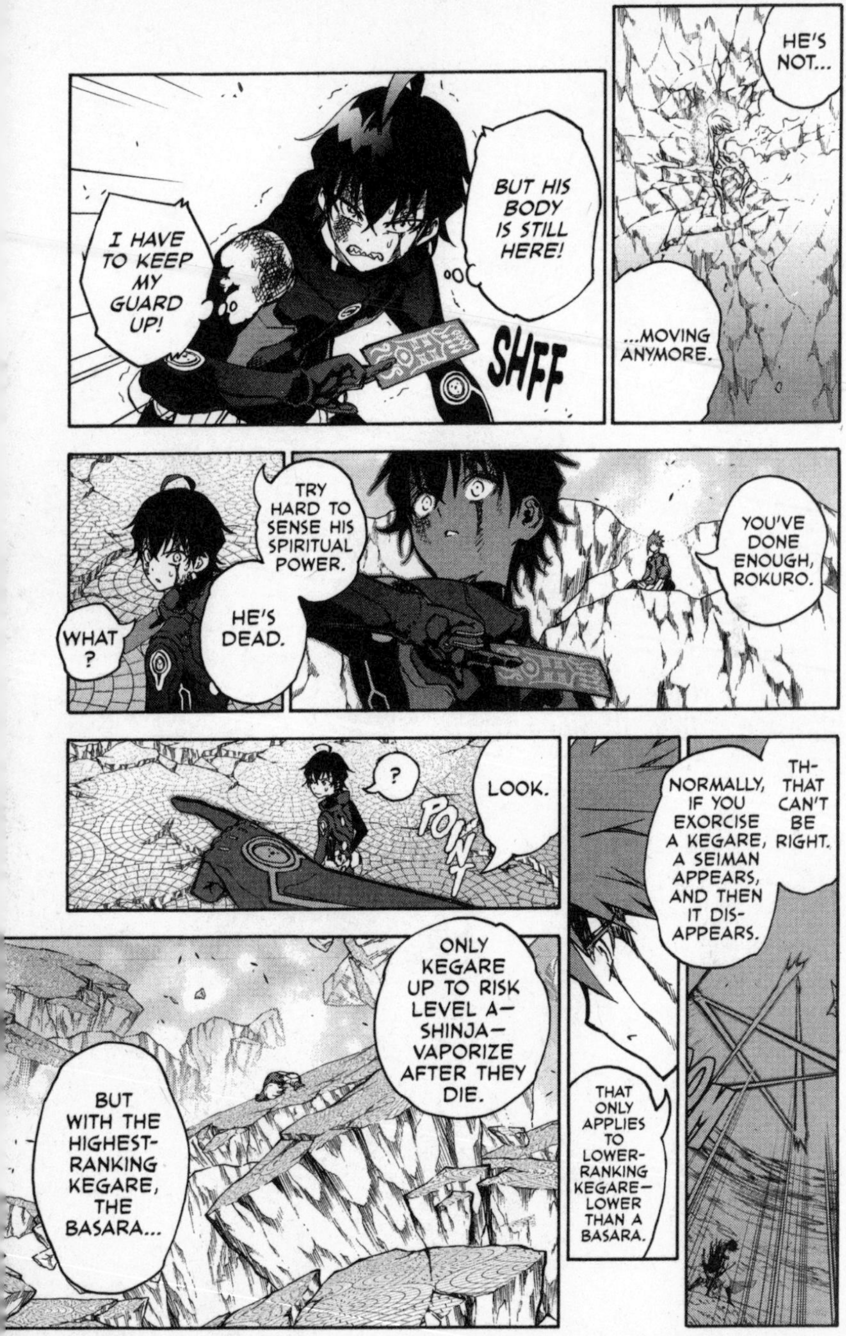
HE'S NOT...
...MOVING ANYMORE.
BUT HIS BODY IS STILL HERE!
SHFF
I HAVE TO KEEP MY GUARD UP!
YOU'VE DONE ENOUGH, ROKURO.
TRY HARD TO SENSE HIS SPIRITUAL POWER.
HE'S DEAD.
WHAT?
TH-THAT CAN'T BE RIGHT.
NORMALLY, IF YOU EXORCISE A KEGARE, A SEIMAN APPEARS, AND THEN IT DIS-APPEARS.
THAT ONLY APPLIES TO LOWER-RANKING KEGARE—LOWER THAN A BASARA.
LOOK.
POINT
?
ONLY KEGARE UP TO RISK LEVEL A—SHINJA—VAPORIZE AFTER THEY DIE.
BUT WITH THE HIGHEST-RANKING KEGARE, THE BASARA...

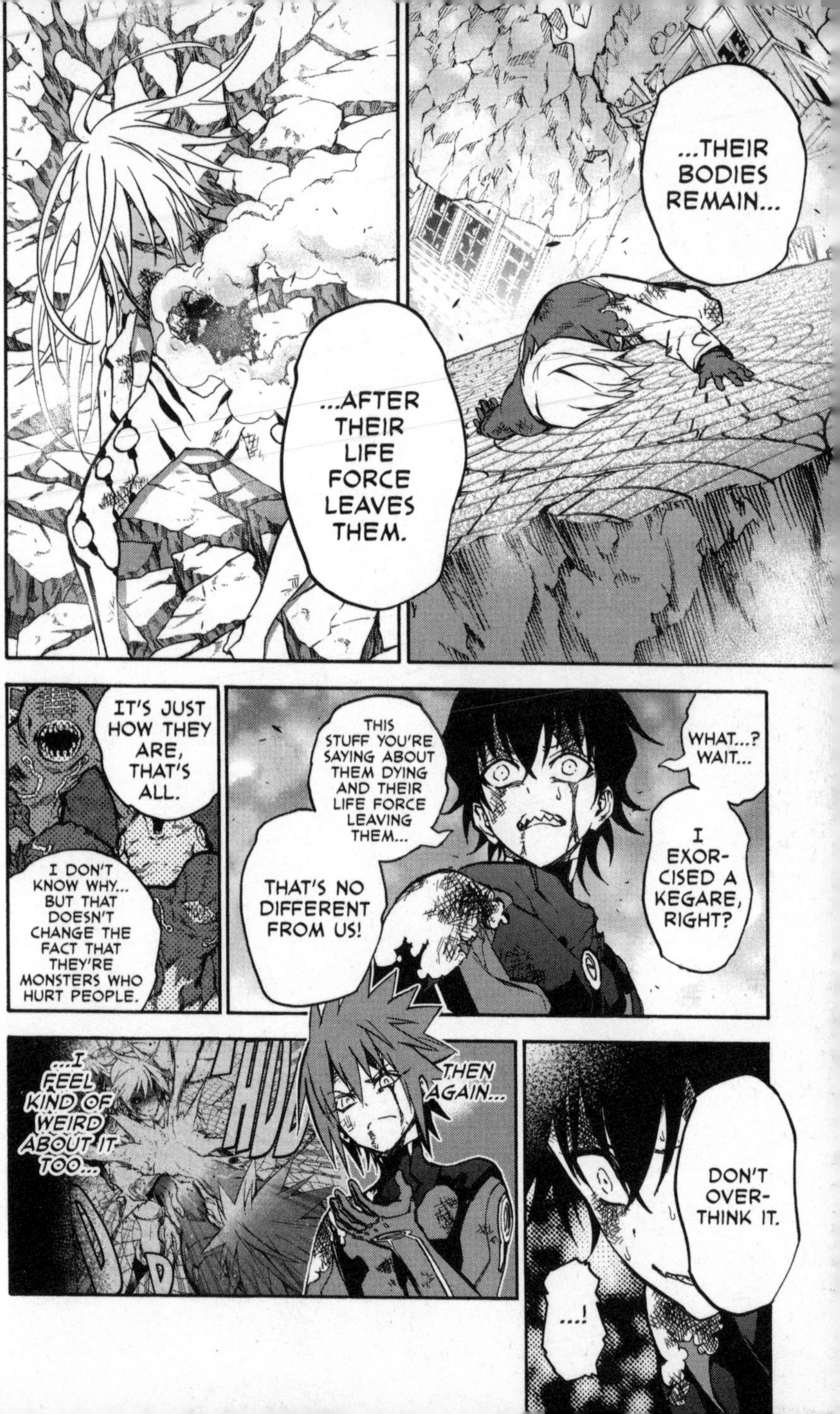
...THEIR BODIES REMAIN...
...AFTER THEIR LIFE FORCE LEAVES THEM.
WHAT...? WAIT...
I EXOR-CISED A KEGARE, RIGHT?
THIS STUFF YOU'RE SAYING ABOUT THEM DYING AND THEIR LIFE FORCE LEAVING THEM...
THAT'S NO DIFFERENT FROM US!
IT'S JUST HOW THEY ARE, THAT'S ALL.
I DON'T KNOW WHY... BUT THAT DOESN'T CHANGE THE FACT THAT THEY'RE MONSTERS WHO HURT PEOPLE.
DON'T OVER-THINK IT.
...!
THEN AGAIN...
...I FEEL KIND OF WEIRD ABOUT IT TOO...

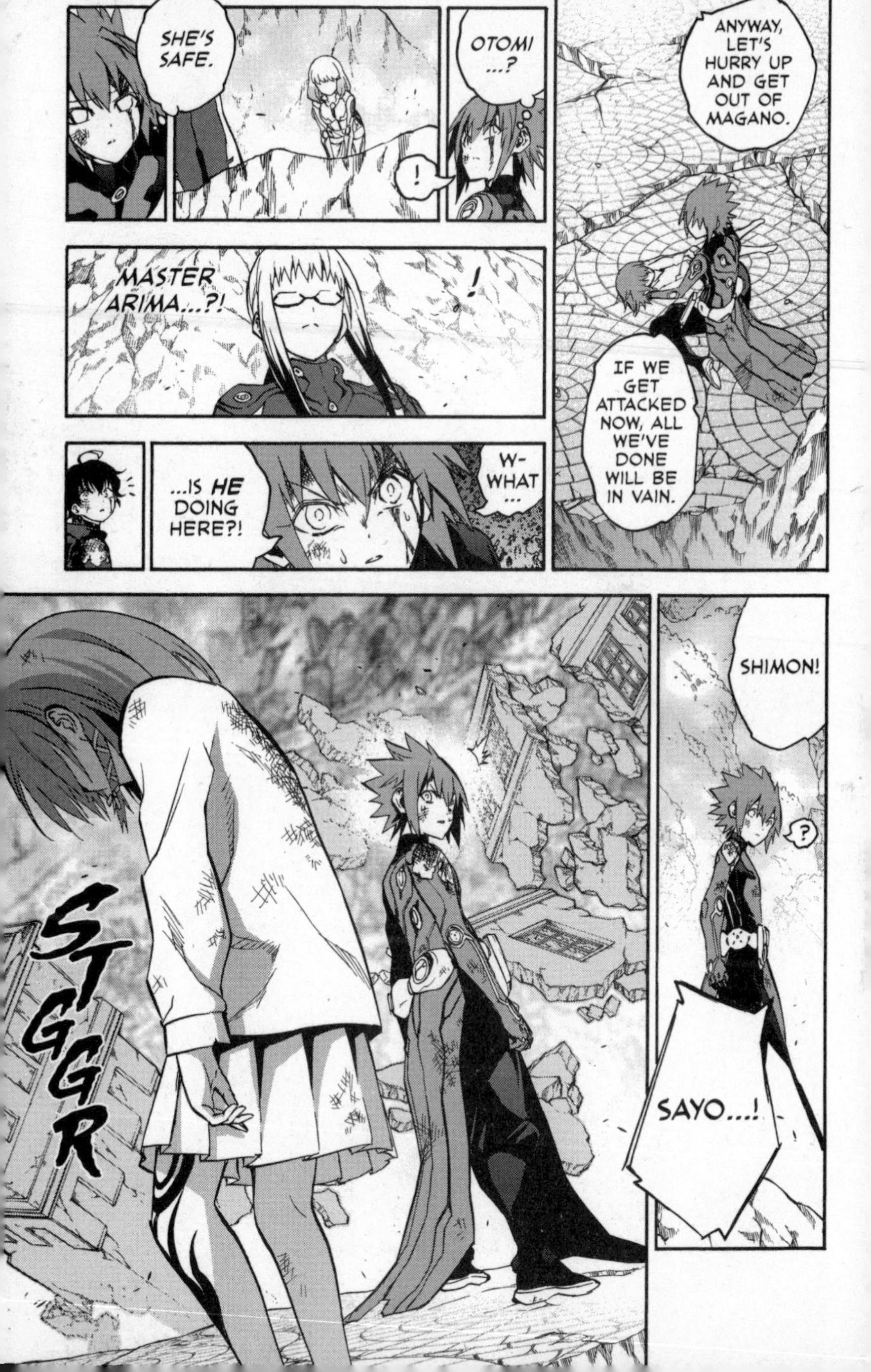
ANYWAY, LET'S HURRY UP AND GET OUT OF MAGANO.
IF WE GET ATTACKED NOW, ALL WE'VE DONE WILL BE IN VAIN.
OTOMI ...?
!
SHE'S SAFE.
!
MASTER ARIMA...?!
W-WHAT ...
...IS HE DOING HERE?!
SHIMON!
?
SAYO...!
STGGR

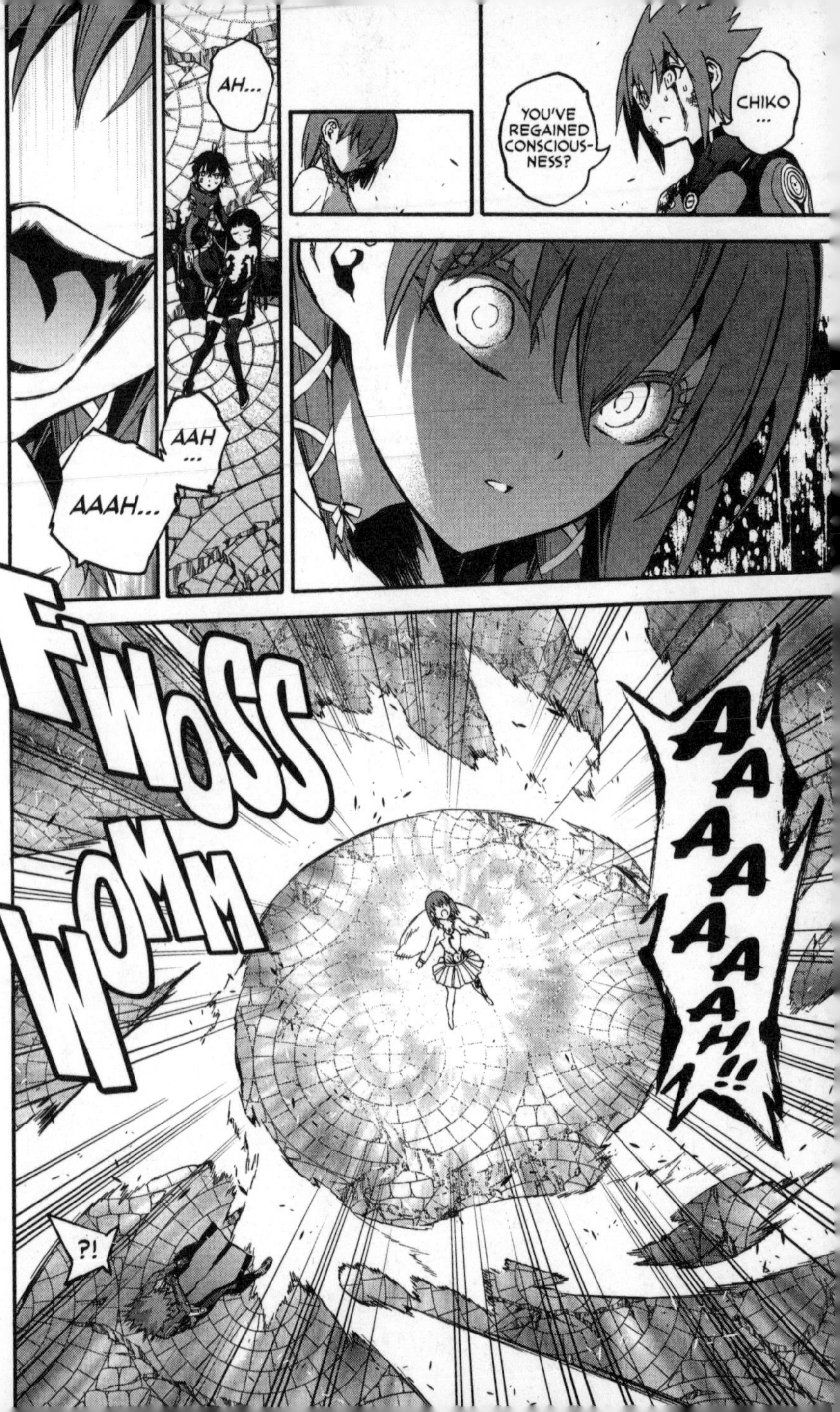
CHIKO ...
YOU'VE REGAINED CONSCIOUS-NESS?
AH...
AAH ...
AAAH...
AAAAAAAAH!!
FWOSS
WOMM
?!

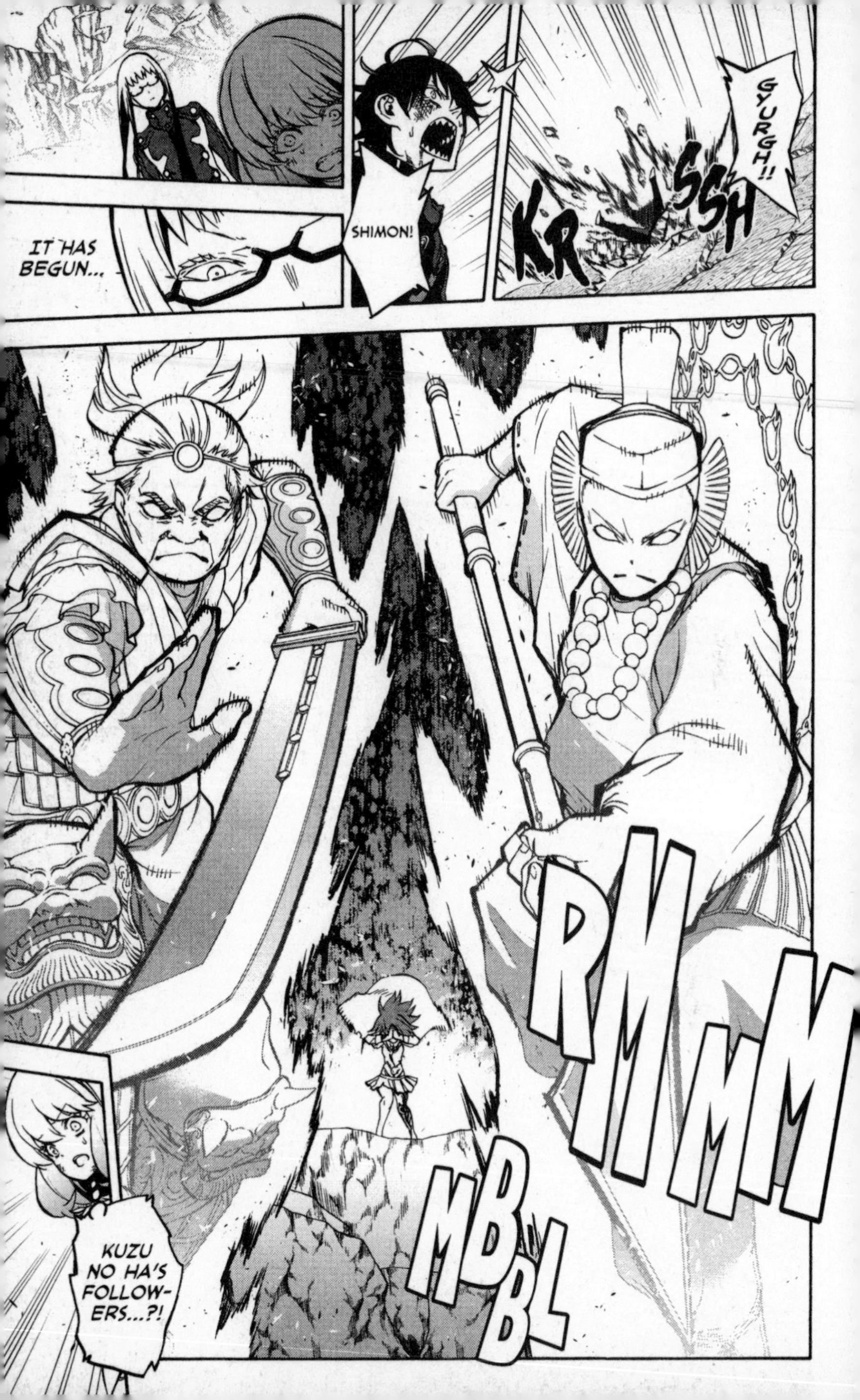
GYURGH!!
KRSSH
SHIMON!
IT HAS BEGUN...
RMMMM
MBDBL
KUZU NO HA'S FOLLOWERS...?!

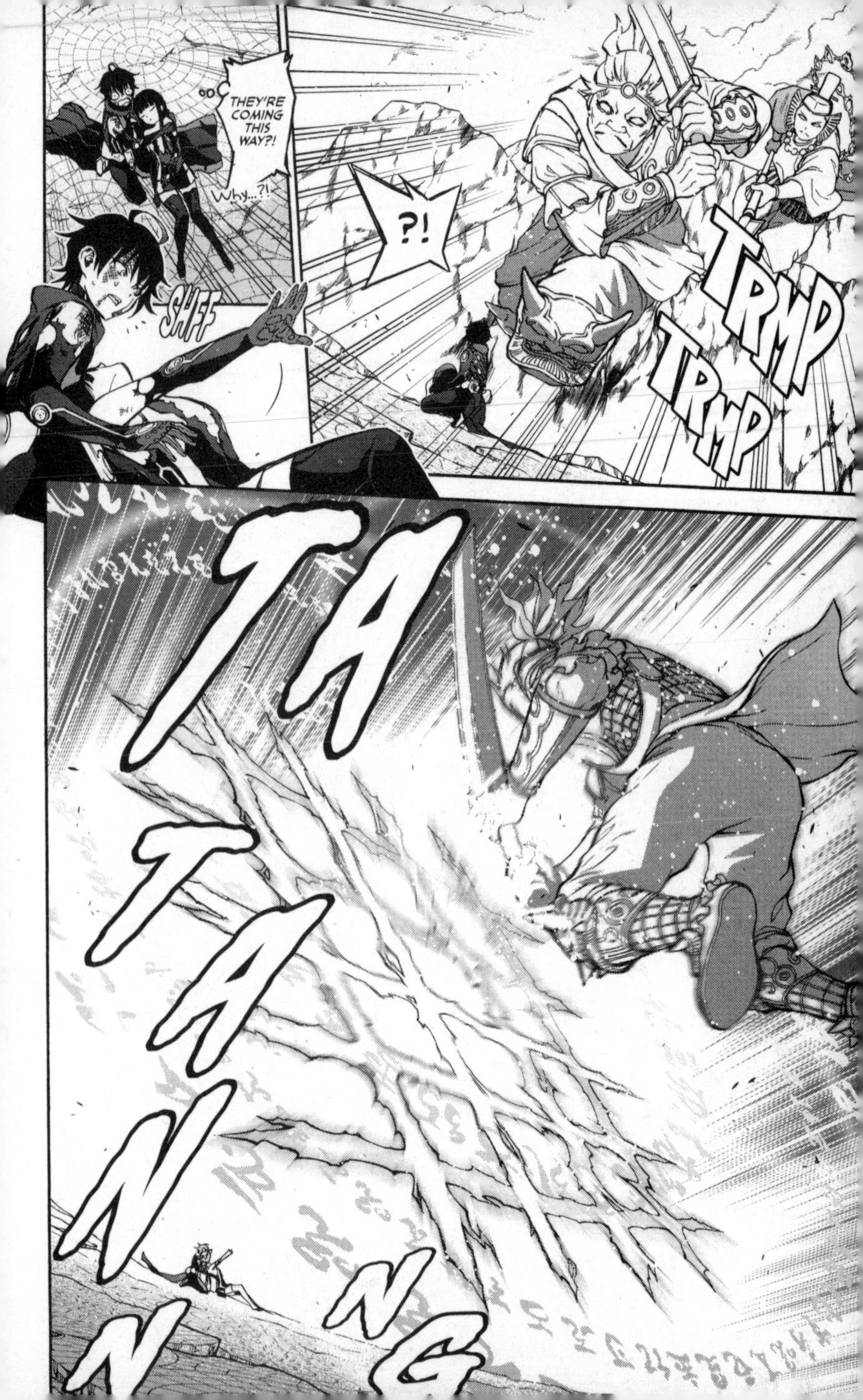
?!
TRMP TRMP
THEY'RE COMING THIS WAY?!
Why...?!
SHFF
TATANNNNG

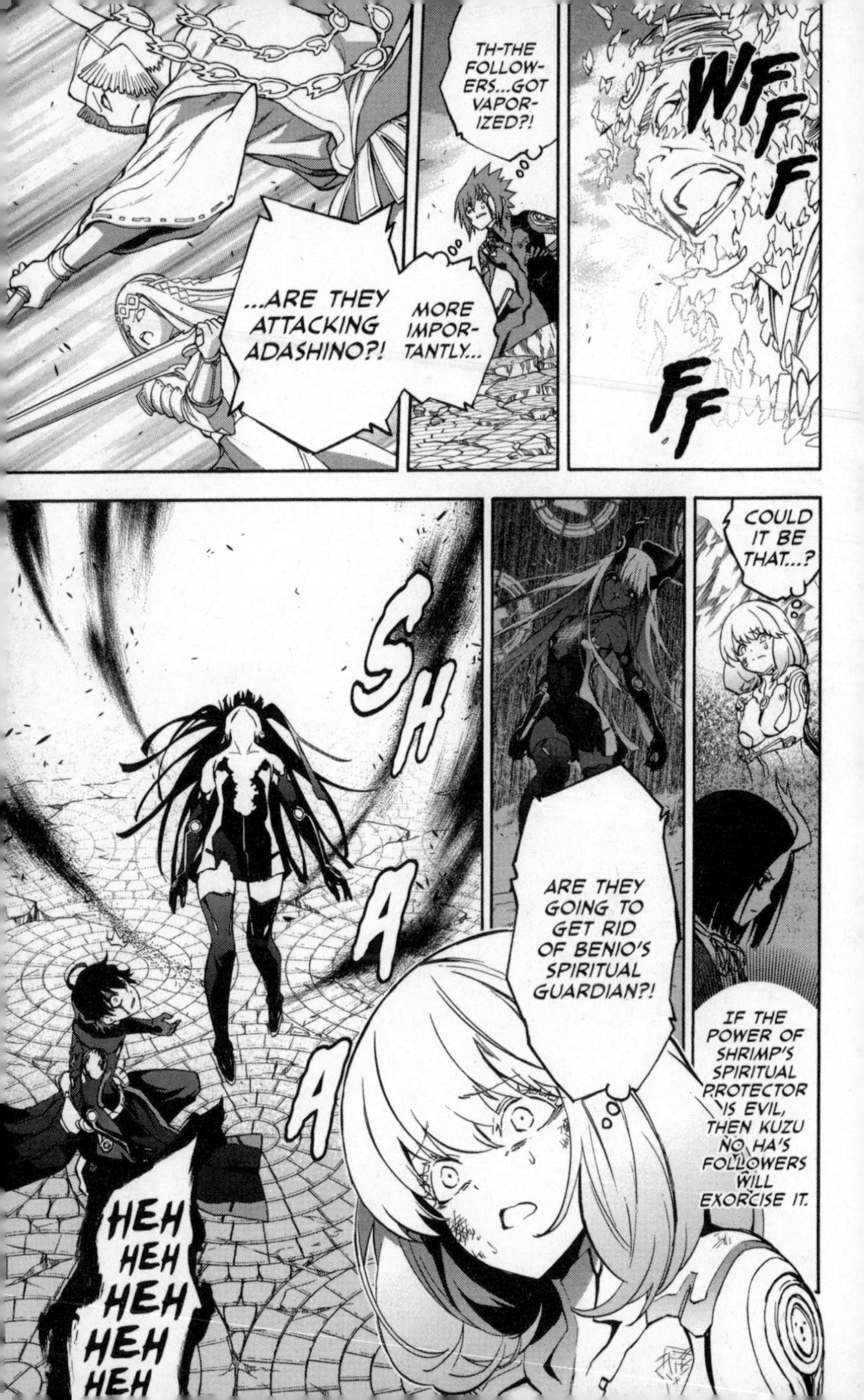
WFF
F
FF
TH-THE FOLLOWERS...GOT VAPORIZED?!
MORE IMPORTANTLY...
...ARE THEY ATTACKING ADASHINO?!
COULD IT BE THAT...?
IF THE POWER OF SHRIMP'S SPIRITUAL PROTECTOR IS EVIL, THEN KUZU NO HA'S FOLLOWERS WILL EXORCISE IT.
ARE THEY GOING TO GET RID OF BENIO'S SPIRITUAL GUARDIAN?!
SHAAA
HEH HEH HEH HEH HEH HEH

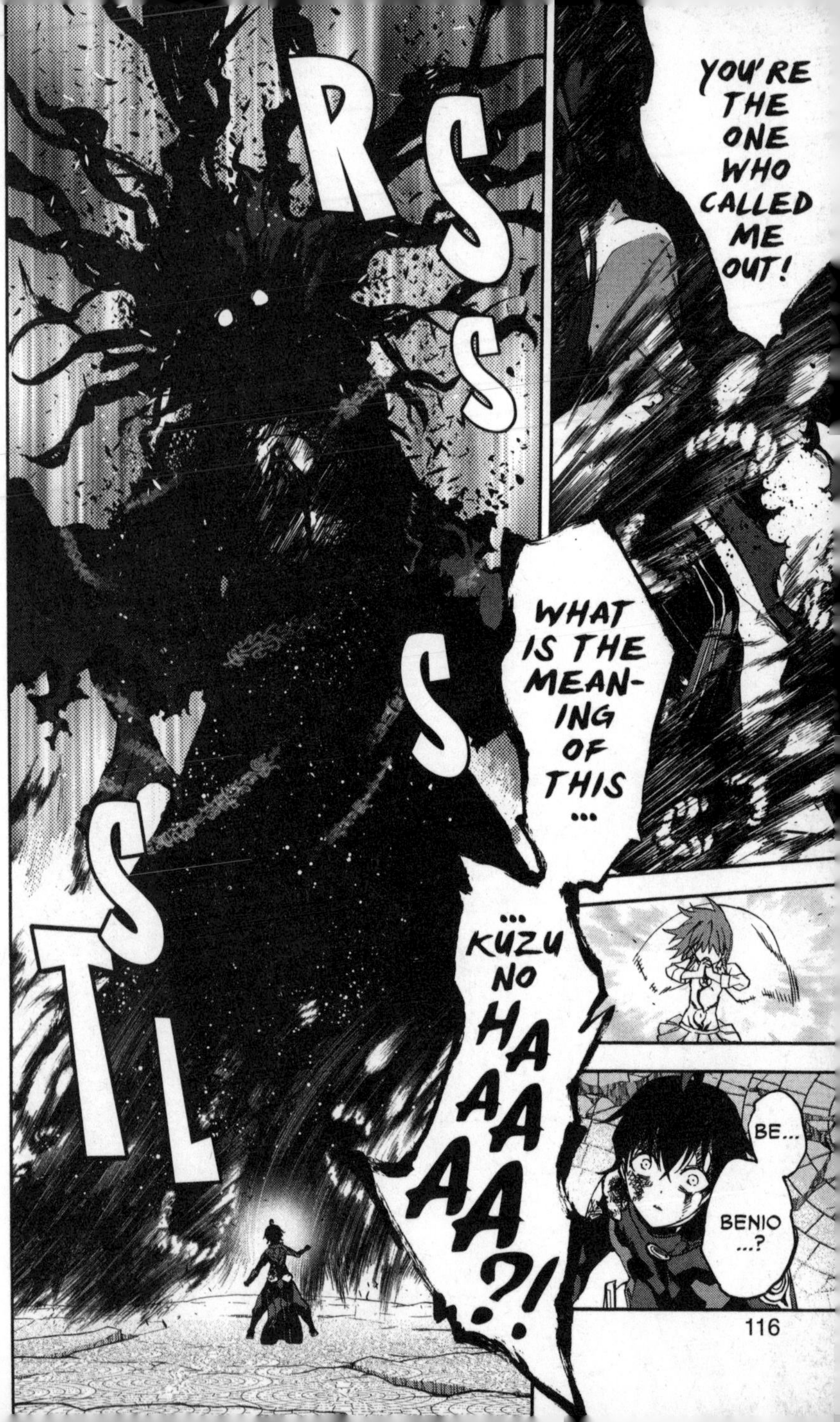
YOU'RE THE ONE WHO CALLED ME OUT!
BE... BENIO ...?
RS
S
S
S
TL
WHAT IS THE MEANING OF THIS ...
... KÜZU NO HAAAAAAA?!

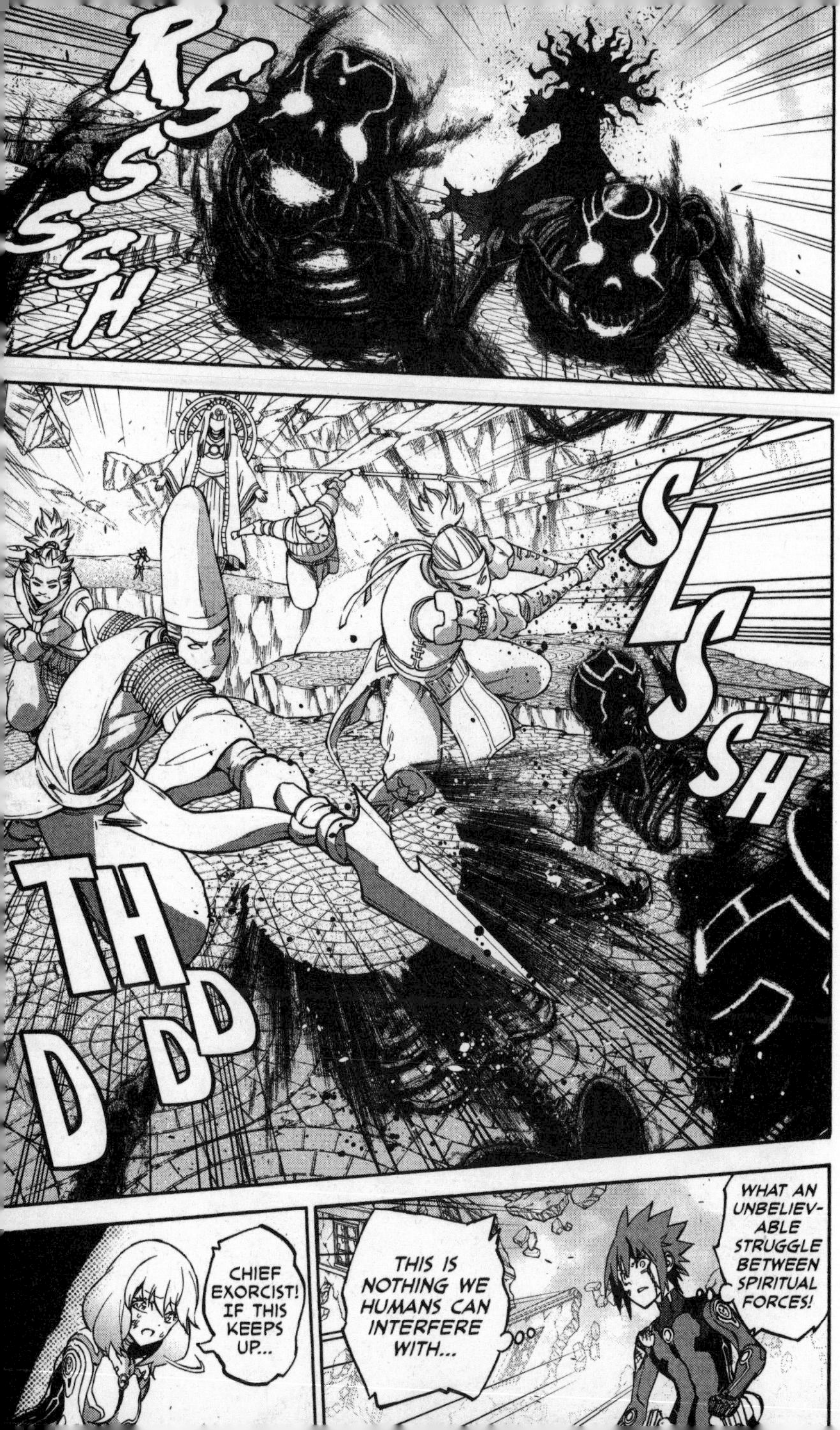
RSSSSH
SLSSH
THDDD
WHAT AN UNBELIEV-ABLE STRUGGLE BETWEEN SPIRITUAL FORCES!
THIS IS NOTHING WE HUMANS CAN INTERFERE WITH...
CHIEF EXORCIST! IF THIS KEEPS UP...

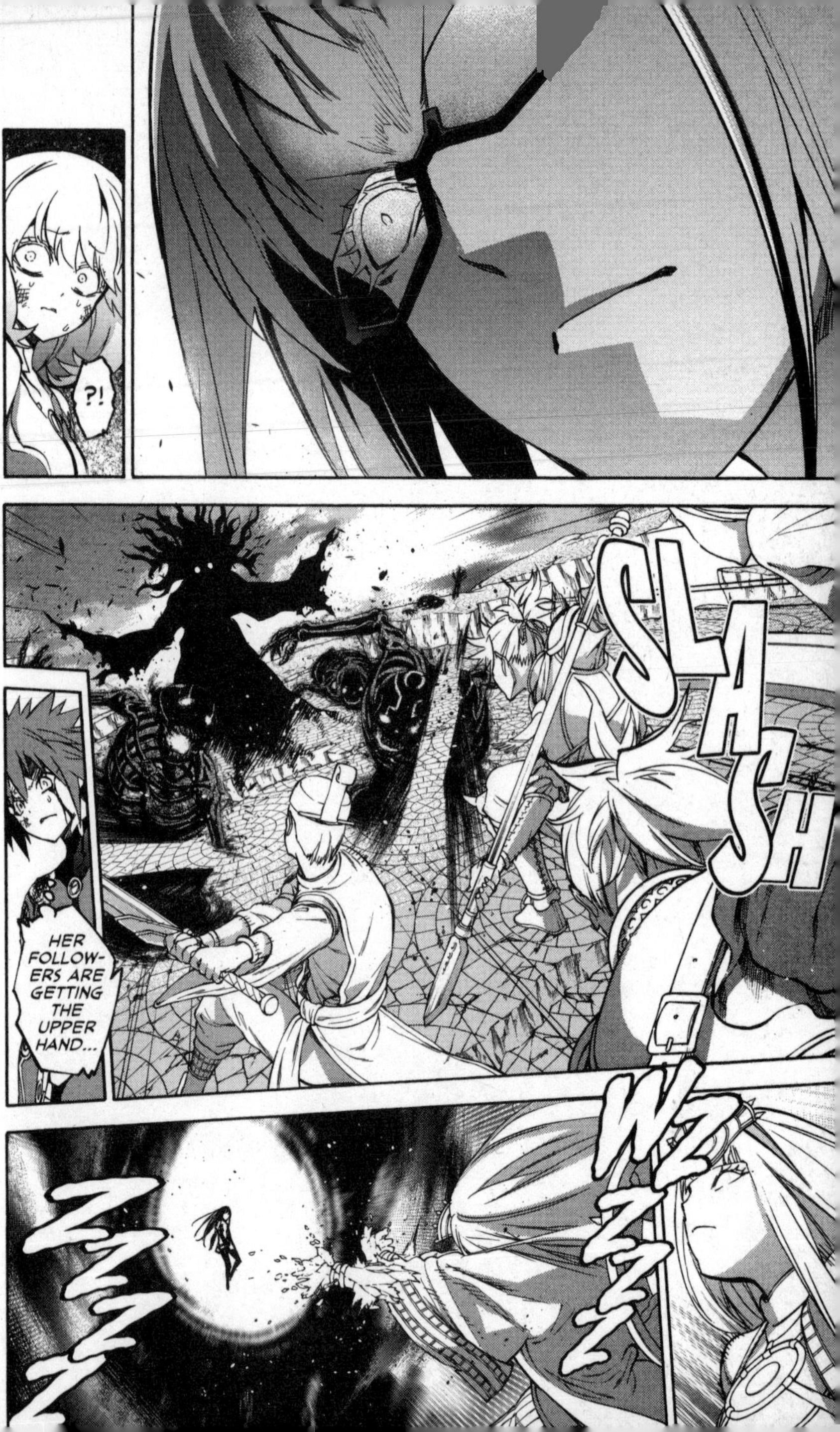
?!
SLASH
HER FOLLOWERS ARE GETTING THE UPPER HAND...
WZZZZ
ZZZZZ

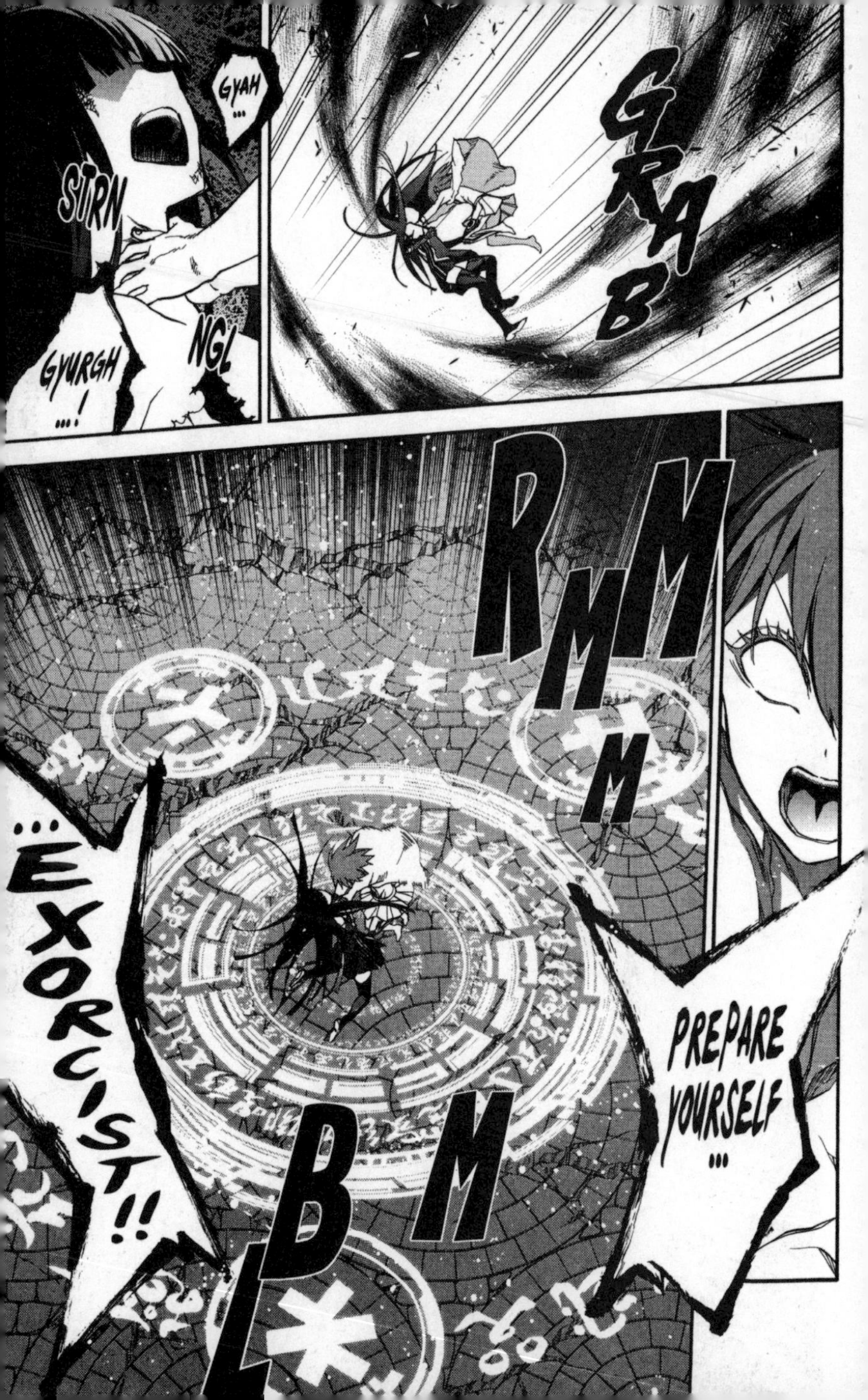
GRAB
GYAH...
STRN
NGL
GYURGH...!
RMMMM
PREPARE YOURSELF...
...EXORCIST!!
BMM

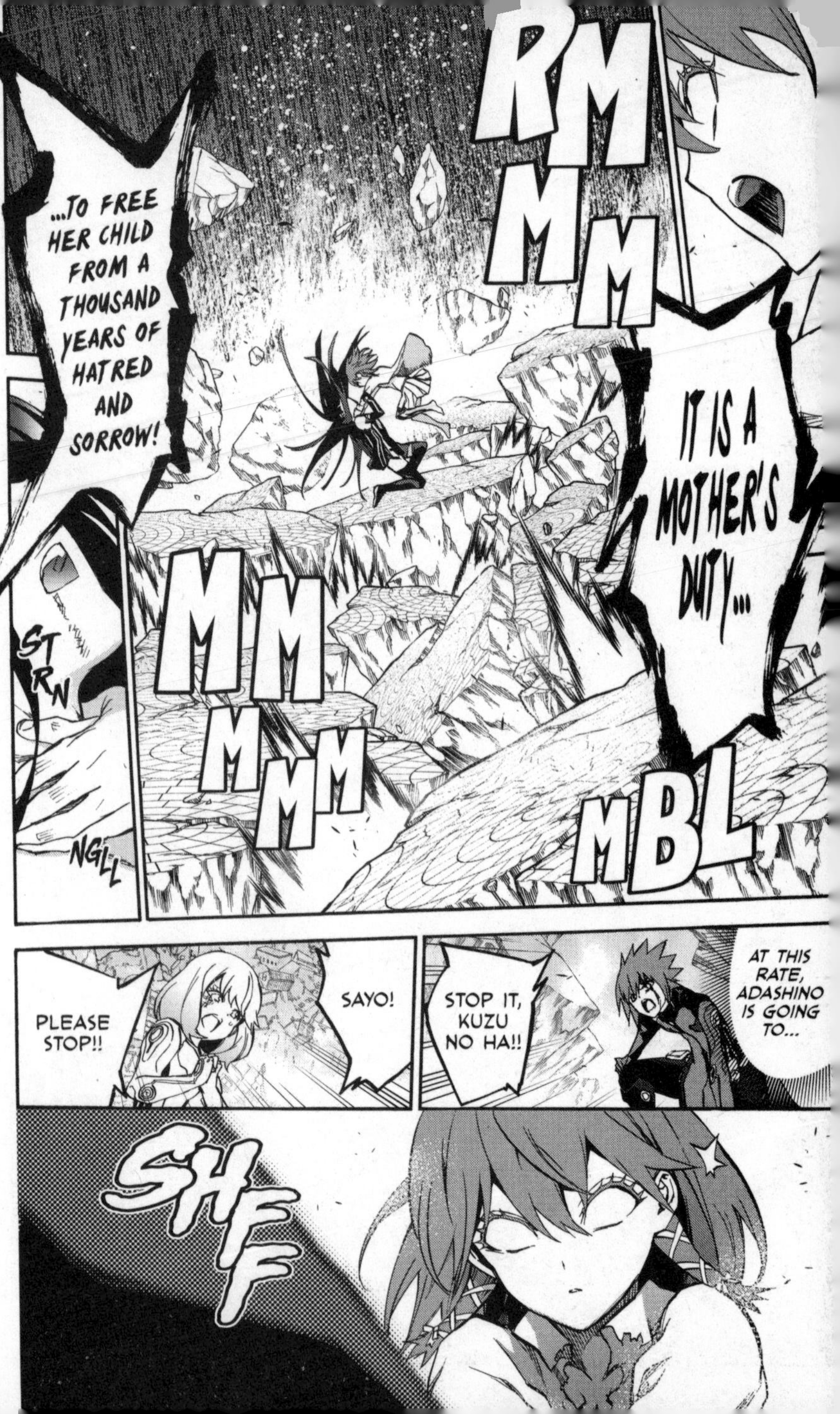
RMMMM
IT IS A MOTHER'S DUTY...
...TO FREE HER CHILD FROM A THOUSAND YEARS OF HATRED AND SORROW!
MMMMMM
MBL
STRN
NGLL
AT THIS RATE, ADASHINO IS GOING TO...
STOP IT, KUZU NO HA!!
SAYO!
PLEASE STOP!!
SHF

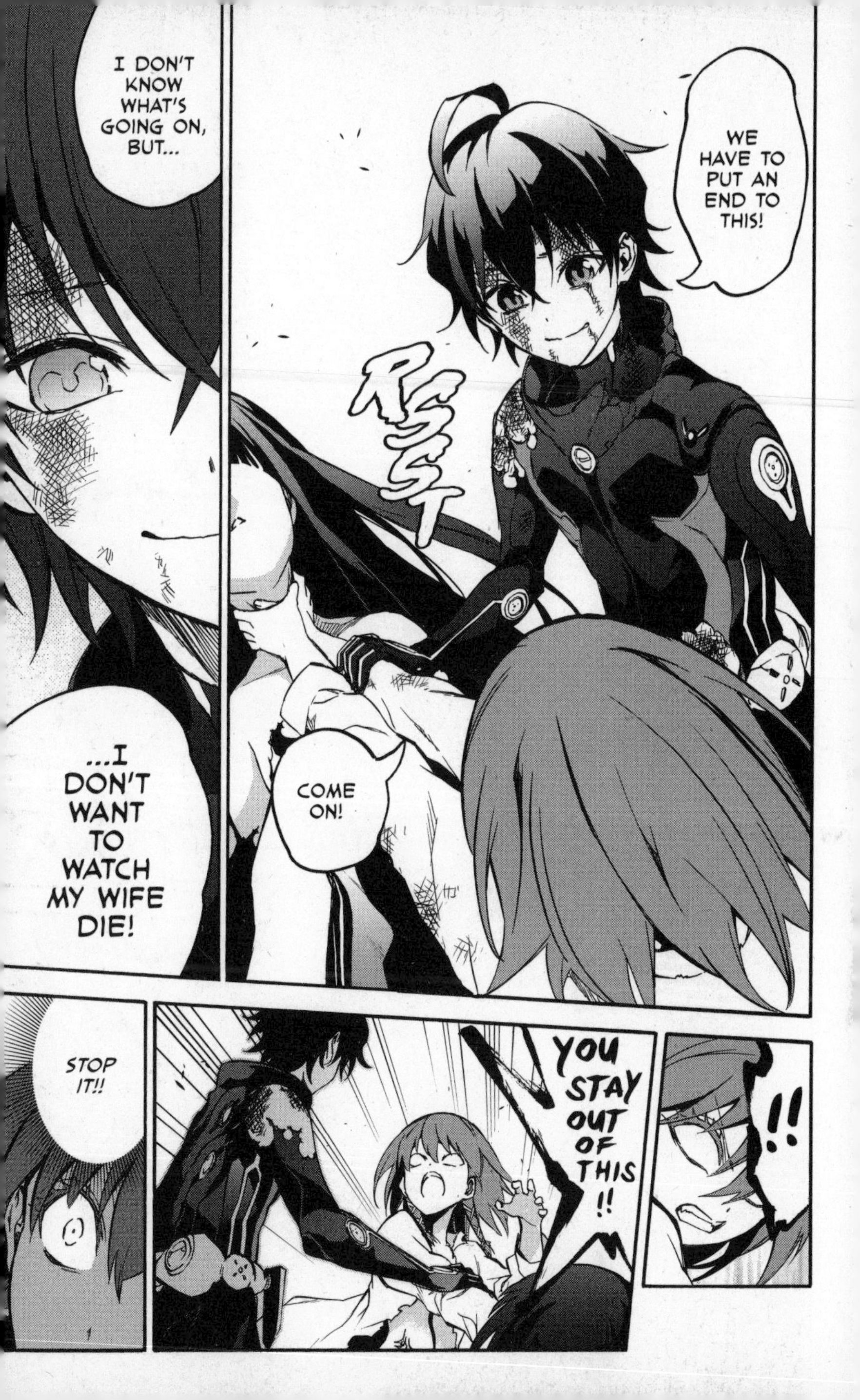
WE HAVE TO PUT AN END TO THIS!
COME ON!
I DON'T KNOW WHAT'S GOING ON, BUT...
...I DON'T WANT TO WATCH MY WIFE DIE!
!!
YOU STAY OUT OF THIS!!
STOP IT!!

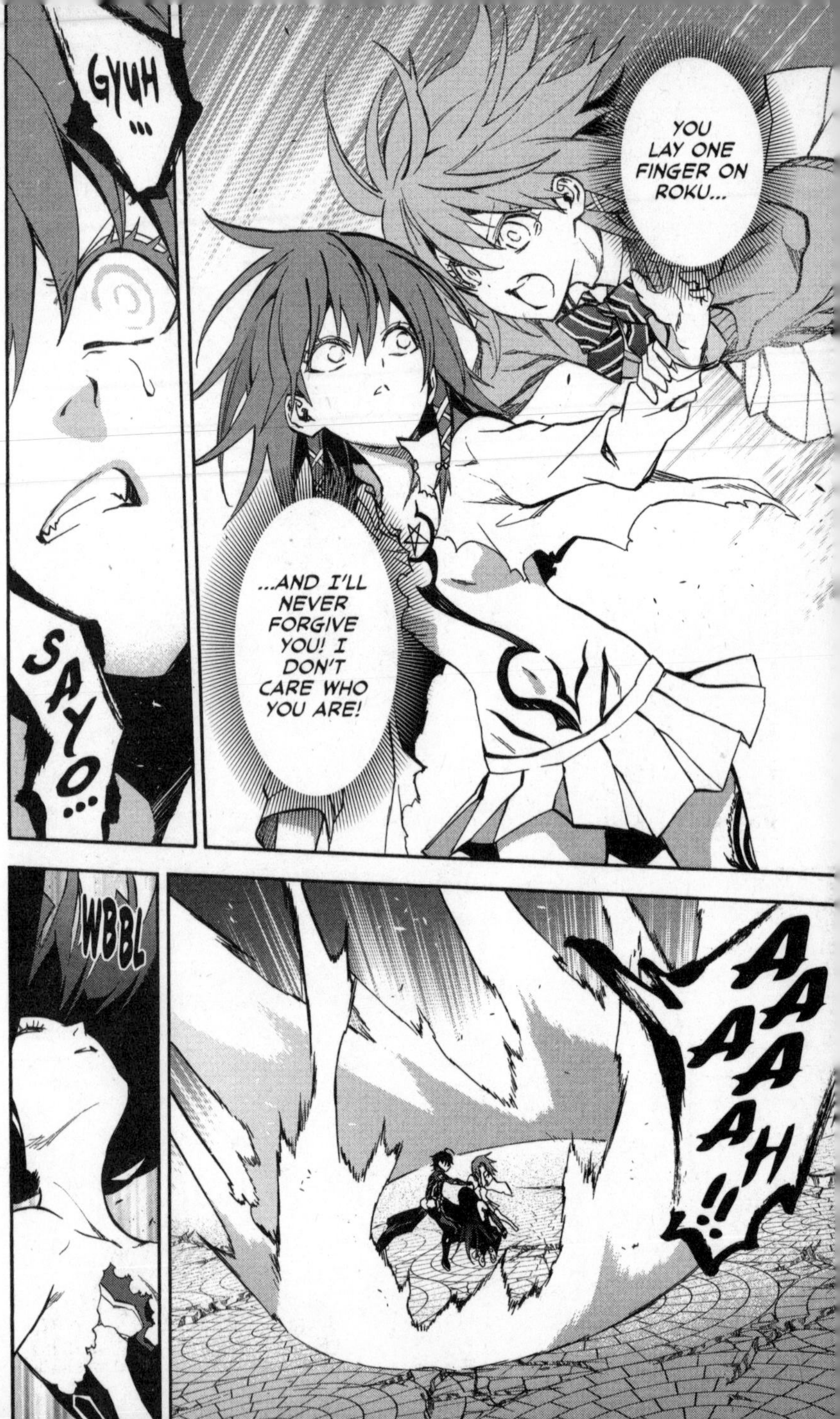
YOU LAY ONE FINGER ON ROKU...
...AND I'LL NEVER FORGIVE YOU! I DON'T CARE WHO YOU ARE!
GYUH...
SAYO...
AAAAAH!!
WBBL

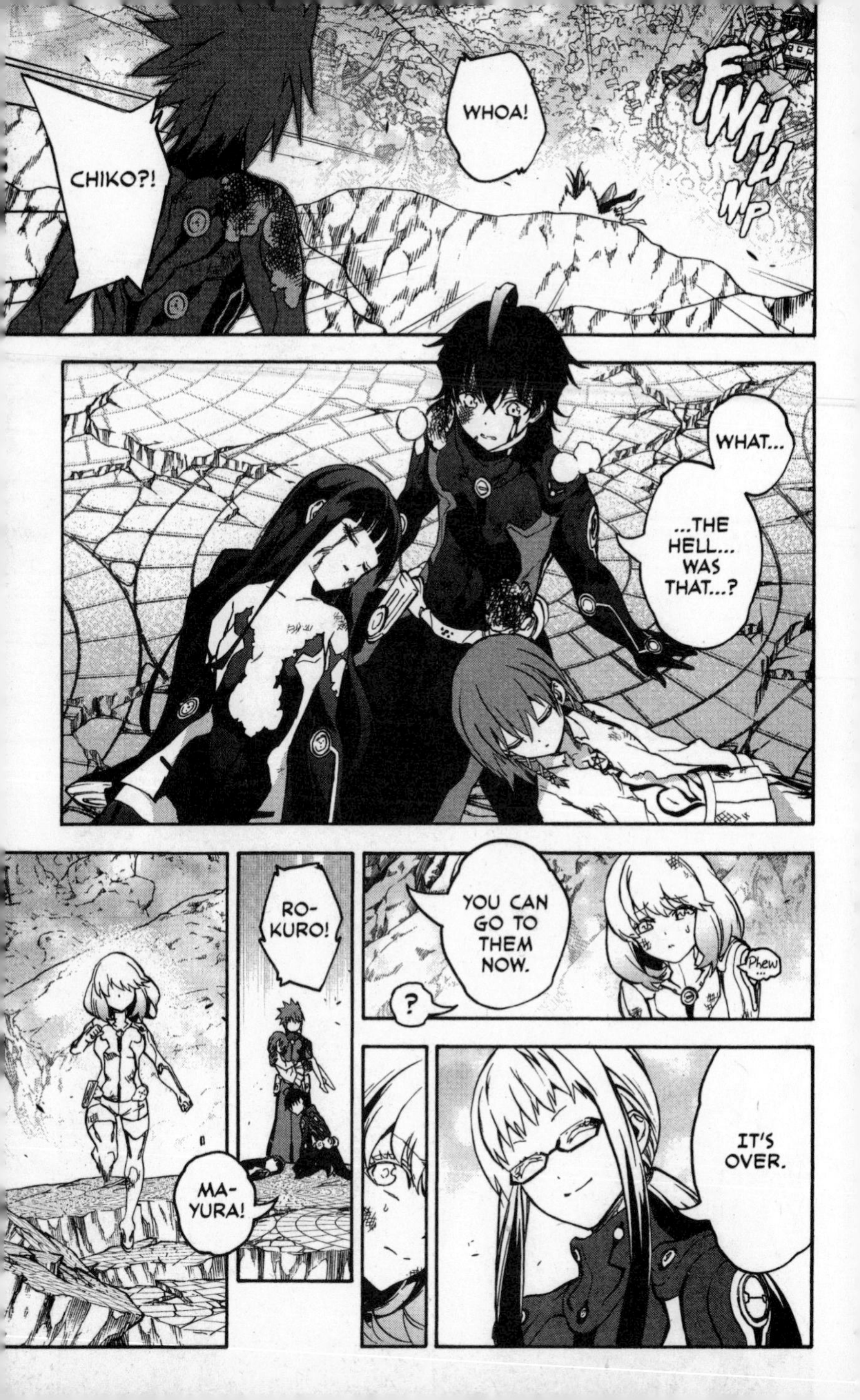
FWHUMP
WHOA!
CHIKO?!
WHAT...
...THE HELL... WAS THAT...?
Phew...
YOU CAN GO TO THEM NOW.
?
IT'S OVER.
RO-KURO!
MA-YURA!

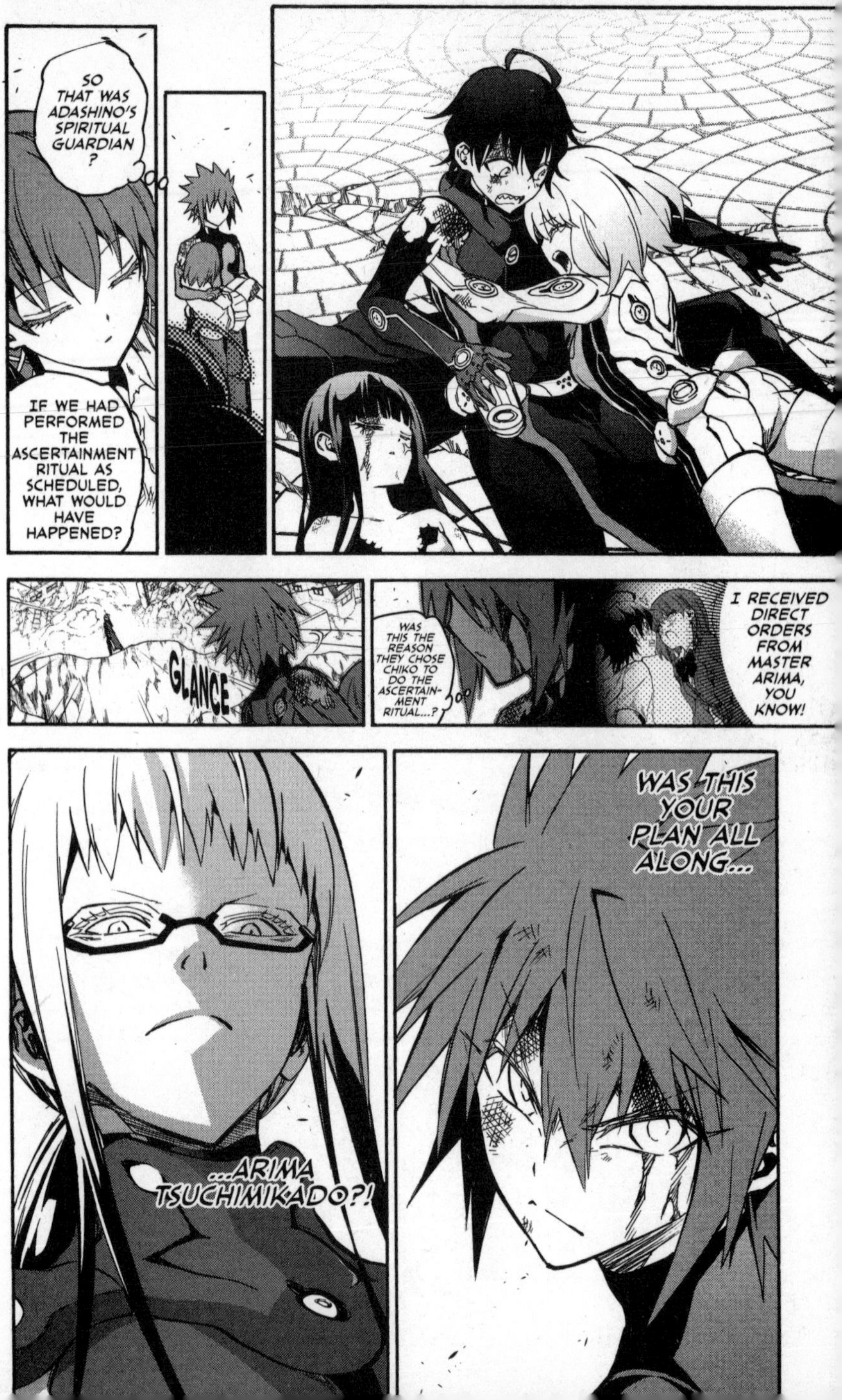
SO THAT WAS ADASHINO'S SPIRITUAL GUARDIAN?
IF WE HAD PERFORMED THE ASCERTAINMENT RITUAL AS SCHEDULED, WHAT WOULD HAVE HAPPENED?
I RECEIVED DIRECT ORDERS FROM MASTER ARIMA, YOU KNOW!
WAS THIS THE REASON THEY CHOSE CHIKO TO DO THE ASCERTAINMENT RITUAL...?
GLANCE
WAS THIS YOUR PLAN ALL ALONG...
...ARIMA TSUCHIMIKADO?!

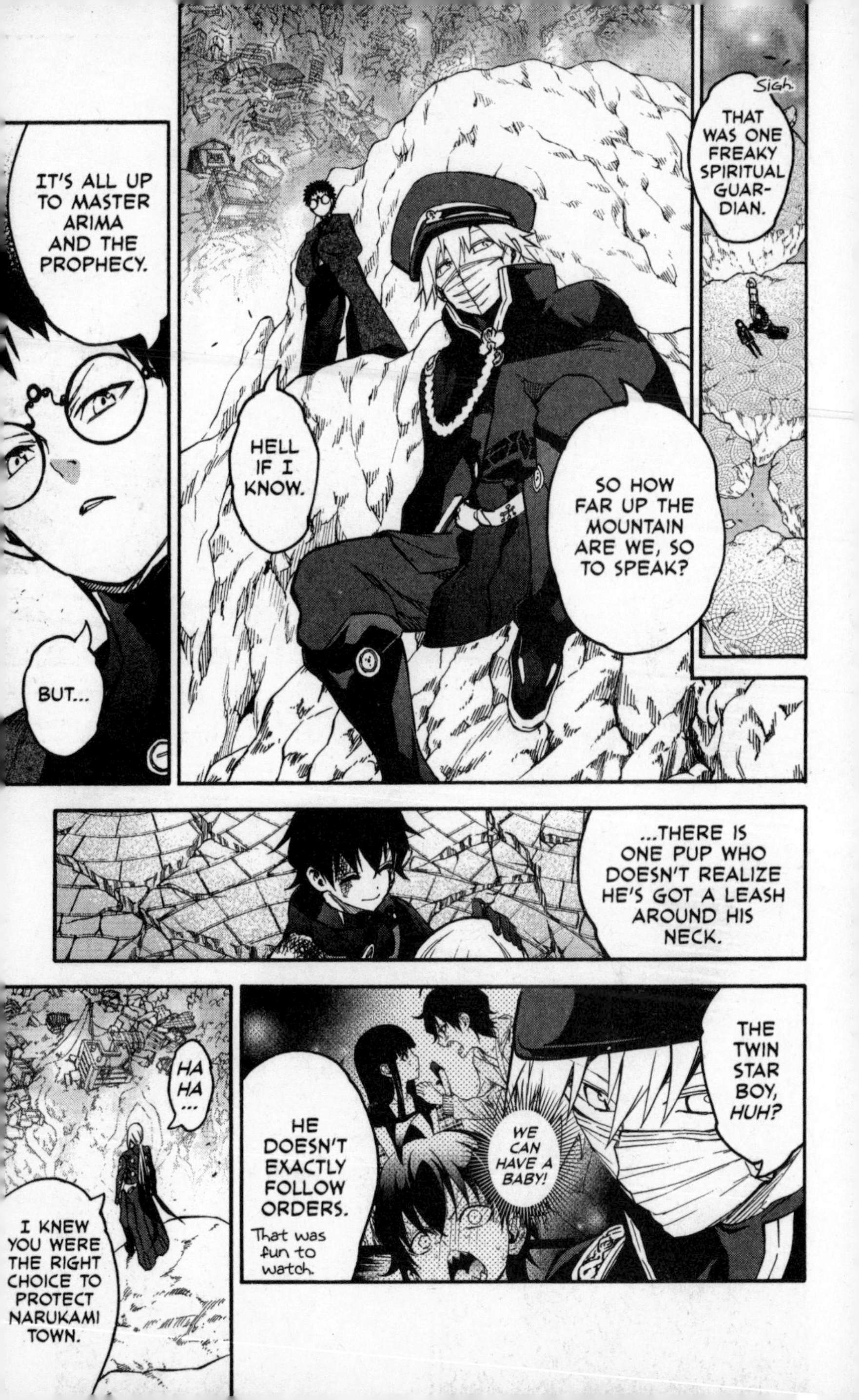
Sigh.
THAT WAS ONE FREAKY SPIRITUAL GUARDIAN.
SO HOW FAR UP THE MOUNTAIN ARE WE, SO TO SPEAK?
HELL IF I KNOW.
IT'S ALL UP TO MASTER ARIMA AND THE PROPHECY.
BUT...
...THERE IS ONE PUP WHO DOESN'T REALIZE HE'S GOT A LEASH AROUND HIS NECK.
THE TWIN STAR BOY, *HUH?*
WE CAN HAVE A BABY!
HE DOESN'T EXACTLY FOLLOW ORDERS.
That was fun to watch.
HA HA...
I KNEW YOU WERE THE RIGHT CHOICE TO PROTECT NARUKAMI TOWN.

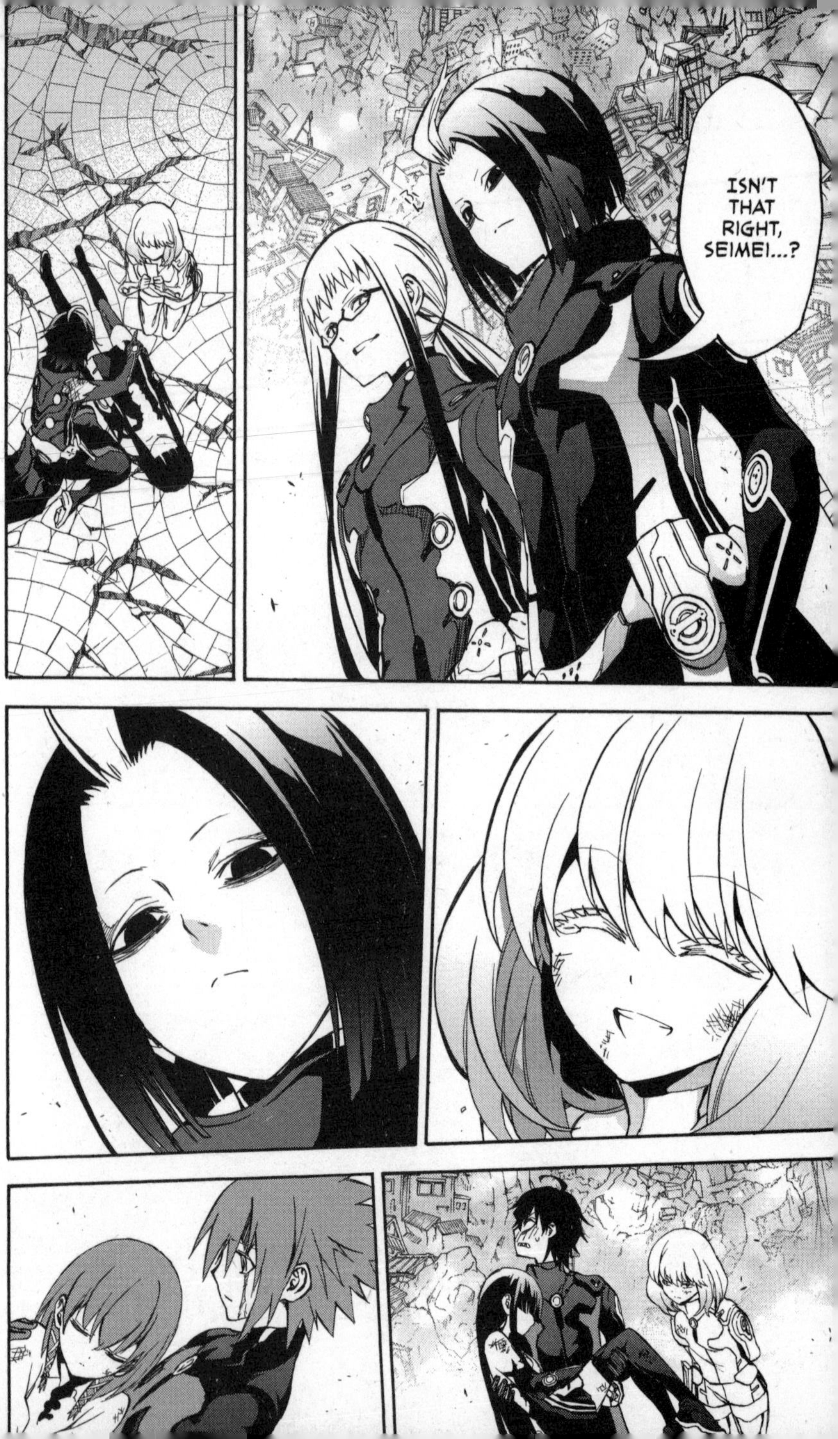
ISN'T THAT RIGHT, SEIMEI...?

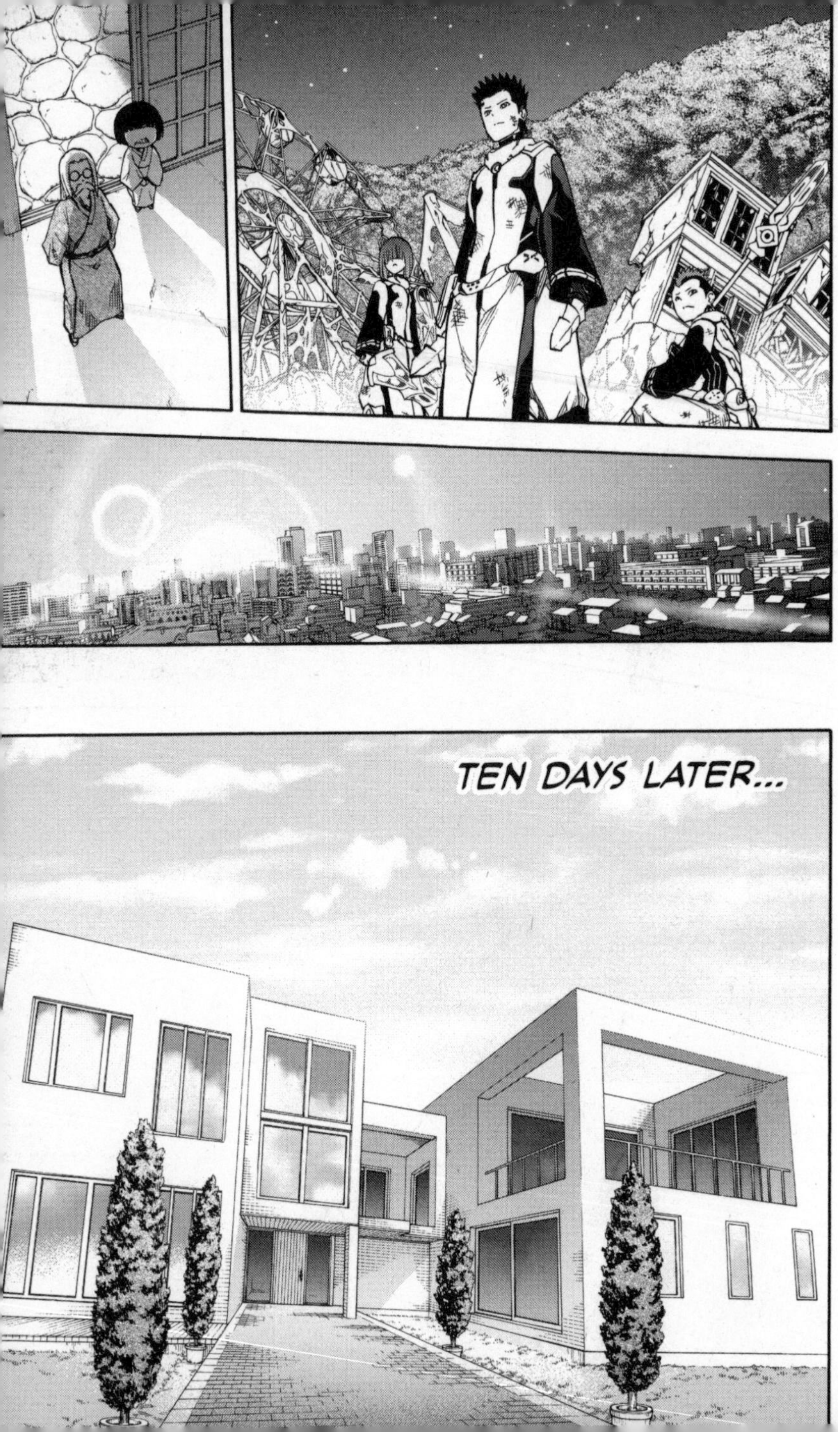
TEN DAYS LATER...

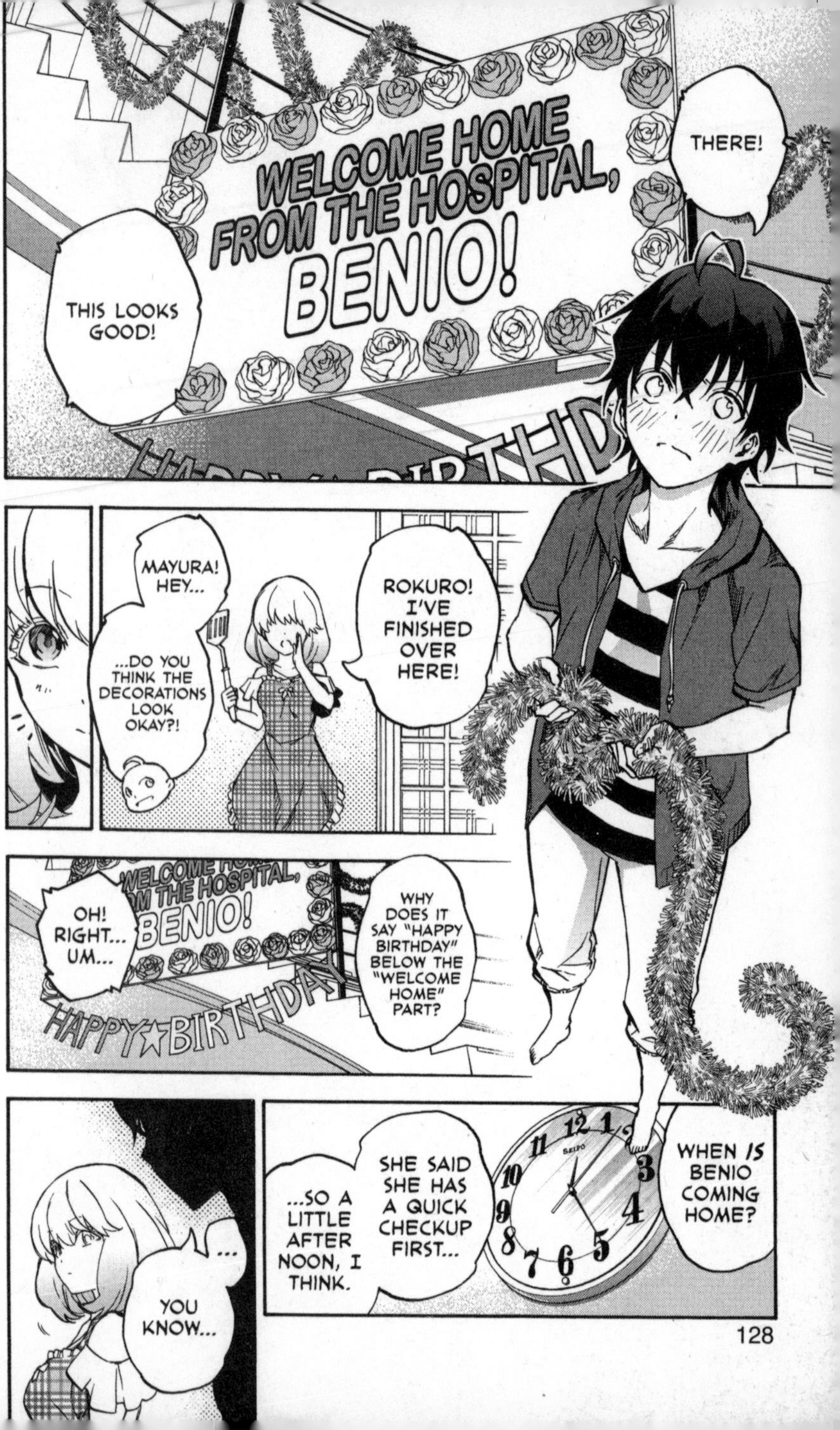
THERE!
WELCOME HOME FROM THE HOSPITAL, BENIO!
THIS LOOKS GOOD!
HAPPY BIRTHD
ROKURO! I'VE FINISHED OVER HERE!
MAYURA! HEY...
...DO YOU THINK THE DECORATIONS LOOK OKAY?!
WHY DOES IT SAY "HAPPY BIRTHDAY" BELOW THE "WELCOME HOME" PART?
WELCOME HOME FROM THE HOSPITAL, BENIO!
HAPPY☆BIRTHDAY
OH! RIGHT... UM...
WHEN *IS* BENIO COMING HOME?
SHE SAID SHE HAS A QUICK CHECKUP FIRST...
...SO A LITTLE AFTER NOON, I THINK.
...
YOU KNOW...

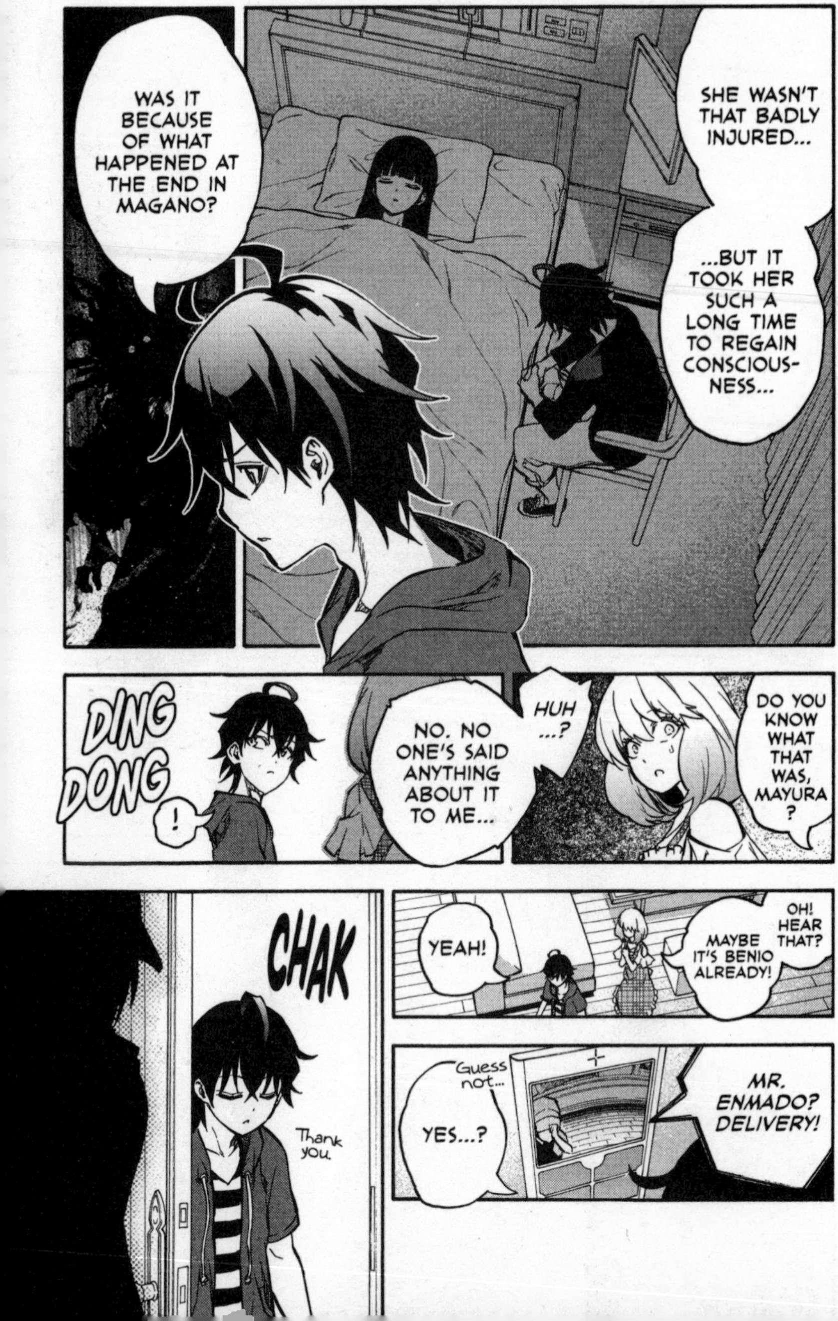
SHE WASN'T THAT BADLY INJURED...
...BUT IT TOOK HER SUCH A LONG TIME TO REGAIN CONSCIOUS-NESS...
WAS IT BECAUSE OF WHAT HAPPENED AT THE END IN MAGANO?
DO YOU KNOW WHAT THAT WAS, MAYURA?
HUH ...?
NO. NO ONE'S SAID ANYTHING ABOUT IT TO ME...
DING DONG
!
OH! HEAR THAT?
MAYBE IT'S BENIO ALREADY!
YEAH!
MR. ENMADO? DELIVERY!
YES...?
Guess not...
CHAK
Thank you.

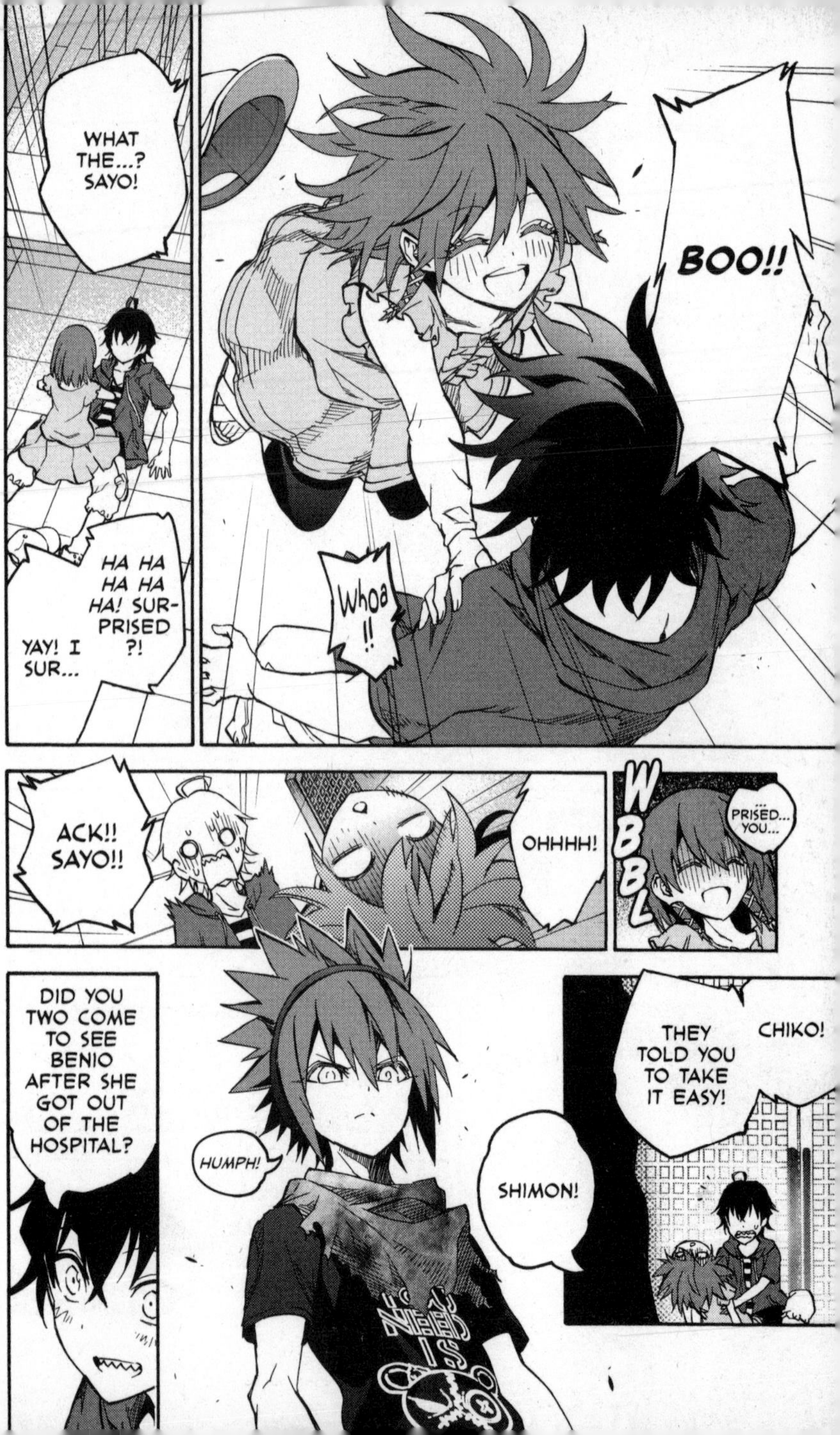
BOO!!
Whoa!!
WHAT THE...? SAYO!
HA HA HA HA HA! SURPRISED?!
YAY! I SUR...
WBBL
...PRISED... YOU...
OHHHH!
ACK!! SAYO!!
CHIKO! THEY TOLD YOU TO TAKE IT EASY!
SHIMON!
HUMPH!
DID YOU TWO COME TO SEE BENIO AFTER SHE GOT OUT OF THE HOSPITAL?

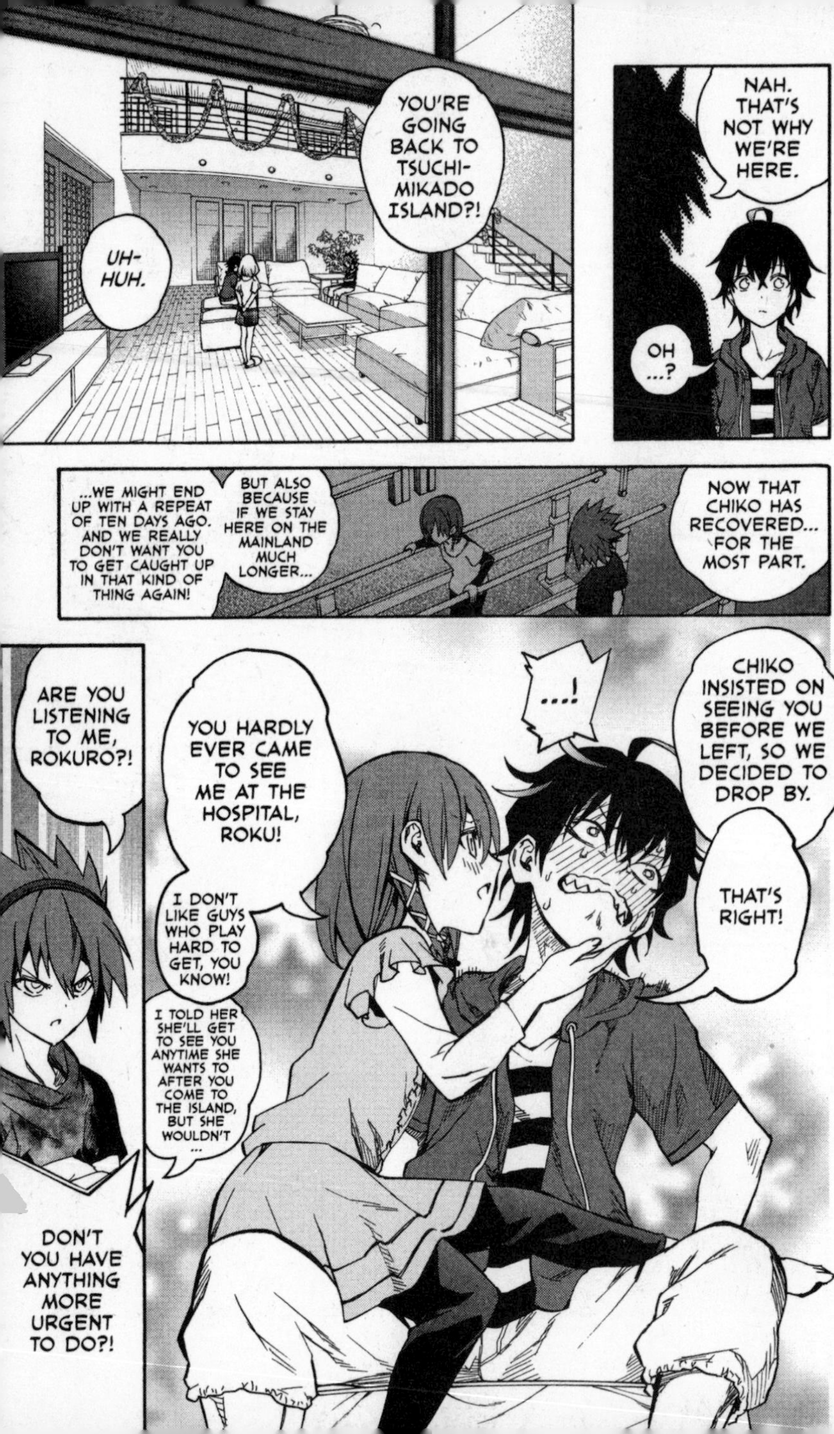

NAH. THAT'S NOT WHY WE'RE HERE.
OH ...?
YOU'RE GOING BACK TO TSUCHI-MIKADO ISLAND?!
UH-HUH.
NOW THAT CHIKO HAS RECOVERED... FOR THE MOST PART.
BUT ALSO BECAUSE IF WE STAY HERE ON THE MAINLAND MUCH LONGER...
...WE MIGHT END UP WITH A REPEAT OF TEN DAYS AGO. AND WE REALLY DON'T WANT YOU TO GET CAUGHT UP IN THAT KIND OF THING AGAIN!
CHIKO INSISTED ON SEEING YOU BEFORE WE LEFT, SO WE DECIDED TO DROP BY.
THAT'S RIGHT!
...!
YOU HARDLY EVER CAME TO SEE ME AT THE HOSPITAL, ROKU!
I DON'T LIKE GUYS WHO PLAY HARD TO GET, YOU KNOW!
I TOLD HER SHE'LL GET TO SEE YOU ANYTIME SHE WANTS TO AFTER YOU COME TO THE ISLAND, BUT SHE WOULDN'T ...
ARE YOU LISTENING TO ME, ROKURO?!
DON'T YOU HAVE ANYTHING MORE URGENT TO DO?!

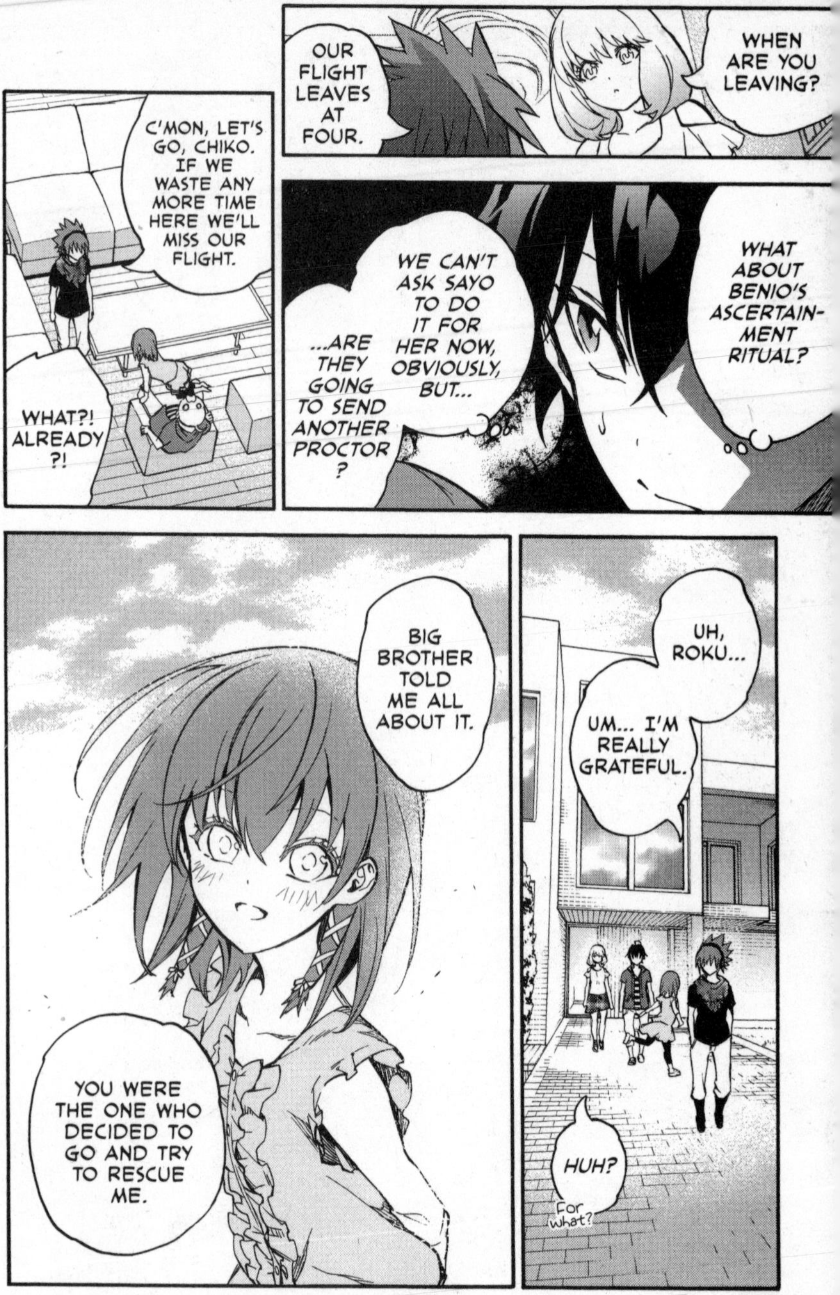
WHEN ARE YOU LEAVING?
OUR FLIGHT LEAVES AT FOUR.
WHAT ABOUT BENIO'S ASCERTAINMENT RITUAL?
WE CAN'T ASK SAYO TO DO IT FOR HER NOW, OBVIOUSLY, BUT...
...ARE THEY GOING TO SEND ANOTHER PROCTOR?
C'MON, LET'S GO, CHIKO. IF WE WASTE ANY MORE TIME HERE WE'LL MISS OUR FLIGHT.
WHAT?! ALREADY?!
UH, ROKU...
UM... I'M REALLY GRATEFUL.
HUH?
For what?
BIG BROTHER TOLD ME ALL ABOUT IT.
YOU WERE THE ONE WHO DECIDED TO GO AND TRY TO RESCUE ME.

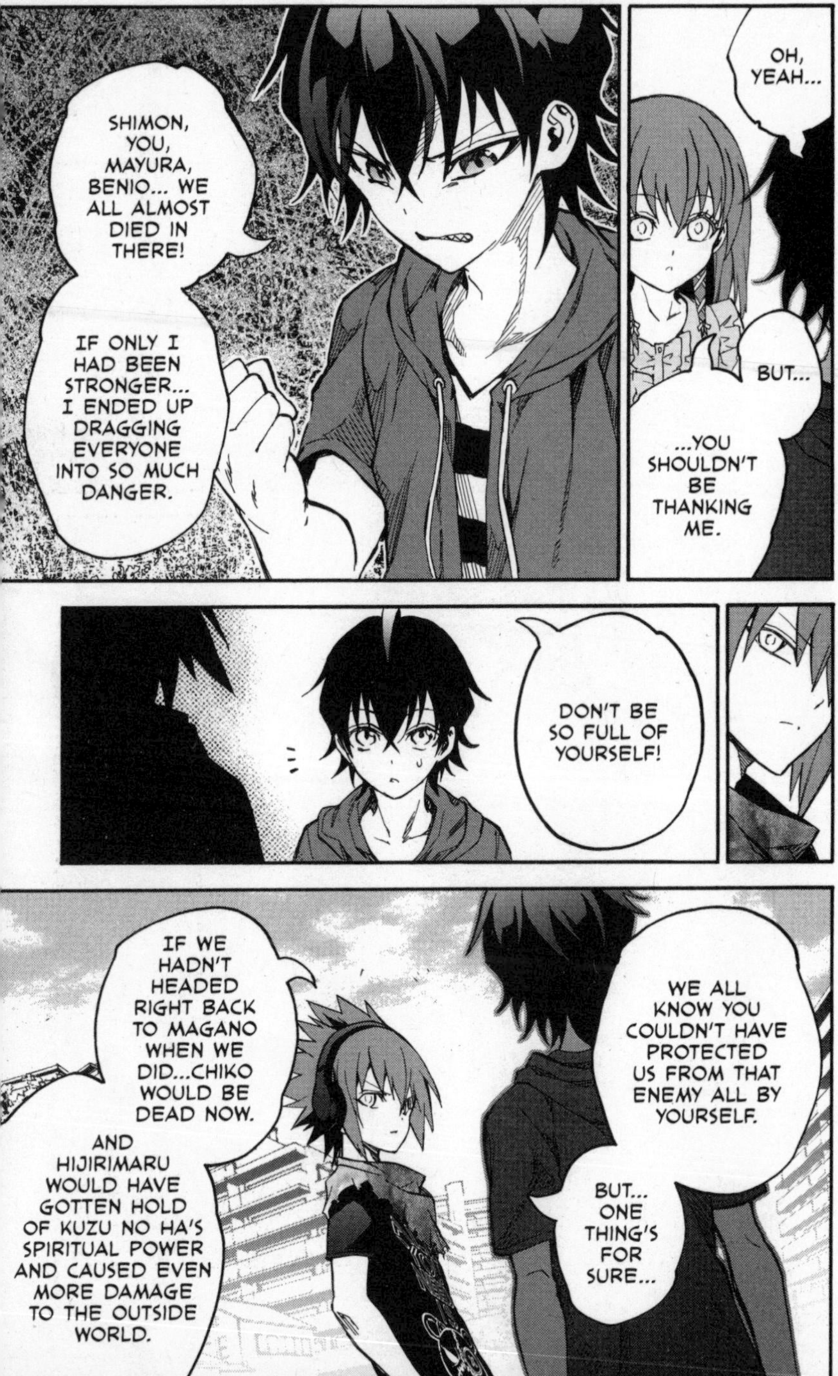
OH, YEAH...
BUT...
...YOU SHOULDN'T BE THANKING ME.
SHIMON, YOU, MAYURA, BENIO... WE ALL ALMOST DIED IN THERE!
IF ONLY I HAD BEEN STRONGER... I ENDED UP DRAGGING EVERYONE INTO SO MUCH DANGER.
DON'T BE SO FULL OF YOURSELF!
WE ALL KNOW YOU COULDN'T HAVE PROTECTED US FROM THAT ENEMY ALL BY YOURSELF.
BUT... ONE THING'S FOR SURE...
IF WE HADN'T HEADED RIGHT BACK TO MAGANO WHEN WE DID...CHIKO WOULD BE DEAD NOW.
AND HIJIRIMARU WOULD HAVE GOTTEN HOLD OF KUZU NO HA'S SPIRITUAL POWER AND CAUSED EVEN MORE DAMAGE TO THE OUTSIDE WORLD.

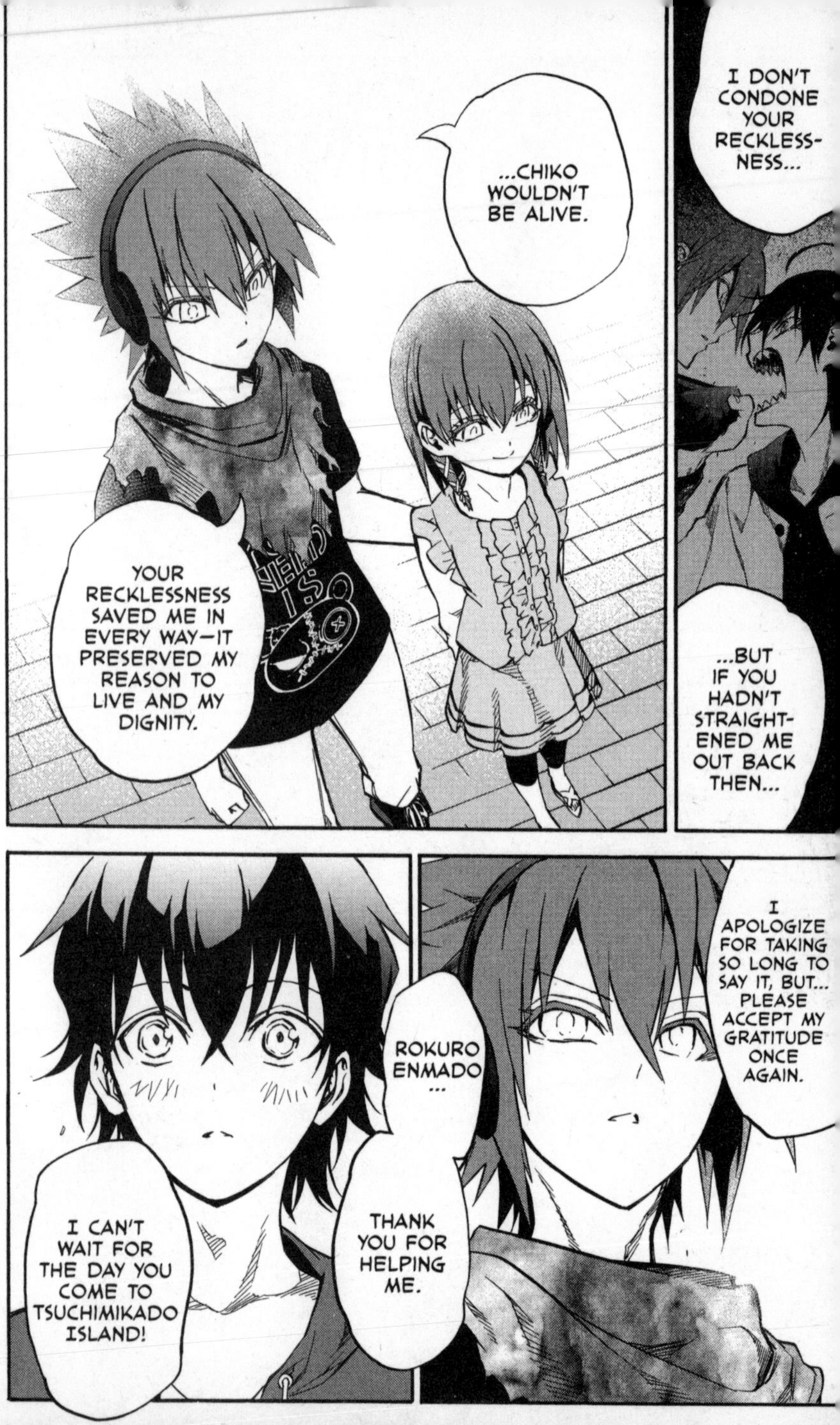
I DON'T CONDONE YOUR RECKLESS-NESS...
...BUT IF YOU HADN'T STRAIGHT-ENED ME OUT BACK THEN...
...CHIKO WOULDN'T BE ALIVE.
YOUR RECKLESSNESS SAVED ME IN EVERY WAY—IT PRESERVED MY REASON TO LIVE AND MY DIGNITY.
I APOLOGIZE FOR TAKING SO LONG TO SAY IT, BUT... PLEASE ACCEPT MY GRATITUDE ONCE AGAIN.
ROKURO ENMADO...
THANK YOU FOR HELPING ME.
I CAN'T WAIT FOR THE DAY YOU COME TO TSUCHIMIKADO ISLAND!

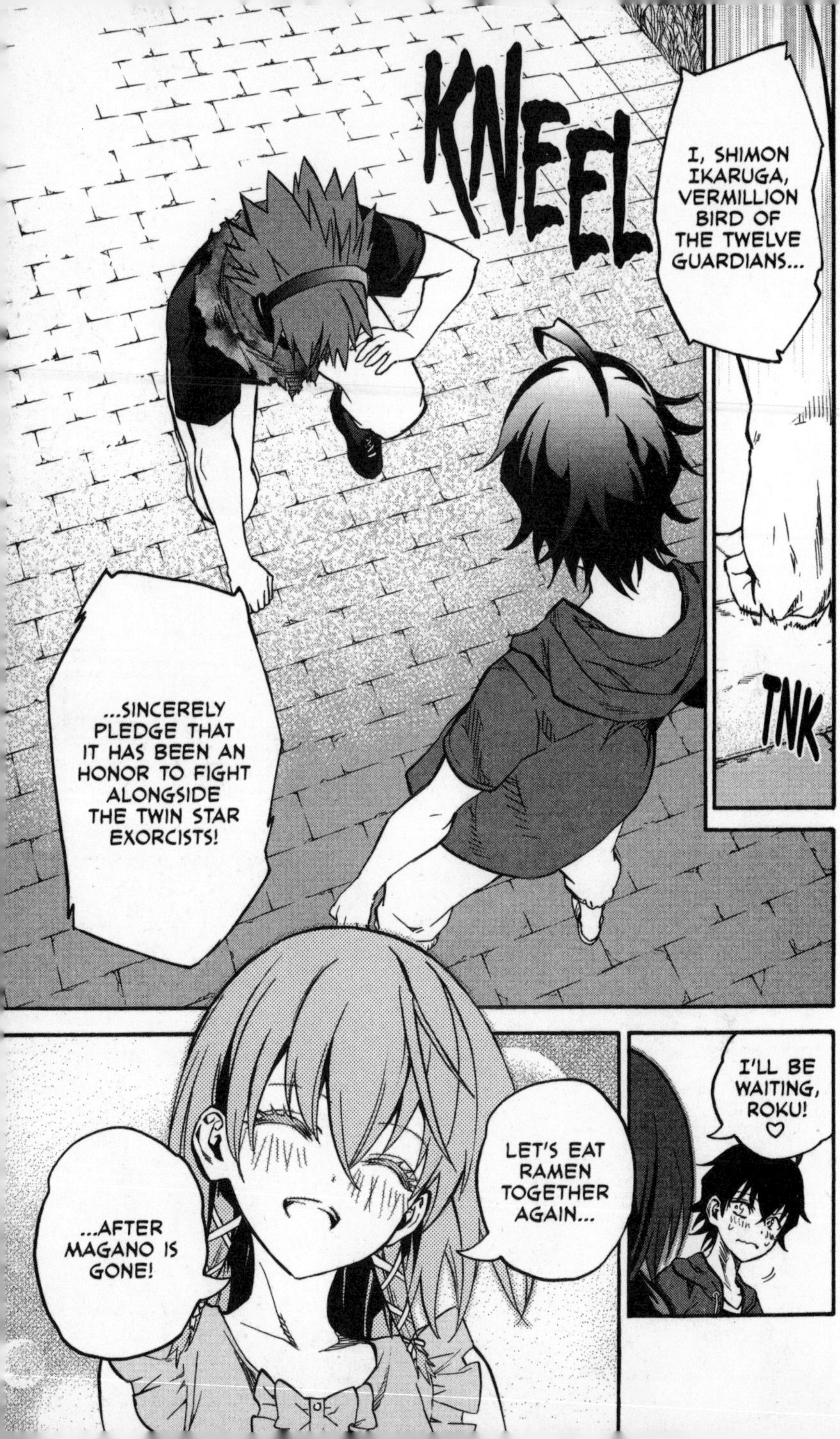
I, SHIMON IKARUGA, VERMILLION BIRD OF THE TWELVE GUARDIANS...
TNK
KNEEL
...SINCERELY PLEDGE THAT IT HAS BEEN AN HONOR TO FIGHT ALONGSIDE THE TWIN STAR EXORCISTS!
I'LL BE WAITING, ROKU! ♡
LET'S EAT RAMEN TOGETHER AGAIN...
...AFTER MAGANO IS GONE!

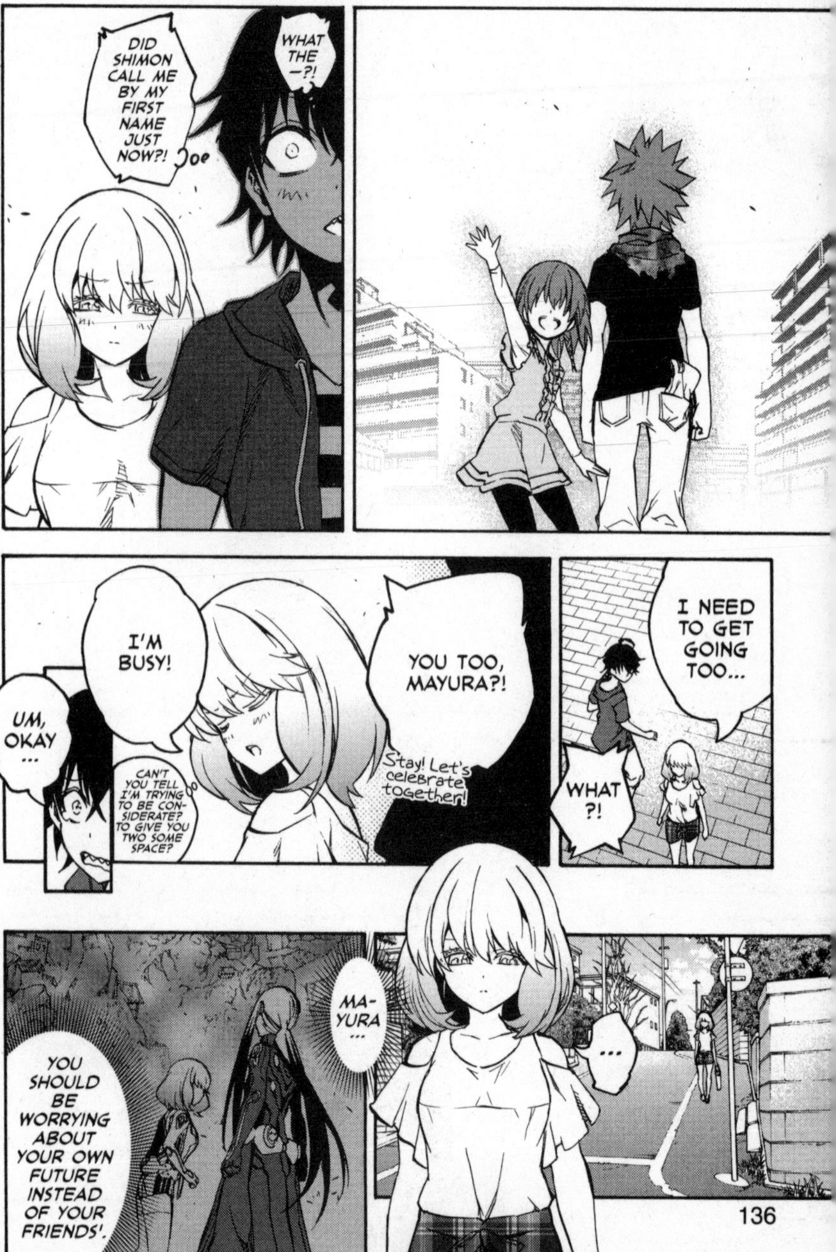
WHAT THE —?!
DID SHIMON CALL ME BY MY FIRST NAME JUST NOW?!
I NEED TO GET GOING TOO...
WHAT ?!
YOU TOO, MAYURA?!
Stay! Let's celebrate together!
I'M BUSY!
CAN'T YOU TELL I'M TRYING TO BE CONSIDERATE? TO GIVE YOU TWO SOME SPACE?
UM, OKAY ...
...
MA-YURA ...
YOU SHOULD BE WORRYING ABOUT YOUR OWN FUTURE INSTEAD OF YOUR FRIENDS'.

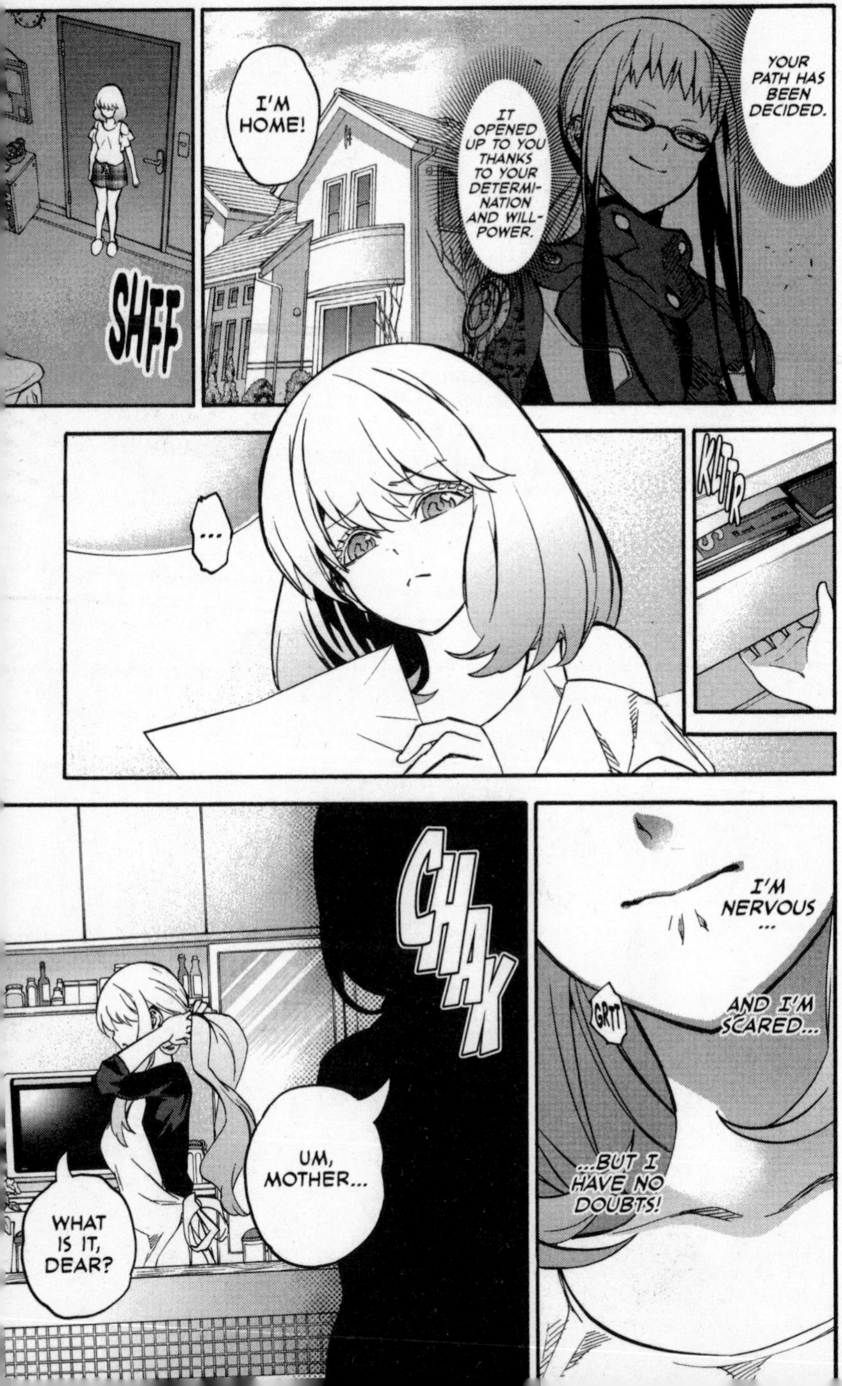
YOUR PATH HAS BEEN DECIDED.
IT OPENED UP TO YOU THANKS TO YOUR DETERMINATION AND WILLPOWER.
I'M HOME!
SHFF
KLTTR
...
I'M NERVOUS...
GRTT
AND I'M SCARED...
...BUT I HAVE NO DOUBTS!
CHAK
UM, MOTHER...
WHAT IS IT, DEAR?

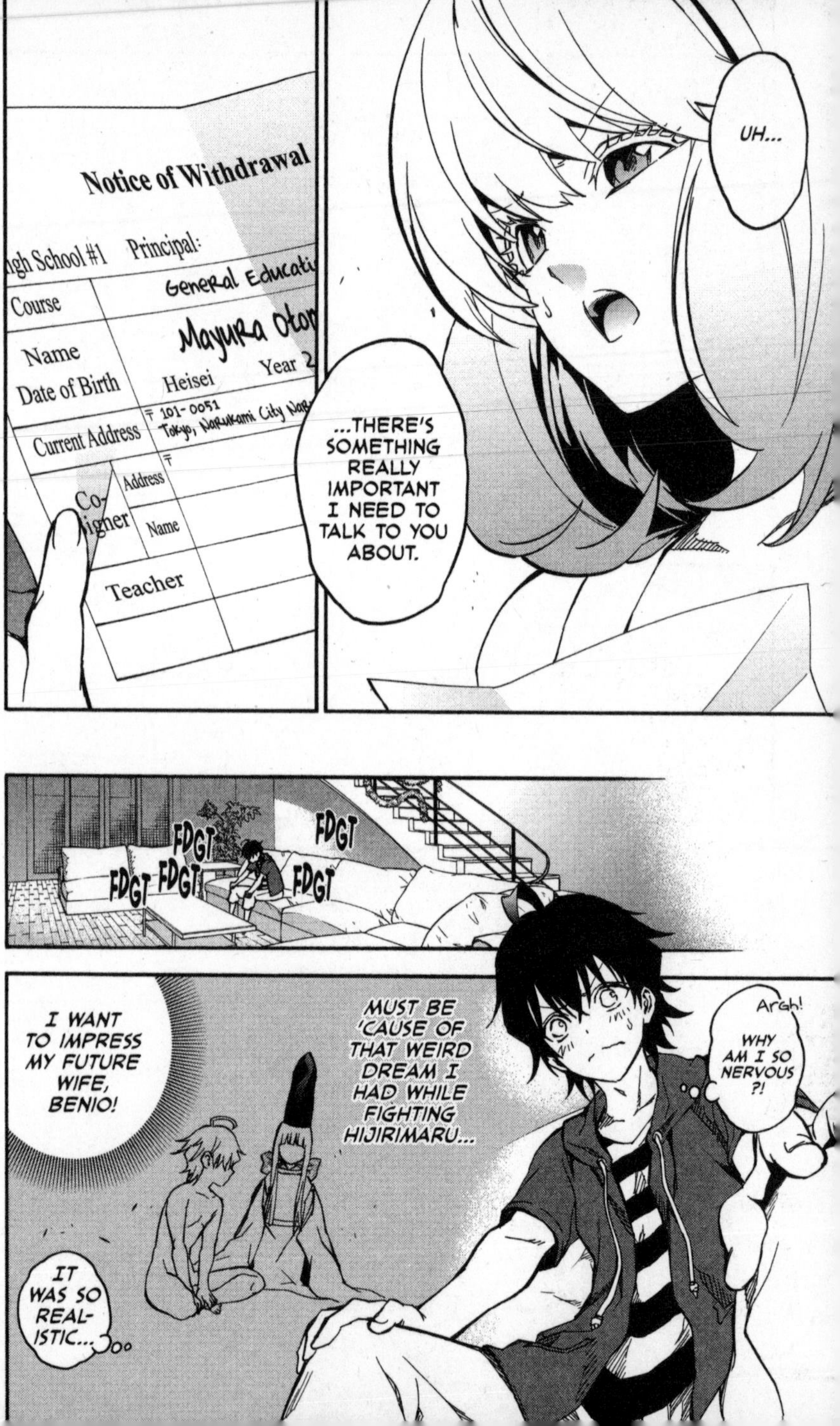
UH...
...THERE'S SOMETHING REALLY IMPORTANT I NEED TO TALK TO YOU ABOUT.
Notice of Withdrawal
igh School #1 Principal:
Course
General Educati
Name
Mayura Oto
Date of Birth
Heisei
Year 2
Current Address
〒 101-0051
Tokyo, Narukami City
〒
Co-Signer
Address
Name
Teacher
FDGT
FDGT
FDGT
FDGT
FDGT
Argh!
WHY AM I SO NERVOUS?!
MUST BE 'CAUSE OF THAT WEIRD DREAM I HAD WHILE FIGHTING HIJIRIMARU...
I WANT TO IMPRESS MY FUTURE WIFE, BENIO!
IT WAS SO REAL-ISTIC...

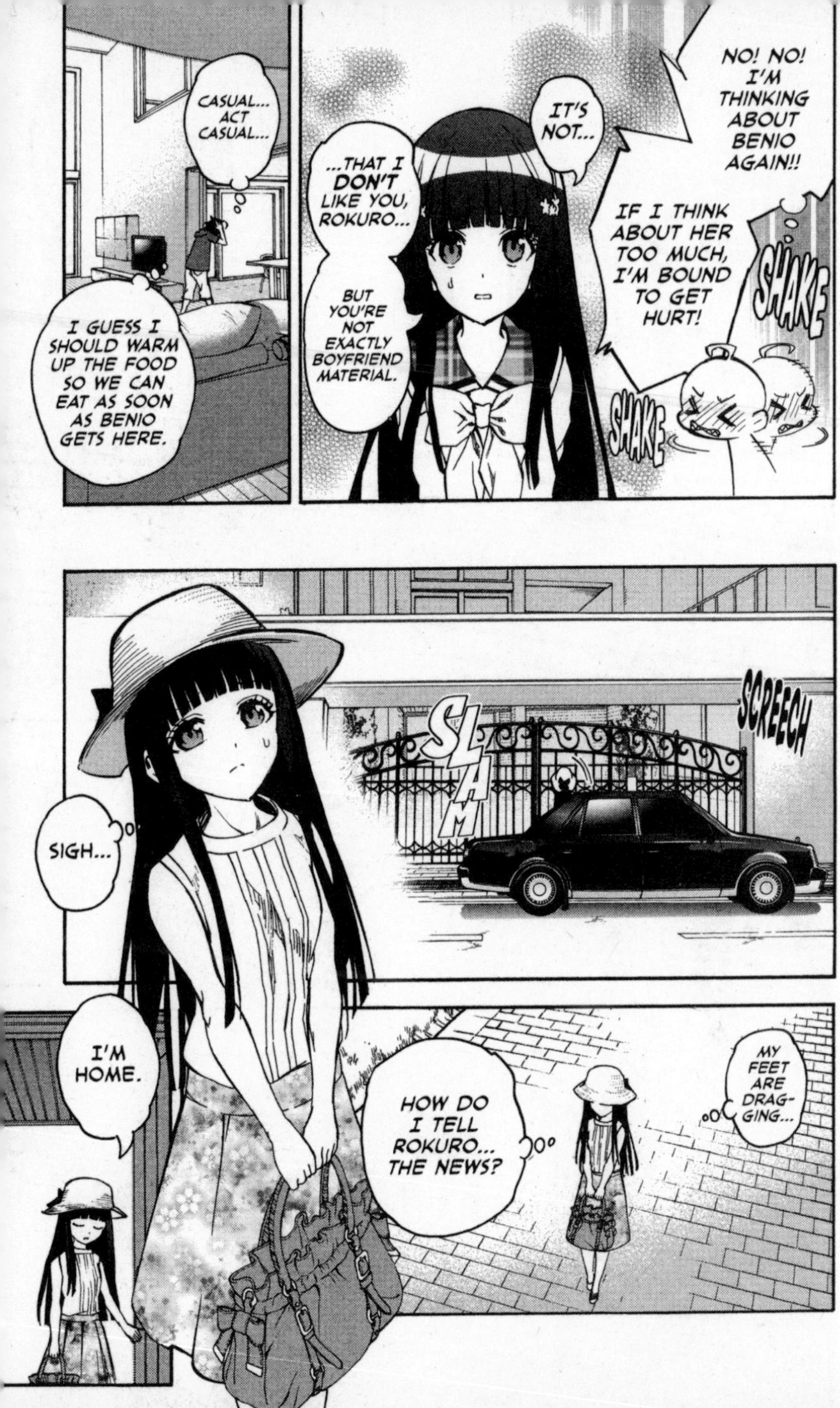
NO! NO! I'M THINKING ABOUT BENIO AGAIN!!
IF I THINK ABOUT HER TOO MUCH, I'M BOUND TO GET HURT!
SHAKE
SHAKE
IT'S NOT...
...THAT I DON'T LIKE YOU, ROKURO...
BUT YOU'RE NOT EXACTLY BOYFRIEND MATERIAL.
CASUAL... ACT CASUAL...
I GUESS I SHOULD WARM UP THE FOOD SO WE CAN EAT AS SOON AS BENIO GETS HERE.
SCREECH
SLAM
SIGH...
MY FEET ARE DRAG-GING...
HOW DO I TELL ROKURO... THE NEWS?
I'M HOME.

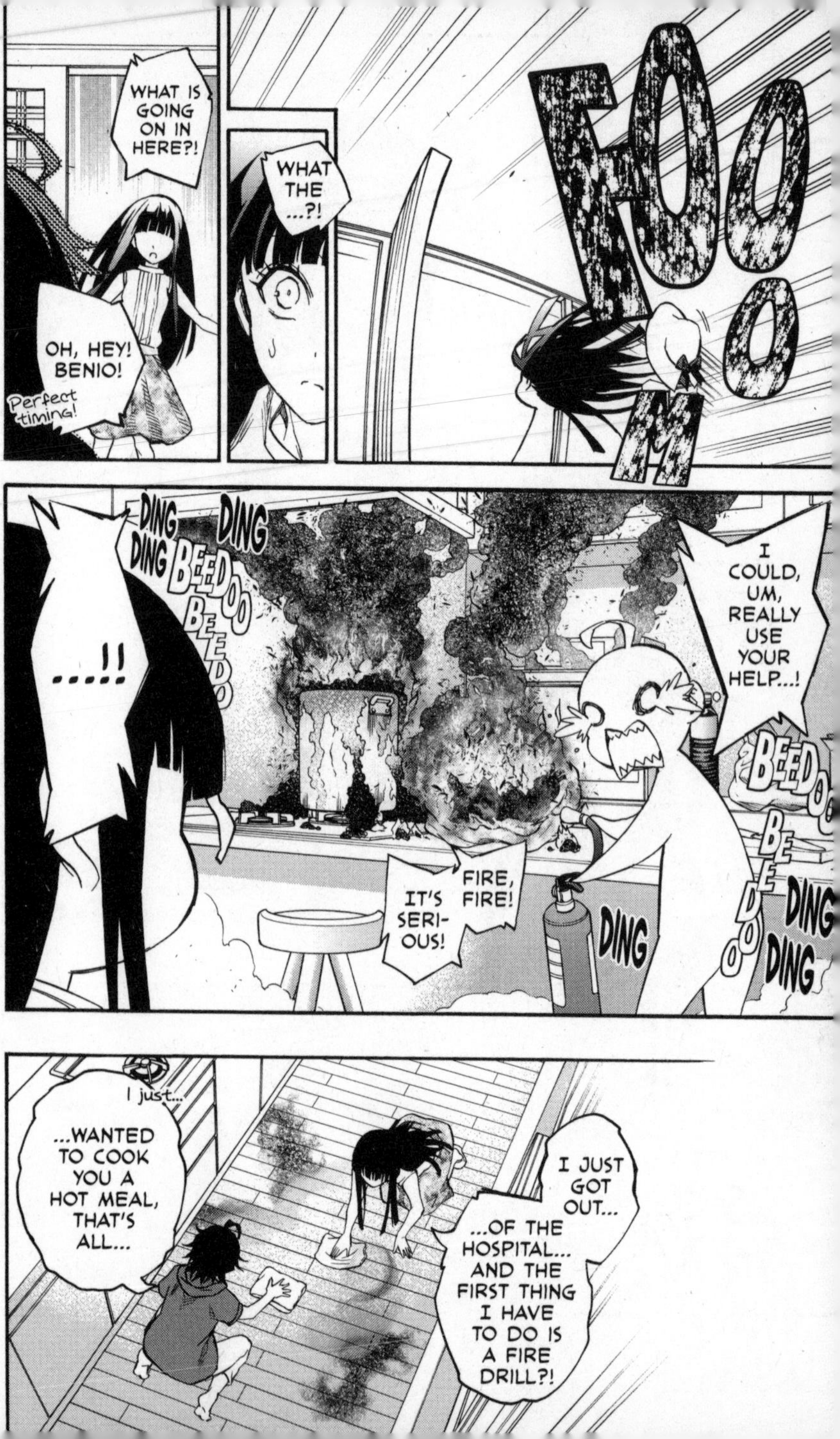
FOOOM
WHAT THE ...?!
WHAT IS GOING ON IN HERE?!
OH, HEY! BENIO!
Perfect timing!
I COULD, UM, REALLY USE YOUR HELP...!
DING DING BEEDOO BEEDOO
DING DING BEEDOO BEEDOO
...!!
BEEDOO BEEDOO DING DING
DING
FIRE, FIRE!
IT'S SERIOUS!
I JUST GOT OUT...
...OF THE HOSPITAL... AND THE FIRST THING I HAVE TO DO IS A FIRE DRILL?!
I just...
...WANTED TO COOK YOU A HOT MEAL, THAT'S ALL...

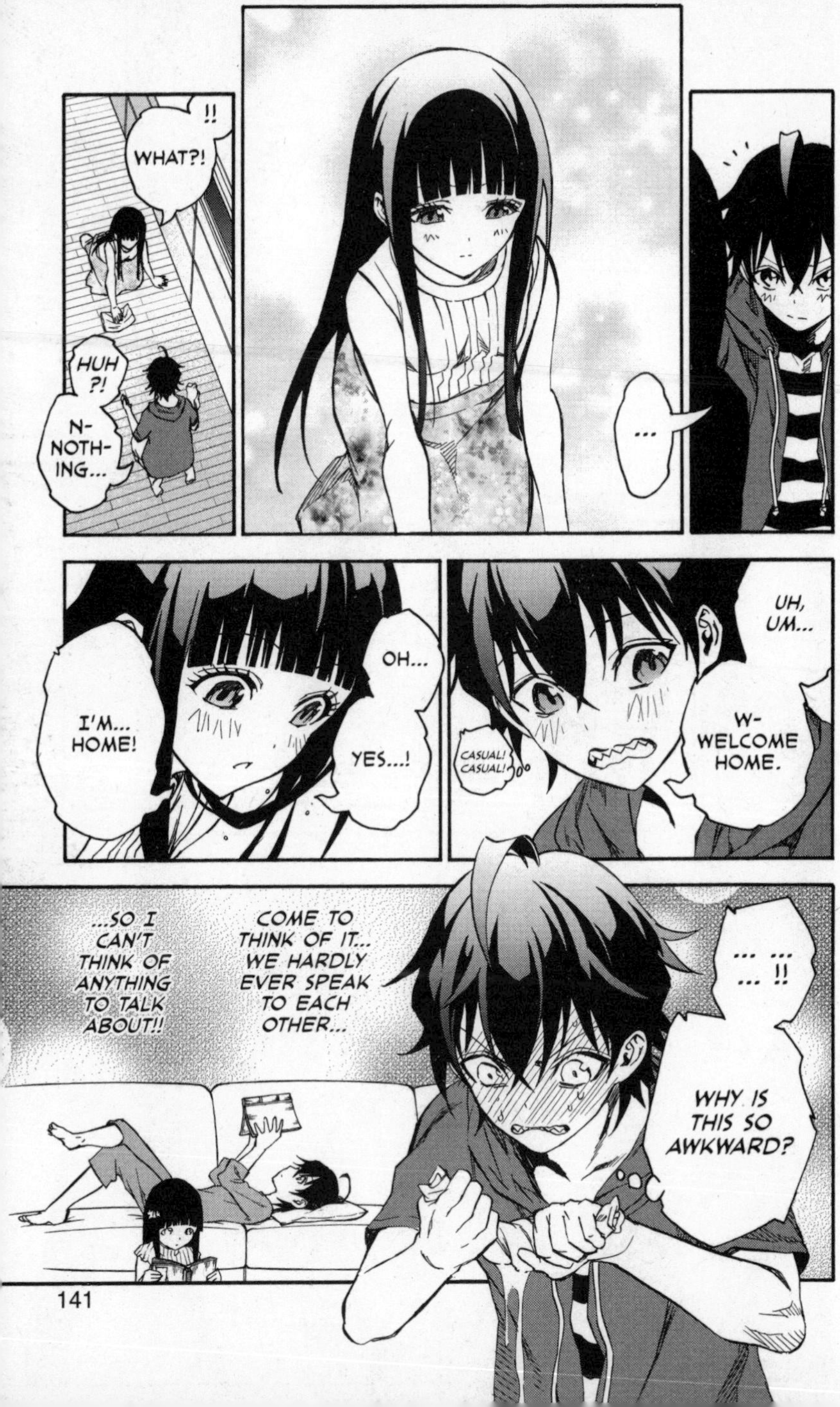
...
!!
WHAT?!
HUH?!
N-NOTHING...
UH, UM...
W-WELCOME HOME.
CASUAL! CASUAL!
OH...
YES...!
I'M... HOME!
... ... !!
WHY IS THIS SO AWKWARD?
COME TO THINK OF IT... WE HARDLY EVER SPEAK TO EACH OTHER...
...SO I CAN'T THINK OF ANYTHING TO TALK ABOUT!!

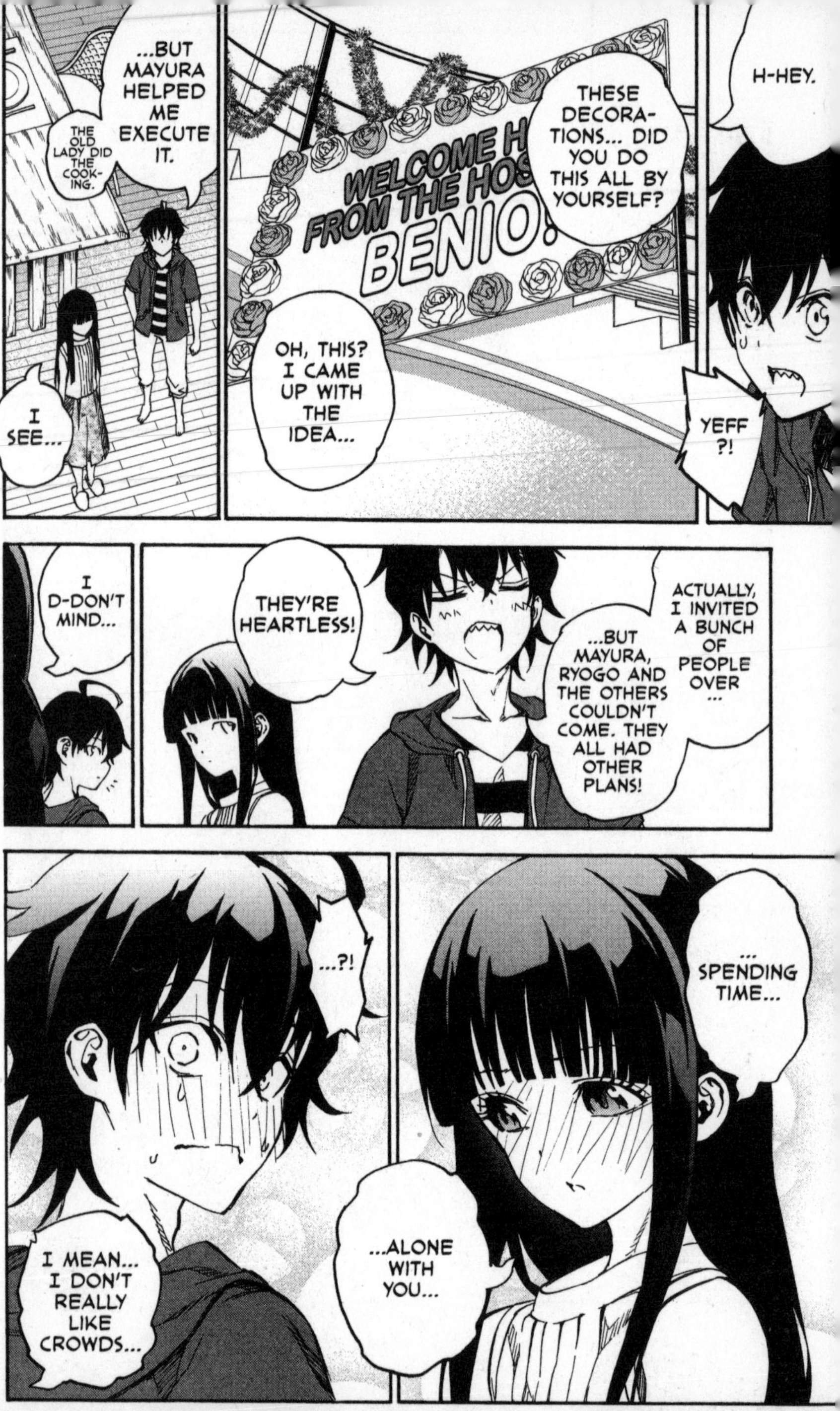
H-HEY.
YEFF ?!
THESE DECORATIONS... DID YOU DO THIS ALL BY YOURSELF?
WELCOME H
FROM THE HOS
BENIO!
OH, THIS? I CAME UP WITH THE IDEA...
...BUT MAYURA HELPED ME EXECUTE IT.
THE OLD LADY DID THE COOKING.
I SEE...
ACTUALLY, I INVITED A BUNCH OF PEOPLE OVER...
...BUT MAYURA, RYOGO AND THE OTHERS COULDN'T COME. THEY ALL HAD OTHER PLANS!
THEY'RE HEARTLESS!
I D-DON'T MIND...
...SPENDING TIME...
...ALONE WITH YOU...
...?!
I MEAN... I DON'T REALLY LIKE CROWDS...

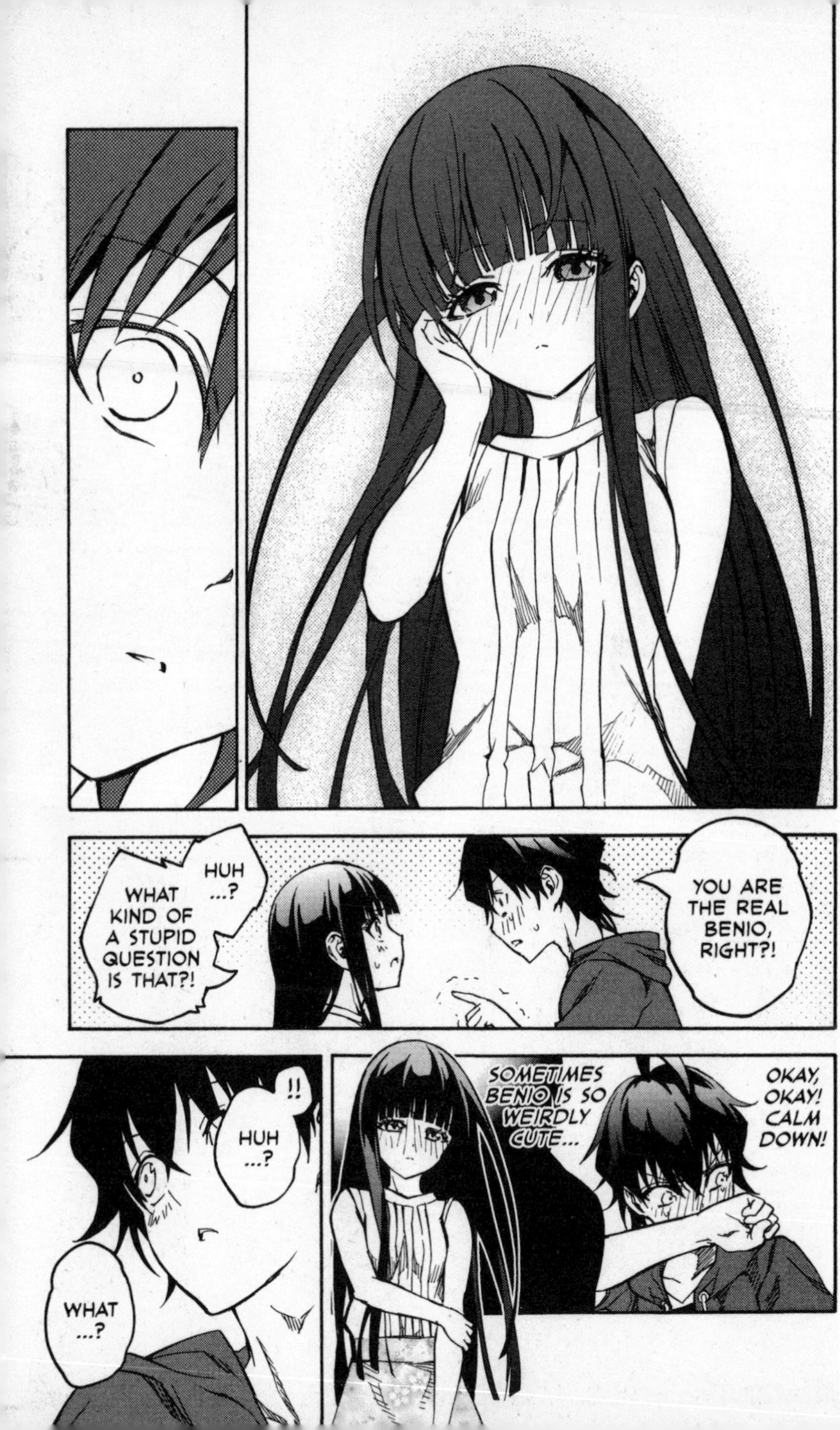
YOU ARE THE REAL BENIO, RIGHT?!
HUH ...?
WHAT KIND OF A STUPID QUESTION IS THAT?!
OKAY, OKAY! CALM DOWN!
SOMETIMES BENIO IS SO WEIRDLY CUTE...
!!
HUH ...?
WHAT ...?

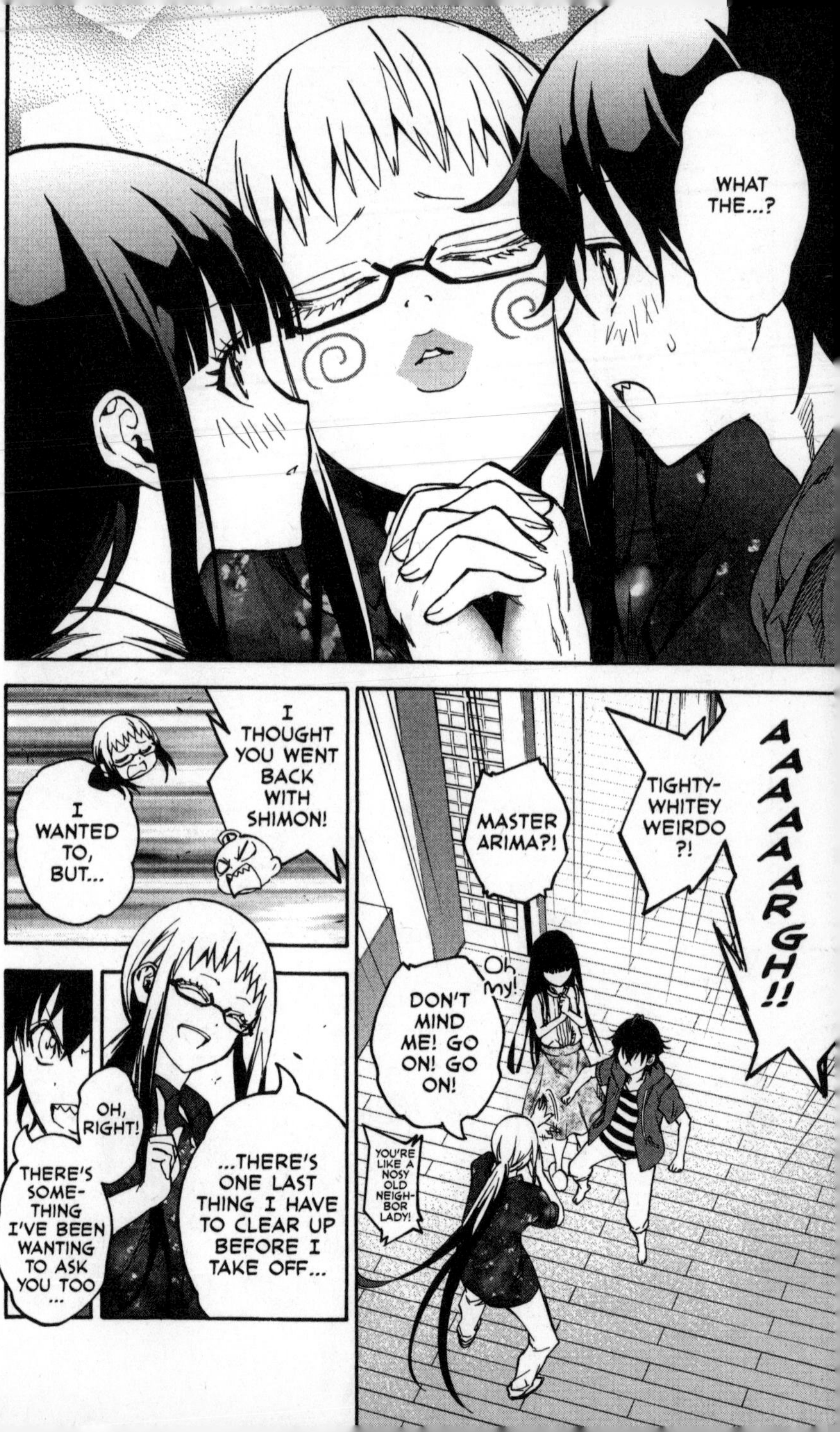
WHAT THE...?
AAAAARGH!!
TIGHTY-WHITEY WEIRDO?!
MASTER ARIMA?!
Oh my!
DON'T MIND ME! GO ON! GO ON!
YOU'RE LIKE A NOSY OLD NEIGHBOR LADY!
I THOUGHT YOU WENT BACK WITH SHIMON!
I WANTED TO, BUT...
...THERE'S ONE LAST THING I HAVE TO CLEAR UP BEFORE I TAKE OFF...
OH, RIGHT!
THERE'S SOMETHING I'VE BEEN WANTING TO ASK YOU TOO...

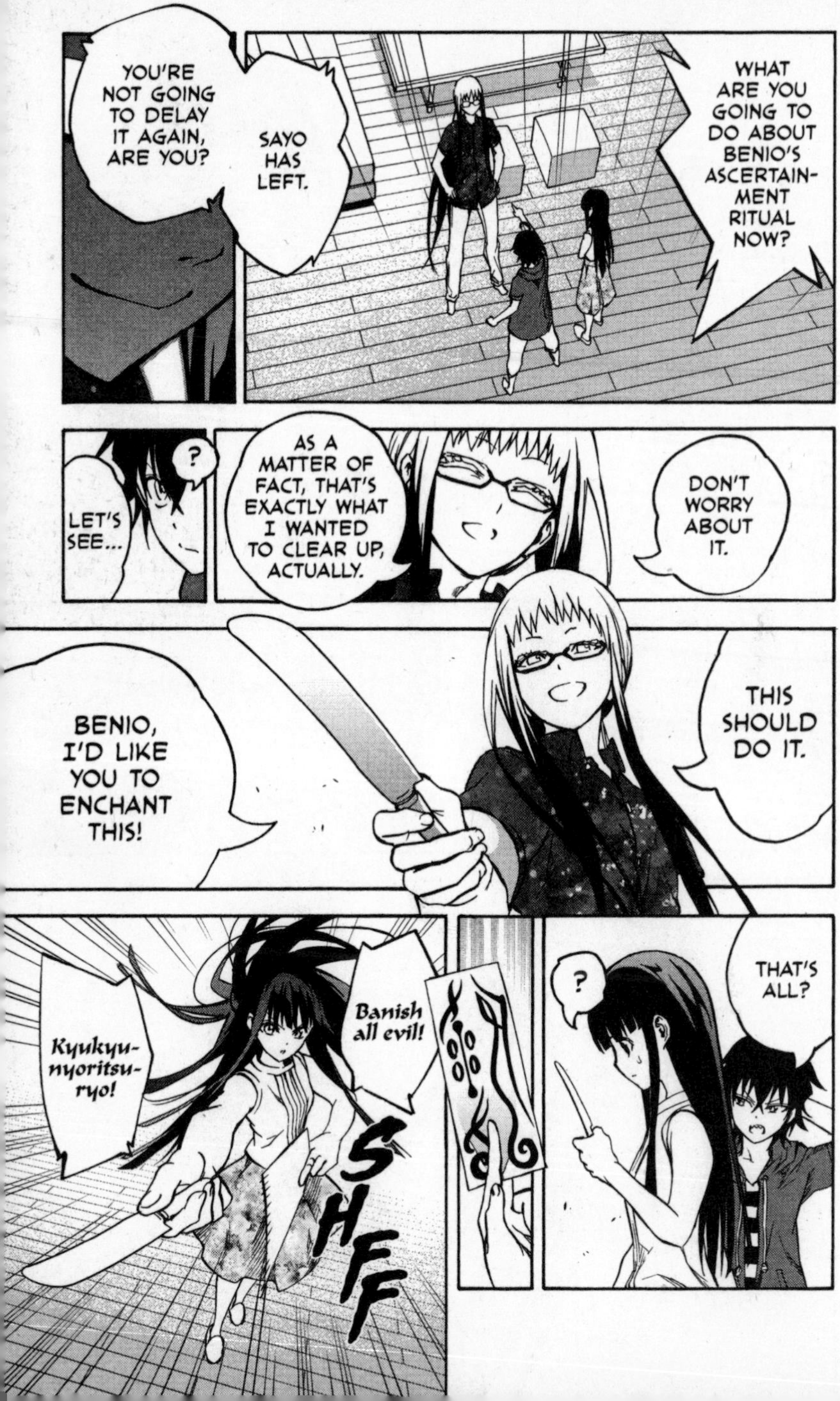
WHAT ARE YOU GOING TO DO ABOUT BENIO'S ASCERTAINMENT RITUAL NOW?
SAYO HAS LEFT.
YOU'RE NOT GOING TO DELAY IT AGAIN, ARE YOU?
DON'T WORRY ABOUT IT.
AS A MATTER OF FACT, THAT'S EXACTLY WHAT I WANTED TO CLEAR UP, ACTUALLY.
?
LET'S SEE...
THIS SHOULD DO IT.
BENIO, I'D LIKE YOU TO ENCHANT THIS!
THAT'S ALL?
?
Banish all evil!
Kyukyu-nyoritsu-ryo!
SHFF

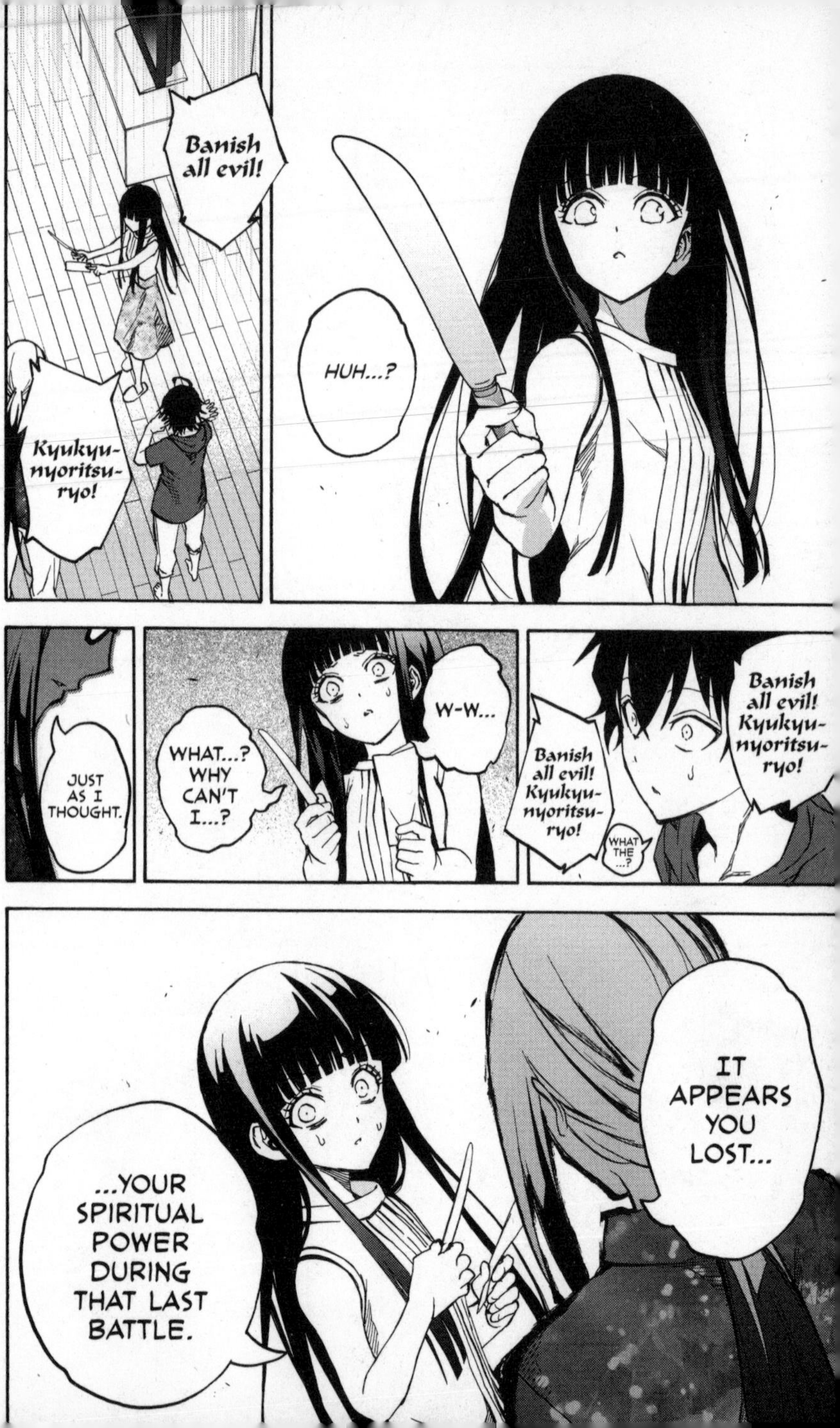
HUH...?
Banish all evil!
Kyukyu-nyoritsu-ryo!
Banish all evil! Kyukyu-nyoritsu-ryo!
Banish all evil! Kyukyu-nyoritsu-ryo!
WHAT THE ...?
W-W...
WHAT...? WHY CAN'T I...?
JUST AS I THOUGHT.
IT APPEARS YOU LOST...
...YOUR SPIRITUAL POWER DURING THAT LAST BATTLE.

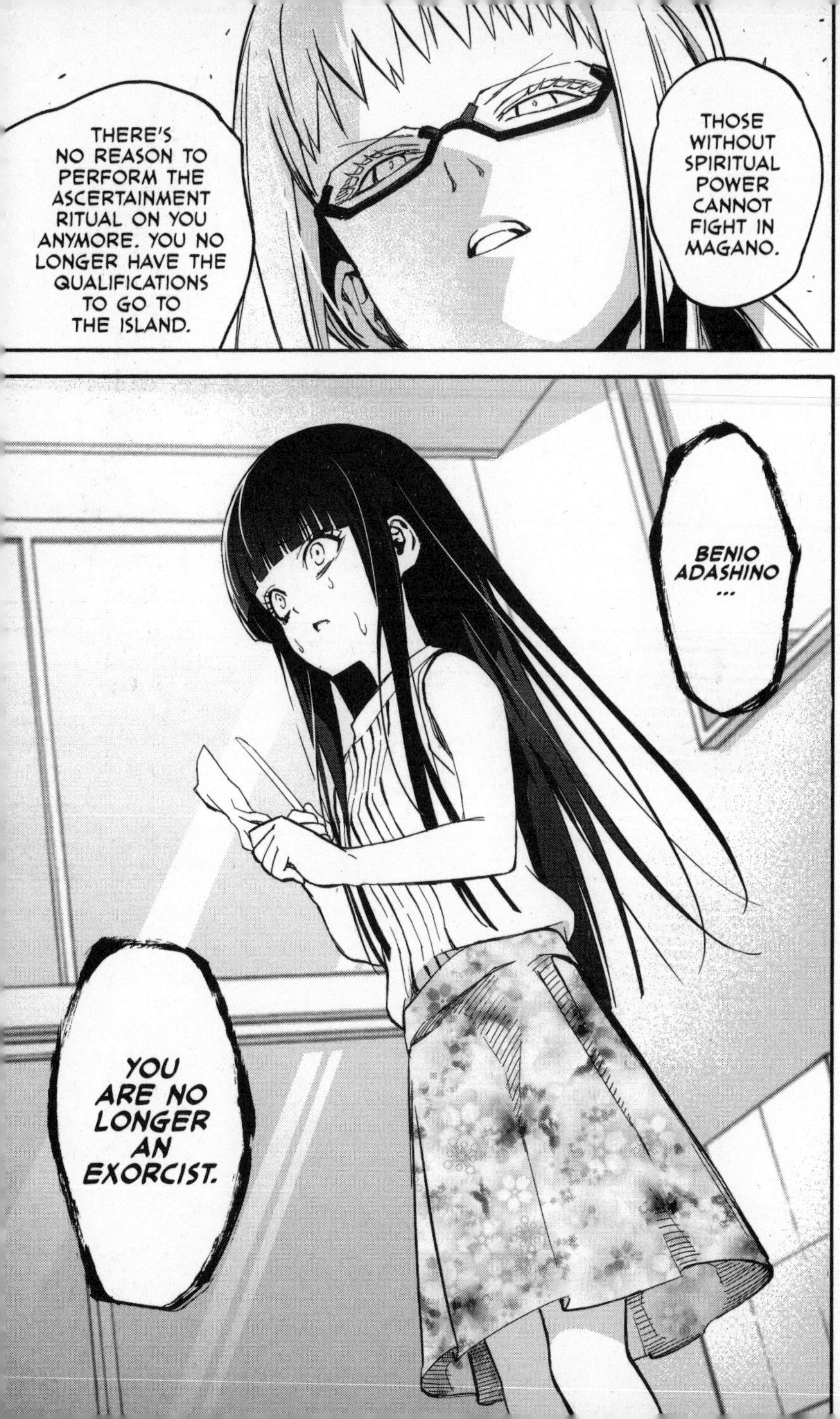
THOSE WITHOUT SPIRITUAL POWER CANNOT FIGHT IN MAGANO.
THERE'S NO REASON TO PERFORM THE ASCERTAINMENT RITUAL ON YOU ANYMORE. YOU NO LONGER HAVE THE QUALIFICATIONS TO GO TO THE ISLAND.
BENIO ADASHINO...
YOU ARE NO LONGER AN EXORCIST.

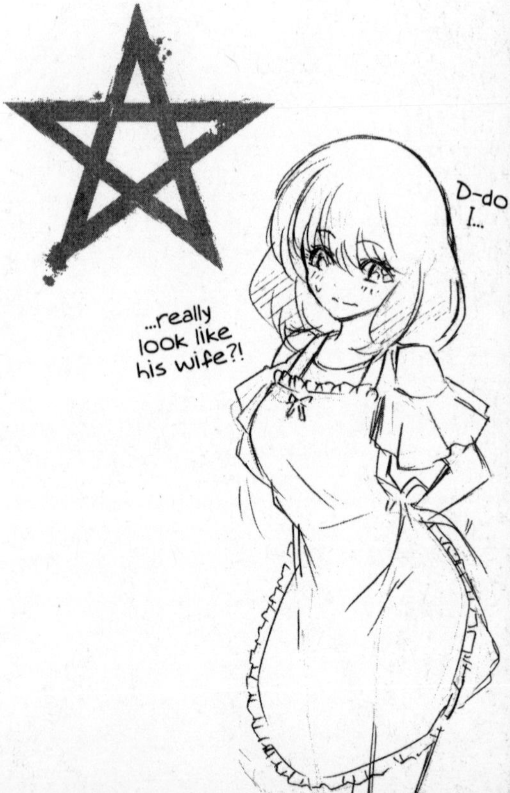
D-do I...
...really look like his wife?!

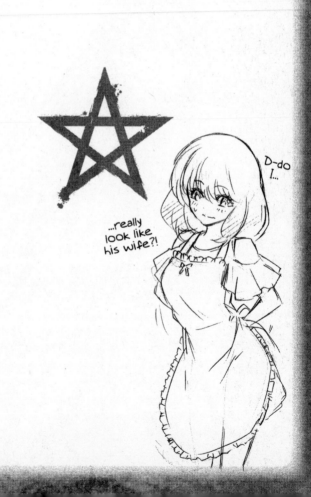

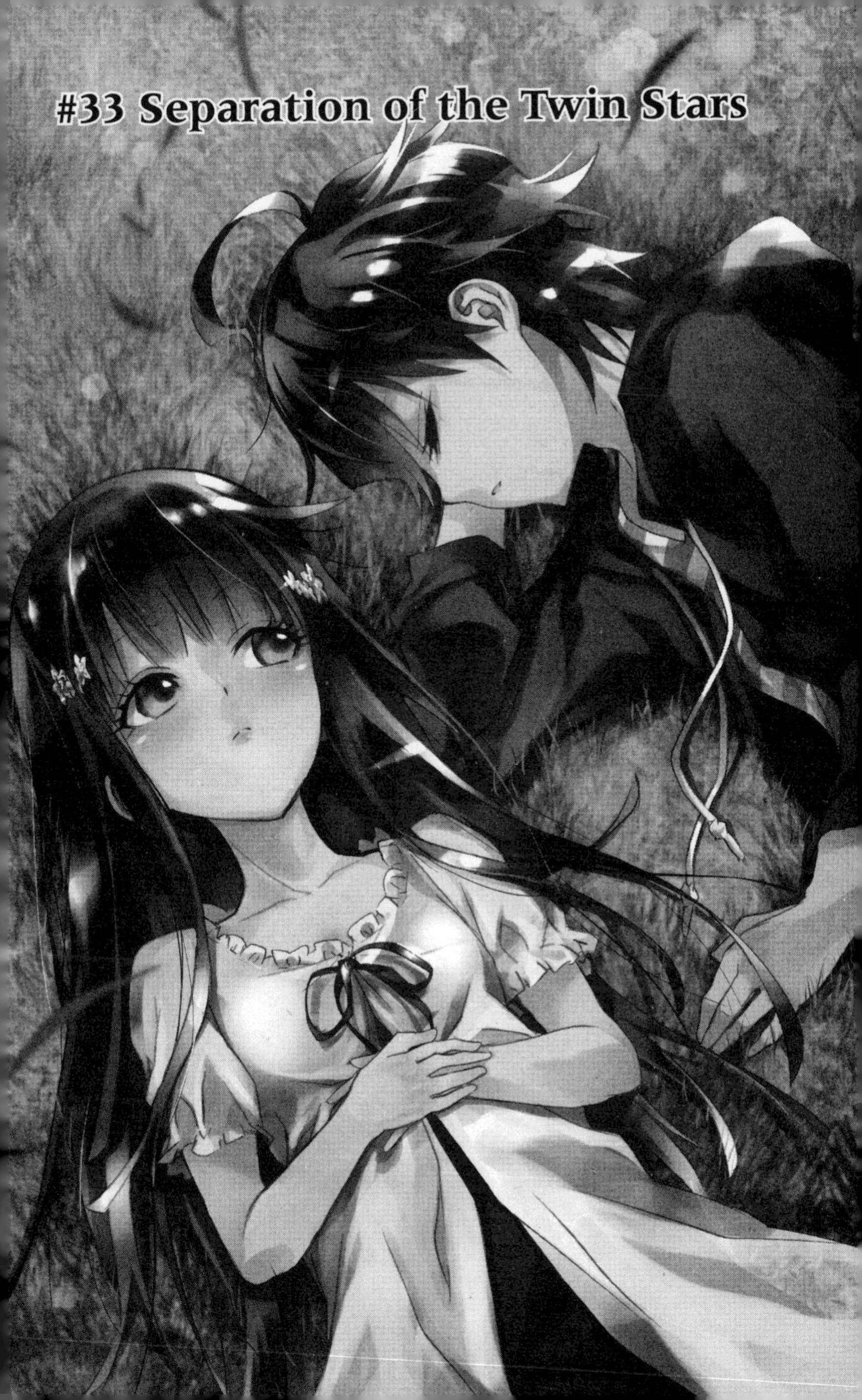
#33 Separation of the Twin Stars

Twin Star Exorcists
ONMYOJI

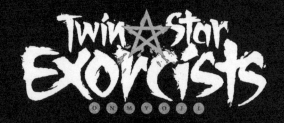

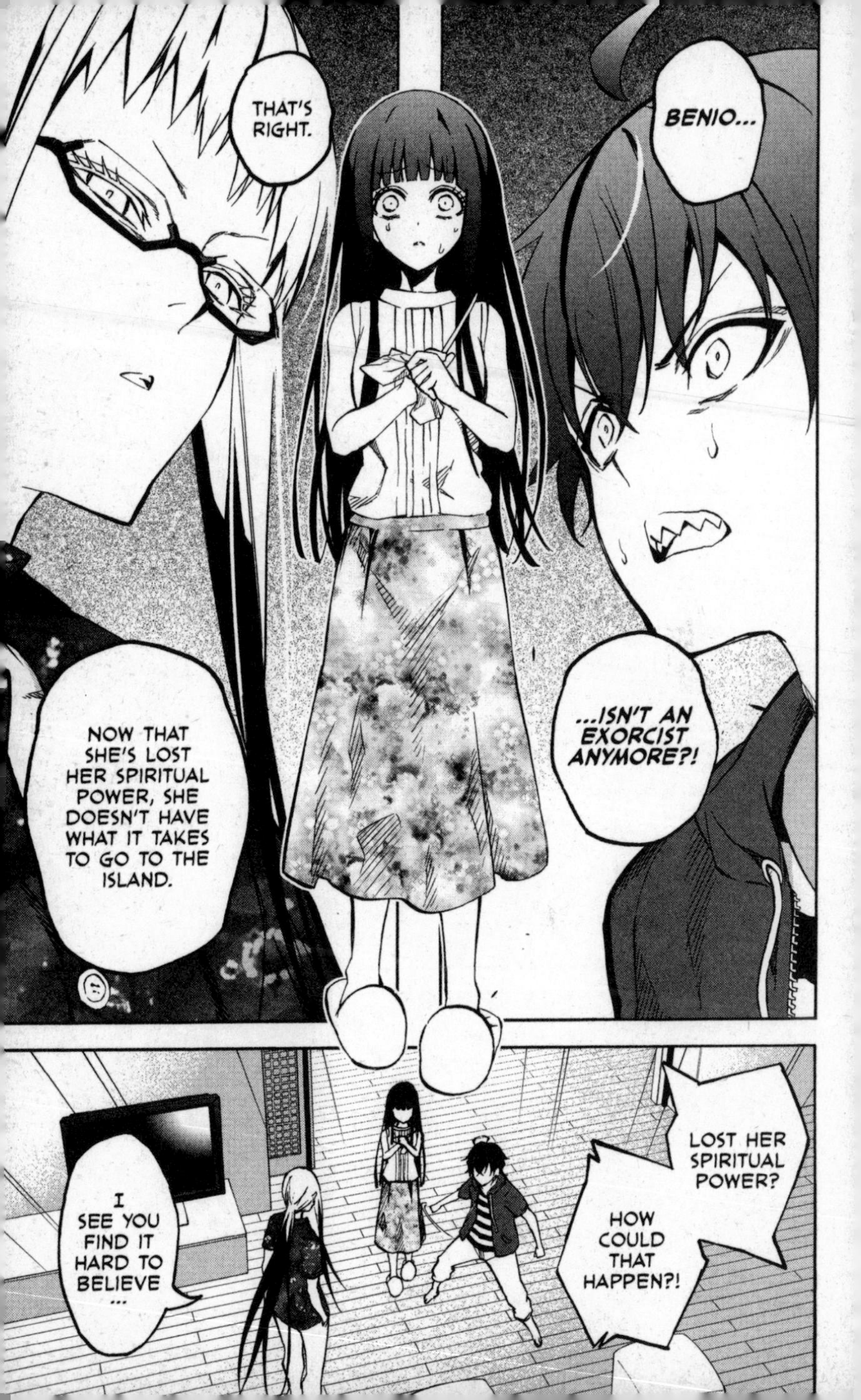
BENIO...
...ISN'T AN EXORCIST ANYMORE?!
THAT'S RIGHT.
NOW THAT SHE'S LOST HER SPIRITUAL POWER, SHE DOESN'T HAVE WHAT IT TAKES TO GO TO THE ISLAND.
LOST HER SPIRITUAL POWER?
HOW COULD THAT HAPPEN?!
I SEE YOU FIND IT HARD TO BELIEVE...

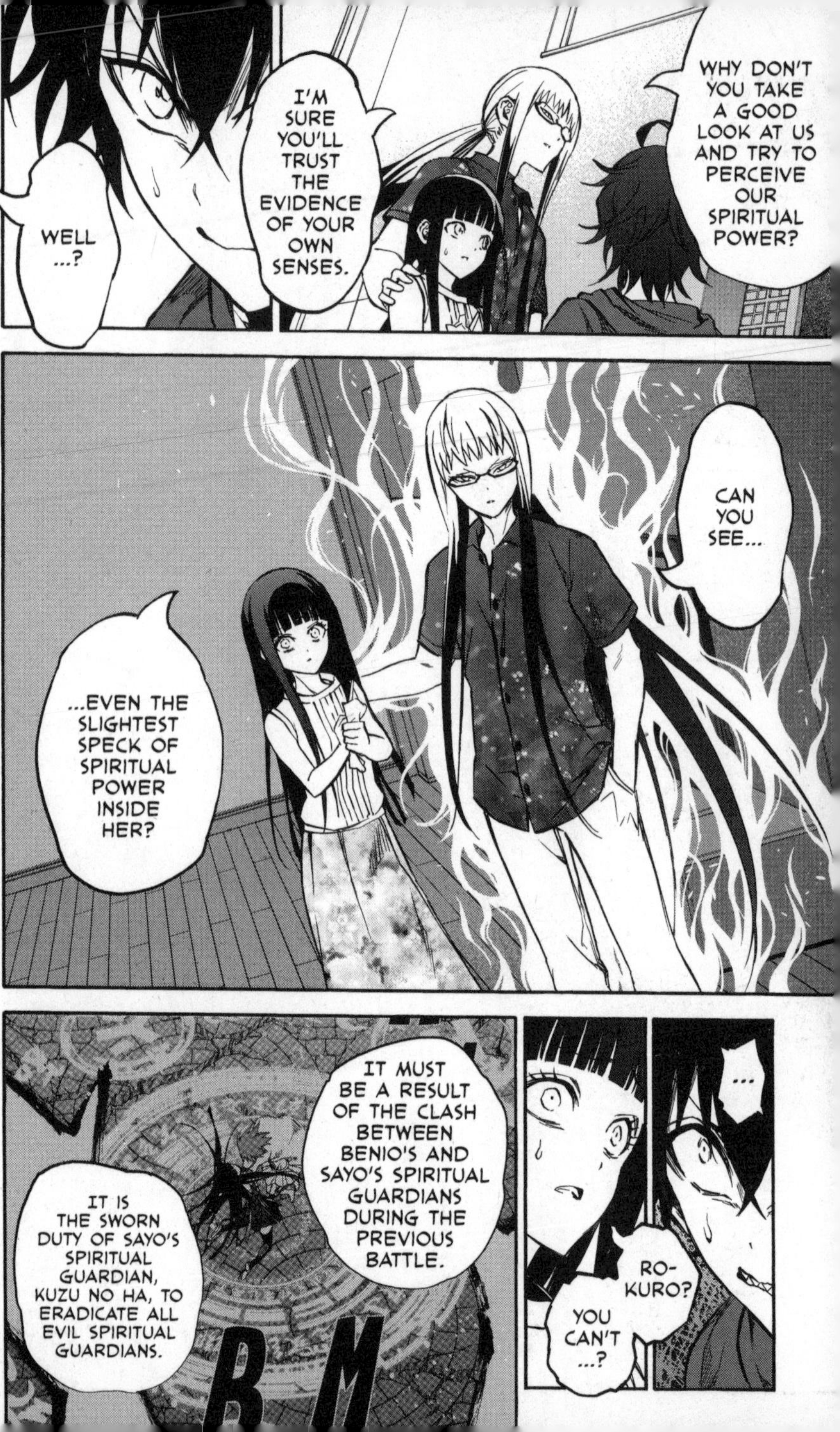
WHY DON'T YOU TAKE A GOOD LOOK AT US AND TRY TO PERCEIVE OUR SPIRITUAL POWER?
I'M SURE YOU'LL TRUST THE EVIDENCE OF YOUR OWN SENSES.
WELL ...?
CAN YOU SEE...
...EVEN THE SLIGHTEST SPECK OF SPIRITUAL POWER INSIDE HER?
...
RO-KURO?
YOU CAN'T ...?
IT MUST BE A RESULT OF THE CLASH BETWEEN BENIO'S AND SAYO'S SPIRITUAL GUARDIANS DURING THE PREVIOUS BATTLE.
IT IS THE SWORN DUTY OF SAYO'S SPIRITUAL GUARDIAN, KUZU NO HA, TO ERADICATE ALL EVIL SPIRITUAL GUARDIANS.

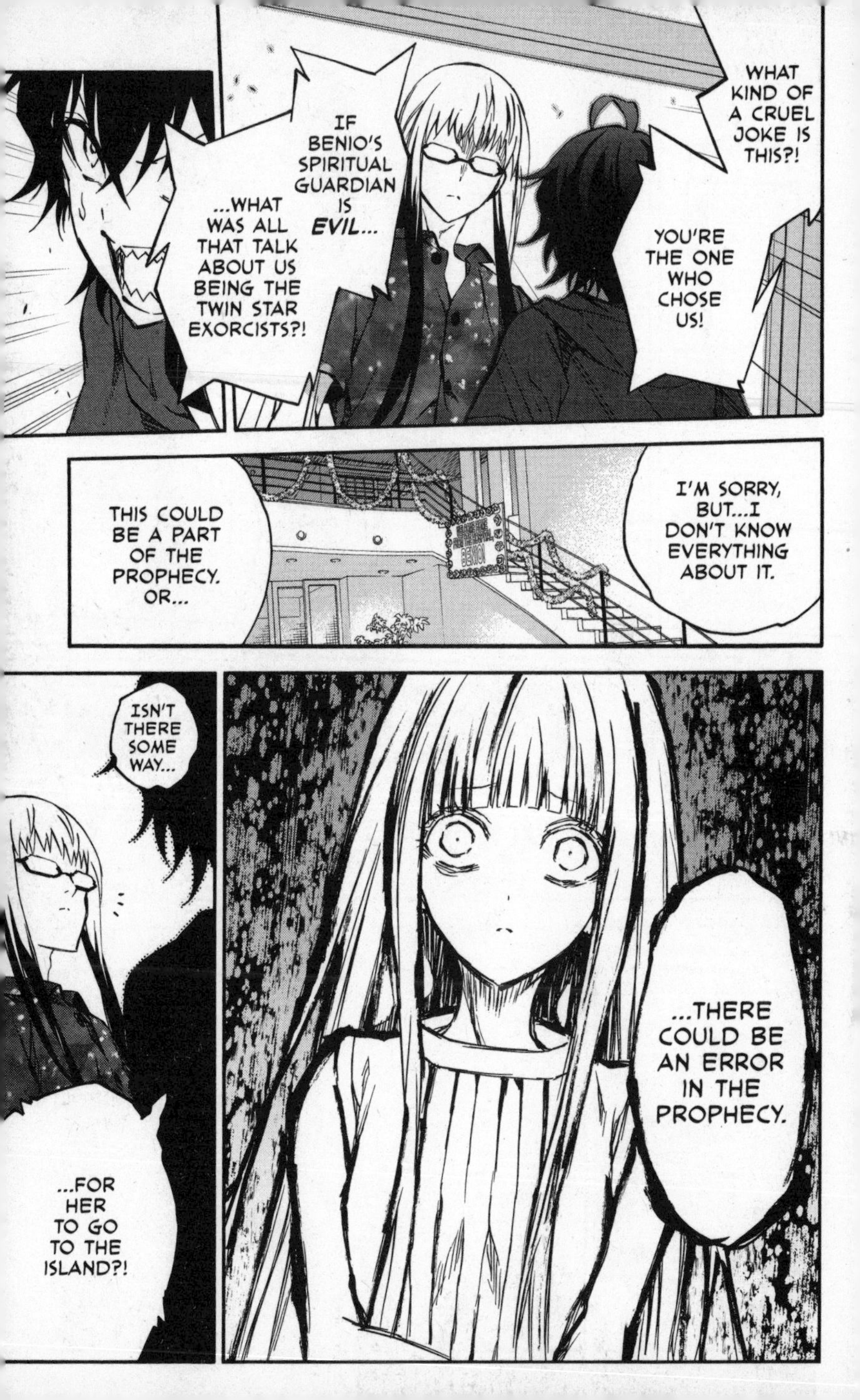
WHAT KIND OF A CRUEL JOKE IS THIS?!
YOU'RE THE ONE WHO CHOSE US!
IF BENIO'S SPIRITUAL GUARDIAN IS *EVIL*...
...WHAT WAS ALL THAT TALK ABOUT US BEING THE TWIN STAR EXORCISTS?!
I'M SORRY, BUT...I DON'T KNOW EVERYTHING ABOUT IT.
THIS COULD BE A PART OF THE PROPHECY. OR...
...THERE COULD BE AN ERROR IN THE PROPHECY.
ISN'T THERE SOME WAY...
...FOR HER TO GO TO THE ISLAND?!

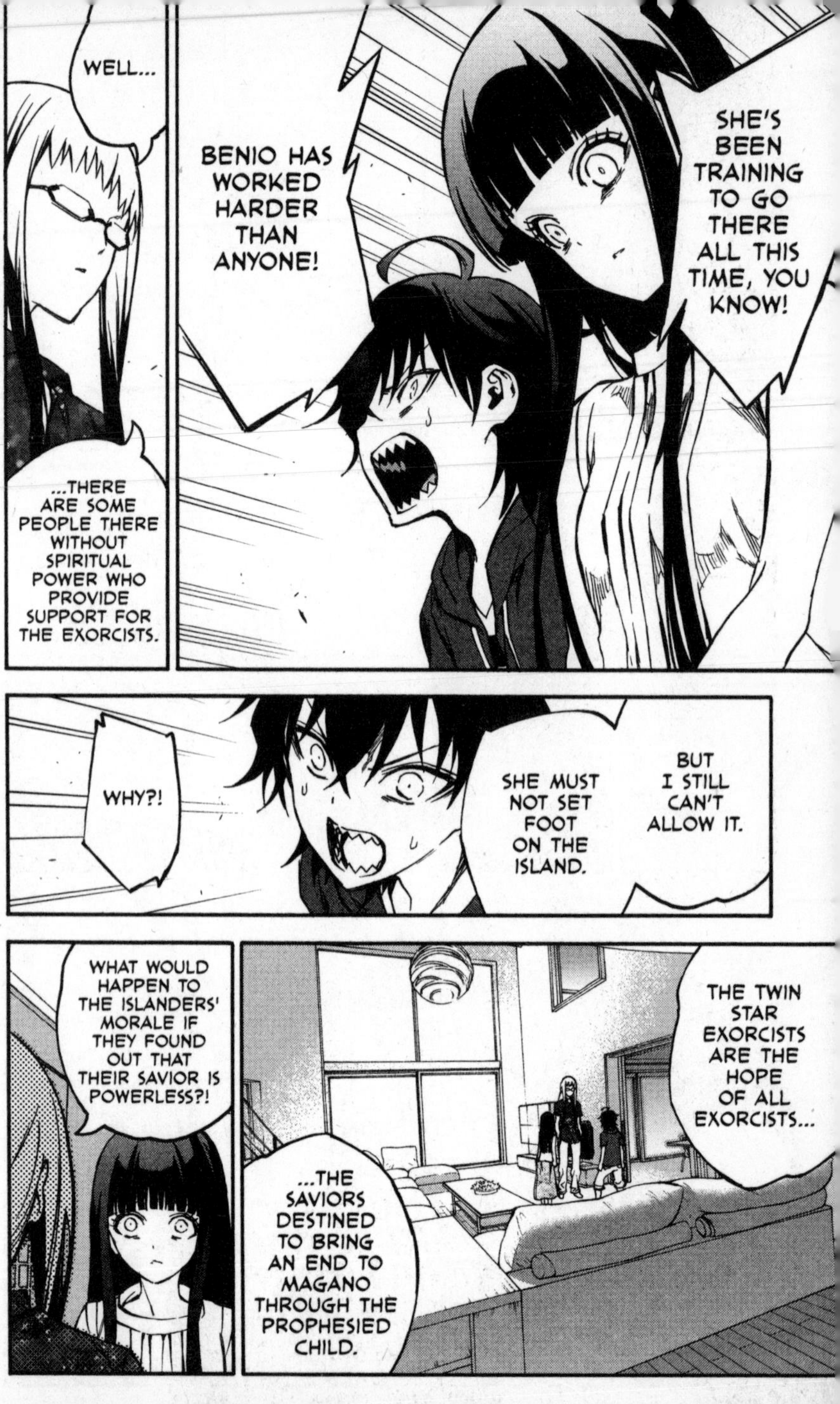
SHE'S BEEN TRAINING TO GO THERE ALL THIS TIME, YOU KNOW!
BENIO HAS WORKED HARDER THAN ANYONE!
WELL...
...THERE ARE SOME PEOPLE THERE WITHOUT SPIRITUAL POWER WHO PROVIDE SUPPORT FOR THE EXORCISTS.
BUT I STILL CAN'T ALLOW IT.
SHE MUST NOT SET FOOT ON THE ISLAND.
WHY?!
THE TWIN STAR EXORCISTS ARE THE HOPE OF ALL EXORCISTS...
...THE SAVIORS DESTINED TO BRING AN END TO MAGANO THROUGH THE PROPHESIED CHILD.
WHAT WOULD HAPPEN TO THE ISLANDERS' MORALE IF THEY FOUND OUT THAT THEIR SAVIOR IS POWERLESS?!

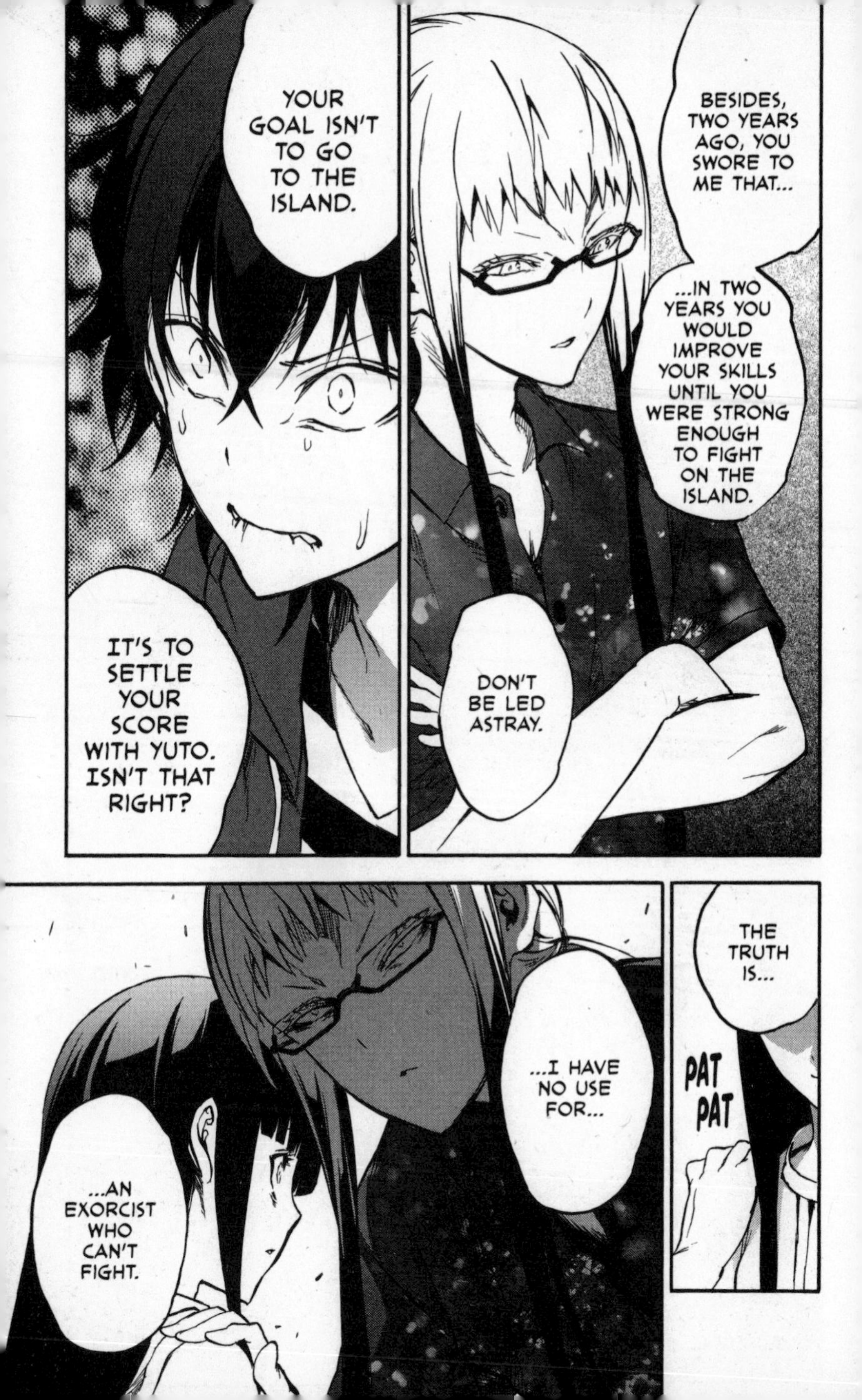
BESIDES, TWO YEARS AGO, YOU SWORE TO ME THAT...
...IN TWO YEARS YOU WOULD IMPROVE YOUR SKILLS UNTIL YOU WERE STRONG ENOUGH TO FIGHT ON THE ISLAND.
DON'T BE LED ASTRAY.
YOUR GOAL ISN'T TO GO TO THE ISLAND.
IT'S TO SETTLE YOUR SCORE WITH YUTO. ISN'T THAT RIGHT?
THE TRUTH IS...
PAT PAT
...I HAVE NO USE FOR...
...AN EXORCIST WHO CAN'T FIGHT.

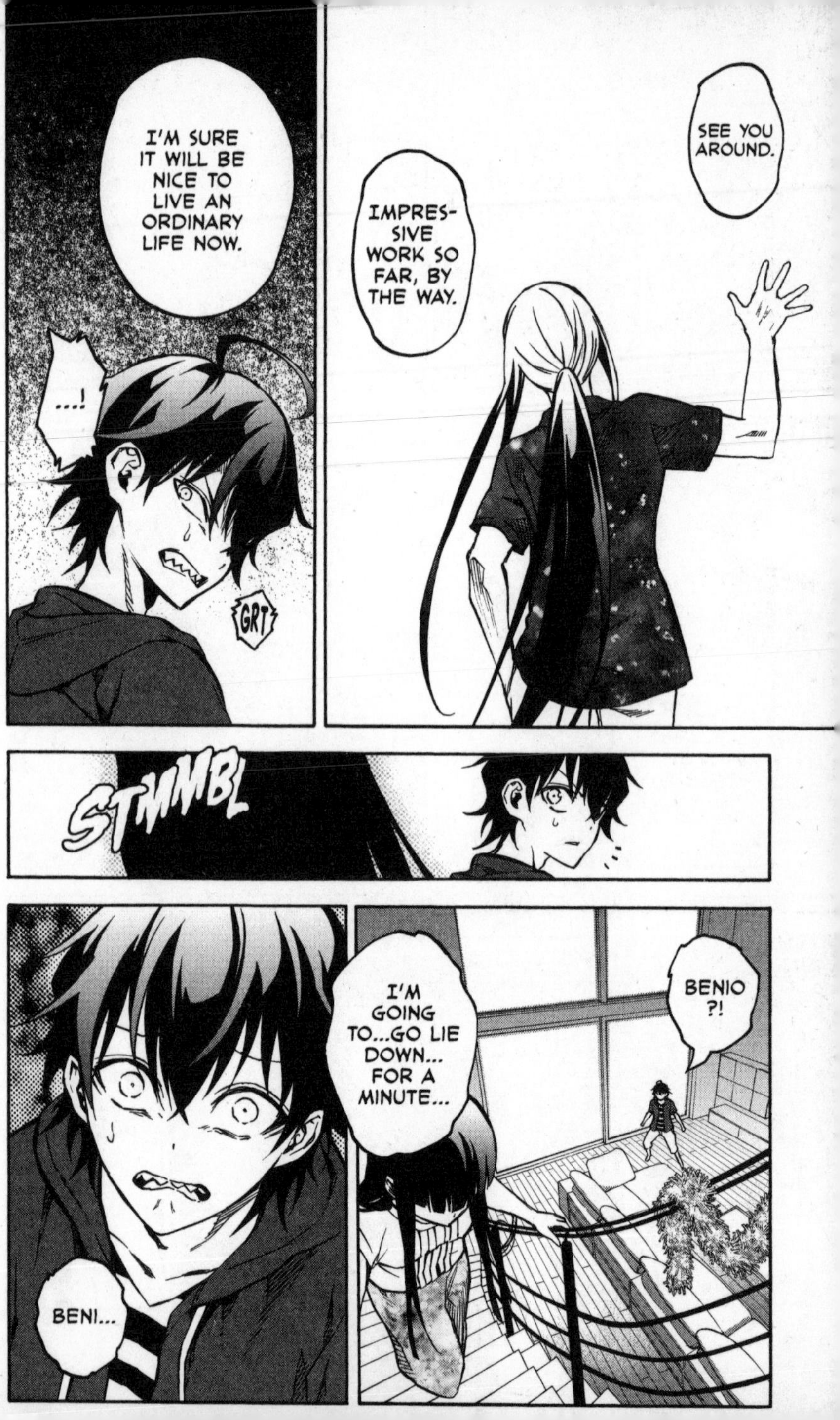
SEE YOU AROUND.
IMPRES-SIVE WORK SO FAR, BY THE WAY.
I'M SURE IT WILL BE NICE TO LIVE AN ORDINARY LIFE NOW.
...!
GRT
STMMBL
BENIO?!
I'M GOING TO...GO LIE DOWN... FOR A MINUTE...
BENI...

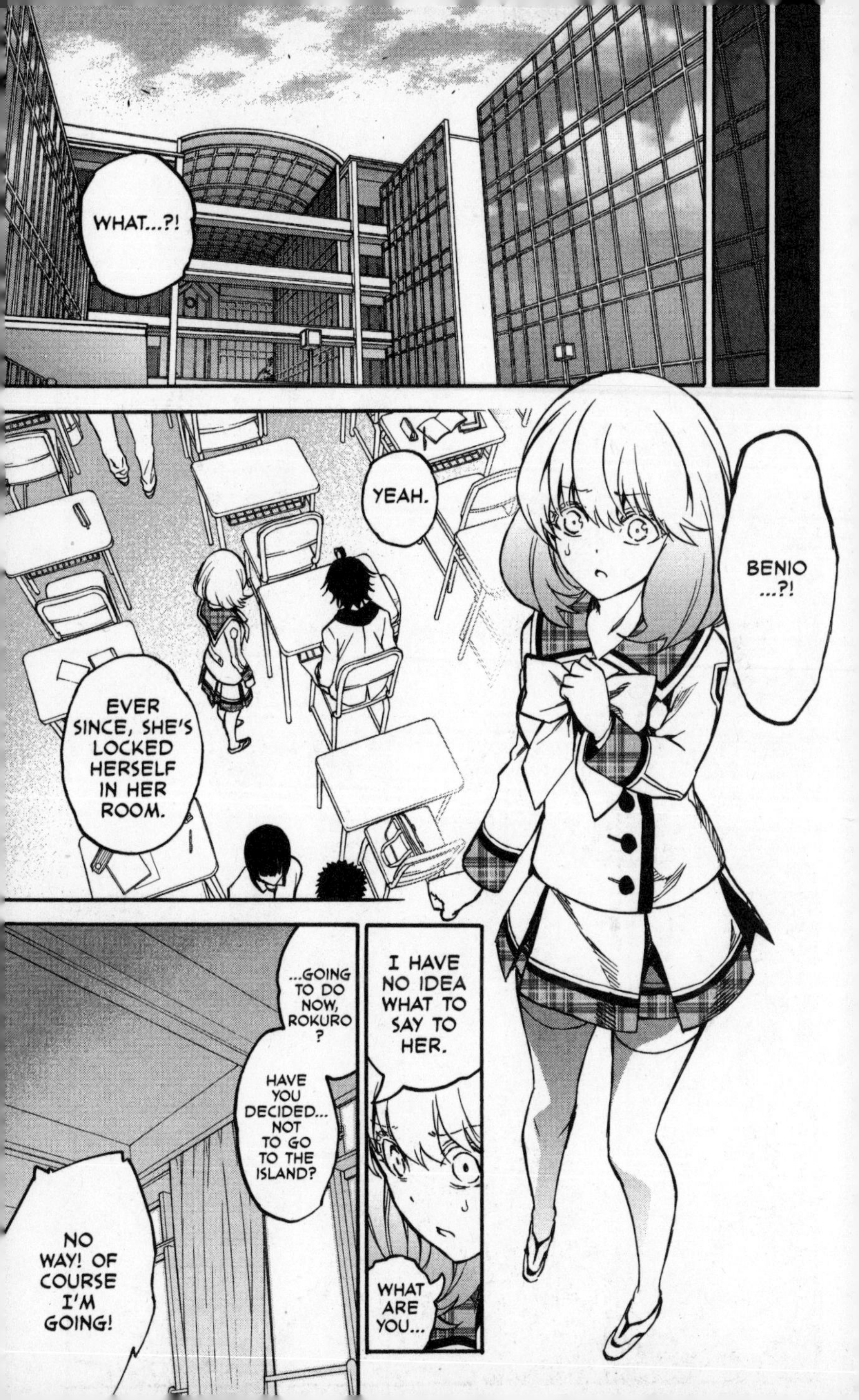
WHAT...?!
BENIO ...?!
YEAH.
EVER SINCE, SHE'S LOCKED HERSELF IN HER ROOM.
I HAVE NO IDEA WHAT TO SAY TO HER.
WHAT ARE YOU...
...GOING TO DO NOW, ROKURO?
HAVE YOU DECIDED... NOT TO GO TO THE ISLAND?
NO WAY! OF COURSE I'M GOING!

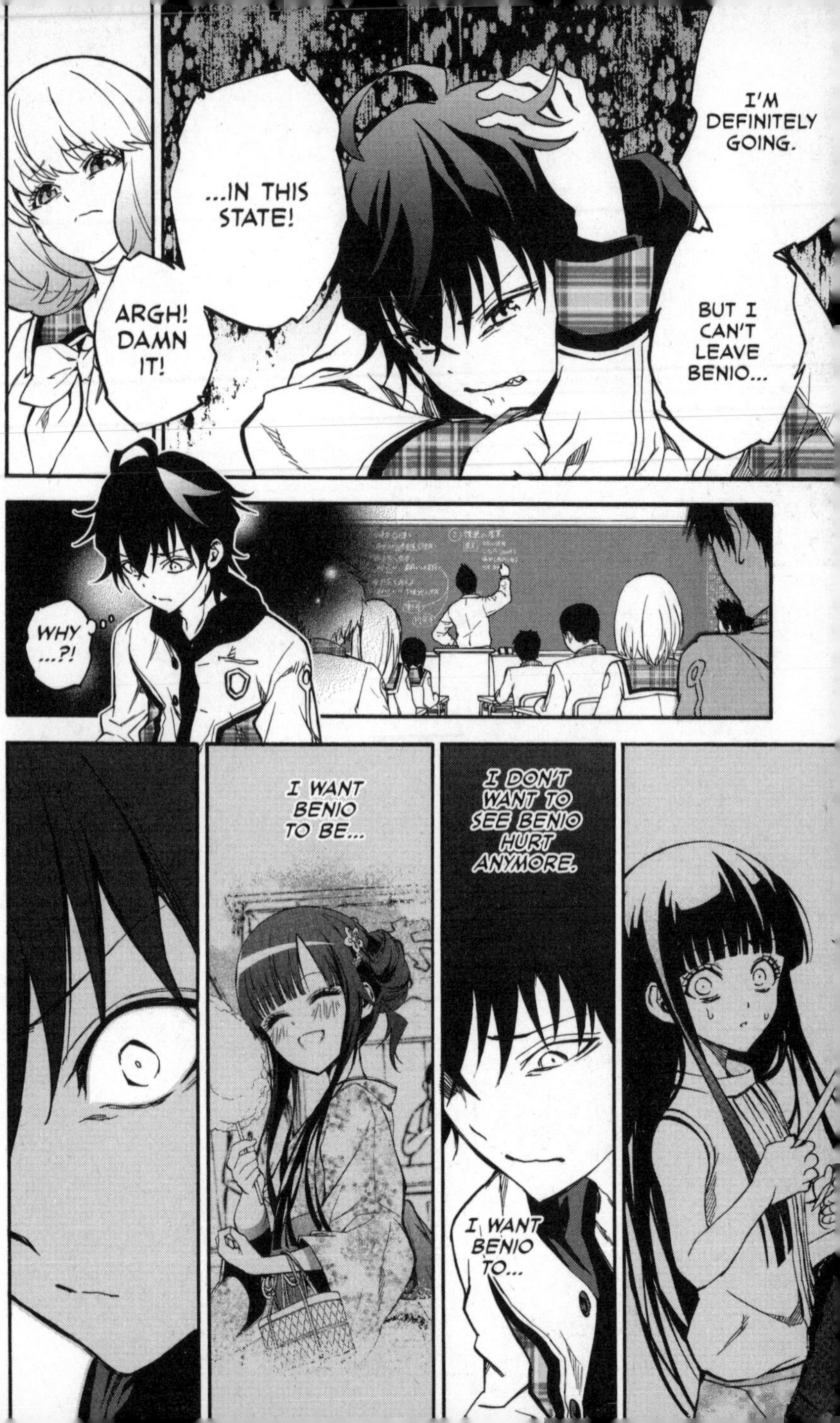
I'M DEFINITELY GOING.
BUT I CAN'T LEAVE BENIO...
...IN THIS STATE!
ARGH! DAMN IT!
WHY ...?!
I DON'T WANT TO SEE BENIO HURT ANYMORE.
I WANT BENIO TO...
I WANT BENIO TO BE...

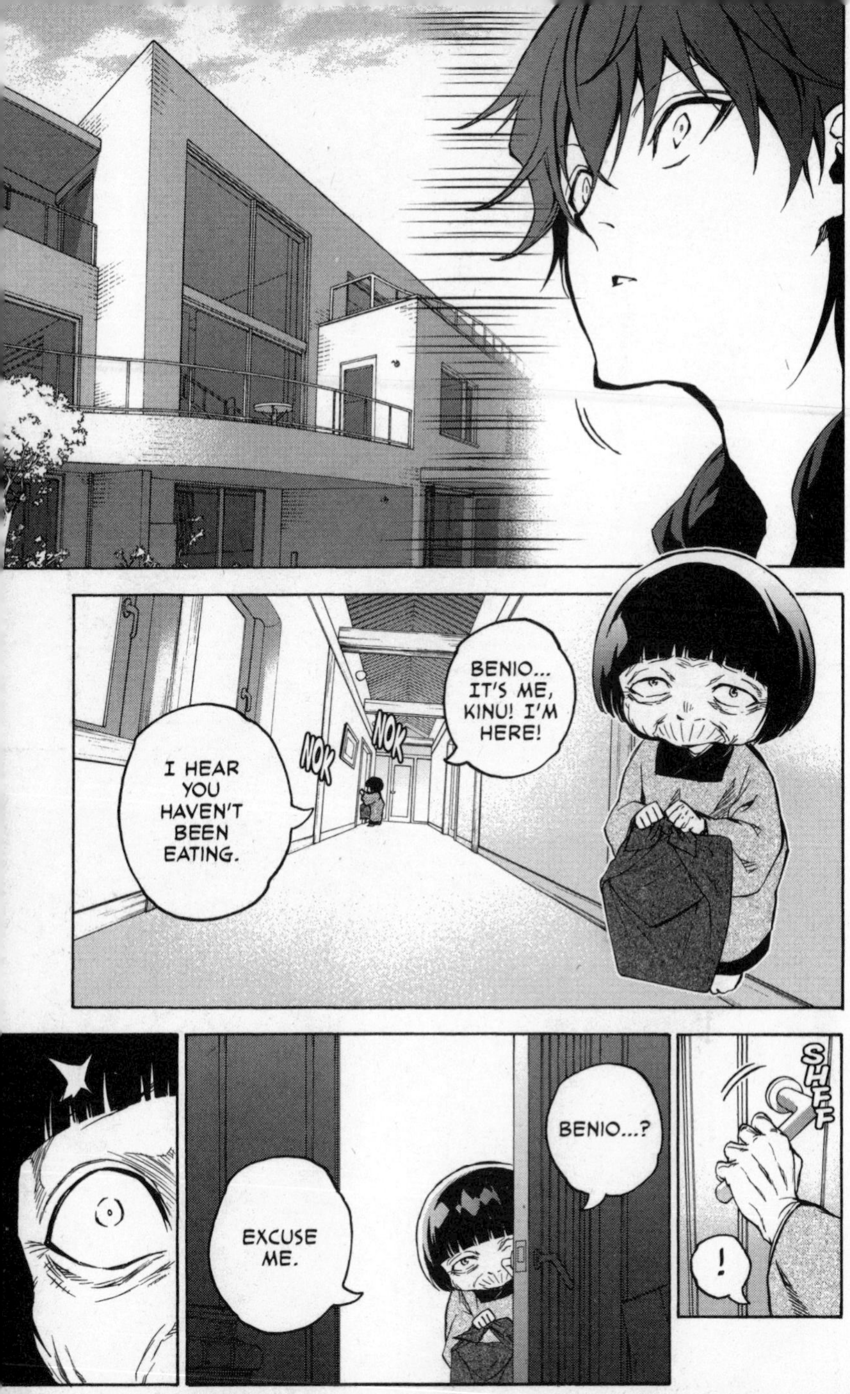
BENIO... IT'S ME, KINU! I'M HERE!
NOK
NOK
I HEAR YOU HAVEN'T BEEN EATING.
SHFF
!
BENIO...?
EXCUSE ME.

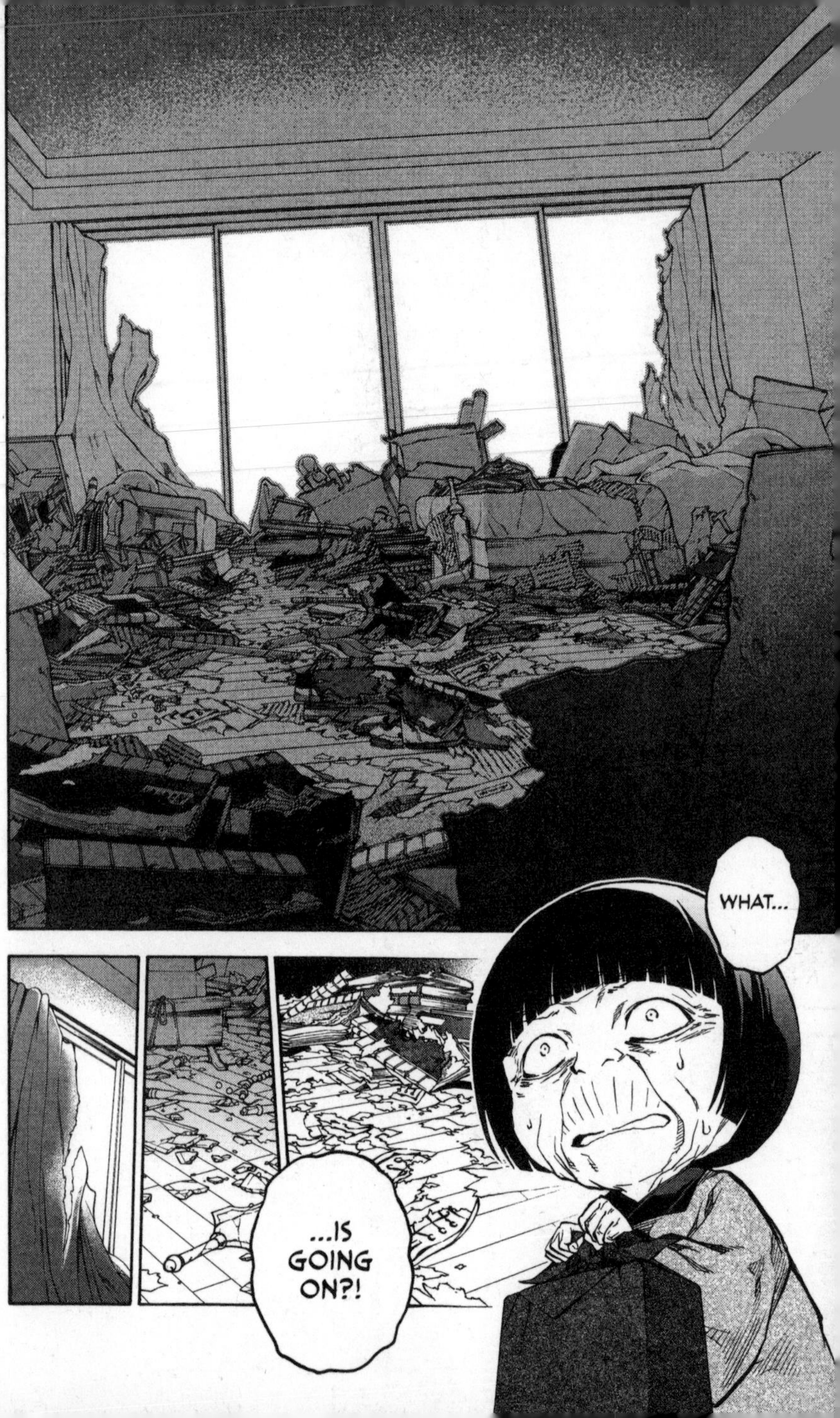
WHAT...
...IS GOING ON?!

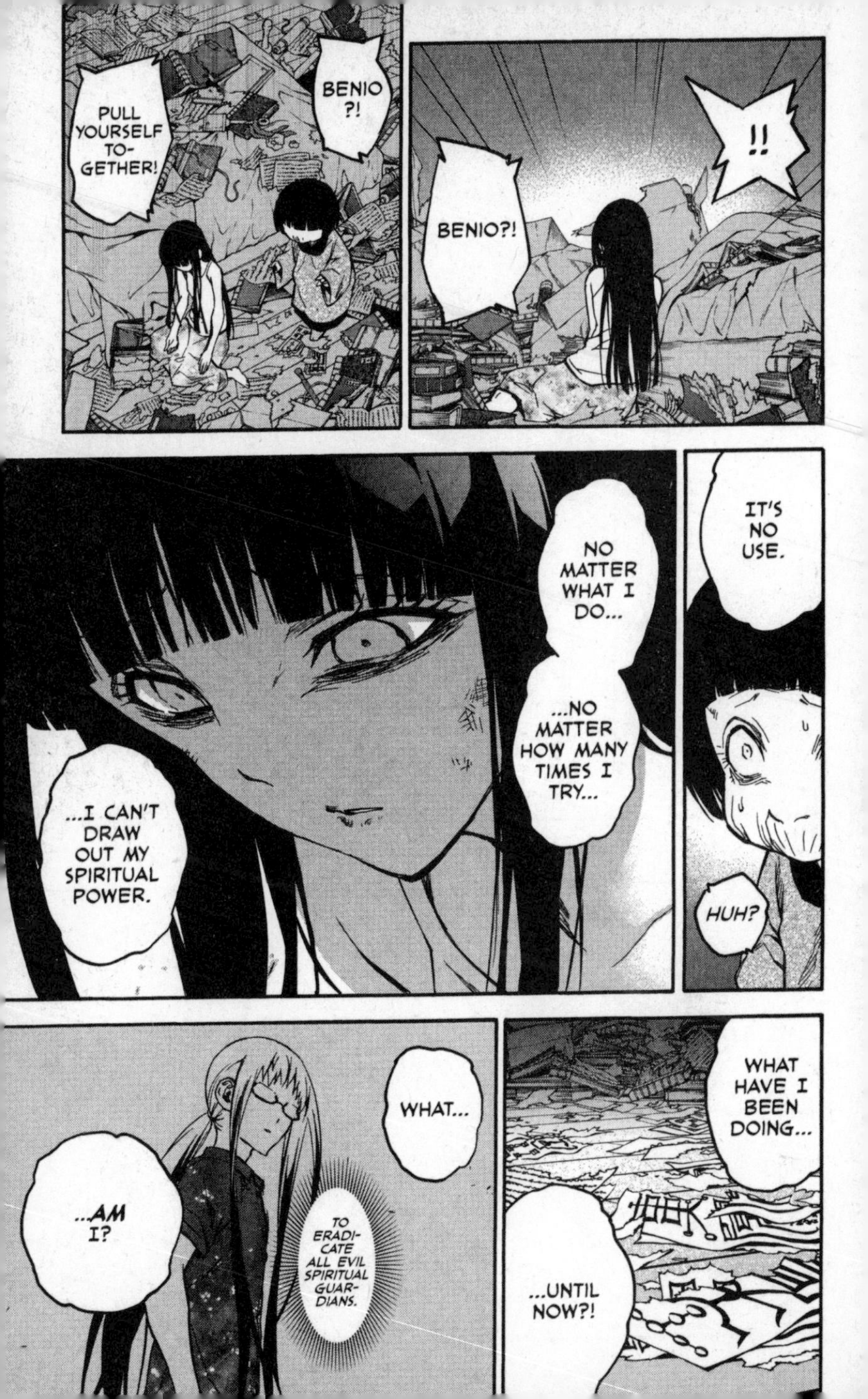
!!
BENIO?!
BENIO ?!
PULL YOURSELF TO-GETHER!
IT'S NO USE.
HUH?
NO MATTER WHAT I DO...
...NO MATTER HOW MANY TIMES I TRY...
...I CAN'T DRAW OUT MY SPIRITUAL POWER.
WHAT HAVE I BEEN DOING...
...UNTIL NOW?!
WHAT...
TO ERADI-CATE ALL EVIL SPIRITUAL GUAR-DIANS.
...AM I?

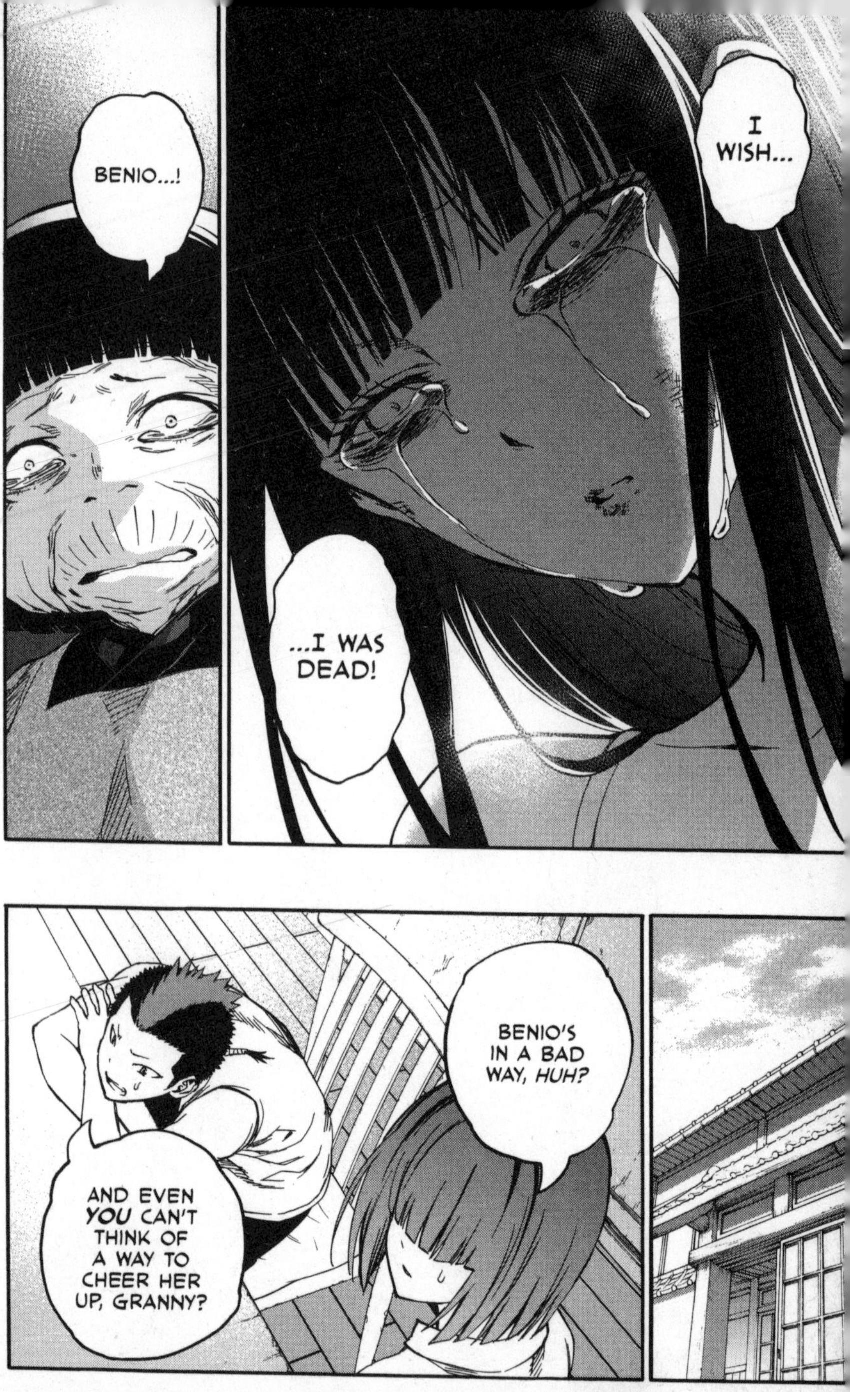
I WISH...
...I WAS DEAD!
BENIO...!
BENIO'S IN A BAD WAY, *HUH?*
AND EVEN *YOU* CAN'T THINK OF A WAY TO CHEER HER UP, GRANNY?

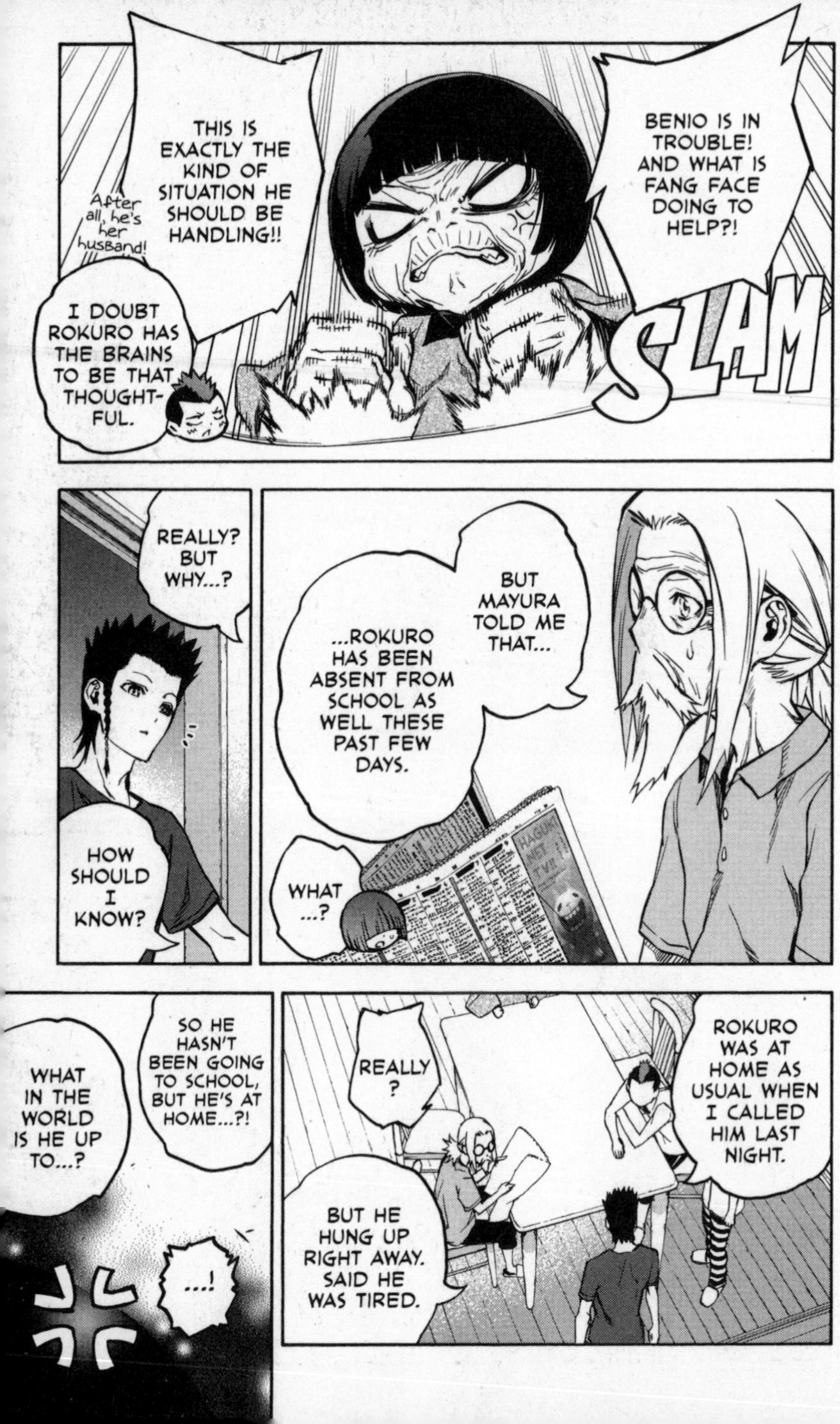
BENIO IS IN TROUBLE! AND WHAT IS FANG FACE DOING TO HELP?!
SLAM
THIS IS EXACTLY THE KIND OF SITUATION HE SHOULD BE HANDLING!!
After all, he's her husband!
I DOUBT ROKURO HAS THE BRAINS TO BE THAT THOUGHTFUL.
BUT MAYURA TOLD ME THAT...
...ROKURO HAS BEEN ABSENT FROM SCHOOL AS WELL THESE PAST FEW DAYS.
WHAT ...?
REALLY? BUT WHY...?
HOW SHOULD I KNOW?
ROKURO WAS AT HOME AS USUAL WHEN I CALLED HIM LAST NIGHT.
REALLY?
BUT HE HUNG UP RIGHT AWAY. SAID HE WAS TIRED.
SO HE HASN'T BEEN GOING TO SCHOOL, BUT HE'S AT HOME...?!
WHAT IN THE WORLD IS HE UP TO...?
...!

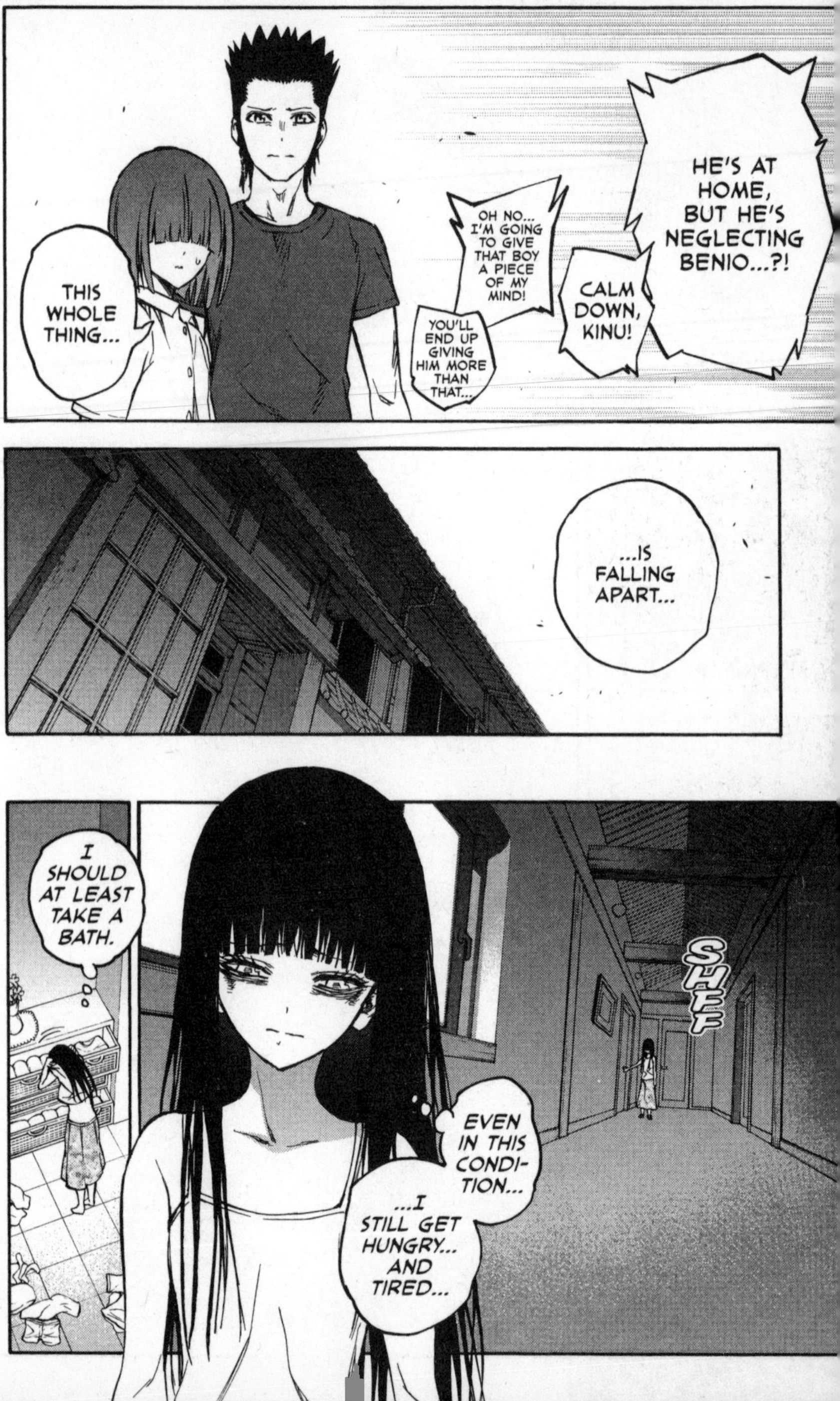
HE'S AT HOME, BUT HE'S NEGLECTING BENIO...?!
CALM DOWN, KINU!
OH NO... I'M GOING TO GIVE THAT BOY A PIECE OF MY MIND!
YOU'LL END UP GIVING HIM MORE THAN THAT...
THIS WHOLE THING...
...IS FALLING APART...
SHFF
EVEN IN THIS CONDITION...
...I STILL GET HUNGRY... AND TIRED...
I SHOULD AT LEAST TAKE A BATH.

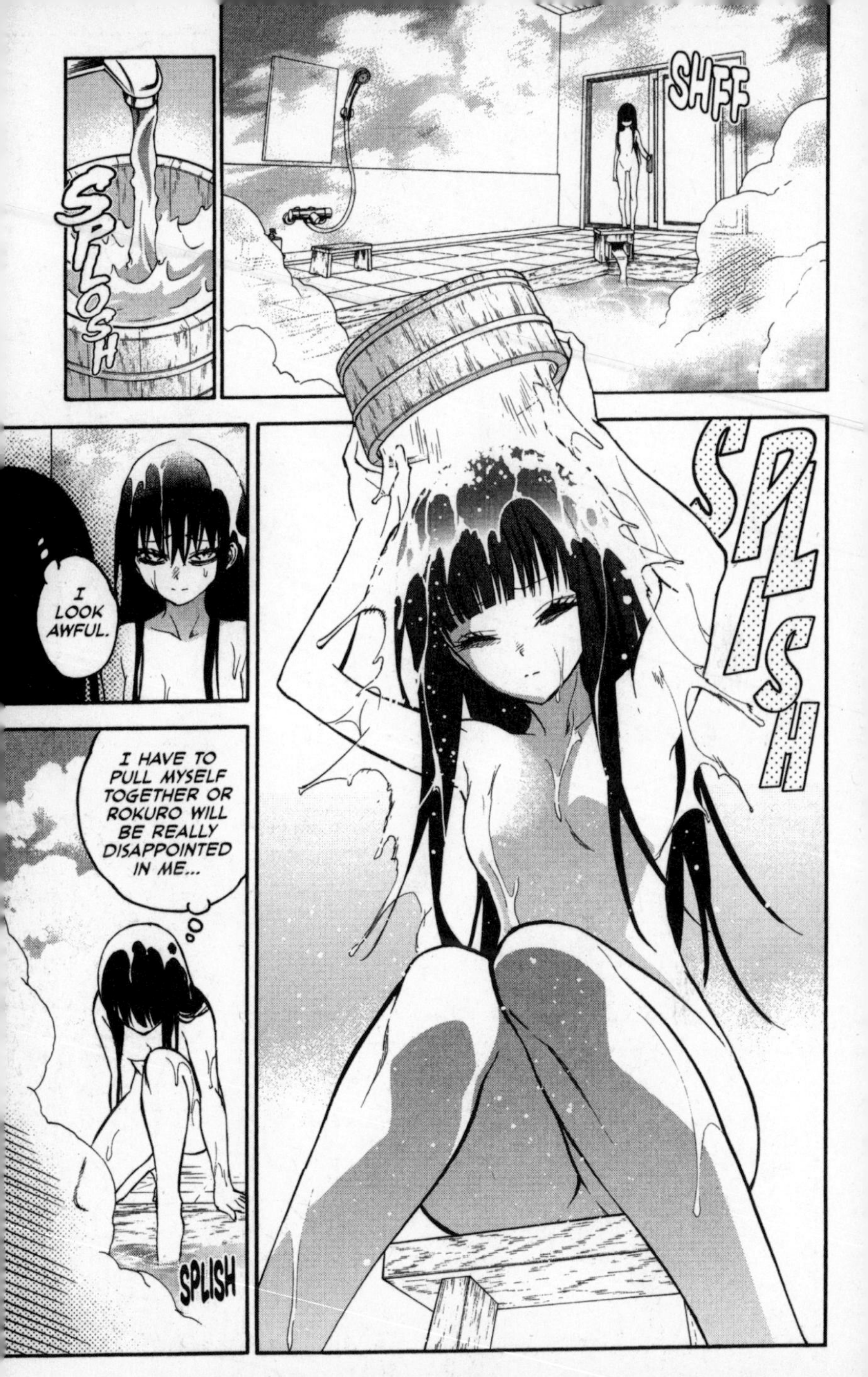
SHFF
SPLOSH
SPLASH
I LOOK AWFUL.
I HAVE TO PULL MYSELF TOGETHER OR ROKURO WILL BE REALLY DISAPPOINTED IN ME...
SPLISH

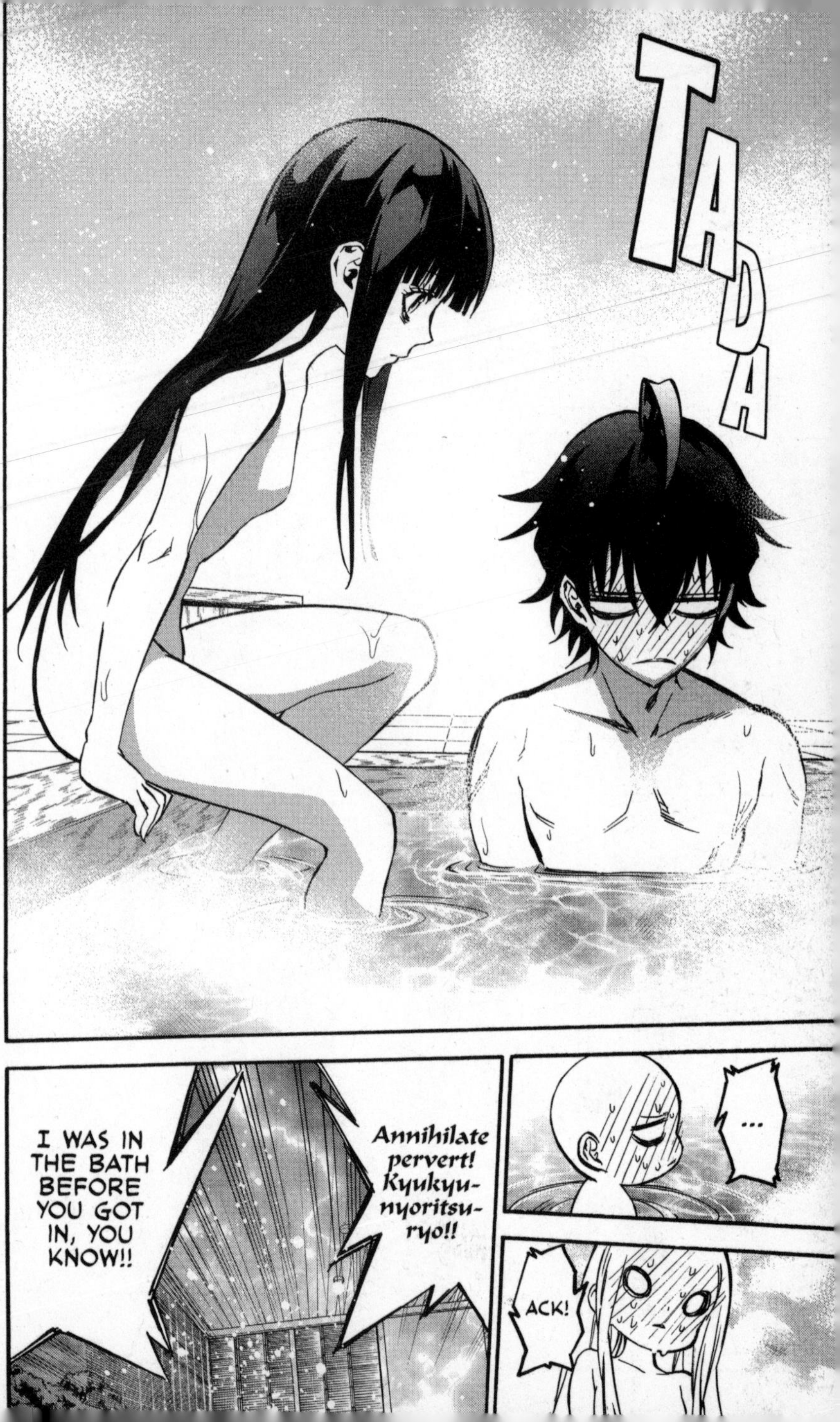
TADADA
...
ACK!
Annihilate pervert! Kyukyu-nyoritsu-ryo!!
I WAS IN THE BATH BEFORE YOU GOT IN, YOU KNOW!!

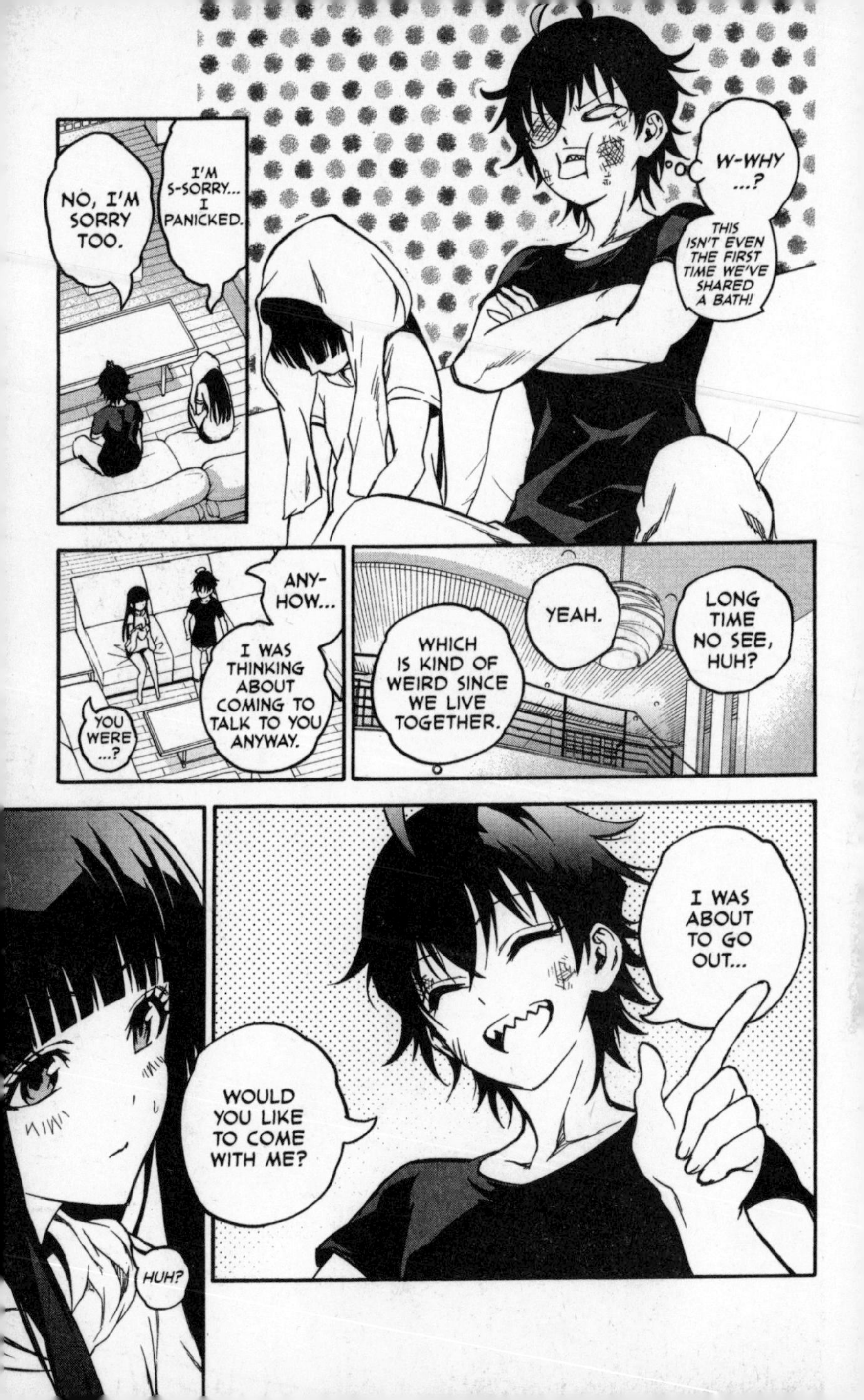
W-WHY ...?
THIS ISN'T EVEN THE FIRST TIME WE'VE SHARED A BATH!
I'M S-SORRY... I PANICKED.
NO, I'M SORRY TOO.
LONG TIME NO SEE, HUH?
YEAH.
WHICH IS KIND OF WEIRD SINCE WE LIVE TOGETHER.
ANY-HOW...
I WAS THINKING ABOUT COMING TO TALK TO YOU ANYWAY.
YOU WERE ...?
I WAS ABOUT TO GO OUT...
WOULD YOU LIKE TO COME WITH ME?
HUH?

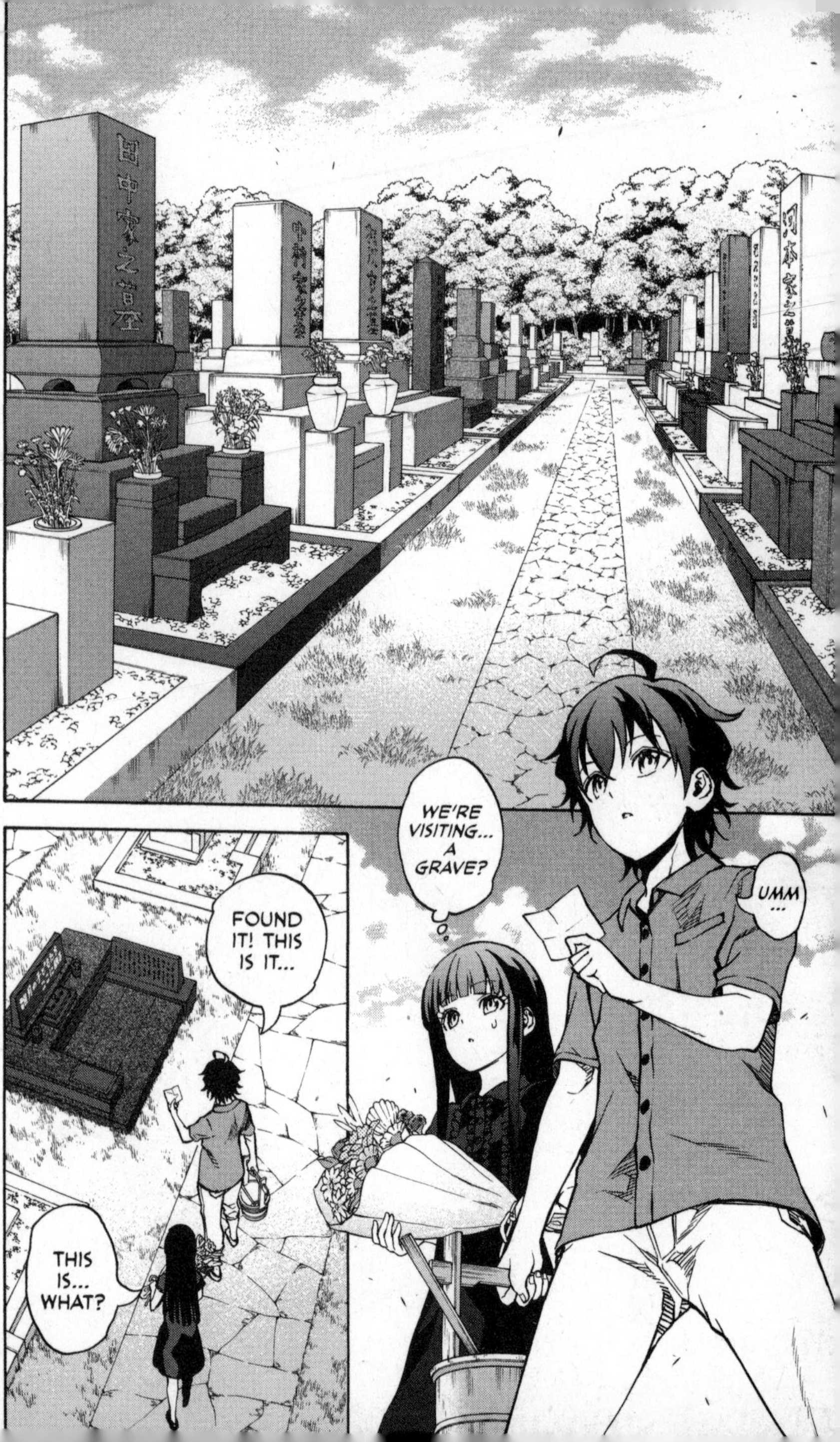
WE'RE VISITING... A GRAVE?
UMM...
FOUND IT! THIS IS IT...
THIS IS... WHAT?

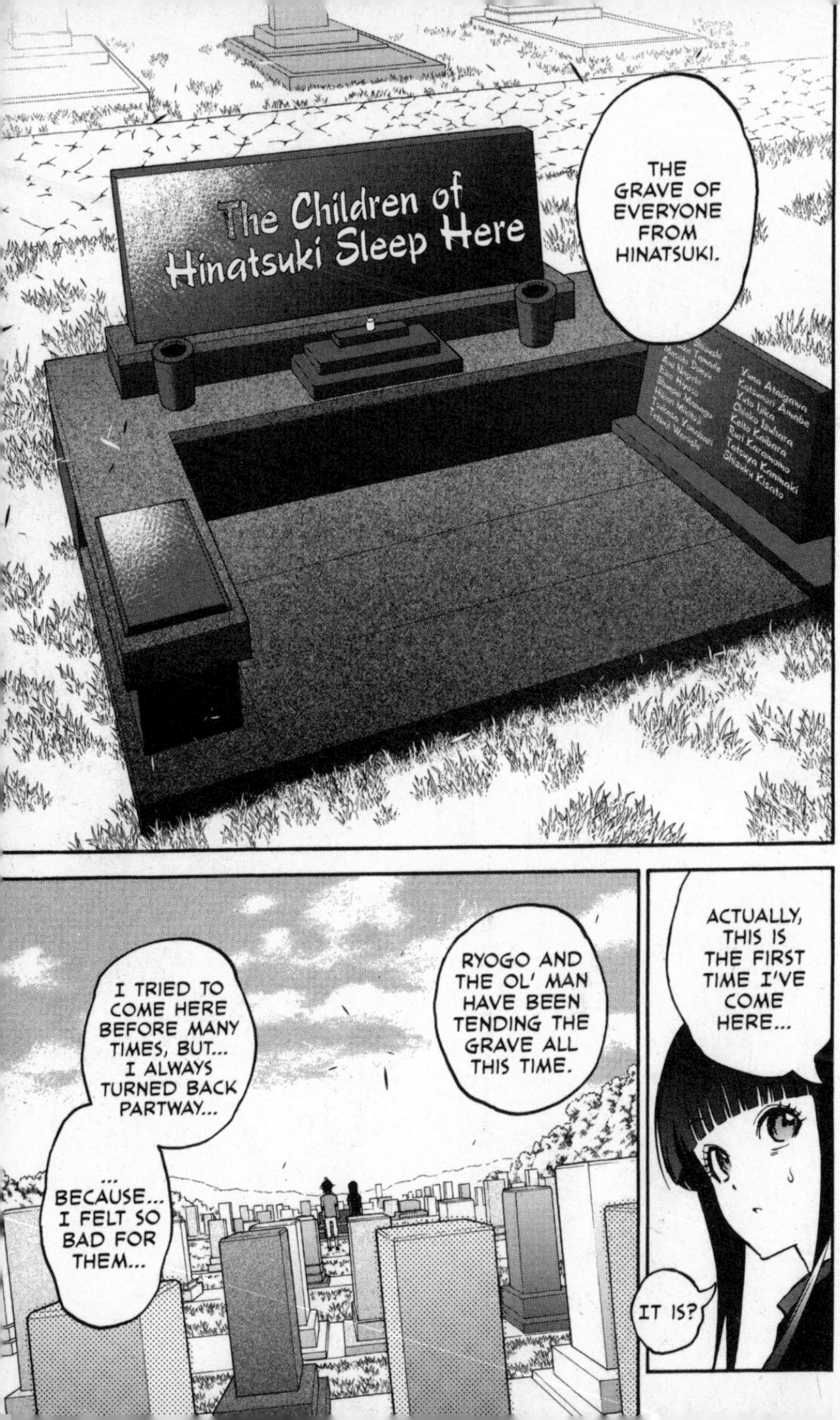
The Children of Hinatsuki Sleep Here
Yuna Ataigawa
Katsunori Amabe
Yuto Iijika
Chieko Izuhara
Keito Kaibara
Ruri Karamoto
Tatsuya Kanmaki
Shizuku Kisato
THE GRAVE OF EVERYONE FROM HINATSUKI.
ACTUALLY, THIS IS THE FIRST TIME I'VE COME HERE...
IT IS?
RYOGO AND THE OL' MAN HAVE BEEN TENDING THE GRAVE ALL THIS TIME.
I TRIED TO COME HERE BEFORE MANY TIMES, BUT... I ALWAYS TURNED BACK PARTWAY...
...BECAUSE... I FELT SO BAD FOR THEM...

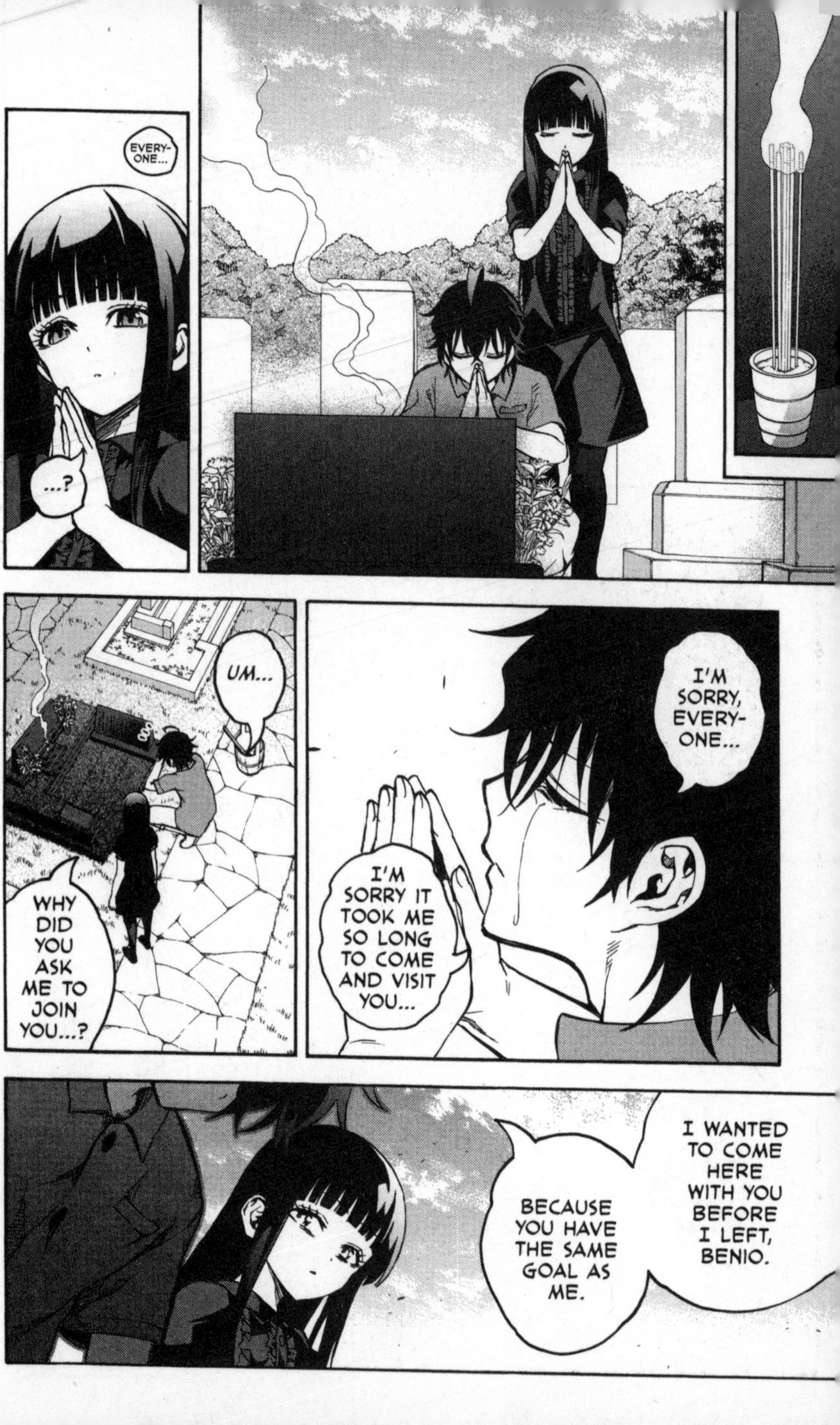
EVERY-ONE...
...?
I'M SORRY, EVERY-ONE...
I'M SORRY IT TOOK ME SO LONG TO COME AND VISIT YOU...
UM...
WHY DID YOU ASK ME TO JOIN YOU...?
I WANTED TO COME HERE WITH YOU BEFORE I LEFT, BENIO.
BECAUSE YOU HAVE THE SAME GOAL AS ME.

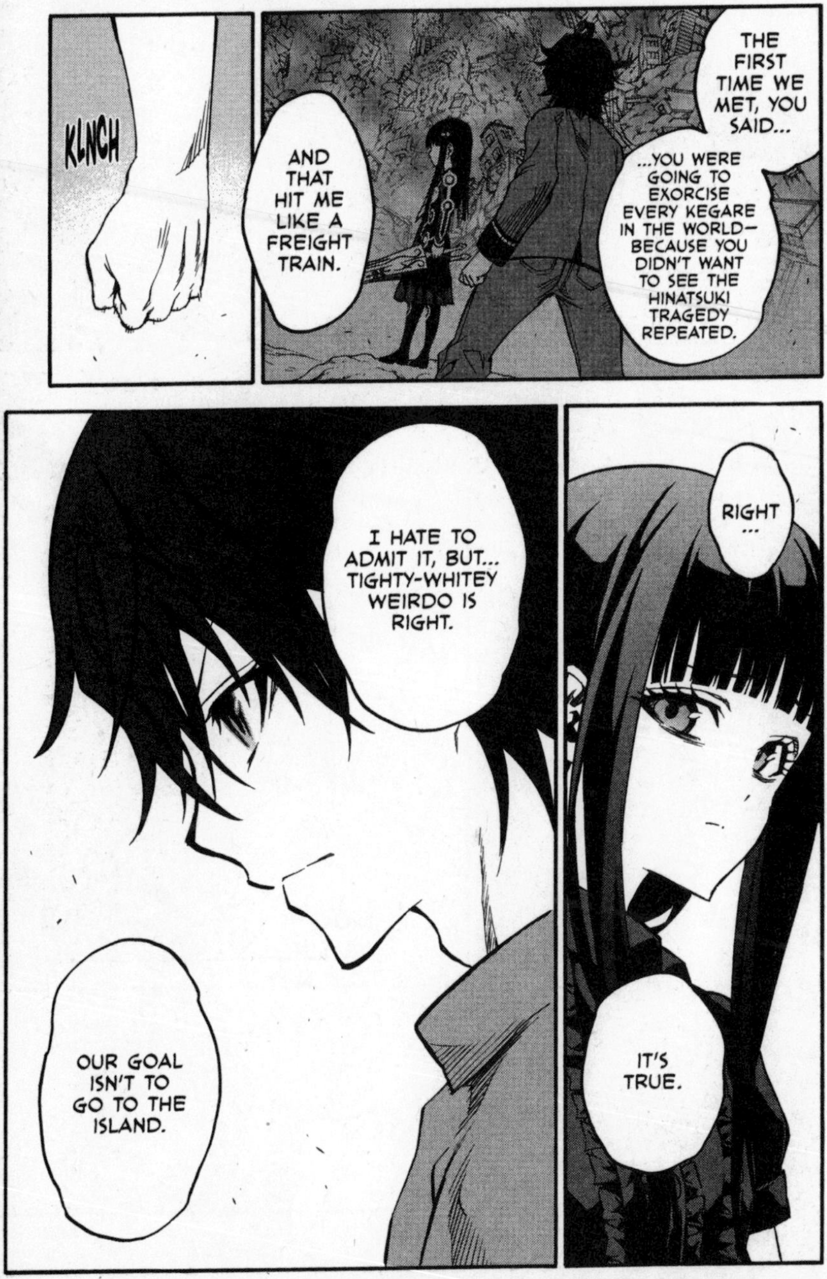
THE FIRST TIME WE MET, YOU SAID...
...YOU WERE GOING TO EXORCISE EVERY KEGARE IN THE WORLD—BECAUSE YOU DIDN'T WANT TO SEE THE HINATSUKI TRAGEDY REPEATED.
AND THAT HIT ME LIKE A FREIGHT TRAIN.
KLNCH
RIGHT...
IT'S TRUE.
I HATE TO ADMIT IT, BUT... TIGHTY-WHITEY WEIRDO IS RIGHT.
OUR GOAL ISN'T TO GO TO THE ISLAND.

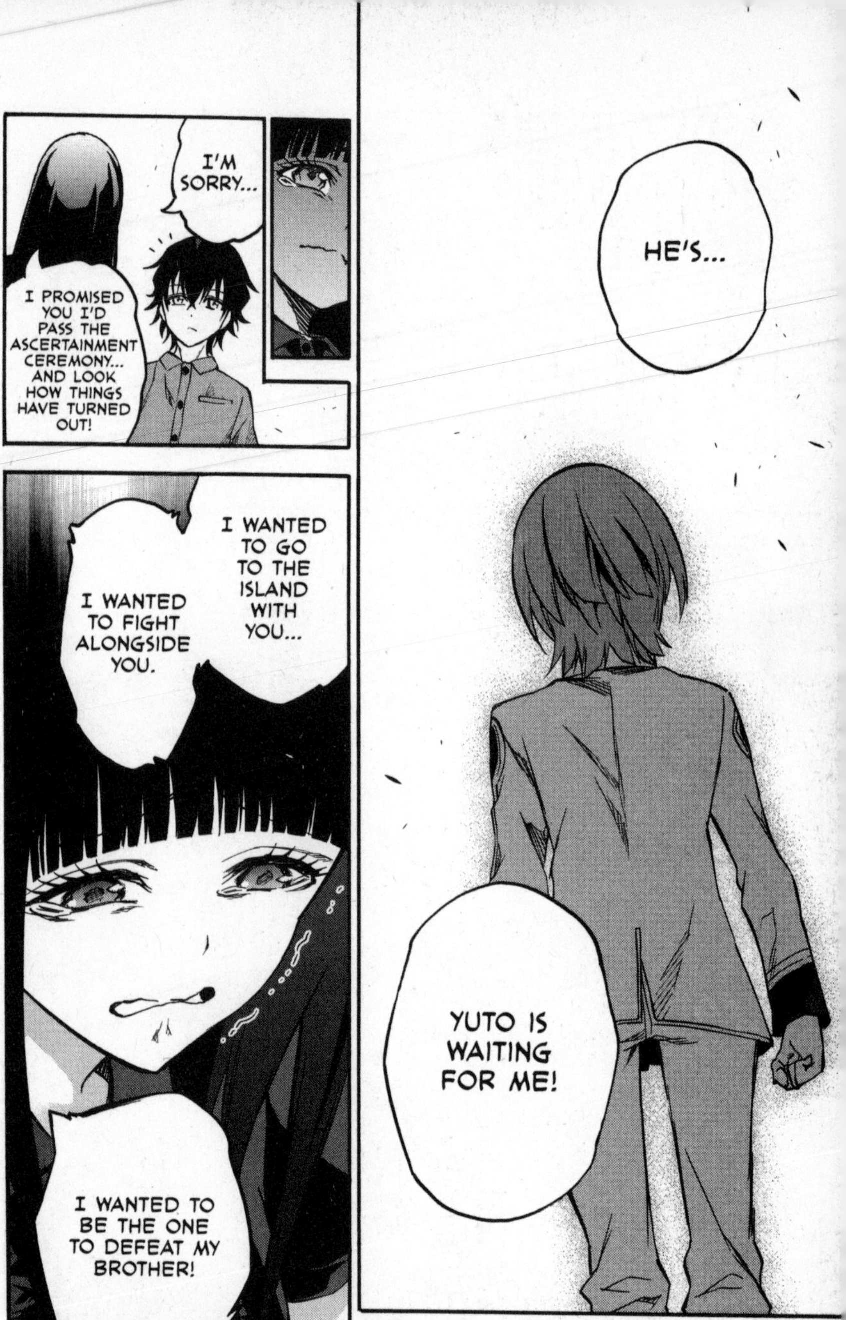
HE'S...
YUTO IS WAITING FOR ME!
I'M SORRY...
I PROMISED YOU I'D PASS THE ASCERTAINMENT CEREMONY... AND LOOK HOW THINGS HAVE TURNED OUT!
I WANTED TO GO TO THE ISLAND WITH YOU...
I WANTED TO FIGHT ALONGSIDE YOU.
I WANTED TO BE THE ONE TO DEFEAT MY BROTHER!

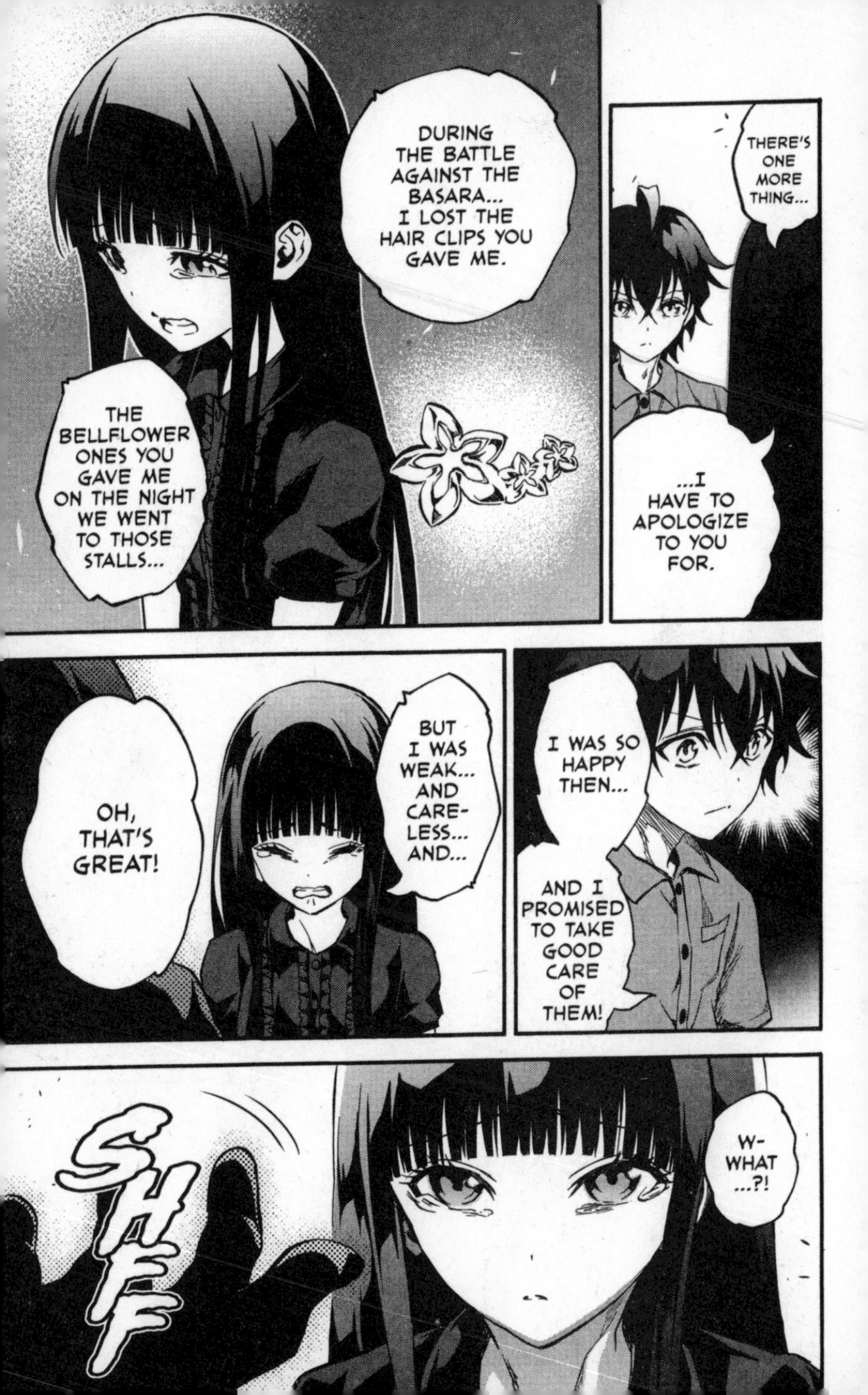
THERE'S ONE MORE THING...
...I HAVE TO APOLOGIZE TO YOU FOR.
DURING THE BATTLE AGAINST THE BASARA... I LOST THE HAIR CLIPS YOU GAVE ME.
THE BELLFLOWER ONES YOU GAVE ME ON THE NIGHT WE WENT TO THOSE STALLS...
I WAS SO HAPPY THEN...
AND I PROMISED TO TAKE GOOD CARE OF THEM!
BUT I WAS WEAK... AND CARE-LESS... AND...
OH, THAT'S GREAT!
W-WHAT ...?!
SHF

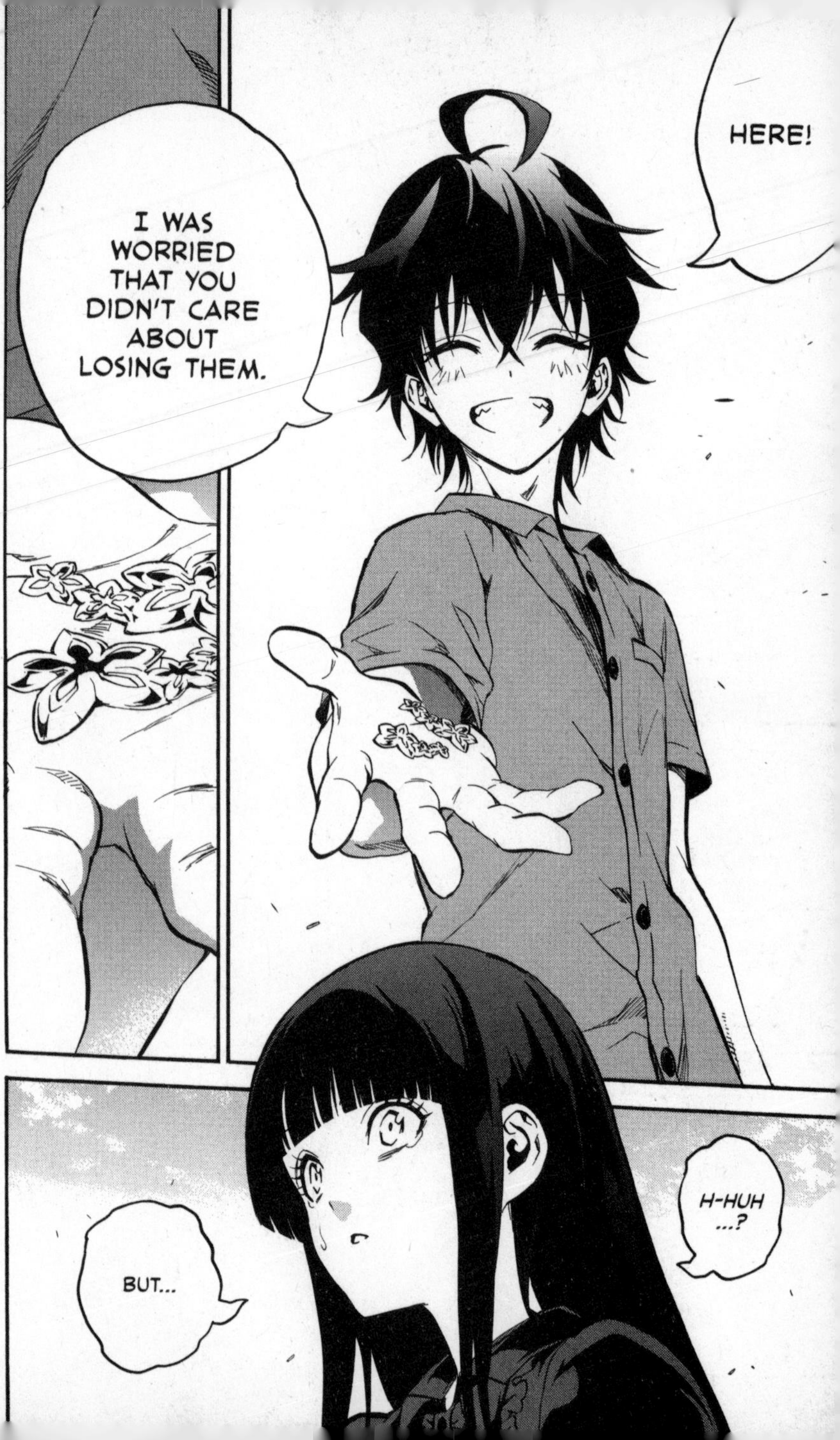
HERE!
I WAS WORRIED THAT YOU DIDN'T CARE ABOUT LOSING THEM.
H-HUH ...?
BUT...

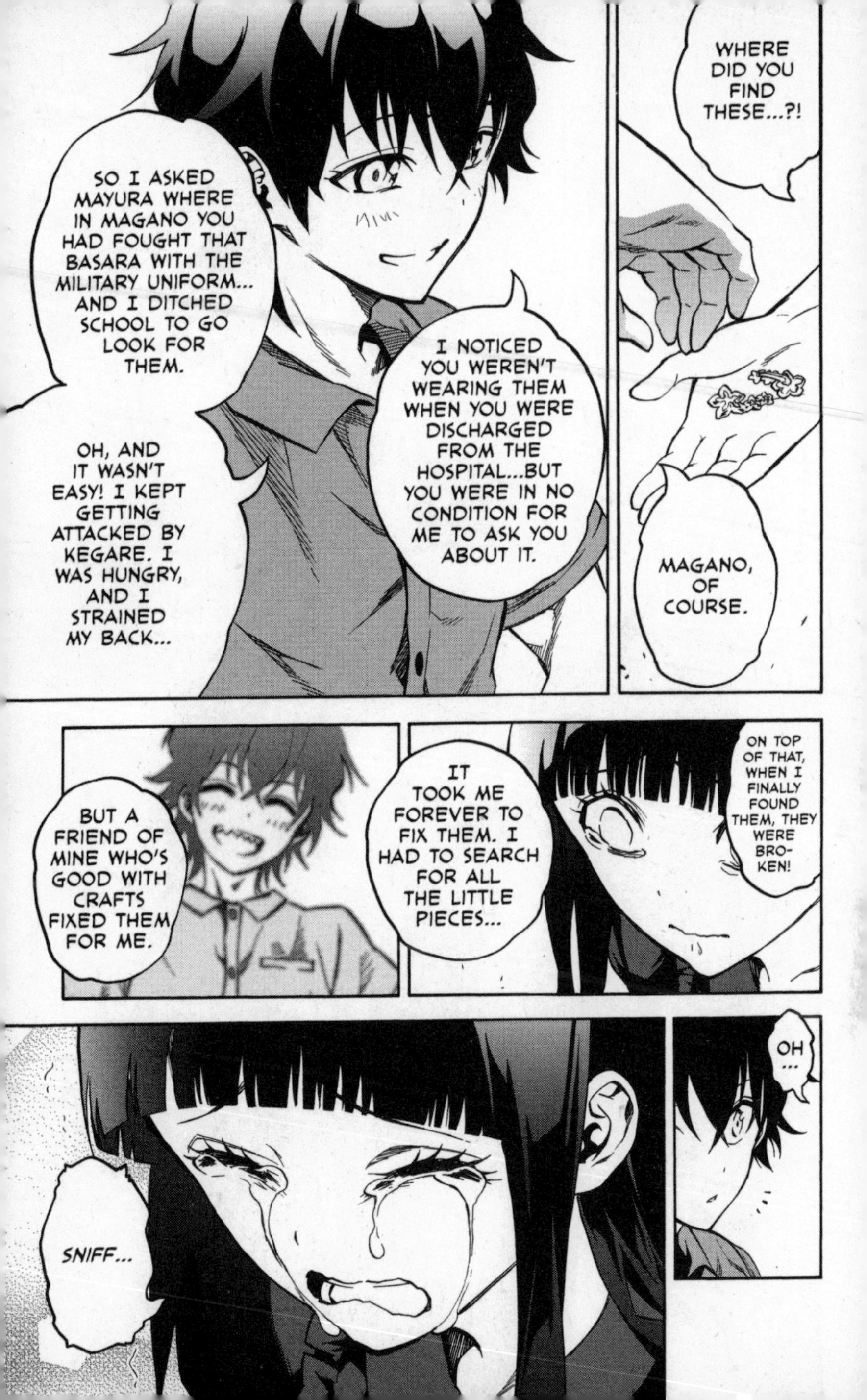
WHERE DID YOU FIND THESE...?!
MAGANO, OF COURSE.
I NOTICED YOU WEREN'T WEARING THEM WHEN YOU WERE DISCHARGED FROM THE HOSPITAL...BUT YOU WERE IN NO CONDITION FOR ME TO ASK YOU ABOUT IT.
SO I ASKED MAYURA WHERE IN MAGANO YOU HAD FOUGHT THAT BASARA WITH THE MILITARY UNIFORM... AND I DITCHED SCHOOL TO GO LOOK FOR THEM.
OH, AND IT WASN'T EASY! I KEPT GETTING ATTACKED BY KEGARE. I WAS HUNGRY, AND I STRAINED MY BACK...
ON TOP OF THAT, WHEN I FINALLY FOUND THEM, THEY WERE BRO-KEN!
IT TOOK ME FOREVER TO FIX THEM. I HAD TO SEARCH FOR ALL THE LITTLE PIECES...
BUT A FRIEND OF MINE WHO'S GOOD WITH CRAFTS FIXED THEM FOR ME.
OH ...
SNIFF...

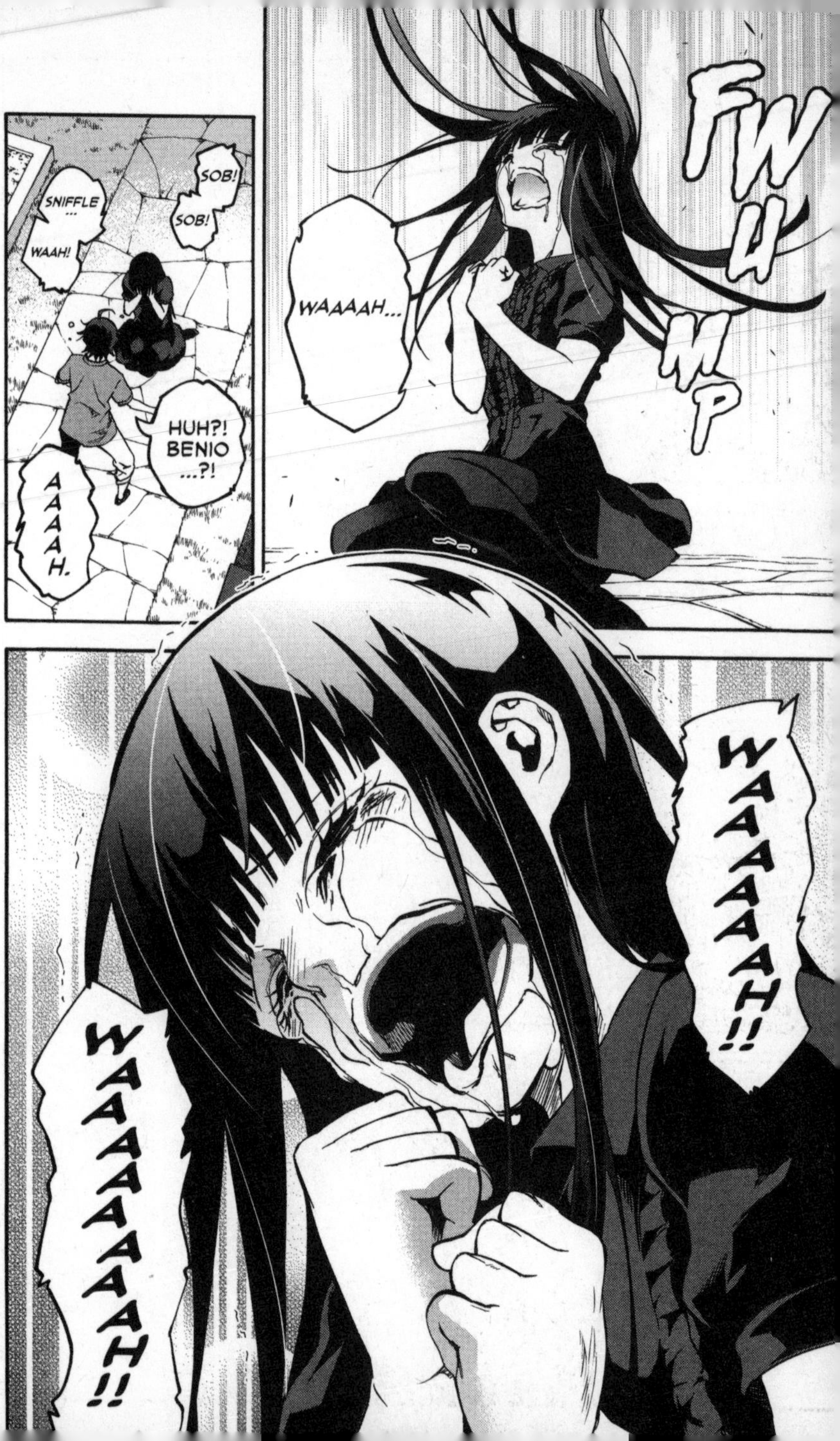
FWUMP
WAAAAH...
SOB! SOB!
SNIFFLE... WAAH!
HUH?! BENIO...?!
AAAAAH.
WAAAAAAH!!
WAAAAAAAAH!!

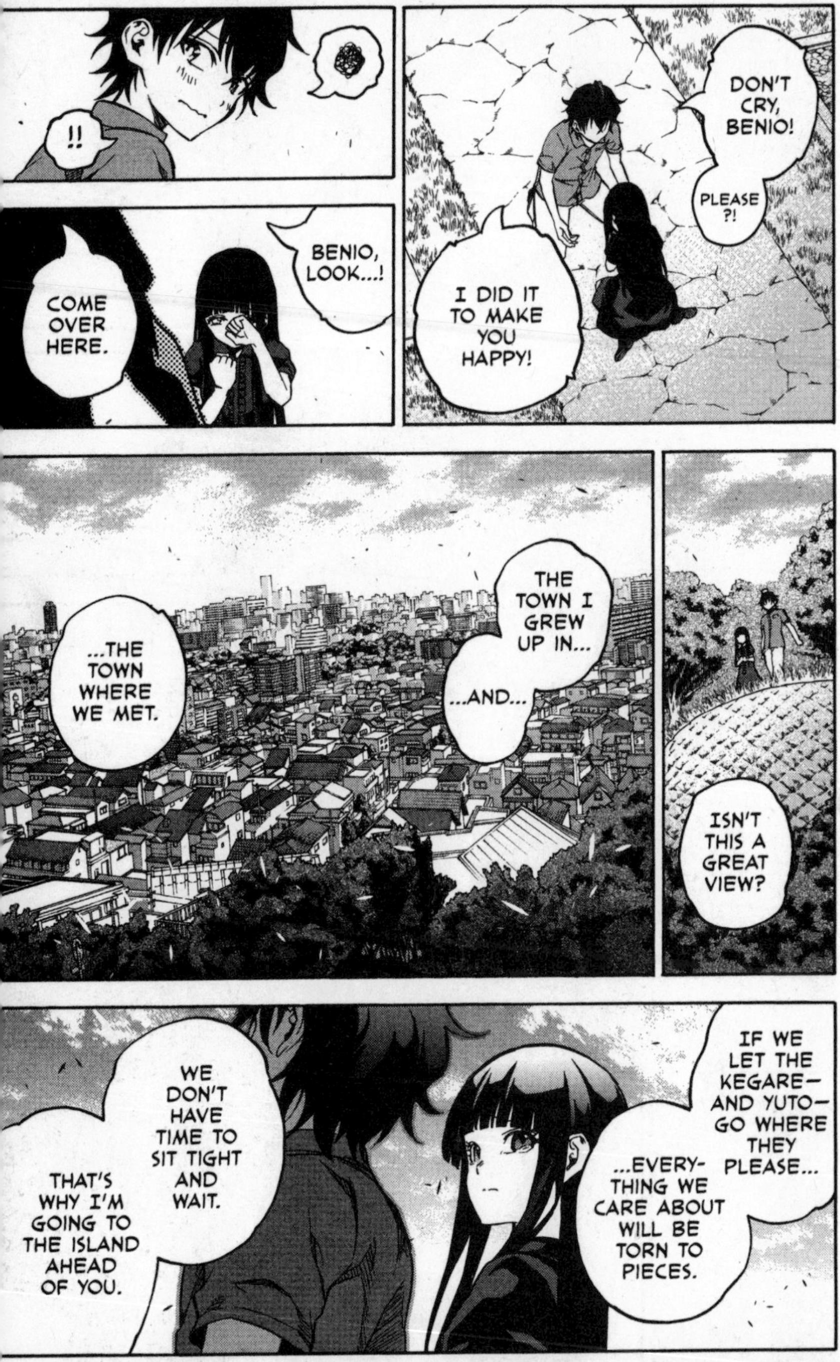
DON'T CRY, BENIO!
PLEASE ?!
I DID IT TO MAKE YOU HAPPY!
!!
BENIO, LOOK...!
COME OVER HERE.
ISN'T THIS A GREAT VIEW?
THE TOWN I GREW UP IN...
...AND...
...THE TOWN WHERE WE MET.
IF WE LET THE KEGARE—AND YUTO—GO WHERE THEY PLEASE...
...EVERY-THING WE CARE ABOUT WILL BE TORN TO PIECES.
WE DON'T HAVE TIME TO SIT TIGHT AND WAIT.
THAT'S WHY I'M GOING TO THE ISLAND AHEAD OF YOU.

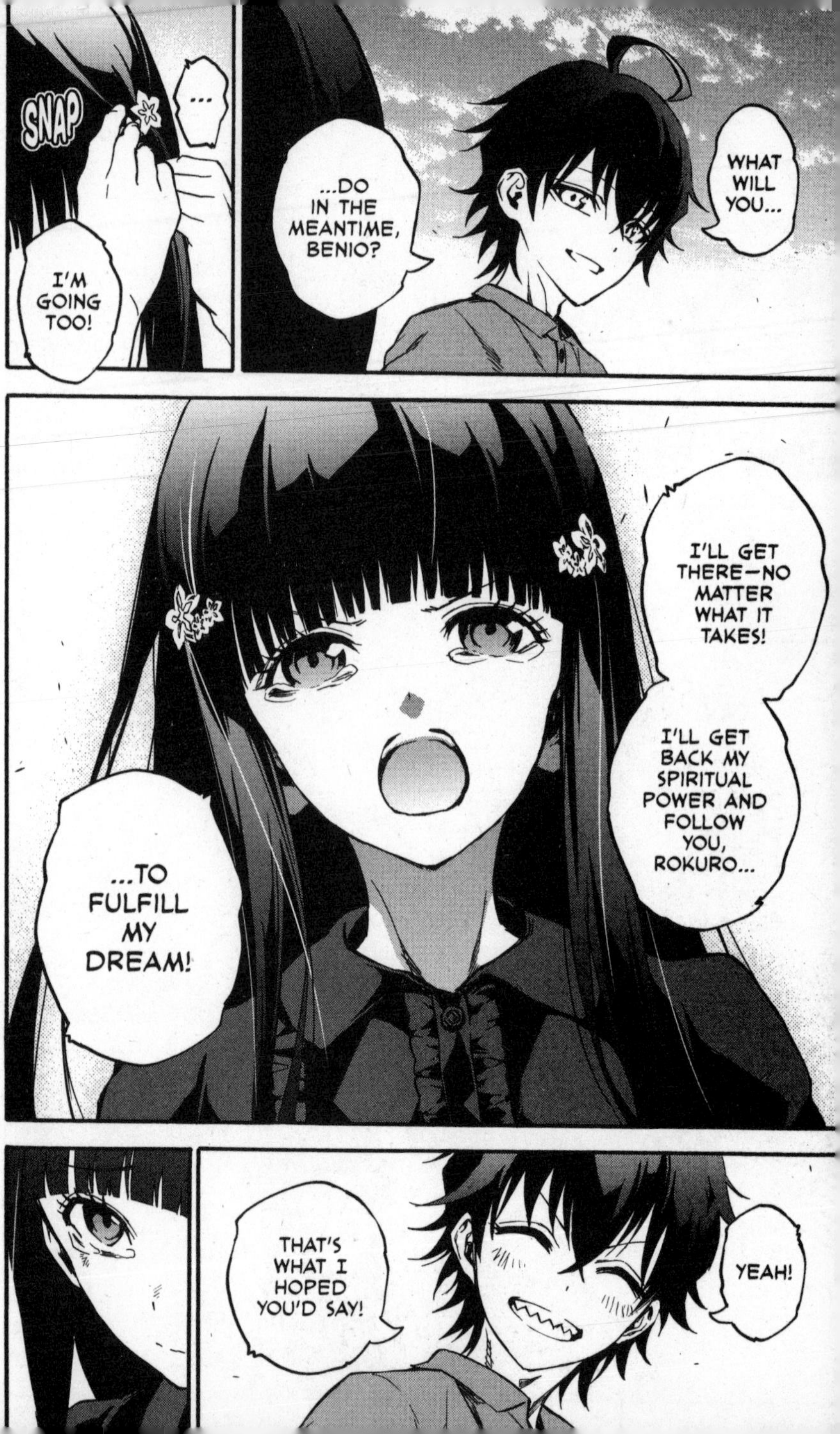
WHAT WILL YOU...
...DO IN THE MEANTIME, BENIO?
...
SNAP
I'M GOING TOO!
I'LL GET THERE—NO MATTER WHAT IT TAKES!
I'LL GET BACK MY SPIRITUAL POWER AND FOLLOW YOU, ROKURO...
...TO FULFILL MY DREAM!
YEAH!
THAT'S WHAT I HOPED YOU'D SAY!

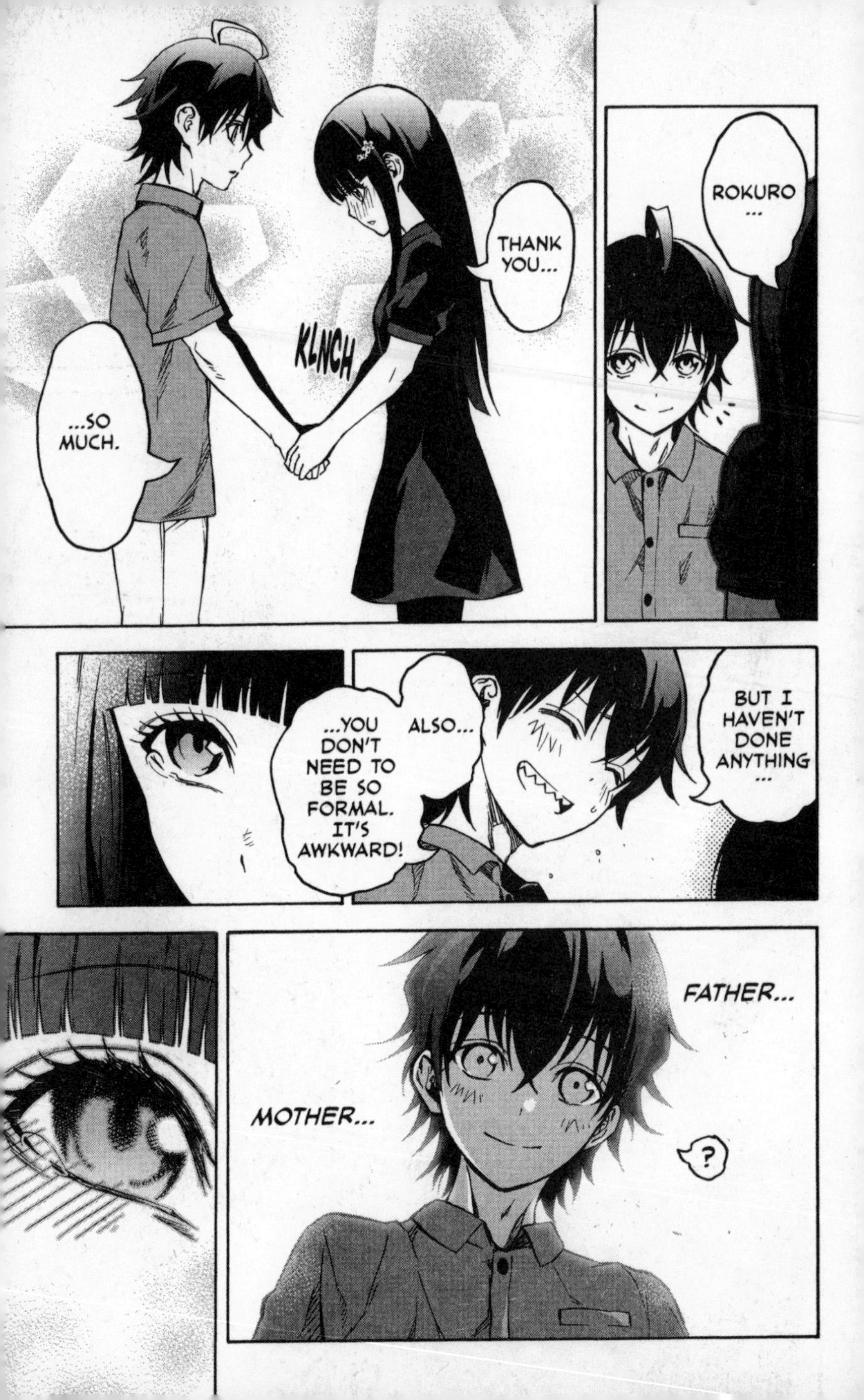
ROKURO...
THANK YOU...
KLNCH
...SO MUCH.
BUT I HAVEN'T DONE ANYTHING...
ALSO...
...YOU DON'T NEED TO BE SO FORMAL. IT'S AWKWARD!
FATHER...
MOTHER...
?

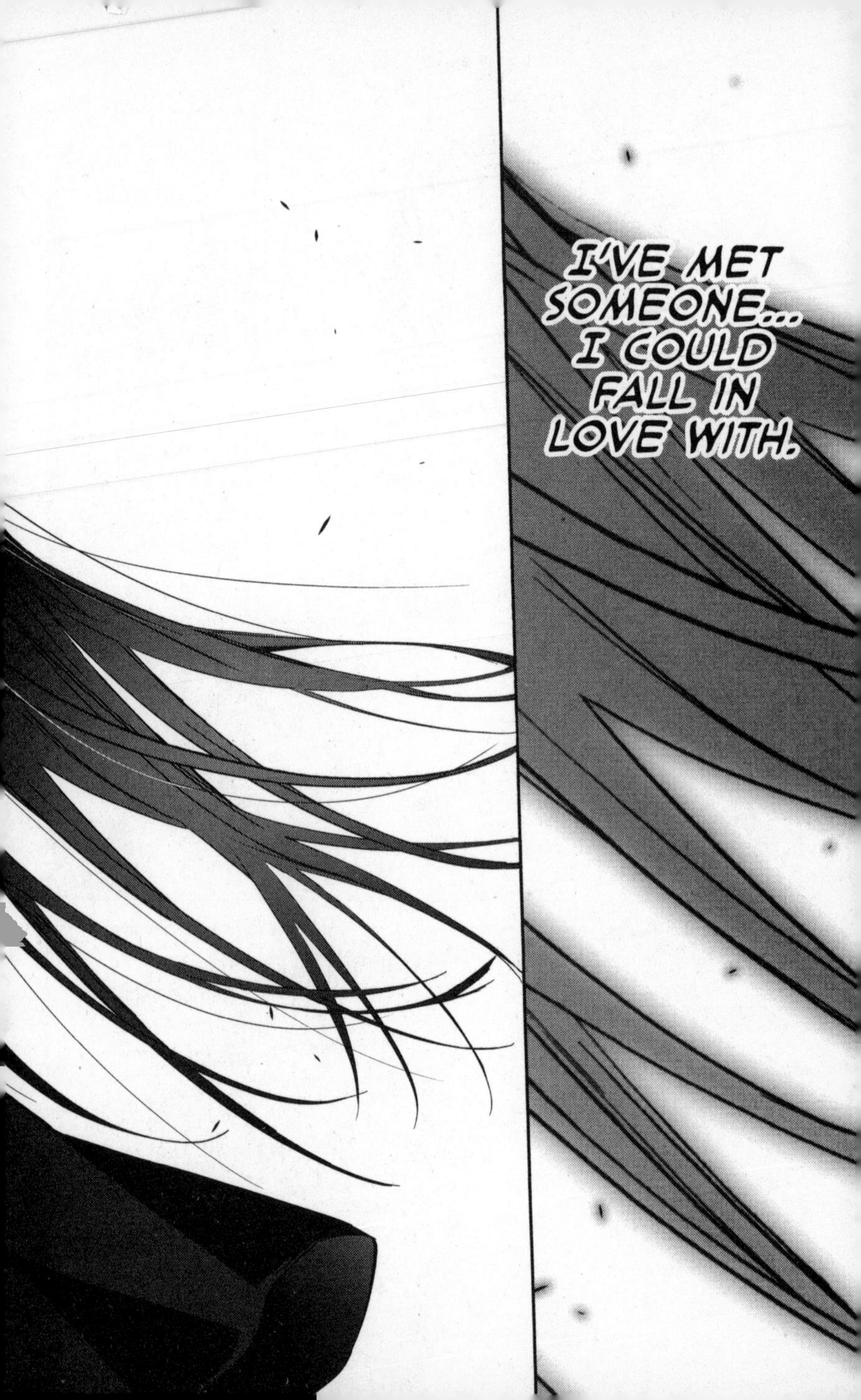
I'VE MET SOMEONE... I COULD FALL IN LOVE WITH.

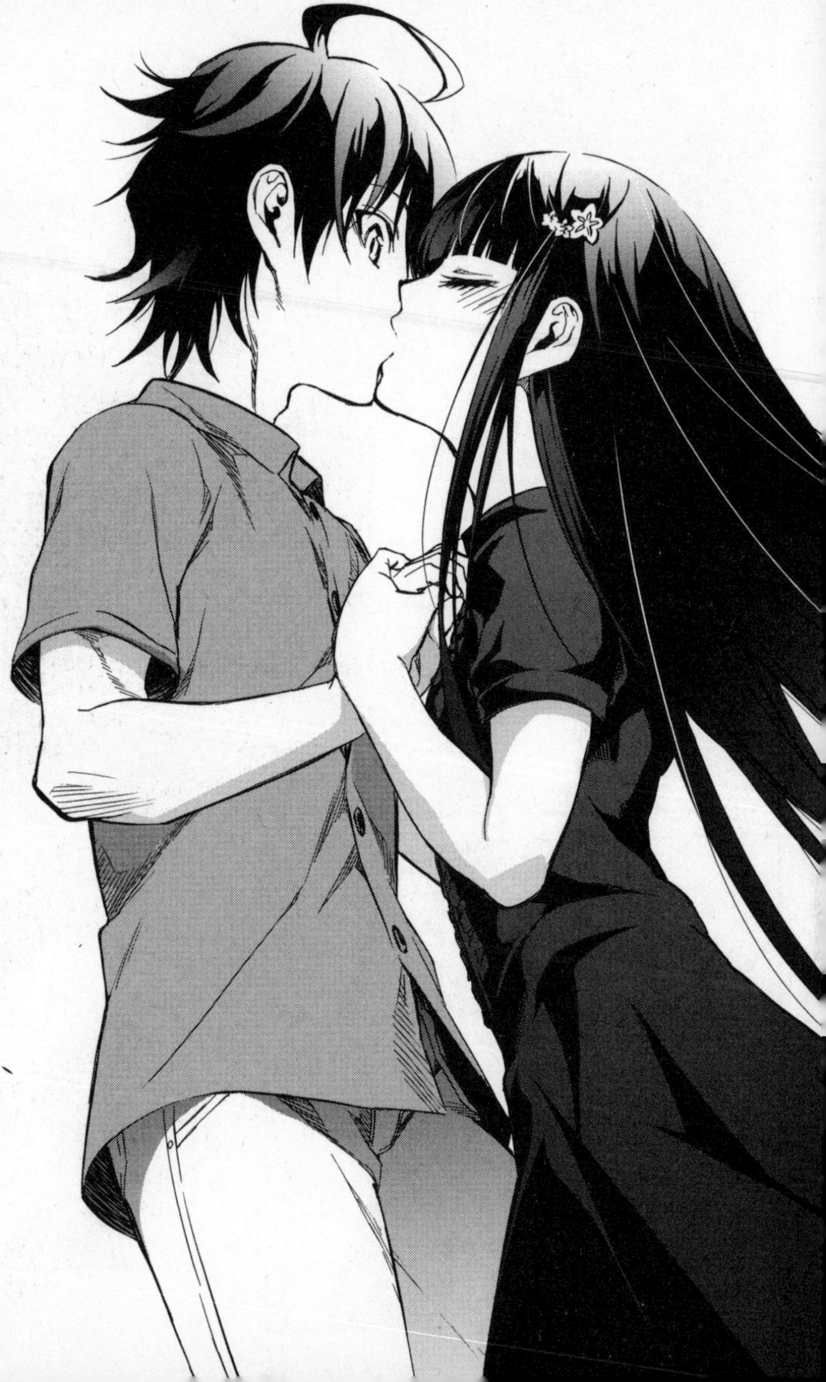

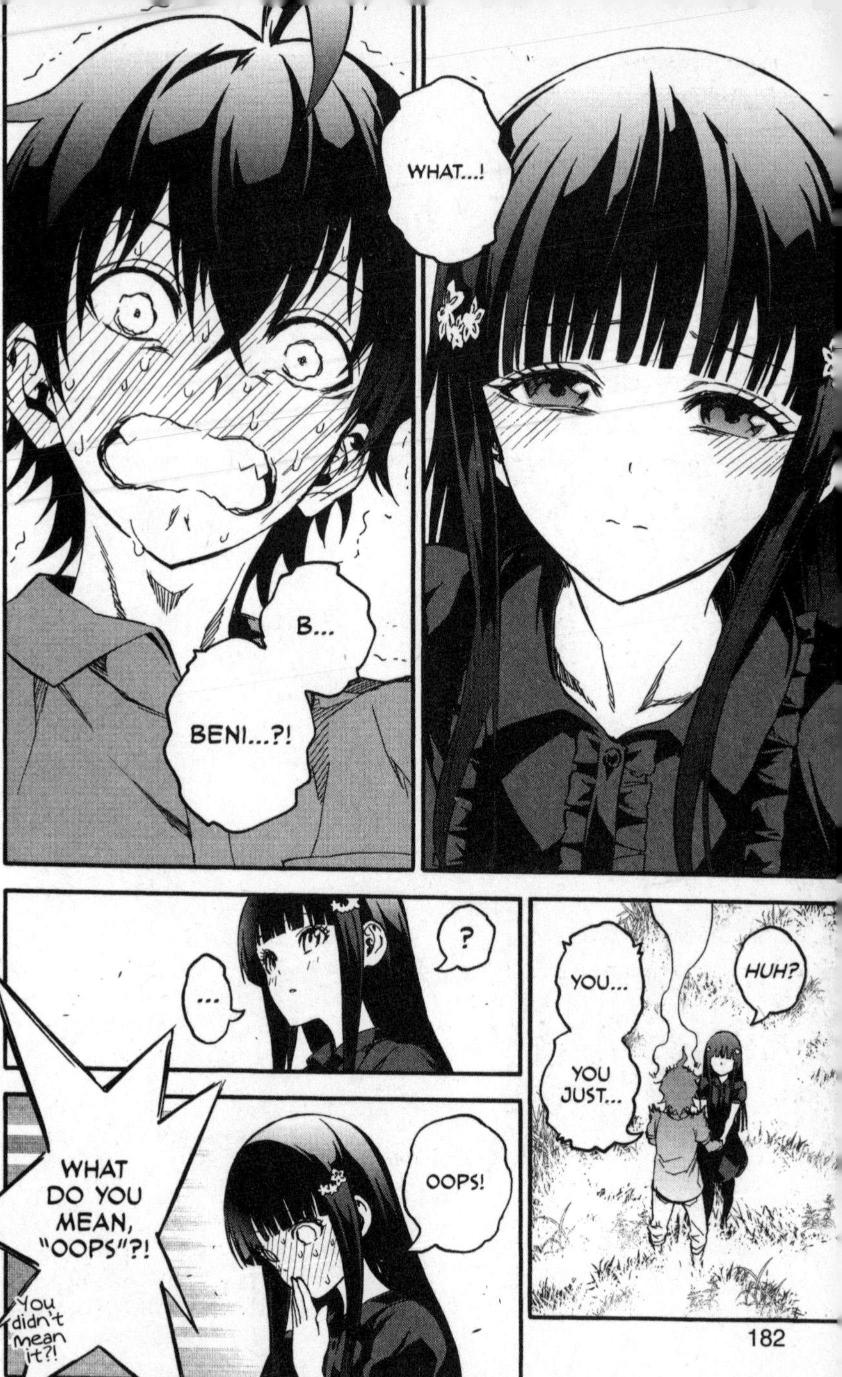
WHAT...!
B...
BENI...?!
HUH?
YOU...
YOU JUST...
?
...
OOPS!
WHAT DO YOU MEAN, "OOPS"?!
You didn't mean it?!

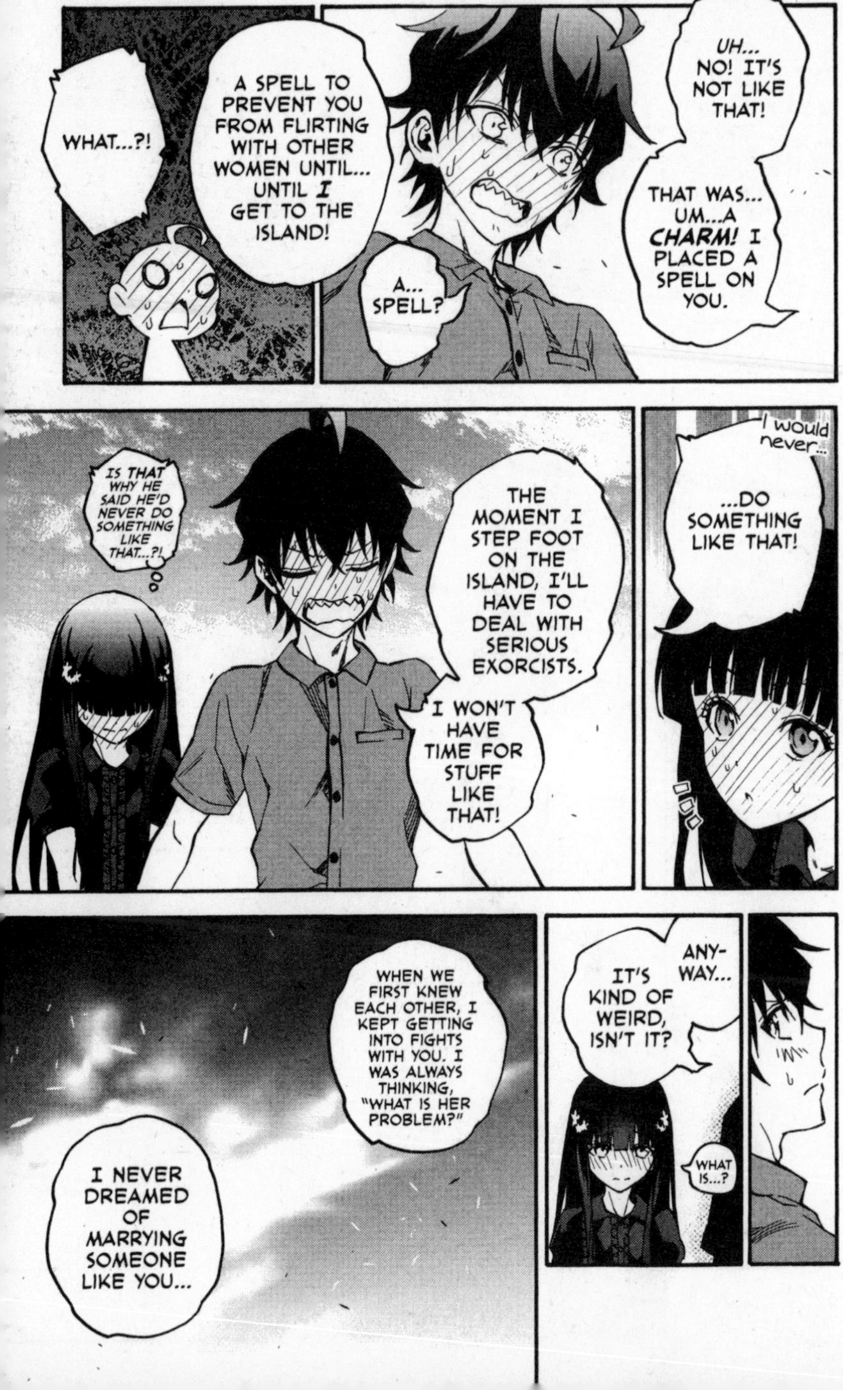
UH... NO! IT'S NOT LIKE THAT!
THAT WAS... UM...A CHARM! I PLACED A SPELL ON YOU.
A... SPELL?
A SPELL TO PREVENT YOU FROM FLIRTING WITH OTHER WOMEN UNTIL... UNTIL I GET TO THE ISLAND!
WHAT...?!
I would never...
...DO SOMETHING LIKE THAT!
THE MOMENT I STEP FOOT ON THE ISLAND, I'LL HAVE TO DEAL WITH SERIOUS EXORCISTS.
I WON'T HAVE TIME FOR STUFF LIKE THAT!
IS THAT WHY HE SAID HE'D NEVER DO SOMETHING LIKE THAT...?!
ANY-WAY...
IT'S KIND OF WEIRD, ISN'T IT?
WHAT IS...?
WHEN WE FIRST KNEW EACH OTHER, I KEPT GETTING INTO FIGHTS WITH YOU. I WAS ALWAYS THINKING, "WHAT IS HER PROBLEM?"
I NEVER DREAMED OF MARRYING SOMEONE LIKE YOU...

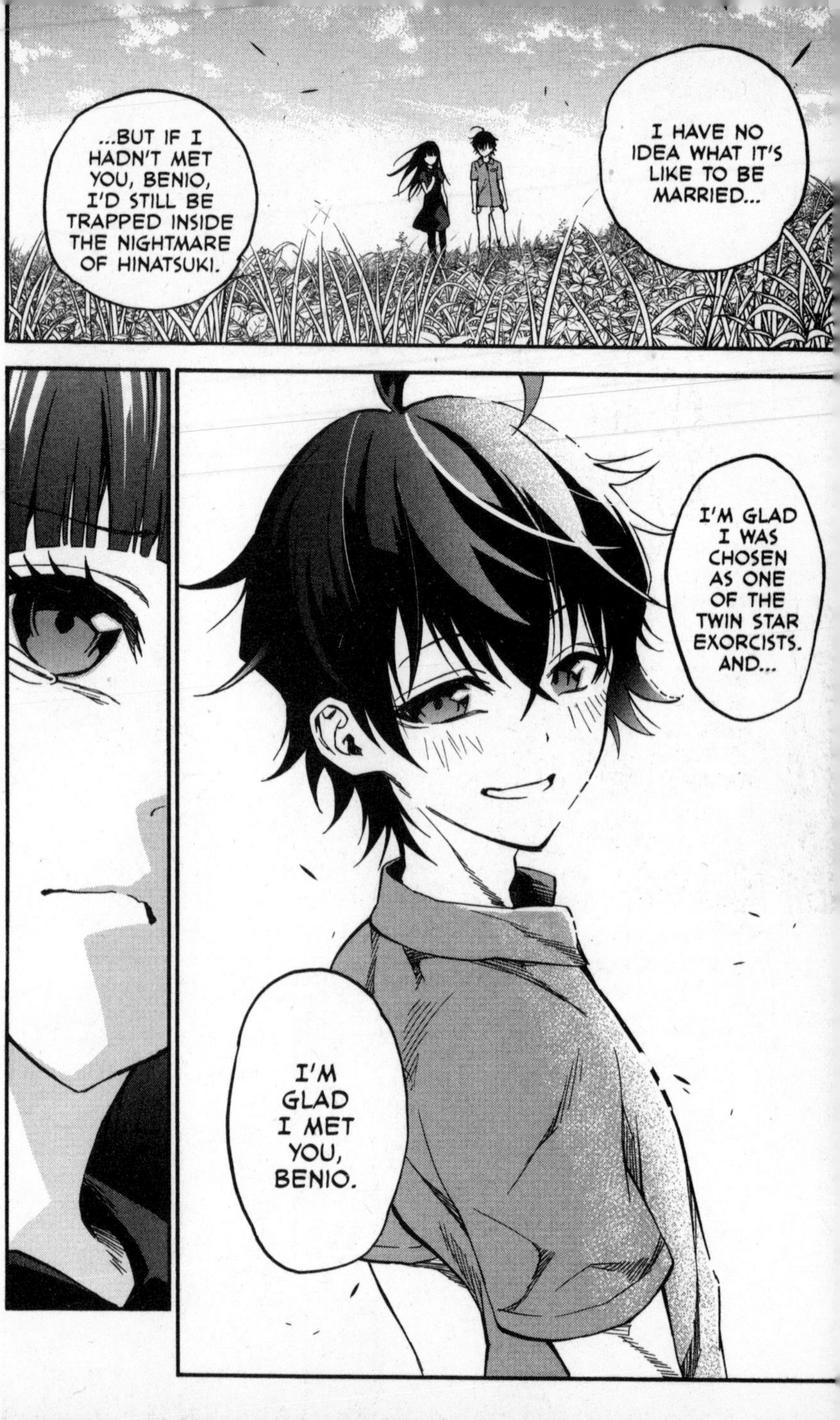
I HAVE NO IDEA WHAT IT'S LIKE TO BE MARRIED...
...BUT IF I HADN'T MET YOU, BENIO, I'D STILL BE TRAPPED INSIDE THE NIGHTMARE OF HINATSUKI.
I'M GLAD I WAS CHOSEN AS ONE OF THE TWIN STAR EXORCISTS. AND...
I'M GLAD I MET YOU, BENIO.

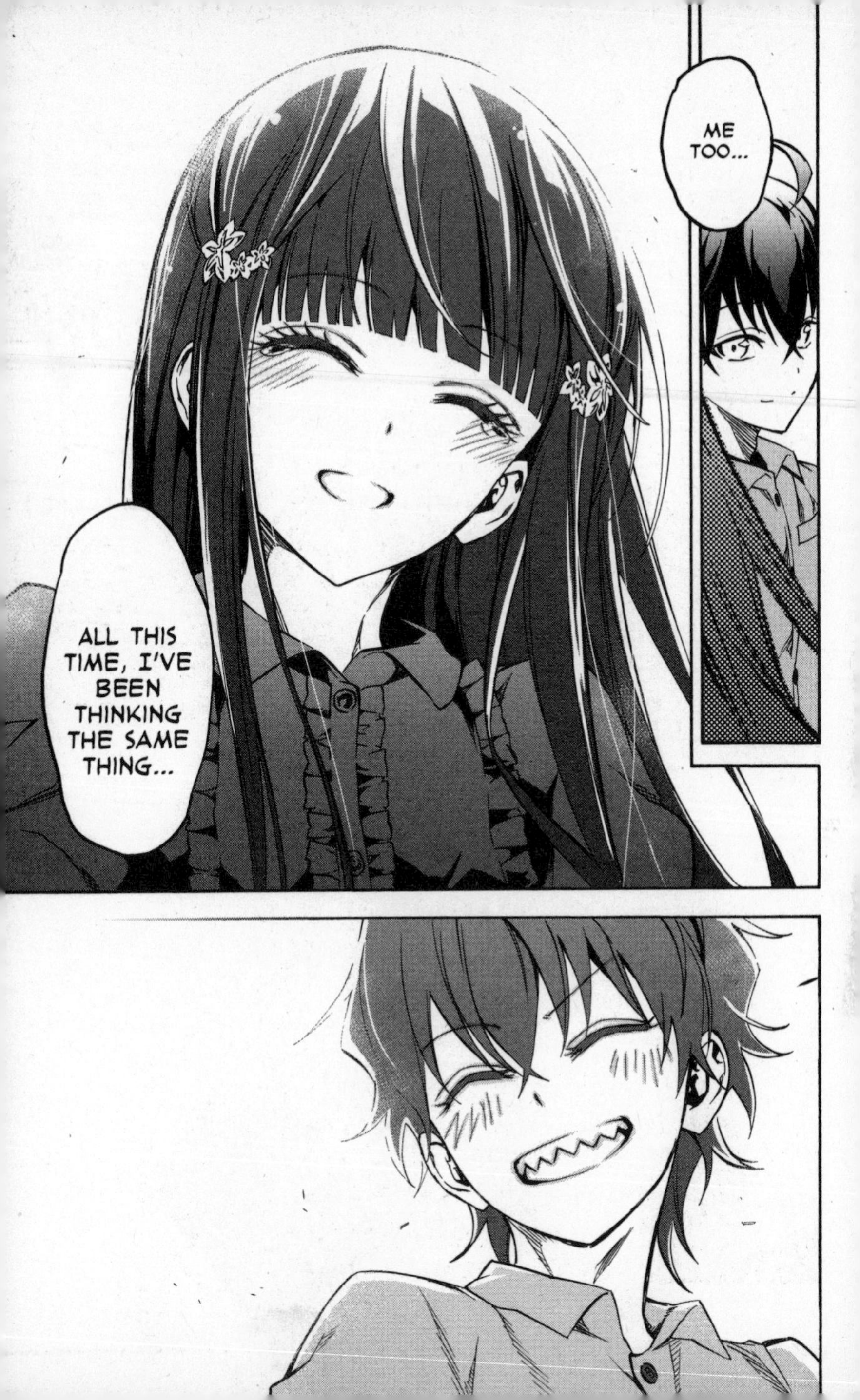
ME TOO...
ALL THIS TIME, I'VE BEEN THINKING THE SAME THING...

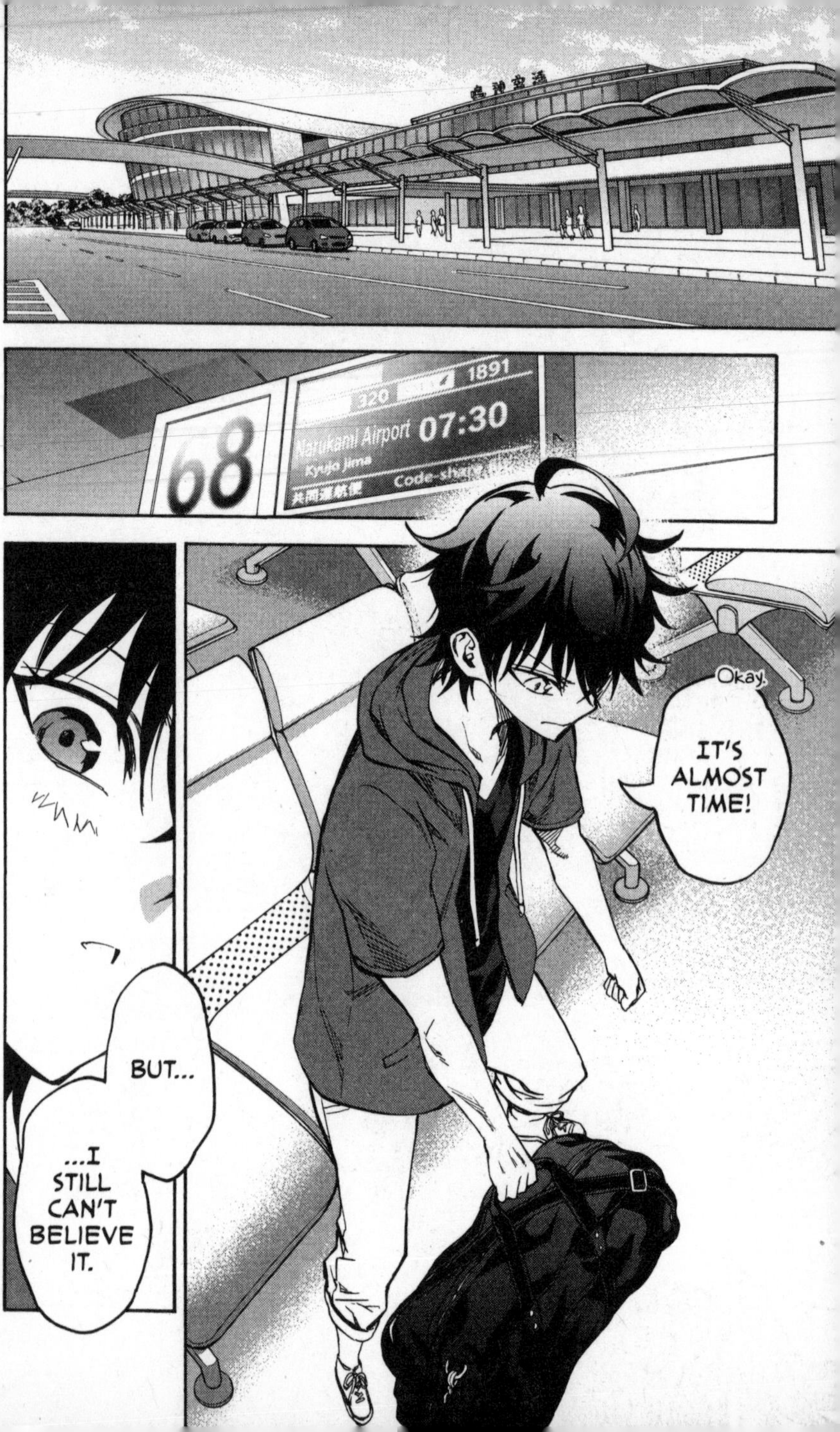
1891
320
Narukami Airport 07:30
Kyujo jima
Code-sha
共同運航便
68
Okay.
IT'S ALMOST TIME!
BUT...
...I STILL CAN'T BELIEVE IT.

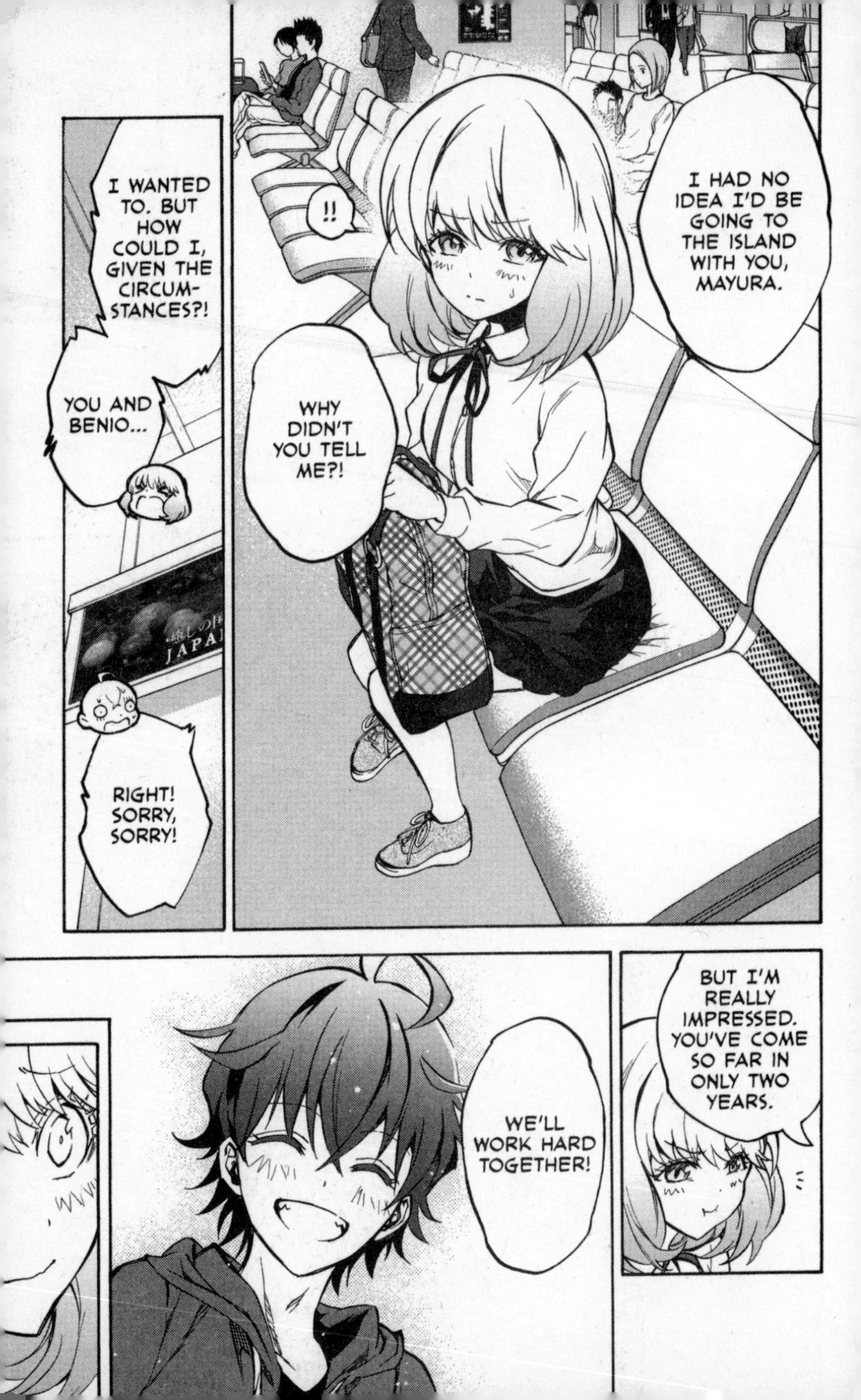
I HAD NO IDEA I'D BE GOING TO THE ISLAND WITH YOU, MAYURA.
!!
WHY DIDN'T YOU TELL ME?!
I WANTED TO. BUT HOW COULD I, GIVEN THE CIRCUM-STANCES?!
YOU AND BENIO...
RIGHT! SORRY, SORRY!
BUT I'M REALLY IMPRESSED. YOU'VE COME SO FAR IN ONLY TWO YEARS.
WE'LL WORK HARD TOGETHER!

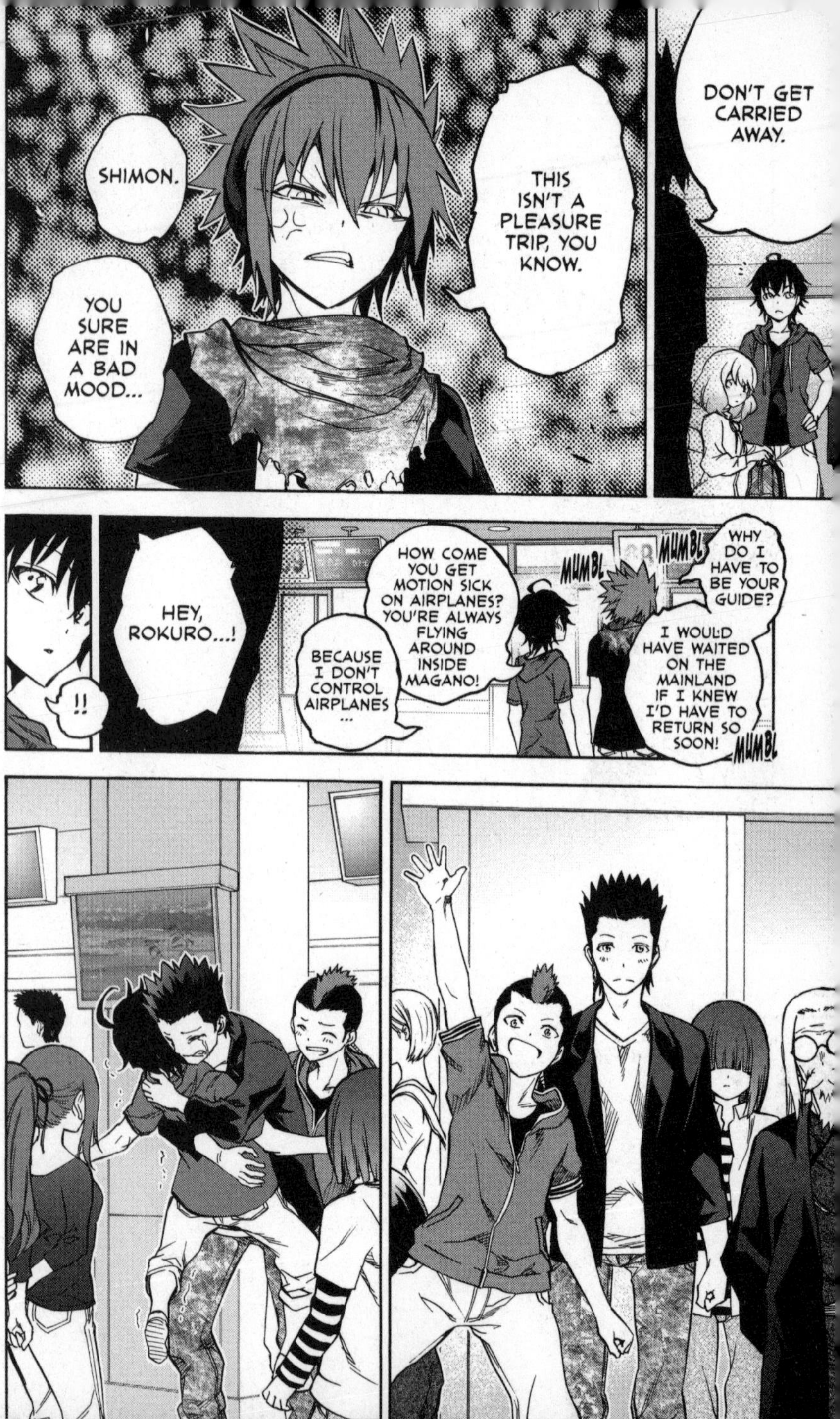
DON'T GET CARRIED AWAY.
THIS ISN'T A PLEASURE TRIP, YOU KNOW.
SHIMON.
YOU SURE ARE IN A BAD MOOD...
WHY DO I HAVE TO BE YOUR GUIDE?
MUMBL
I WOULD HAVE WAITED ON THE MAINLAND IF I KNEW I'D HAVE TO RETURN SO SOON!
MUMBL
MUMBL
HOW COME YOU GET MOTION SICK ON AIRPLANES? YOU'RE ALWAYS FLYING AROUND INSIDE MAGANO!
BECAUSE I DON'T CONTROL AIRPLANES ...
HEY, ROKURO...!
!!

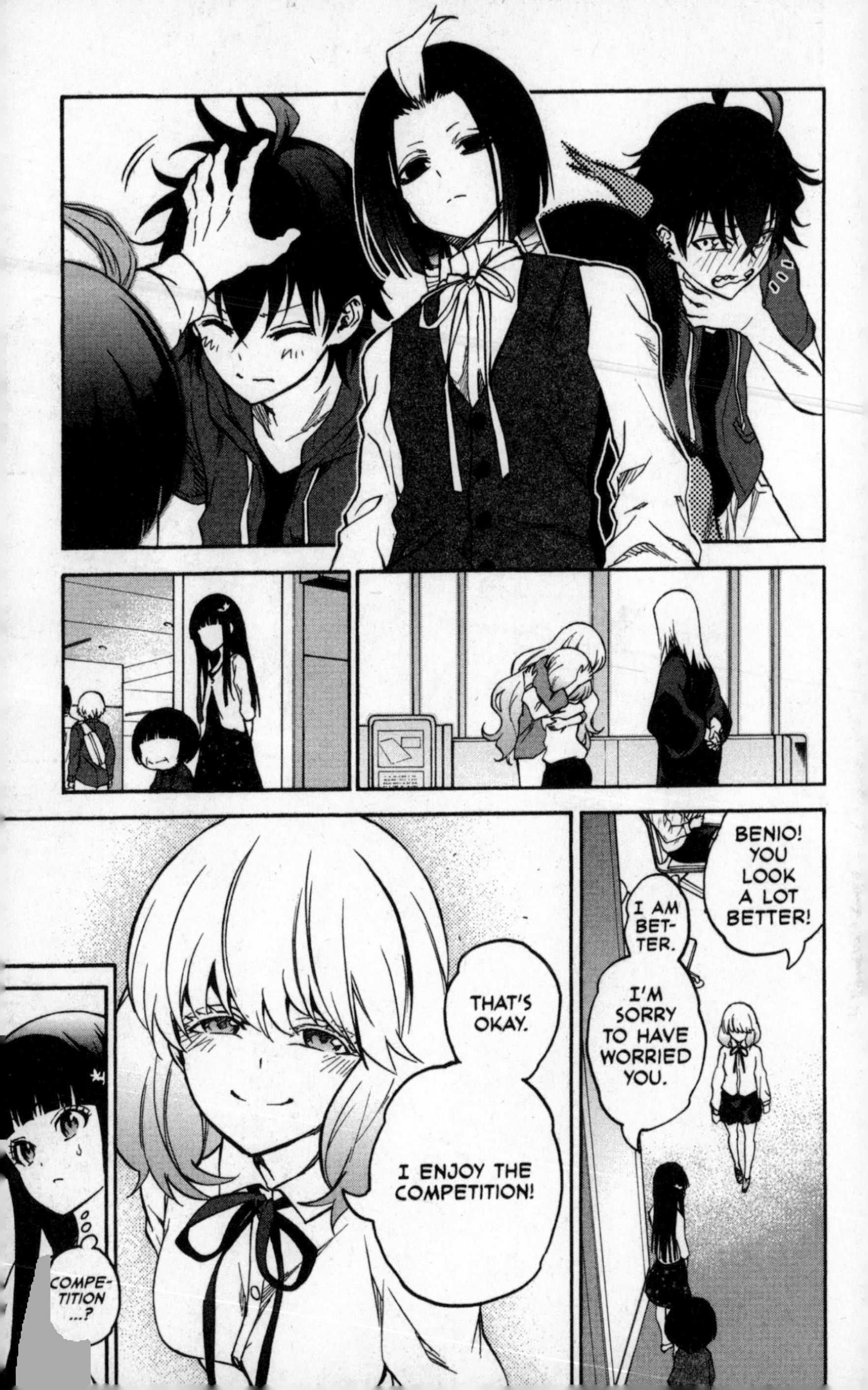
BENIO! YOU LOOK A LOT BETTER!
I AM BETTER.
I'M SORRY TO HAVE WORRIED YOU.
THAT'S OKAY.
I ENJOY THE COMPETITION!
COMPETITION ...?

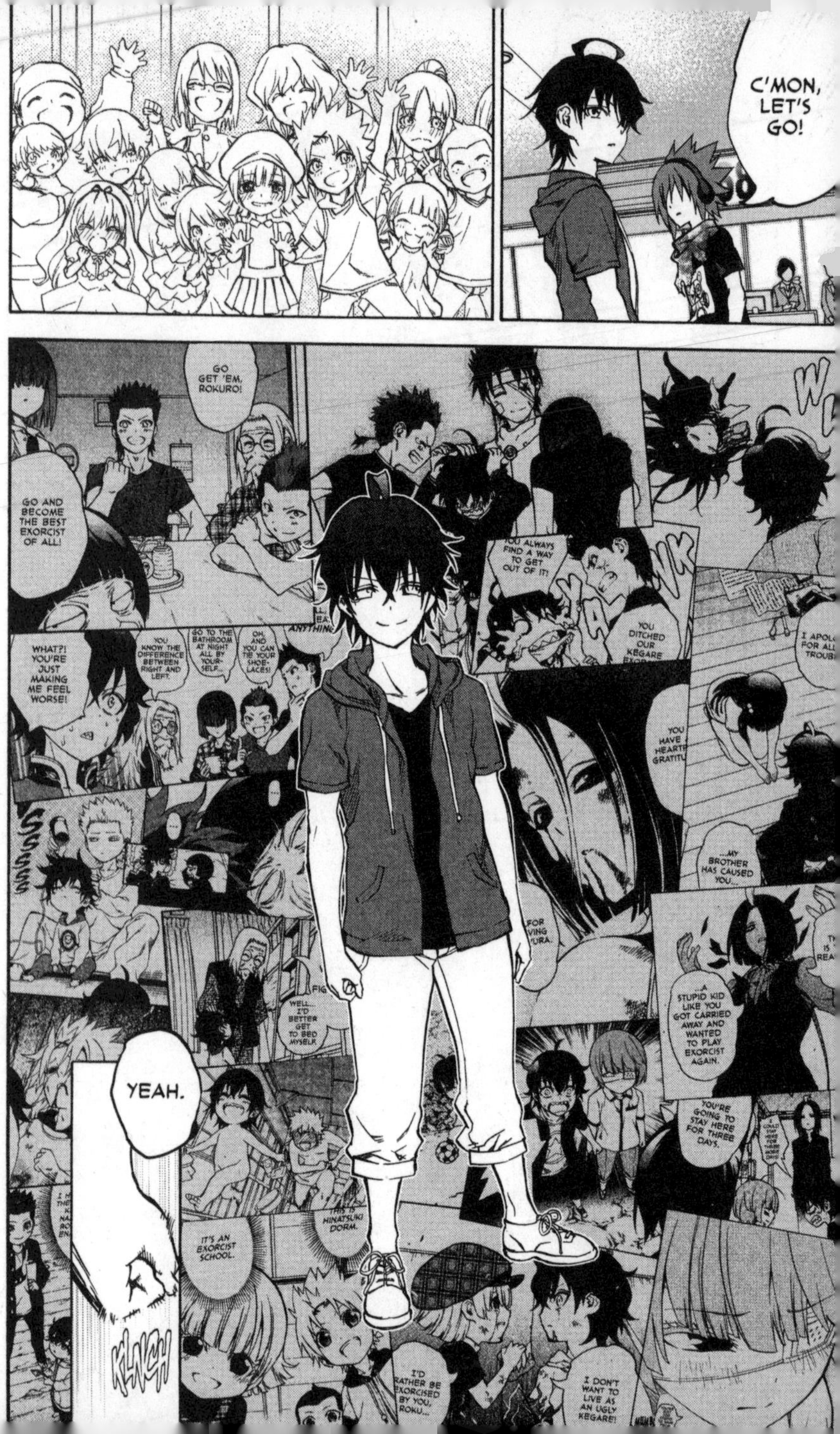
C'MON, LET'S GO!
YOU ALWAYS FIND A WAY TO GET OUT OF IT!
GO GET 'EM, ROKURO!
GO AND BECOME THE BEST EXORCIST OF ALL!
YOU DITCHED OUR KEGARE
OH, AND YOU CAN TIE YOUR SHOELACES!
GO TO THE BATHROOM AT NIGHT ALL BY YOURSELF...
YOU KNOW THE DIFFERENCE BETWEEN RIGHT AND LEFT.
WHAT?! YOU'RE JUST MAKING ME FEEL WORSE!
...MY BROTHER HAS CAUSED YOU...
...A STUPID KID LIKE YOU GOT CARRIED AWAY AND WANTED TO PLAY EXORCIST AGAIN.
WELL... I'D BETTER GET TO BED MYSELF.
YOU'RE GOING TO STAY HERE FOR THREE DAYS.
YEAH.
THIS IS HINATSUKI DORM.
IT'S AN EXORCIST SCHOOL.
KLINCH
I DON'T WANT TO LIVE AS AN UGLY KEGARE!
I'D RATHER BE EXORCISED BY YOU, ROKU...

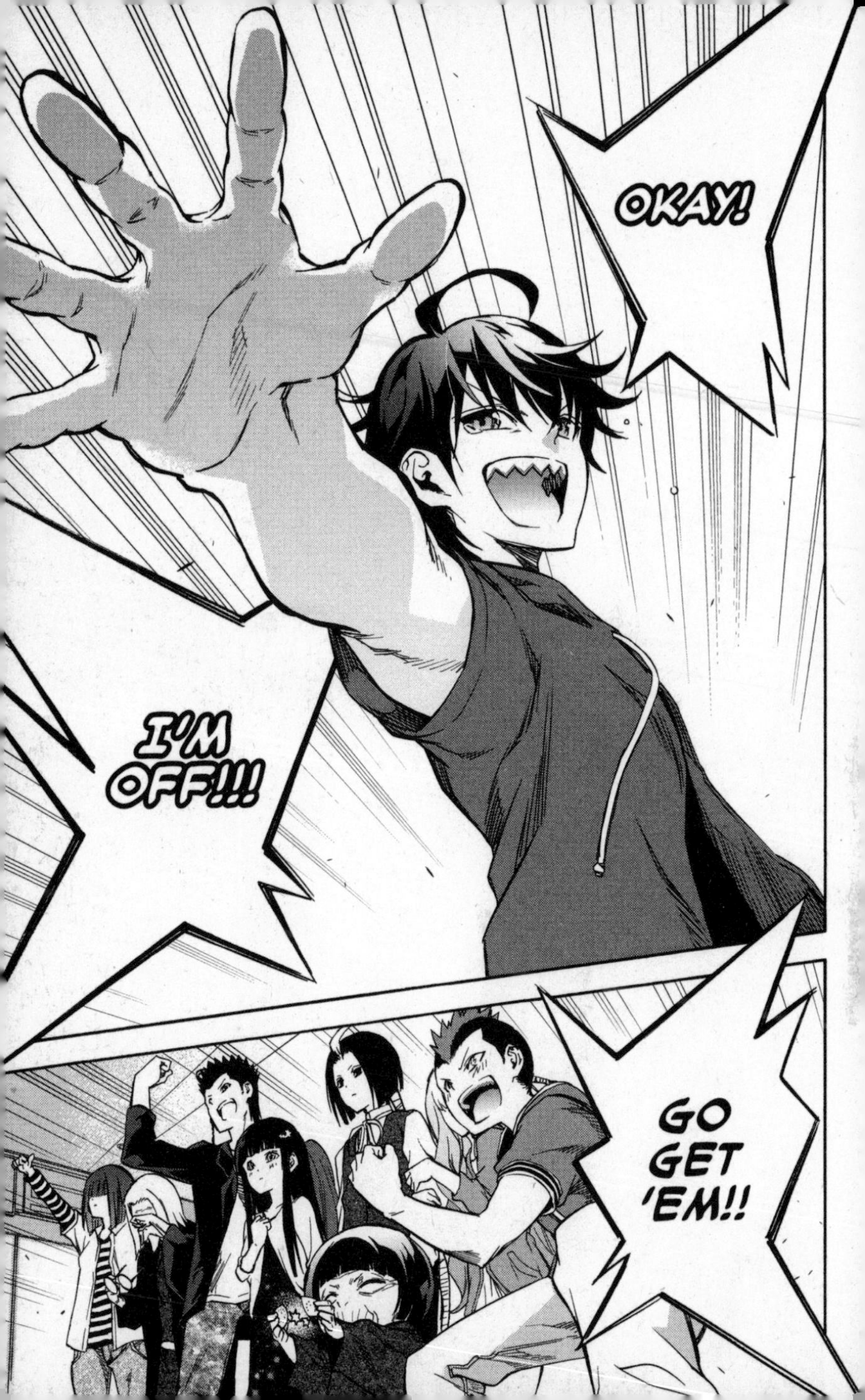
OKAY!
I'M OFF!!!
GO GET 'EM!!

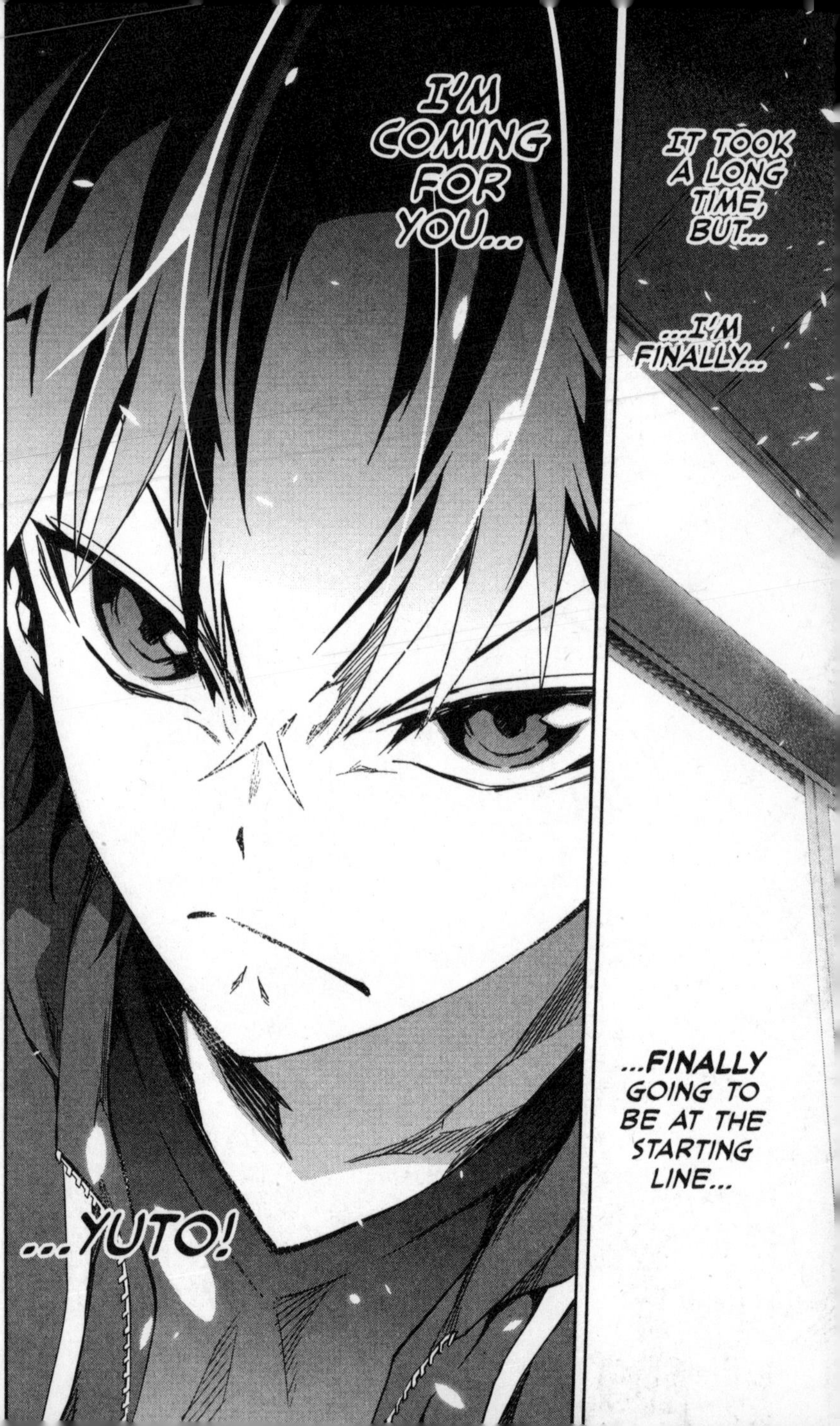
IT TOOK A LONG TIME, BUT...
...I'M FINALLY...
...FINALLY GOING TO BE AT THE STARTING LINE...
I'M COMING FOR YOU...
...YUTO!

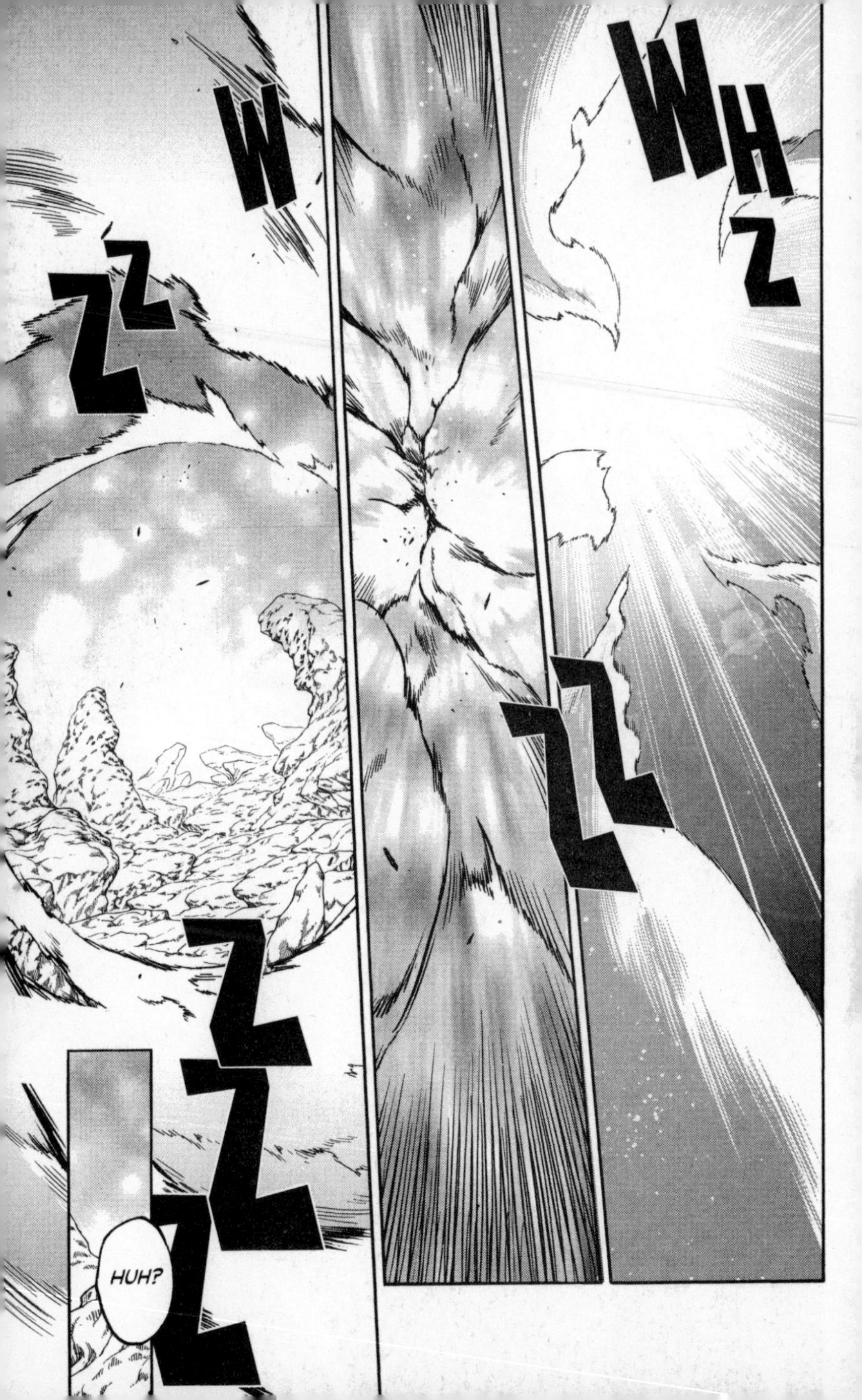
WHZ
ZZZ
W
ZZ
ZZZZ
HUH?

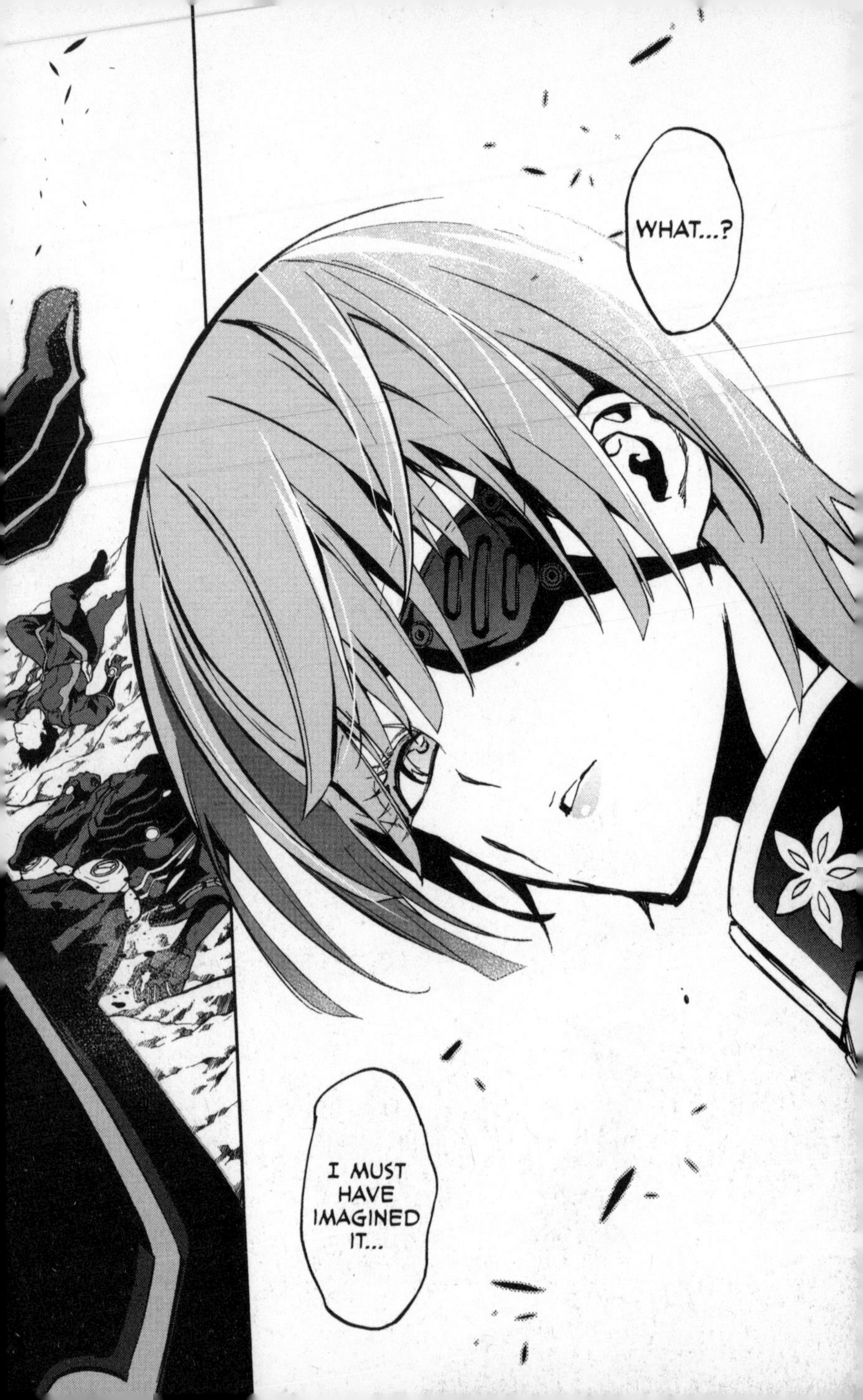
WHAT...?
I MUST HAVE IMAGINED IT...

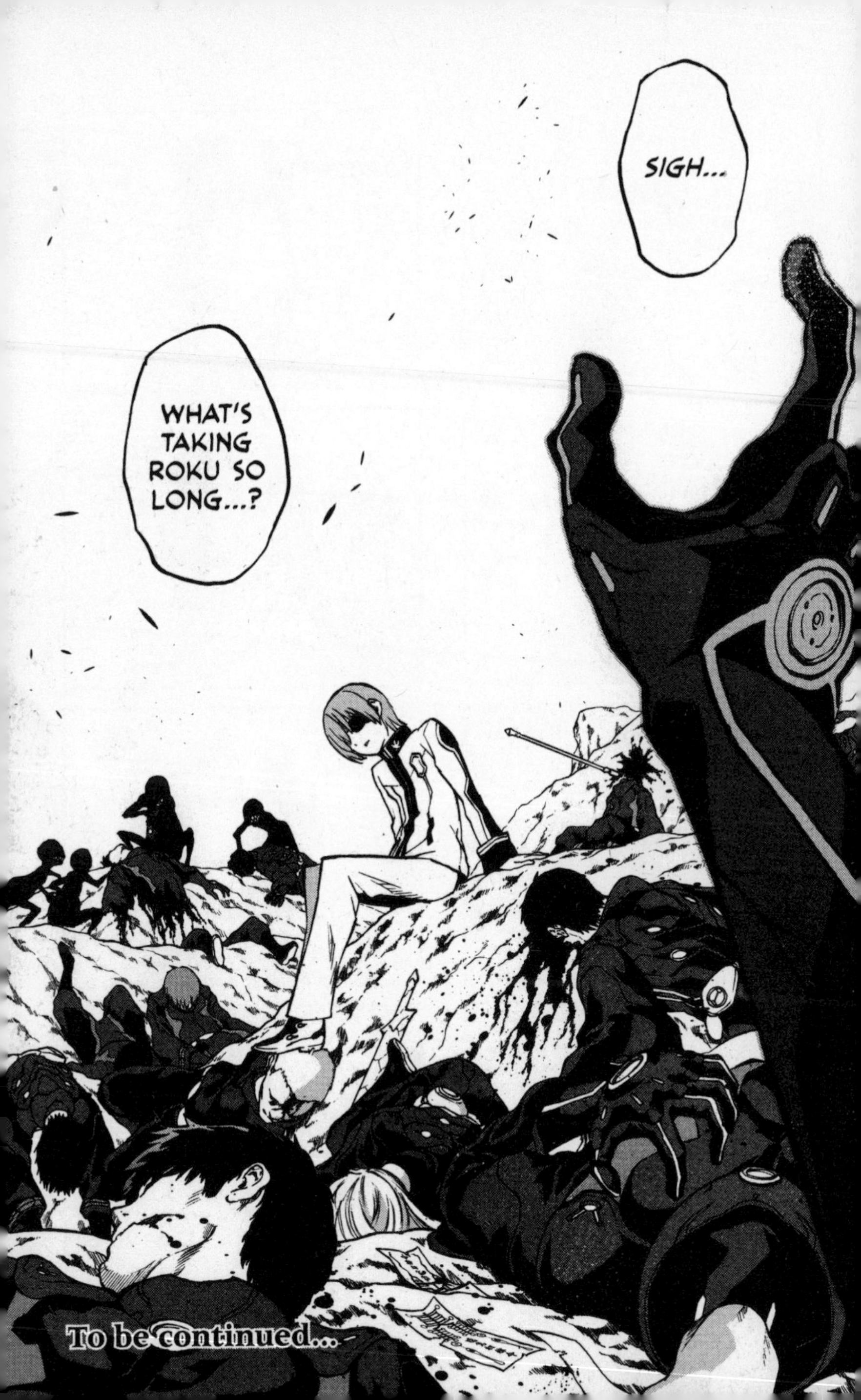
SIGH...
WHAT'S TAKING ROKU SO LONG...?
To be continued...

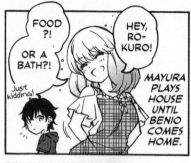

...AND THAT'S WHY MAYURA SHOULDN'T STAY...
SOMEONE HAS TO PUSH HER OUT OF THE NEST SOMETIME!
BUT WHAT IF WHITE TIGER HADN'T HELPED HER?!
BUT WHY WORRY ABOUT WHAT-IFS...?
HOW MANY TIMES DO I HAVE TO TELL YOU? I HAVE FAITH IN HER.
SHE'S A CHIP OFF THE OLD BLOCK!
WHY WON'T YOU LOOK ME IN THE EYE?!
RMMMBL
SHE'S SCARIER THAN A KEGARE ...
RMBL
MAYURA PLAYS HOUSE UNTIL BENIO COMES HOME.
HEY, RO-KURO!
FOOD?! OR A BATH?!
Just kidding!
HMM... ALL RIGHT, THEN...
BATH!
WHAT...?
NOOO! THAT'S NOT WHAT I MEANT! ROKURO, YOU HAVE A WIFE—BENIO. HOW COULD YOU EVEN THINK OF HAVING AN AFFAIR?! BOYS ARE ALL SO—
AFTER ALL, I CAN'T COOK...
...SO CLEAN-ING THE BATH IS PROBABLY EASIER.

*FAMILY MEETING

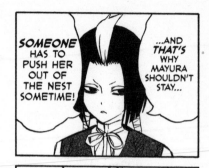

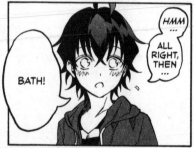

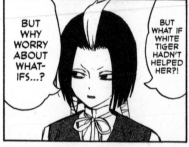

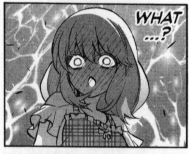

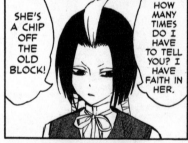

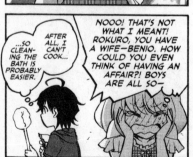

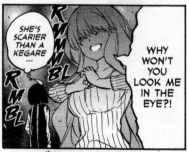

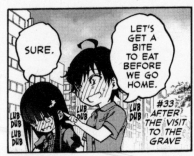

#33 AFTER THE VISIT TO THE GRAVE
LET'S GET A BITE TO EAT BEFORE WE GO HOME.
LUB DUB
LUB DUB
SURE.
LUB DUB
LUB DUB
I'VE TAKEN MY BATH, SO IT'S YOUR TURN, RO-KURO...
LUB DUB
LUB DUB
LUB DUB
YEAH!
LUB DUB
LUB DUB
LUB DUB
LUB DUB
OKAY... G-GOOD NIGHT, THEN!
LUB DUB
LUB DUB
LUB DUB
LUB DUB
YES. GOOD N-NIGHT...
LUB DUB
HUH?!
NOTHING HAP-PENED...

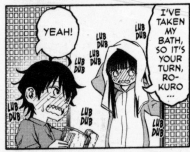

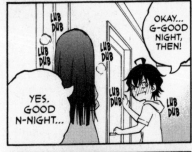

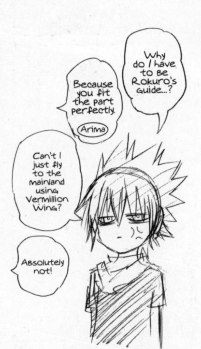

Why do I have to be Rokuro's guide...?
Because you fit the part perfectly.
Arima
Can't I just fly to the mainland using Vermillion Wing?
Absolutely not!

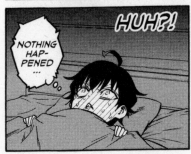

TSUCHIMIKADO ISLAND TRAVELOGUE 3

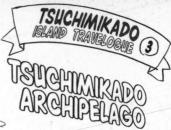

TSUCHIMIKADO ARCHIPELAGO

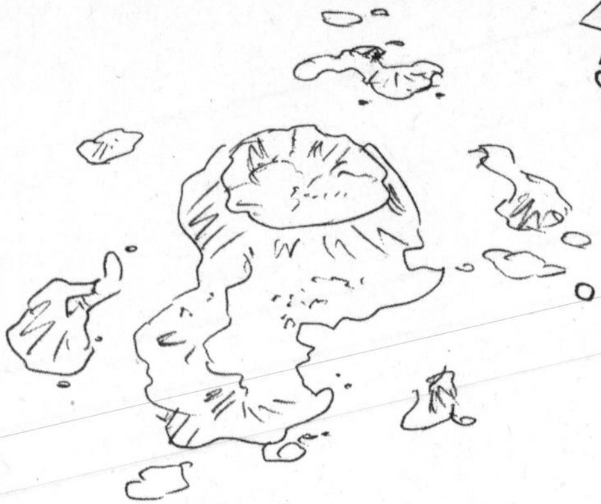

- Tsuchimikado consists of the main island, Tsuchimikado (a.k.a. the Masado) and more than twenty smaller surrounding islands (a.k.a. the Urasato).

- The largest island, the Masado, where over 90 percent of the population lives, is the administrative and business center. Reserve-duty exorcists study at the Seiyoin Institute there. This is also the location of the Great Black Torii and has the only entrance to Magano. Various stores and services required for everyday life, such as supermarkets and hospitals, are concentrated on the Masado as well.

- Each of the Urasato islands has a unique characteristic. One island has only Shikigami (Spirit Servants) living on it, while another is inhabited by the craftsmen who create the exorcists' special weapons and equipment. There is even an island inhabited by a clan of assassins who have mastered the craft of killing people instead of Kegare.

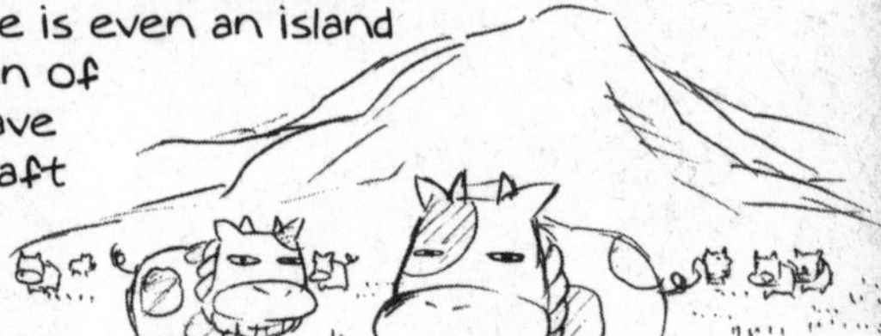

- Gozu: A bovine-like Shikigami whose sole purpose is to graze the island it inhabits. Unfortunately, being Shikigami, their meat is inedible and they do not produce milk. They are absolutely useless as livestock. But they still feed on the grass.

★ Artwork ★
Tetsuro Kakiuchi
Kosuke Ono
Takumi Kikuta
koppy
Yoshiaki Sukeno

★ Editor ★
Junichi Tamada

★ Graphic Novel Editor ★
Naomi Maehara

★ Graphic Novel Design ★
Tatsuo Ishino (Freiheit)

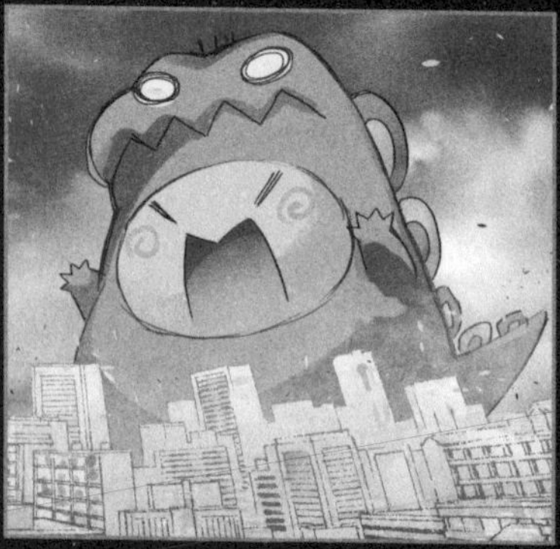

This volume finally concludes the mainland story, and now we move on to Tsuchimikado Island, the home base of the exorcists!

To tell the truth, in my first draft, Rokuro was scheduled to leave the mainland at the end of chapter one, and his story on the island was to begin in chapter two. (By the way, Mayura was the main heroine of the first chapter and Benio was to appear in the second chapter in that version).

So originally the mainland arc was only supposed to last for a month...but I ended up working on it for nearly three years...

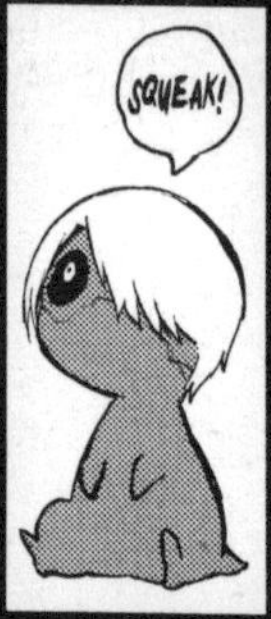
SQUEAK!

YOSHIAKI SUKENO was born July 23, 1981, in Wakayama, Japan. He graduated from Kyoto Seika University, where he studied manga. In 2006, he won the Tezuka Award for Best Newcomer Shonen Manga Artist. In 2008, he began his previous work, the supernatural comedy *Binbougami ga!*, which was adapted into the anime *Good Luck Girl!* in 2012.

#33 Unused Scene ① ~At the airport~

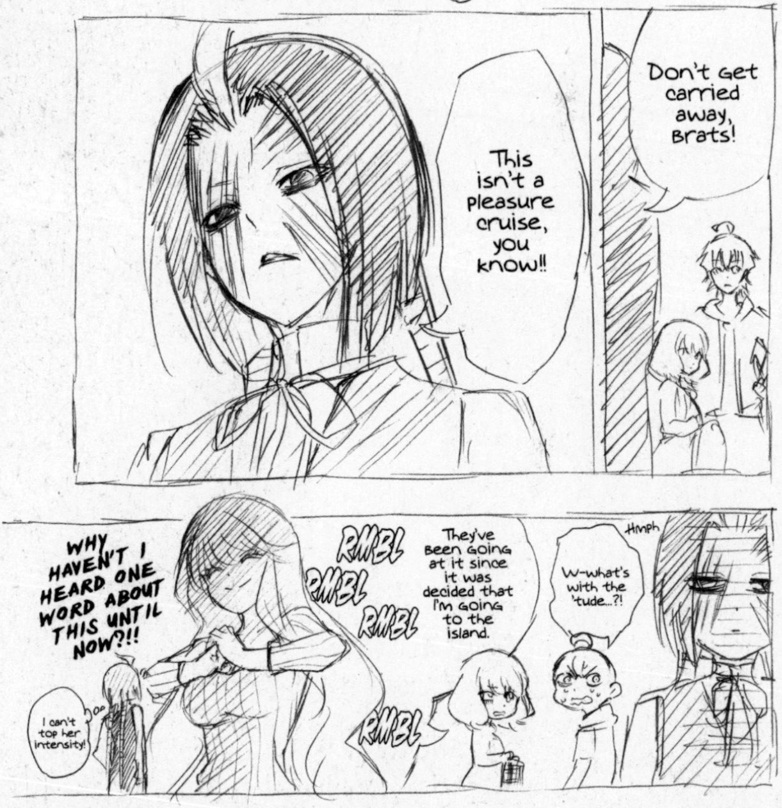
Don't get carried away, Brats!
This isn't a pleasure cruise, you know!!
Hmph
W-what's with the 'tude...?!
They've been going at it since it was decided that I'm going to the island.
RMBL
RMBL
RMBL
RMBL
WHY HAVEN'T I HEARD ONE WORD ABOUT THIS UNTIL NOW?!!
I can't top her intensity!

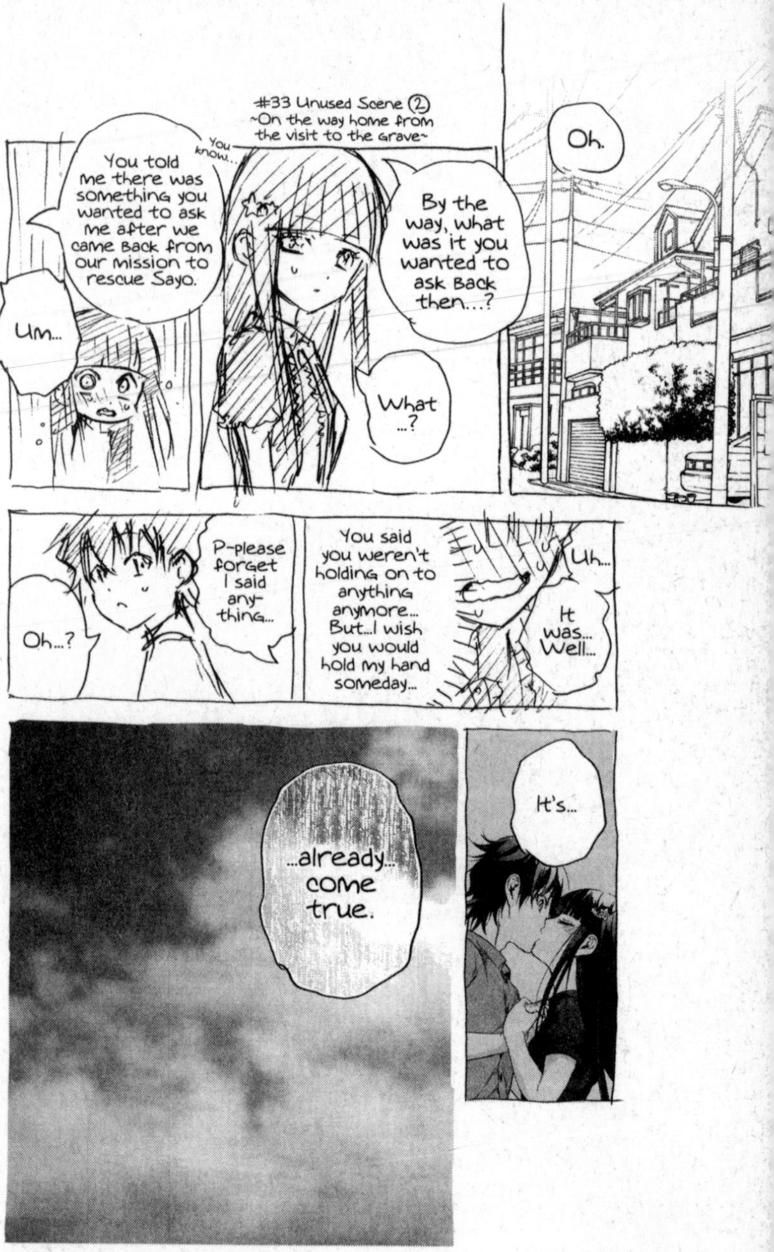
#33 Unused Scene ②
~On the way home from the visit to the grave~
Oh.
By the way, what was it you wanted to ask back then...?
What...?
You know...
You told me there was something you wanted to ask me after we came back from our mission to rescue Sayo.
Um...
Uh...
It was... Well...
You said you weren't holding on to anything anymore... But...I wish you would hold my hand someday...
P-please forget I said any-thing...
Oh...?
It's...
...already... come true.

— SHONEN JUMP Manga Edition —

STORY & ART **Yoshiaki Sukeno**

TRANSLATION **Tetsuichiro Miyaki**
ENGLISH ADAPTATION **Bryant Turnage**
TOUCH-UP ART & LETTERING **Stephen Dutro**
DESIGN **Shawn Carrico**
EDITOR **Annette Roman**

SOUSEI NO ONMYOJI © 2013 by Yoshiaki Sukeno
All rights reserved.
First published in Japan in 2013 by SHUEISHA Inc., Tokyo.
English translation rights arranged by SHUEISHA Inc.

The stories, characters and incidents mentioned in this
publication are entirely fictional.

Printed in the U.S.A.

Published by VIZ Media, LLC
P.O. Box 77010
San Francisco, CA 94107

10 9 8 7 6 5 4 3 2 1
First printing, July 2017

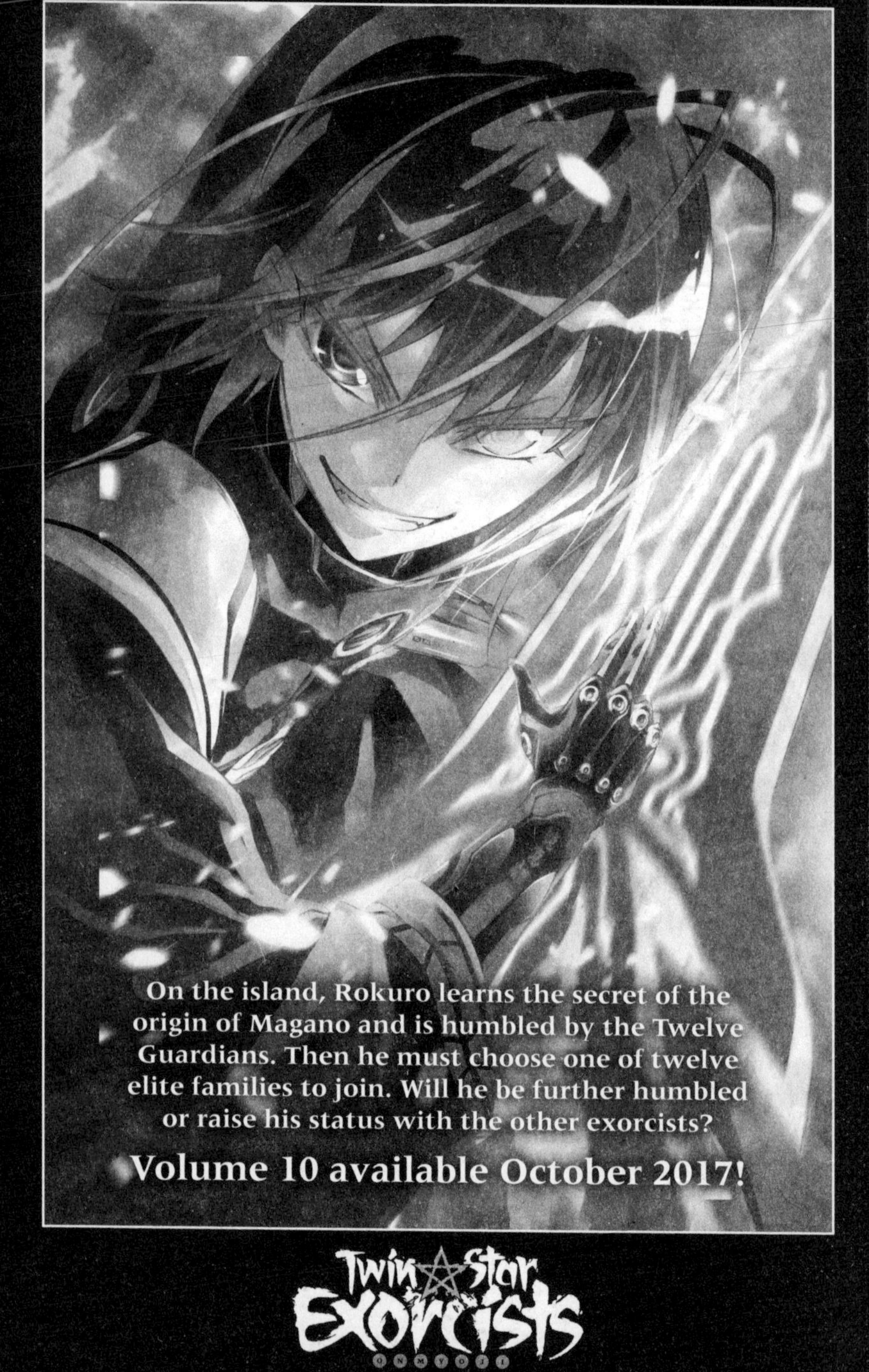
On the island, Rokuro learns the secret of the origin of Magano and is humbled by the Twelve Guardians. Then he must choose one of twelve elite families to join. Will he be further humbled or raise his status with the other exorcists?
Volume 10 available October 2017!

Twin Star Exorcists
ONMYOJI

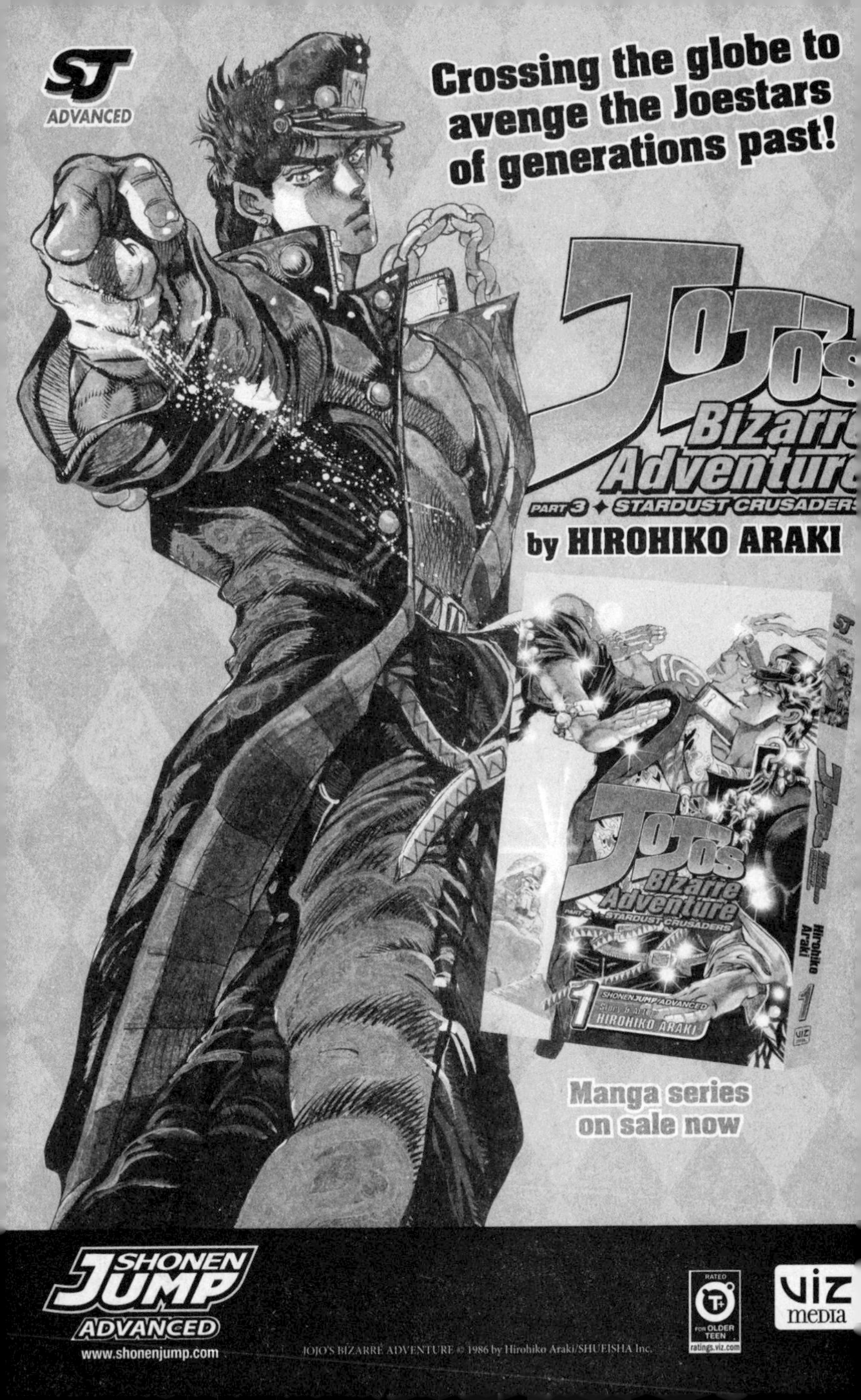
SJ ADVANCED
Crossing the globe to avenge the Joestars of generations past!
JoJo's Bizarre Adventure
PART 3 ✦ STARDUST CRUSADERS
by HIROHIKO ARAKI
Manga series on sale now
SHONEN JUMP ADVANCED
www.shonenjump.com
JOJO'S BIZARRE ADVENTURE © 1986 by Hirohiko Araki/SHUEISHA Inc.
RATED T+ FOR OLDER TEEN
ratings.viz.com
VIZ media

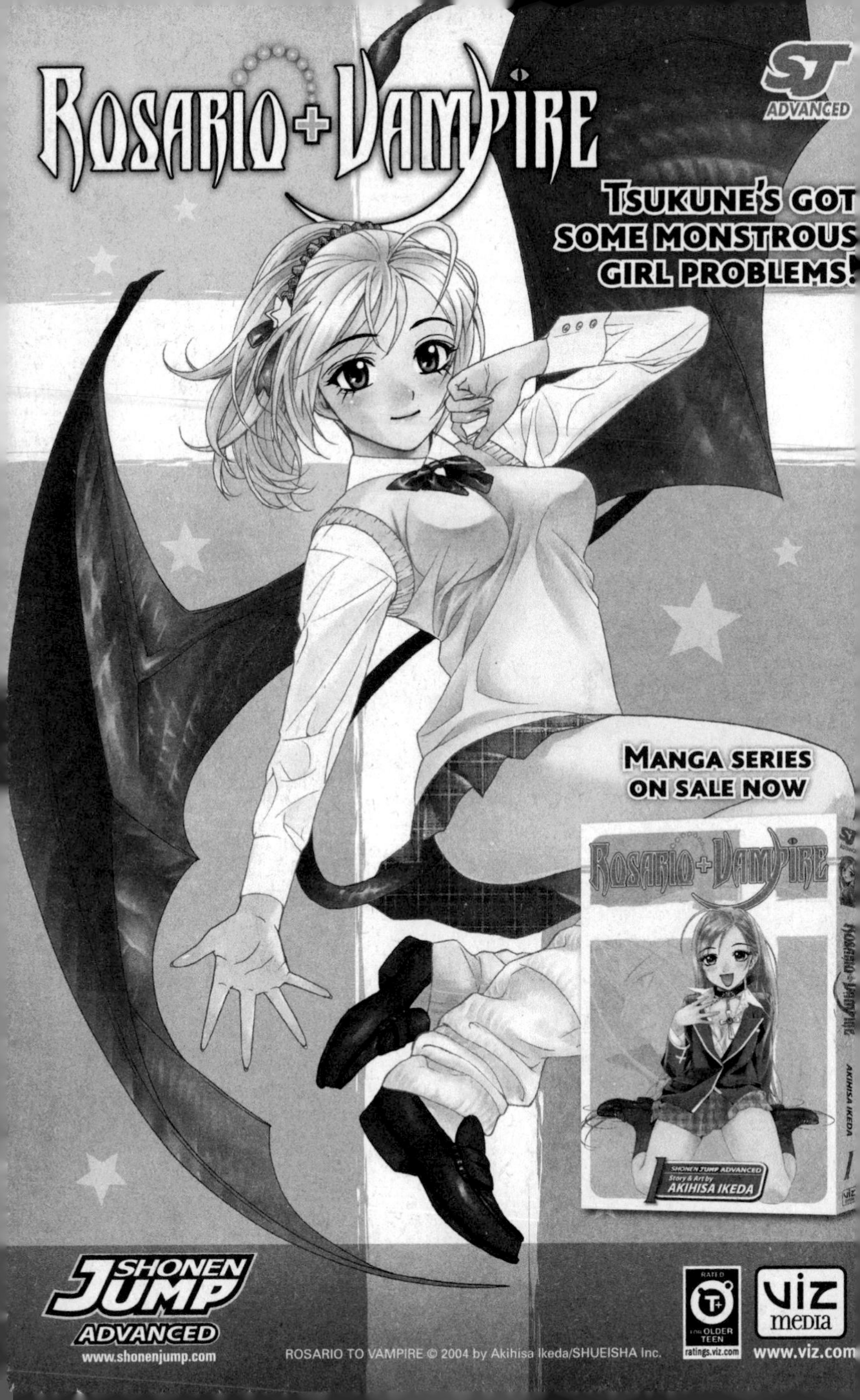
ROSARIO+VAMPIRE
SJ ADVANCED
TSUKUNE'S GOT SOME MONSTROUS GIRL PROBLEMS!
MANGA SERIES ON SALE NOW
ROSARIO+VAMPIRE
SHONEN JUMP ADVANCED
Story & Art by
AKIHISA IKEDA
SHONEN JUMP ADVANCED
www.shonenjump.com
ROSARIO TO VAMPIRE © 2004 by Akihisa Ikeda/SHUEISHA Inc.
RATED T+ FOR OLDER TEEN
ratings.viz.com
VIZ media
www.viz.com

YOU'RE READING THE

WRONG WAY!

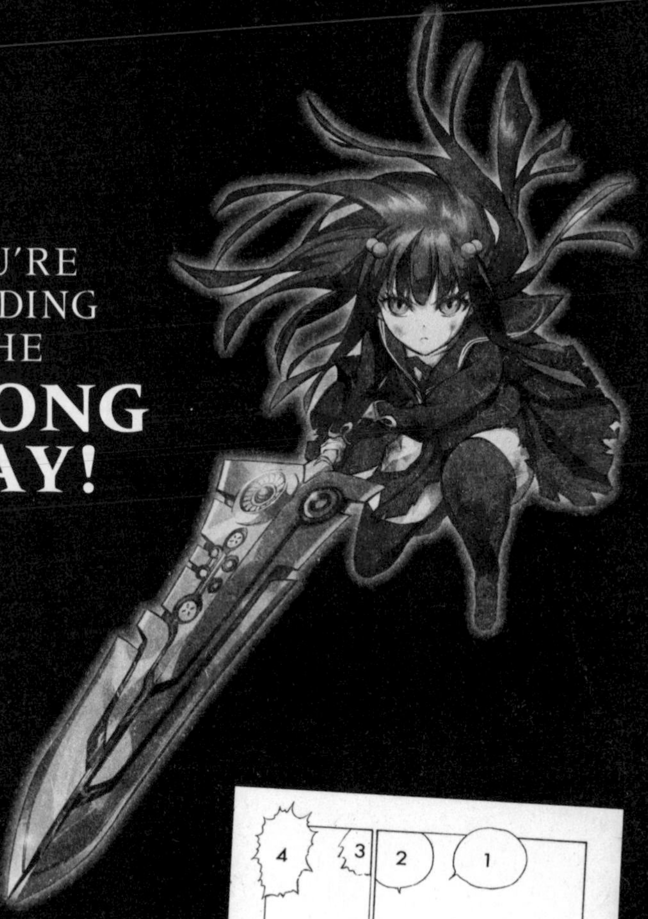

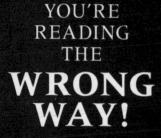

Twin Star Exorcists reads from right to left, starting in the upper-right corner. Japanese is read from right to left, meaning that action, sound effects and word-balloon order are completely reversed from English order.

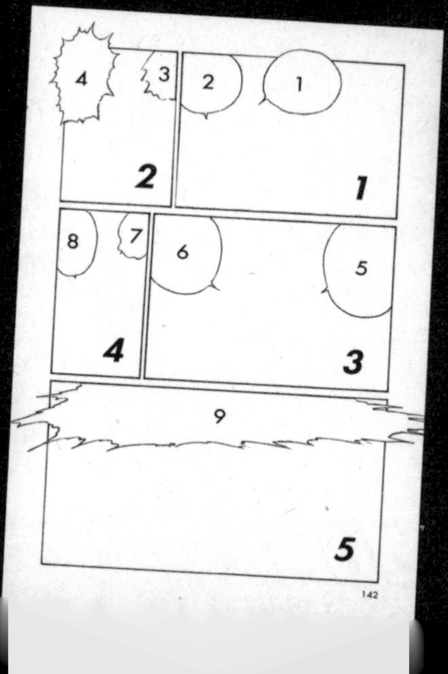
1
2
3
4
5
6
7
8
9
1
2
3
4
5
142